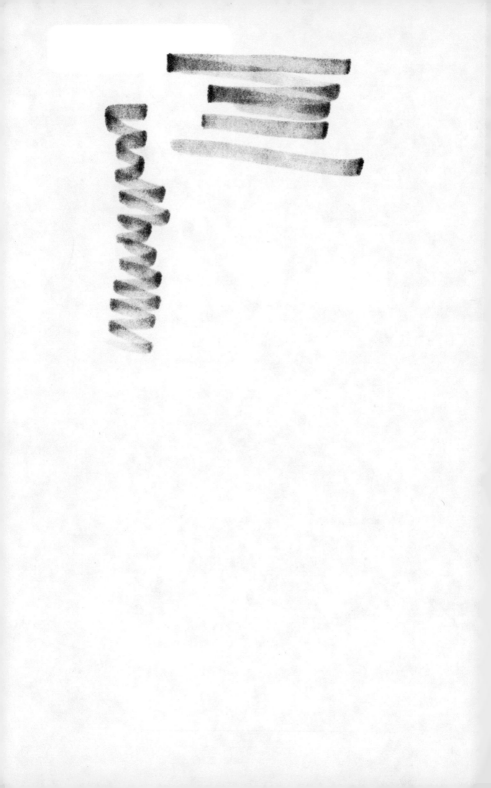

TO
LIVE THE WORD,
INSPIRED AND INCARNATE

To my parents, brothers, and sisters,
to all of whom I owe so much for their
love, example, and encouragement,
this work is gratefully dedicated.

A lamp to my feet is your word,
a light to my path . . .
O Lord, give me life according
to your word! (Ps 119:105, 107)

In the beginning was the word,
and the word was with God,
and the word was God . . .
In him was life, and the life
was the light of men. (Jn 1:1, 4)

TO

LIVE THE WORD,

INSPIRED AND INCARNATE:

An   Integral   Biblical   Spirituality

by

Warren Dicharry,
C.M., S.T.L., S.S.L.

"The Word of God
is a Tree of Life"
(*St. Ephrem*)

ALBA · HOUSE   NEW · YORK

SOCIETY OF ST. PAUL, 2187 VICTORY BLVD., STATEN ISLAND, NEW YORK 10314

Library of Congress Cataloging in Publication Data

Dicharry, Warren F.
  To Live the Word, Inspired and Incarnate.

  Includes bibliographies and indexes.
  1. Spiritual life—Catholic authors. I. Title.
BX2350.2.D495   1985   248.4'82   85-7386
ISBN 0-8189-0476-3

Imprimatur:
Most Rev. Philip M. Hannan
Archbishop of New Orleans
April 19, 1985

Nihil Obstat:
Rev. William Maestri
Censor Librorum
Archdiocese of New Orleans

Imprimi Potest:
Rev. Dennis Martin, C.M., Provincial
Vincentian Fathers and Brothers of the Southern Province

Designed, printed and bound in the United States of
America by the Fathers and Brothers of the
Society of St. Paul, 2187 Victory Boulevard,
Staten Island, New York 10314, as part of their
communications apostolate.

1 2 3 4 5 6 7 8 9 (Current Printing: first digit).

PREFACE

To write an article, and all the more so a book, on spirituality always becomes a cryptic autobiography. It expresses the story of one's life in another cadence. Anyone who reads this book will gradually acquire a warm, personal bond with Fr. Warren F. Dicharry, C.M. This preface, accordingly, will not introduce the author whom you will come to know better than I can describe for you. I prefer to reflect on the method of writing a book like this one.

An example may put it all together for us. It is as close to home as repairing doors, windows, electric fixtures and the kitchen sink. A man or woman rightly feels a tinge of pride if they fix a jammed lock on the front door *or* the pulleys on a window *or* a short in the electric wiring *or* a stopped up pipe beneath the kitchen sink. To remedy any single one of these home disasters deserves a long triumphant conversation over the neighbor's fence or cup of tea. It is, however, a far superior accomplishment to be that handyperson mending anything and everything that goes wrong. A person breaks into the ranks of the professionals when he or she can draw the blueprints and construct the home from scratch.

Fr. Dicharry, as we gather from the table of contents, lays before us the blueprints of a spirituality from the raw biblical material of Old and New Testaments. I am reminded of the man chosen by God to construct and furnish the Israelite sanctuary for worship. We read in the Book of Exodus:

The Lord said to Moses, "See, I have chosen Bezalel, son of Uri, son of Hur, of the tribe of Judah, and I have *filled him with a divine spirit* of skill and understanding and knowledge in every craft (Ex 31:1-3).

A little later we read again:

> Bezalel, therefore, will set to work with Oholiab and with all the experts whom the Lord has endowed with skill and understanding in knowing how to execute *all the work* for the service of the sanctuary, just as the Lord has commanded (Ex 36:1).

A unique gift of the spirit, similar to Bezalel's, must be bestowed for writing a book like this one. The entire history of Israel, of Jesus and of the first disciples of Jesus converges in a harmonious blend. This synthesis, in turn, reaches us and calls us to prayer, to reflection, to conversion of morals, to discipleship ever more sincere, God-fearing, God-loving. Under the direction of Fr. Dicharry the entire house of our lives, individually and as family, community and church keeps functioning smoothly and effectively according to the biblical model of Jesus.

It is difficult enough to write a book centering on a single biblical topic, like the love and justice of God, or prayer and worship, or the question of peace and war, or the various ministries of prophet, priest and laity, or marriage and the single state, or death and dying. Biblical theology writes about all of these *at once,* showing how one topic interacts with the others, enriches, challenges and develops.

Biblical theology is not a dictionary, listing its topics alphabetically. It is a way of life in which all the parts of the body grow together. St. Paul expressed it this way:

> Let us profess the truth in love and grow to the full maturity of Christ the head. Through him the whole body grows, and with the proper functioning of the members joined firmly together by each supporting ligament, builds itself up in love (Ep 4:15-16).

Fr. Dicharry has gone a step further. He is writing a biblical *spirituality* and therefore looks at each doctrine and practice in the Bible to see how they lead us *today* to still more fervent living for God, with God and in God.

Biblical spirituality, because it is *biblical* reaches into ancient times, and because it is *spirituality* touches our daily lives today. It requires a firm rooting in the Bible, a strong sense of tradition that spans the ages of Christianity, and a healthy attitude that looks out at our contemporary world with appreciation and wisdom. Fr. Dicharry reveals himself to be a person open to goodness across the Bible, through the centuries of Christian writers, to philosophy and literature of the twentieth century. St Paul described the quality of soul necessary to undertake a book of spirituality:

> Your thoughts should be wholly directed to all that is true, all that deserves respect, all that is honest, pure, admirable, decent, virtuous or worthy of praise. Live according to what you have learned and accepted, what you have heard me say and seen me do (Ph 4:8-9).

Biblical spirituality seeks what is true, honest, pure, admirable, virtuous and worthy of praise *throughout the Bible*. As a branch of theology these are united in a focus or central insight.

In this book, as is rightly evident from the title page onward, life is focused on Jesus Christ, the Word Incarnate. This book is alive in Jesus who lived by every word that came forth from the mouth of God — his answer to the tempter in the desert (Mt 4:4). Jesus, the Word Incarnate, was sustained in peace and wisdom by the inspired Word. Under the able direction of Fr. Dicharry, we search the Scriptures to know all that had to happen to Jesus because of them, and if to Jesus, then certainly to ourselves (Lk 24:25-27).

It is a privilege to introduce this book, a still greater delight to read it, a lasting reward in virtuous living to take it to heart.

Carroll Stuhlmueller, C.P.
Catholic Theological Union at Chicago

ABBREVIATIONS

Old Testament

Genesis	Gn	Proverbs	Pr
Exodus	Ex	Ecclesiastes	Ec
Leviticus	Lv	Songs of Songs	Sg
Numbers	Nb	Wisdom	Ws
Deuteronomy	Dt	Sirach	Si
Joshua	Jos	Isaiah	Is
Judges	Jg	Jeremiah	Jr
Ruth	Rt	Lamentations	Lm
1 Samuel	1 S	Baruch	Ba
2 Samuel	2 S	Ezekiel	Ezk
1 Kings	1 K	Daniel	Dn
2 Kings	2 K	Hosea	Ho
1 Chronicles	1 Ch	Joel	Jl
2 Chronicles	2 Ch	Amos	Am
Ezra	Ezr	Obadiah	Ob
Nehemiah	Ne	Jonah	Jon
Tobit	Tb	Micah	Mi
Judith	Jdt	Nahum	Na
Esther	Est	Habakkuk	Hab
1 Maccabees	1 M	Zephaniah	Zp
2 Maccabees	2 M	Haggai	Hg
Job	Jb	Malachi	Ml
Psalms	Ps	Zechariah	Zc

New Testament

Matthew	Mt	1 Timothy	1 Tm
Mark	Mk	2 Timothy	2 Tm
Luke	Lk	Titus	Tt
John	Jn	Philemon	Phm
Acts	Ac	Hebrews	Heb
Romans	Rm	James	Jm
1 Corinthians	1 Cor	1 Peter	1 P
2 Corinthians	2 Cor	2 Peter	2 P
Galatians	Gal	1 John	1 Jn
Ephesians	Ep	2 John	2 Jn
Philippians	Ph	3 John	3 Jn
Colossians	Col	Jude	Jude
1 Thessalonians	1 Th	Revelation	Rv
2 Thessalonians	2 Th		

TABLE OF CONTENTS

INTRODUCTION

WHY AN INTEGRAL BIBLICAL SPIRITUALITY?
The Wonderful Way of the Word!

On December 4, 1963, the Second Vatican Council issued its first two documents: *Constitution on the Sacred Liturgy*[1] and the *Decree on the Means of Social Communication*.[2] Within just two more years, there would emanate from the Council an unprecedented collection of documents, culminating on December 7, 1965 in the *Pastoral Constitution on the Church in the Modern World*.[3] Thus was ushered in what Pope John XXIII, the Council's inspiration, loved to call a "new Pentecost."[4] And, as with the first Christian Pentecost, there began to develop a groundswell of "living water" (Jn 7:38) bringing dynamic life to the Church and dividing, after the manner of the river of Eden (Gn 2:10), into four streams of renewal: Scripture and Liturgy, Spirituality and Ministry.

In response to the spreading hunger in these four areas, many articles, pamphlets, books and even new periodicals began to appear almost overnight. New or renewed movements quickly gathered thousands of enthusiastic members, for example: the Liturgical, Charismatic, amd Ecumenical Movements, as well as the Family Life, Marriage Encounter, Cursillo, and Basic Community Movements. Permanent Diaconate and Lay Ministry Programs proliferated. Prayer and Bible Study Groups became commonplace. Youth Programs of all kinds flourished. Adult Education and Parish Councils became indispensable. More recently, Diocesan and Parish,

Priestly and Religious, Renewal Programs, featuring retreats and days of reflection, have grown in popularity. And currently, the Renew Program of extensive Parish participation, especially in Bible sharing groups, is kindling enthusiasm all around the country. In addition, workshops in Eastern prayer methods, Jungian psychology, and intensive journals have drawn an impressive number of devotees. Besides all these phenomena, there has been a rapid growth of interest in and commitment to all kinds of programs promoting peace and justice.

This groundswell of renewal has indeed been edifying, but rather uneven and often faddish. One cannot help observing how quickly so many devotees embrace enthusiastically a particular form of renewal, only to abandon it soon afterwards in order to "jump on the bandwagon" of the latest "discovery." Why is this? Perhaps, there is an element of wanting to "join the crowd," but I suspect that the explanation lies deeper than that. Underneath all this apparent mobility and even instability, I detect something very positive — a genuine hunger for true spirituality and a desperate hunger for the Word of God in Sacred Scripture. To me, these two hungers are really one, the hunger for God! Nor is this surprising. After all, as St. Augustine expressed it so eloquently in his *Confessions,* God has made us for himself and our hearts are restless until they rest in him[5] — especially in times such as ours when the world about us seems to be literally falling apart.

Maybe the hunger for Scripture has something to do with the unfortunate biblical starvation from which most Catholics have suffered for centuries, especially since the Protestant Reformation, but here again I believe there is a deeper explanation. In their hunger for God, the faithful instinctively turn to the Word of God as containing his own "roadmap" for finding him. And has this not been confirmed in the *Dogmatic Constitution on Divine Revelation*[6] of Vatican II? In its sublime final chapter, it declares that the Bible is the "very soul of sacred theology,"[7] as well as "a pure and lasting fount of spiritual life"[8] to such an extent that "all the preaching of the Church, as indeed the entire Christian religion, should be nourished and ruled by Sacred Scripture''!⁹

In fact, the principal key to understanding Vatican II is the realization that, after centuries of reliance on philosophical theology and various kinds of law, the Church has at long last made Sacred Scripture the clear basis of her thought and teaching. Hence, her declared hope in the unforgettable conclusion to the *Constitution on Divine Revelation*:¹⁰

> So may it come that, by the reading and study of the sacred books, ''the Word of God may speed on and triumph'' (2 Th 3:1) and the treasure of Revelation entrusted to the Church may more and more fill the hearts of men. Just as from constant attendance at the Eucharistic mystery the life of the Church draws increase, so a *new impulse of spiritual life may be expected from increased veneration of the Word of God,* which ''stands forever'' (Is 40:8; cf. 1 P 1:23-25).

Surely, the growing phenomenon of consuming interest in Sacred Scripture and Spirituality is nothing less than the fulfillment of the Council's expectations!

Yes, Christians in general, and Catholics in particular, impelled by the Holy Spirit, ''hunger and thirst for holiness'' (Mt 5:6) and for the Word of God (Dt 8:3, Mt 4:4, Lk 4:4) or, in other words, for *Biblical Spirituality.* Consciously or unconsciously, they want to learn how they can live in closer union with God according to God's own Word. But here, regrettably, there has not been the abundant supply of published works that they might have expected to satisfy their hunger. Oh, there have been plenty of books on Spirituality, especially on prayer, and plenty of books on Scripture. But works that bring the two together, books on Biblical Spirituality, have been few and far between. Those that have appeared, such as the ones that I have recommended for further reading after Chapter One, have been excellent. But the hunger is so great and the subject so crucial that we need a veritable flood rather than a trickle of such works. It is principally for this reason that I have undertaken this "labor of love" (1 Th 1:3).

For me, it represents the fulfillment of a long-cherished desire. Even before the first document of Vatican II appeared in 1963, my deep personal interest in the Spiritual Life ever since my seminary days in the early forties and my missionary years in China (including two under Communism) in the late forties and early fifties, coupled with my Scripture studies and teaching for the rest of the fifties, had given me the intense desire to formulate a biblical spirituality which I could both live personally and share with others through preaching, teaching, counseling, and writing. But alas! The fulfillment of my cherished hope, at least so far as writing was concerned, had to be postponed. The heavy responsibility of teaching, administration, and various ministries, as well as the writing and revisions of my book on New Testament Greek entitled *Greek Without Grief* [11] precluded the possibility of finding the time needed for my favorite project, at least until now. And I truly believe that this twenty-year delay has been a "blessing in disguise," for it has allowed my biblical spirituality to develop, mature, and be tested by time, life-experience, and mutual sharing with others. After all, to borrow the blind *Milton's* touching assurance, "They also serve who only stand and wait"![12]

Now, after teaching Sacred Scripture for twenty-eight years to seminarians, priests, ministers, permanent deacon candidates, religious, and lay people (especially those preparing for ministry), I am happy to "launch out into the deep" (Lk 5:4) by embarking full time on a ministry of evangelization (in the true sense of preaching and teaching the Gospel) through biblical missions, retreats, and workshops in an effort to satisfy the ever-growing hunger for biblical spirituality. (Actually, this is the original work of our Community, whose sainted founder, *Vincent de Paul*, chose as our motto those stirring words of Is 61:1 which, in Lk 4:18, Jesus uses as his Messianic Manifesto: "To preach the Gospel to the poor the Lord has sent me.") And, after thirty-nine years of priesthood, I am attempting to concretize in book form my twenty-year-old project of biblical spirituality, both as a follow-up to my preaching and teaching and, hopefully, as a help to others interested in this vital subject. I am under no illusions about writing "the Great American Spiritual Classic" or about saying the last word on the subject, but I do hope that *To Live the Word, Inspired and Incarnate* will contribute something worthwhile and, even more importantly, will stimulate others of greater knowledge, holiness, and talent than I to make their own contributions in this important field.

The *Title* I have chosen describes the dual focus of the work itself, namely *living the life of Jesus Christ, the Incarnate Word, by living the inspired Word of Sacred Scripture*. While the book takes up many themes, they are all viewed in relation to this dual focus. It is written out of a Catholic tradition and directed primarily to Catholics, but it is my fond hope that it contains at least some material which will appeal to a *wider readership*, especially to my beloved fellow-Christians and even my cherished Jewish friends. (Such adjectives do not exaggerate my feelings, for I became ecumenical in China a decade before Vatican II, and my long, close relationship with the Jewish Community of Houston has endeared Jews everywhere to me for life.)

The *Subtitle* of my book, *An Integral Biblical Spirituality*, needs some explanation. The word *integral* possesses a number of meanings and connotations that are relevant here, but the ones I prefer are "complete, integrated, and essential." In contrast with collections of articles or monographs of narrower focus (which seem to comprise most works on this important subject), I am attempting to present an *overview* of biblical spirituality which is fairly *complete* in itself, *integrated* in all of its parts, and confined to *essential* considerations according to the dual focus mentioned above. My purpose and my prayerful hope is to provide a biblical spirituality which is thoroughly *livable*.

In addition to many Scripture references, I have also seen fit to include a number of quotations from and allusions to the Fathers of the

Church, Papal and Conciliar Documents, and writings or sayings of various spiritual authors, both canonized and otherwise. However, in no way is this an eclectic survey of the Spiritual Life such as that of *Tanquerey*, [13] the standby classic in seminaries for many years before Vatican II. References included in this work are chosen solely for their usefulness as confirmation and "color commentary" by acknowledged experts whose word carries far more weight than mine.

A remarkable thing happened when I finally decided on the title and subtitle for this book. Upon typing them out, together with my name as author, I found to my surprise that it all came together symmetrically to form a *well-defined tree*. How very appropriate! In almost all cultures, and particularly in the Judeo-Christian tradition reflected in the Bible, the symbolism of trees is extremely rich. Above all, the *"Tree of Life"* featured at the beginning and end of *Sacred Scripture* (Gn 2:9; 3:22, 24; Rv 2:7; 22:2, 14) represents Eternal Life, while Psalm 1:3 and Proverbs 3:18 connect it with the Word and Wisdom of God which lead to it.

The *Fathers of the Church* not only continue but expand the symbolism of God's Tree of Life, of Word, and of Wisdom. For example, St. Ephrem the Syrian Deacon, in his *Commentary on the Diatessaron* (of Tatian), declares, "The Word of God is a tree of life that offers us blessed fruit from each of its branches." [14] St. Augustine, in his monumental *City of God,* expounds, "The 'Tree of Life' would seem to have been in the terrestrial Paradise what the Wisdom of God is in the spiritual, of which it is written, 'She is a Tree of Life to them that lay hold upon her' (Pr 3:18)," and again, "The 'Tree of Life' is the holy of holies, Christ!" [15] And finally the trusty (and sometimes crusty) St. Jerome, in his *Treatise on Psalm One,* includes both the Inspired and the Incarnate Word,

> One river comes forth from the throne of God — the grace of the Holy Spirit — and this grace of the Holy Spirit is found in the river of the Sacred Scriptures. This river, moreover, has two banks, the Old Testament and the New Testament, and the tree planted on both sides is Christ. [16]

Is this mere coincidence? Or farfetched imagining unworthy of a Scripture scholar? Maybe, but I believe that highly symbolic sections of the Bible, such as we find at the beginning of Genesis and at the end of Revelation, do lend themselves to a certain amount of imaginative ''reading between the lines.'' At any rate, I know that I will never see a Christmas tree (or any tree for that matter) without discerning in it that ''Tree of Life'' which is the *''Word (or Wisdom) of God, Inspired and Incarnate''*!

A glance at the *Table of Contents* indicates an uneven threefold division into the *Nature* (five chapters), *Features* (four chapters), and *Means* (three chapters) of the Spiritual Life. Within these divisions, I have arranged the twelve chapters of material in such a way as to comprise all the essentials in a step-by-step manner, each chapter building on the preceding one. In doing so, I have tried to fulfill Jesus' description of a ''scribe . . ., a disciple of the kingdom of heaven'' who, ''like a householder . . . brings out from his storeroom things both new and old'' (Mt 13:51). But, even in the case of ''old things,'' I have endeavored to treat them in a new way, particularly in reference to my dual focus of the Inspired Word and the Incarnate Word. *''Non nova, sed nove!''* (''Not new things, but in a new way!'')

In an effort not to ''miss the forest for the trees,'' I have tried to paint my portrait of biblical spirituality with *''broad brush strokes.''* Also, I have found it useful to employ, sometimes unconsciously, a method of development called *''concentric circles''* which is particularly dear to biblical writers, for example, St. John. This simply involves the presentation of the main ideas at the beginning, followed by the periodic return to these ideas for fuller expansion, much like the ripples that form in ever-widening circles around the place where a pebble is dropped into water. A certain amount of repetition occurs, but only for the sake of clarification and further development.

In referring to *Sacred Scripture,* I have generally used the *New American Bible* translation, the one most familiar to Catholics, but I have not hesitated to employ whatever translation best captures the meaning of the original text in keeping with my own emphases in this work, and in quite a few instances I have had to make my own translations from the texts themselves. However, to avoid confusion, I have carefully indicated the source of each translated passage, as follows: JB for the *Jerusalem Bible*, RSV for the *Revised Standard Version*, NIV for the *New International Version*, NEB for the *New English Bible*, WD for *my own translation,* and no letters at all for the *New American Bible*. Even in employing translations, I have felt it necessary at times to go back to the *original words* in Hebrew or Greek (or to various etymologies), not for the purpose of impressing the reader but rather to share the richness of meaning involved which, unfortunately, does not always survive the translations, no matter how good they are. "Everything suffers in translation!" I have tried to quote Scripture texts in full, but in many instances I have had to summarize by providing only the references. Because of this, I urge the reader to peruse this book with a Bible handy, so that the texts referred to can be read and reflected on in their original context.

Finally, I have included a generous amount of other *quotations,* many of them poetic, which I have carefully selected for their challenging impact. Poetry is the oldest and still the most moving form of literature. But, whether in poetry or prose, God can and does speak to us through the ideas and experiences of others. Besides, this represents a less cerebral and more holistic approach, whose value in Scripture studies has recently been confirmed by various authors, notably Walter Wink in *Transforming Bible Study.*[17] In the same spirit, I have provided at the end of each chapter a brief *list of books* for further reading and a number of *questions,* which I hope will be useful both for personal reflection and for group discussion.

I cannot conclude this Introduction without expressing, however inadequately, my deep gratitude to all who have encouraged and assisted me in this work, including my brothers and sisters, relatives and friends, confreres and colleagues, superiors and students. In particular, I am deeply indebted to Mrs. Linda Thomas who helped me so much with typing and word processing, Mr. and Mrs. Clint Holmes who enabled me to enter the mysterious world of computers,

Father Carroll Stuhlmueller, C.P. who was kind enough to supply a very inspiring and encouraging Preface, and finally the staff of Alba House, especially Fathers Anthony Chenevey and Edmund Lane, and Brothers Paschal Duesman and Emmanuel Caña, all of the Society of St. Paul (S.S.P.), without whose perception and patience this "labor of love" (1 Th 1:3) might never have seen the light of day.

If this very imperfect work helps even one reader to understand and embrace the Spiritual Life more completely, to read and live the Inspired Word of God more effectively, and to be united to the Incarnate Word, Jesus Christ, more lovingly, then it will have accomplished its purpose. May it enable the Word of God to be truly for us seekers "a lamp to our feet, a light to our path" (Ps 119:105), leading us safely and surely to our cherished goal where —

Through blest eternity,
All things will come to be
Forever clear and bright,
And open to our sight!

Warren F. Dicharry, C.M.
Saint Stephen Church,
New Orleans, LA

SECTION ONE:
THE NATURE OF THE SPIRITUAL LIFE

CHAPTER   ONE

THE HEART OF THE SPIRITUAL LIFE: RELATIONSHIP!
The Mutuality of Scripture and Spirituality

An old familiar story, put into poetry in the past century by *John Godfrey Saxe*, is that of the *six blind men of Hindustan*[1] who chanced to encounter an elephant. Each examined by touch a different part of the animal's anatomy, the result being six entirely diverse conclusions about the nature of an elephant, ranging from a wall, a spear, and a snake to a tree, a fan, and a rope!

Now, it is certainly true, as we have all learned from the late beloved *Helen Keller* (who was blind and deaf from infancy), that blind people are able to "see," not with their eyes, "but through the inner faculty, to serve which eyes were given to us,"[2] and "the greatest calamity that could befall a person is" not blindness but "to have sight and fail to see!"[3] Therefore, while the "elephant story" may be a misleading commentary on physical blindness, it is nonetheless valid in dramatizing our human tendency to accept a part for the whole, to jump to incomplete and often wrong conclusions because of our own self-imposed "tunnel vision."

Perhaps nowhere is this more evident than in the current confusion regarding the nature of spirituality. For example, to some, spirituality is totally identified with ascetical practices, to others with mystical phenomena, to others with charismatic enthusiasm, to others with the "social gospel," to still others with quiet contemplation. Yet true spirituality can be limited to none of these alone. Still less can it be reduced to "stiff upper lip" Stoicism, "do it yourself" Pelagianism, or "positive thinking" psychologism. Rather, it transcends them all and yet, like Wisdom in Pr 8:1-9:11, it makes itself perfectly accessible to all sincere seekers.

But in order to understand what spirituality really is, we need to view it in a broader context, namely that of Christianity in general and even that of religion as a whole.

RELIGION:

Religion is defined in *Webster's Ninth New Collegiate Dictionary* as "The service and worship of God or the supernatural; commitment or devotion to religious faith or observance; a personal set or institutionalized system of religious attitudes, beliefs, and practices; a cause, principle, or system of beliefs held to with ardor and faith."[4] This descriptive definition is traditional and apparently all-inclusive, but basically inadequate. Why? Because it fails to mention the most essential characteristic of religion, namely that of *relationship*. Even archaeology, anthropology, and comparative religion normally point out this phenomenon. For example, John B. Noss, in *Man's Religions,* declares, "All religions imply in one way or another that man does not, and cannot, stand alone, that he is *vitally related with* and even dependent on powers in nature and society external to himself."[5] And the very word *religion*, from Latin *religio* and ultimately (it seems) from the verb *religare* (to bind again), effectively describes the aforementioned relationship. But nothing gives a clearer profile of religion than the *Bible* which, from Genesis to Revelation details the ongoing *relationship between a personal God and humankind, especially by covenant*.

The word *covenant* is most important; indeed, according to Richard P. McBrien in *Catholicism,* it is the very foundation of all Judeo-Christian spirituality.[6] Derived from the French *couvenant* and ultimately from the Latin *convenire* (to come together), a covenant is an agreement (a "coming together") which establishes a bond of personal and/or communal relationship between God and humans and/or between humans alone. For example, the Covenant at Sinai, which biblical archaeologists have shown to be closely akin to Hittite suzerainty treaties,[7] established a *lasting bond of relationship between Yahweh and Israel*, as described so beautifully in one of the Bible's most poignant passages:

> Thus shall you say to the house of Jacob; tell the Israelites: you have seen for yourselves how I treated the Egyptians and how I bore you up on eagle wings and brought you here to myself. Therefore, if you hearken to my voice and keep my *covenant*, you shall be my special possession, dearer to me than all other people, though all the earth is mine. You shall be to me a kingdom of priests, a holy nation. That is what you must tell the Israelites (Ex 19:3-6; see also Dt 32:11).

The conditions or stipulations of this covenant, corresponding to the suzerain's requirements of his vassals in Hittite treaties, were the Ten Commandments, while the many laws of the "Book of the Covenant" in Exodus and especially those of Leviticus, Numbers, and Deuteronomy were so many regulations developed in the course of time among the Israelites to insure the keeping of the Commandments and thereby the preservation of the Covenant. Unfortunately, Israel, especially under the monarchy, often proved faithless through idolatry which the Prophets such as Hosea, Isaiah, Jeremiah, and Ezekiel described as adultery, since the Covenant had established a *"spiritual marriage"* between Yahweh and Israel. Finally, Yahweh allowed his "spouse" to be taken into exile to purge her of idolatry and bring her back to himself (Ho 2:16-22; Is 54:6-8; 62:4-5). Of particular importance, he promised to establish a *new covenant*, as described in the prophecy of Jeremiah 31:31-34,

> The days are coming, says the Lord, when I will make *a new covenant* with the house of Israel and the house of Judah. It will not be like the covenant I made with their fathers the day I took

them by the hand to lead them forth from the land of Egypt; for they broke my covenant, and I had to show myself their master, says the Lord. But this is the covenant which I will make with the house of Israel after those days, says the Lord. *I will place my law within them, and write it upon their hearts*; I will be their God, and they shall be my people. No longer will they have need to teach their friends and kinsmen how to know the Lord. All, from the least to the greatest, shall know me, says the Lord, for I will forgive their evildoing and remember their sin no more.

But alas! Human nature does strange things. Cleansed of idolatry, many Jews returned to their homeland, renewing the Covenant and rebuilding the Temple, only to fall prey in time to exaggerated legalism, especially among the "Scribes and Pharisees," as was evident at the time of Jesus. It is important, however, for us Christians to keep things in perspective by bearing in mind two things: (1) that there were good and holy Jews in Jesus' time, even among the Scribes and Pharisees, and (2) that the Jews of Jesus' time, and indeed of all time, are still God's Chosen People in a unique way, for as Paul insists in Romans 11:29, "God's gifts and his call are irrevocable."

In a related but more universal sense, we Christians are also God's Chosen People, consecrated to Him by a New Covenant (Jr 31:31-34) in the Blood of Christ as "a chosen race, a royal priesthood, a holy nation, a people He claims for His own . . ." (1 P 2:9). Yet, human nature being what it is, Christianity has also, through much of her history, fallen into exaggerated legalism, emphasizing law more than covenant, legalism more than relation, as is evident to anyone familiar with the history of Canon Law. With Vatican II, however, a "new Pentecost"[8] has occurred, ushering in a renewed emphasis on our Covenant relationship. Reflecting this fundamental new direction, Norbert Schiffers in *Rahner's Encyclopedia of Theology* refers to religion as "the quintessence of one's relationship with God."[9] In short, then, we can conclude that *religion essentially consists in our relationship with God (and with others because of God)*.

CHRISTIANITY:

From the foregoing examination of religion, it should be evident that Christianity is that form of revealed religion which essentially consists in our *relationship with the triune God of the New Testament*, a relationship embodied in a "new covenant, a covenant not of a written law but of spirit" (2 Cor 3:6; Jr 31:31-34), a covenant established not with the blood of animals (Ex 24:5-8; Heb 9:18-22) but with the very blood of the Son of God Himself (Mt 26:27-28; Mk 14:23-24; Lk 22:20; 1 Cor 11:25), the mediator and guarantee of a new and better covenant (Heb 7:22; 8:6-13; 9:15). In fact, the new covenant establishes a relationship which surpasses that of the old covenant so completely as to seem all but unbelievable! If Israel could boast, "What great nation is there that has gods so close to it as the Lord, our God, is to us whenever we call upon him?" (Dt 4:7), how can we possibly express our astonishment that, in the new covenant, God himself actually becomes human in the person of Jesus Christ, lives among us just like one of us in everything except sin, freely sacrifices his life for us and, having risen from the dead, continues to dwell with us in his Church, in his Word, in his Eucharist, indeed, in each of us individually, uniquely, and (if we permit) so completely that, through us, he continues his life and ministry in the world today! No wonder that Paul, in comparing the new covenant with the old, cries out in wonder, "All of us, gazing on the Lord's glory with unveiled faces, are being transformed from glory to glory into his very image by the Lord who is the Spirit" (2 Cor 3:18) and, with an additional note of ministry, "For God who said, 'Let light shine out of darkness' has shone in our hearts, that we in turn might make known the glory of God shining on the face of Christ" (2 Cor 4:6).

However, religion (including Christianity) does not exist in the abstract, but rather in the minds and hearts of human beings. By that very fact, it is subject to being shaped, for better or worse, by certain notable dimensions of the various *human cultures* which it encounters, much as water or wine takes on the shape of the pitcher, bottle, or glass into which it is poured. Thus, in the history of

Christianity, we can discern the influence of Jewish culture with its emphasis on Mosaic Law, of Greek culture with its penchant for philosophical speculation, of Roman culture with its genius for law and order, politics and administration, of European culture with its endless struggles for power and prestige, of Asiatic culture with its strong inclination to quietism, and finally of American culture, with its tendency to emotionalism in South and Central America and to efficiency in North America.

Granted that these brief cultural descriptions are only partial and perhaps too simplistic, granted also that no culture should ever be rejected as such, it is still helpful and even necessary to look beyond the particular cultural clothing of the Christian religion to discover the heart of Christianity as a religion "in spirit and in truth" (Jn 4:23-24) which Jesus established through his apostles. We must, in other words, look beyond the frame to the picture, beyond the wrapping to the gift. This we can best do through a careful reading of the *New Testament*, which provides us, over and over again, with the clear profile of Christianity as Jesus intended it to be: a *religion of loving relationship!*

Matthew and *Luke*, among the Gospels, both contain that magnificent passage in which Jesus thanks his Father for revealing his truths to the humble, and goes on to speak of the *revelatory relationship* existing among the Father, the Son, and true believers (Mt 11:25-27; Lk 10:21-22). Then in Matthew, the "Ecclesial Gospel," Jesus gently invites all who "labor and are burdened," especially under the intolerable written and oral regulations imposed by the Scribes and Pharisees, to "come to him" (in personal relationship) and assume his "easy yoke" in order to find peace and rest of soul (Mt 11:28-30). The word "yoke" here is of special significance on account of its literal usage in linking two animals together and its figurative usage in linking two persons to live and work in unison, e.g., in marriage (2 Cor 6:14) or, more importantly, in a spiritual union (2 Cor 6:14-16; see also 1 Cor 6:13-20).

John, especially in the sublime discourse at the Last Supper, portrays Jesus in *intimate lasting relationship* with his followers, a relationship that also clearly includes the Father and the Spirit. ''Anyone who loves me will be true to my word, and my Father will love him; we will come to him and make our dwelling place with him . . . The Paraclete, the Holy Spirit whom the Father will send in my name, will instruct you in everything, and remind you of all that I told you'' (Jn 14:23, 26). This is further underlined in the rest of John's Gospel, particularly in Jesus' parable of the Good Shepherd in Chapter 10 and of the True Vine in Chapter 15, as well as in his Priestly Prayer in Chapter 17.

The Acts of the Apostles describes this same *relationship* as lived out in the community life of the early Church. Very significantly, Luke begins the work with these words, ''In the first book, O Theophilus, I have dealt with all that *Jesus began to do and teach,* until the day when he was taken up, after he had given commandment through the Holy Spirit to the apostles whom he had chosen'' (Ac 1:1 RSV). This translation from the *Revised Standard Version,* adopted also in the *New International Version,* seems far more natural and accurate a rendering of the Greek verb *erxato* (from *archomai* — I begin) than that of ''from the beginning'' found in the *New American Bible,* the *Jerusalem Bible,* and the *New English Bible.* It is also more meaningful and consonant with Luke's ecclesiology in Acts. In his earthly life, as recorded in Luke's Gospel, Jesus only *began* to do and to teach; he *continues* to do so now and for all time in the *Church* and in individual *Christians,* as is clear in Acts, in the Letters (especially those of Paul), and in the Johannine writings.

Was not this the great lesson taught *Paul* at the very moment of his conversion: ''I am Jesus, the one you are persecuting'' (Ac 9:5)? A lesson which he not only learned but lived: ''This life I live now is not my own; Christ is living in me'' (Gal 2:20) and, ''To me, 'life' means Christ; hence dying is so much gain'' (Ph 1:21). In fact, all of *Paul's* letters expand on the theology of this *redemptive relationship* in a great variety of ways, which we can only indicate for the reader's prayerful reflection. (See Rm 8; 1 Cor 6 and 13; 2 Cor 3-6; Gal

3:26-28; Ep 1 and 5; Ph 1-3; Col 1; to which we might also add the *Epistles of Peter and John*, especially 1 Jn 1:1-14 and 4:7-21).

Finally, the *Apocalypse* or Book of *Revelation* faithfully reflects the foregoing emphasis on *personal and communal relationship*, particularly in the opening and closing chapters (Rv 1-3 and 19-22). Of special significance are the great vision of Jesus, the risen and glorified Christ, in the midst of the seven golden lampstands, which represent the Church, especially the seven churches of the Roman Province of Asia in Western Asia Minor (Rv 1:9-20) and the touching invitation of Jesus to the lukewarm church of Laodicea, "Here I stand, knocking at the door. If anyone hears me calling and opens the door, I will enter his house and have supper with him, and he with me" (Rv 3:20). Do not these beautiful passages reflect and reinforce respectively the more familiar descriptions, referred to above, of Jesus' union with the Church and with Christians in the parable of the Vine and the Branches in John 15 and the Divine Indwelling in John 14:23?

Nor does this sense of personal and communal relationship with Christ and, through him, with the Father and the Holy Spirit, cease at the death of the last apostle, or later when the Church begins to lose her pristine fervor. Instead, it continues unabated in the lives of numerous canonized and innumerable uncanonized *saints* who, while they differ widely among themselves in age, sex, nationality, state of life, social status, and particularly mission (thus truly representing the diversity and catholicity of Christianity), nevertheless have one thing above all in common — *a deep, personal relationship* with Jesus Christ and with his Father and Spirit. Even in the very darkest hours of the Church, God has raised up Saints to shine like the stars in the sky and guide his followers, more by example than by word, safely on their pilgrim journey to their home with him.

Clearly, then, *Christianity* as distinguished from any other form of religion, revealed or otherwise, *is focused on a deep personal and communal relationship with God the Father through Jesus Christ and in the Holy Spirit.* This is the center around which everything else revolves. Truths of faith and the creeds in which they are formulated, laws and the moral conduct which they govern, various forms of prayer and worship, psychological growth and social action, all are extremely important and their neglect inconceivable, yet all exist for the sake of what is at the very heart of religion and especially Christianity, namely our personal and communal relationship with God and with one another in God.

SPIRITUALITY: *ESSENCE*

As we have seen, religion in general and Christianity in particular consist essentially of relationship. But, as is obvious, there are *different degrees* of closeness and commitment in relationships, for example between husband and wife, parents and children, brothers and sisters, friends, associates, or mere acquaintances. Spirituality or, more precisely, *Christian spirituality* implies whole-hearted *commitment* to living and growing as fully as possible in *intimate relationship* with Jesus Christ and, through him, with the Father and the Holy Spirit. The Bible, far from shying away from a concept like intimate relationship, actually emphasizes it, especially in the prophetic descriptions of the old covenant as a marital union between Yahweh and Israel (in Ho 1-3; Is 49-54; Jr 1-3; Ezk 16) and in the spiritual interpretation of the *Song of Songs*, as well as in the revelation of Jesus Christ as "the Bridegroom" not only of the Church as a whole (Mt 9:14-15; Jn 3:25-30; 2 Cor 11:2; Ep 5:22-32; Rv 19:6-9) but also of individual Christians (Rm 7:1-6; 1 Cor 6:16-17; 2 Cor 6:14-16).

However, the very term *spirituality* seems too abstract to adequately describe this intimate relationship. For this reason, I personally prefer the term *spiritual life* or, better still, *Spiritual Life*, capitalized. The former expression connotes life in the spiritual dimension of our human nature, as will be explained in the following chapter. This is also sometimes referred to among spiritual writers as the *interior life* because of the emphasis placed on finding God "within" through solitude, silence, and personal prayer (Col 3:3). The latter expression, the Spiritual Life in capital letters, appeals to

me more because it clearly designates a special or higher kind of life,
the very Life of Jesus Christ himself (Rm 6:23; Gal 2:20; Ph 1:21),
formed and guided by the Holy Spirit (Rm 8:9-17; Gal 4:1-7). But the
most important word in these expressions is the common denominator
life because spirituality is nothing at all if it is not a life to be lived and
lived to the full (Jn 10:10)!

We live in a century when, in so many ways, life has lost much of
its meaning and value. Millions have been put to death at the hands of
totalitarian movements and regimes such as Nazism, Fascism, and
Communism. Even in the free world, millions of innocent lives are
snuffed out in the womb, while war, violence, crime, and accidents
account for an additional wholesale loss of life. Suicide, even among
the young, threatens to become an epidemic. What are the causes?
The solutions? Much has been spoken and written about both, but I
submit that the ultimate reasons and remedies lie in the sphere of the
spiritual. Life is precious only when it has meaning, and it has
meaning only when there are genuine faith and hope and love,
resulting in deep inner peace and happiness, with personal responsibility and mutual respect.

Life was not always "cheap." Not only are we endowed with
that most basic instinct of our nature, self-preservation, but history,
especially the salvation history recounted in Sacred Scripture, gives
abundant evidence of the highest regard for the sacredness of life. The
little Hebrew word for life, *hay* (pronounced much like our common
American greeting, "Hi!", which I like to use with the deeper
meaning of wishing life to all whom I meet), is used over four hundred
and fifty times in the Old Testament. All life is sacred and precious,
for it comes from God and depends entirely upon him, who alone has
the power of life and death. The New Testament emphasizes both the
importance and the richness of life by using three different Greek
words: *bíos* for the quality and more often the duration of life, our
lifespan; *psyché* (which also means *soul*) for natural and especially
human life; and *zoé* for supernatural, eternal, or divine life, what
Teilhard de Chardin calls "ultrahuman" life.[10] For example, "The

one who loves his life (*psyché*) in this world preserves it to life (*zoé*) eternal'' (Jn 12:25). This and other sayings of Jesus, however, are not intended to denigrate our natural human life, God's sacred and precious gift, but to emphasize the even greater value of supernatural, eternal life, whereby we share in God's own life.

When, therefore, I use the expression *Spiritual Life* instead of *spirituality*, I do so in order to call attention to the following depth and richness of meaning:

1. That it is a *life to be lived* and lived fully, not a mere abstraction to be studied and discussed.
2. That, as life and indeed supernatural or ultrahuman, eternal or divine life, *it is most sacred and precious.*
3. That, *as spiritual life,* it is lived in the *spiritual dimension* of our being.
4. That, *as Spiritual Life* (capitalized), it is *Life in the Spirit,* lived under the gentle, peaceful, yet transforming guidance of the Holy Spirit.
5. That it is *Life in Christ,* the crucified and risen Lord, into whom we are incorporated by baptism and transformed by prayer, the Sacraments (especially the Holy Eucharist), and the action of the Holy Spirit.
6. That it is *Christ's life in us,* continuing to live, love, and minister in the world today through our unique human nature surrendered to his possession.
7. That it is even *mystical life* which, shorn of all the romanticized ideas and spectacular phenomena so often identified with it, really means our self-surrender to God's living action, ''letting go and letting God,'' even to possession by and transformation into the risen Christ.

In times past, books of spirituality used to be largely ''how to'' manuals on the various *virtues,* with the implied understanding that their development one by one would make a practitioner perfect. Of course, there is some truth to that, for we cannot dispense with personal effort, but a more fundamental truth is that, if we live in personal relationship with Christ, if we truly live in him and he in us, then his virtues become ours, for he is "our wisdom, our justice, our sanctification, and our redemption" (1 Cor 1:30). Yes, the Spiritual Life or spirituality or "perfection" is not a pursuit of virtues as if they were collectors' items or wild game. In fact, it is not even a pursuit of Christ, but rather *his pursuit of us and our total surrender to him,* as is so magnificently described in Francis Thompson's poetic masterpiece, "The Hound of Heaven."[11]

The Spiritual Life, then, is eminently *dynamic* rather than static, *concrete* rather than abstract, *practical* rather than theoretical, *intuitive* rather than speculative, *existential* rather than "essential" (like Greek philosophy), *personal* rather than impersonal, *communal* rather than individualistic. And, providentially, all of these qualities are likewise characteristic of biblical thought, so that *biblical spirituality* is of its very nature an affirmation of Life and a combination of likes rather than the contradiction in terms that stems from a philosophical or legalistic approach to the Spiritual Life. But to see this clearly, we must now reflect on Sacred Scripture and its relationship with the Spiritual Life as we have delineated it.

SCRIPTURE:

First of all, *Sacred Scripture,* as the Word of God (through words of humans), is *informative and revealing.* It reveals God to us and us to ourselves: our call, our destiny, our dignity, the life of love that we are chosen to live. This is beautifully expressed in Hebrews 4:12-13: "God's word is living and effective, sharper than any two-edged sword. It penetrates and divides soul and spirit, joints and marrow; it judges the reflections and thoughts of the heart." From beginning to end, the Bible is a treasure trove of instruction and guidance in the Spiritual Life. Hence, St. Paul reminds his favorite disciple, Timothy (2 Tm 3:15-17): "From your infancy you have known the Sacred Scriptures, the source of the *wisdom* which through faith in Jesus Christ leads to *salvation.* All Scripture is inspired of God and is useful for teaching, for reproof, correction, and *training in holiness. . .''*

Secondly, the Word of God effects a *relationship* through *communication, dialogue,* and *communion* between God and ourselves. *Louis Bouyer,* using as a starting-point the relational ''I-Thou'' philosophy of *Martin Buber,* remarks in his *Introduction to Spirituality,* that

> . . . no one really becomes a person to us except in speaking, in a *dialogue.* . . . God, the God of Israel, the God of the Bible, the God of Jesus Christ . . . has manifested himself to us as supremely the ''I,'' the One Who has not waited to meet us until we should take the first step, but Who has himself taken the initiative in a dialogue between him and ourselves. . . . We can see already, therefore, that it is in no way an accidental circumstance that the eminently personal, interpersonal character of the Christian spiritual life is connected with a revelation, and still more precisely with a divine Word. . . . God has spoken to us, he has given himself to us in his Word; this is what we believe, and this belief not only dominates our Christian spiritual life, but is its very source, its *unique source.*[12]

In particular, Sacred Scripture as the Word of God forms a communion between God and ourselves. As F. X. Durrwell expresses it in his stimulating book, *In the Redeeming Christ,* ''Scripture establishes a communion . . . of thought between two people who love each other and talk together, one of whom is Christ.''[13] Just as married couples or close friends cannot maintain a loving and lasting relationship without personal communication and communion, so we cannot maintain our loving and lasting relationship with God, which is the essence of religion, Christianity, and the Spiritual Life, without the communication, dialogue, and communion effected by his Word in Sacred Scripture.

St. Ambrose, in a memorable passage quoted in part by the *Constitution on Divine Revelation* of Vatican II,[14] challenges the clergy (and, by extension, all Christians) thus,

Why do you not spend the time . . . in reading? Why do you not go back again to see Christ? Why do you not address Him, and hear His voice? We address Him when we pray, we hear Him when we read the sacred oracles of God.[15]

For our dialogue with God, listening to him in Scripture is at least as important as speaking to him in prayer. In fact, the argument might well be made that listening is even more important than speaking. The famous philosopher *Zeno,* founder of the Stoics, is quoted by *Diogenes Laertius* as saying "to a stripling who was talking nonsense . . . 'The reason why we have two ears and only one mouth is that we may listen the more and talk the less!' "[16] And *Shakespeare,* in his *Hamlet* and *Henry IV* respectively, not only has Polonius caution Laertes, "Give every man thine ear, but few thy voice,"[17] but even has Falstaff (of all people) plead guilty of "the disease of not listening, the malady of not marking"![18]

History might well have turned out quite differently if certain persons had truly listened. For example, if Rehoboam had listened to the people at Shechem and especially to his elders, there might never have been a divided kingdom (1 K 12); if the kings of Israel and Judah had listened to the prophets, there would never have been an Assyrian or Babylonian Captivity. In more modern times, such disasters as Custer's battle at Little Big Horn, the charge of the Light Brigade, and the ill-fated maiden voyage of the Titanic might never have occurred if those in key positions had bothered to listen to orders and advice. So conscious have some businesses become of the importance of listening that they even provide courses in listening for their managers and employees. Must it always be true, as Jesus remarked in the parable of the wily manager, that "the worldly take more initiative than the other-worldly" (Lk 16:1-8)?

If listening is so crucial in history, in business, and in life generally, how much more so in the Spiritual Life, in our loving dialogue with God, especially when we consider the unlimited disparity between his word and ours! Perhaps that is why Luke's "Gospel of

Prayer'' first presents the inspiring picture of Mary of Bethany, ''who seated herself at the Lord's feet and *listened* to his words'' (Lk 10:39) and only then proceeds to record Jesus' teaching about prayer in Chapter 11. Perhaps also that is why Jesus so commonly concludes his discourses and parables with the challenge, ''Let him who has ears to hear me, hear!'' (Mk 4:9, 23; 7:16; Mt 11:15; 13:9, 43; Lk 8:8; 14:35). And note how gently but urgently Jesus connects attention to his Word with openness to his indwelling presence in those ''twin passages'' of Johannine writing to which I referred earlier and which I offer here in my own translation from the Greek original:

> If anyone loves me, he will *keep my word*, and my Father will love him, and we will come to him and *make our home* with him (Jn 14:23, WD).

> If anyone *hears my voice* and opens the door, I will come in to him and *have supper* with him, and he with me (Rv 3:20, WD).

We need, then, to take to heart the urgent invitation in the *Liturgy of the Hours*,[19] ''Today, listen to the voice of the Lord'' (Ps 95:7)! We need to respond with the beautifully simple words of the young Samuel, ''Speak, Lord, for your servant is listening'' (1 S 3:10).

   Thirdly, the Word of God is not only informative and revealing, communicative and communion-forming, but actually *creative, formative, life-giving, redemptive*, and *transforming*. To appreciate this amazing fact, we need to know something about the Hebrew understanding of *word* (Hebrew *davar*, Greek *rhēma* or *lógos*) as not only something spoken or written but something *done*, not only word but *deed!* This comes through in many passages of the Bible, beginning with the Old Testament, from the description of creation and formation (Gn 1-2) through God's saving word in *Exodus-Numbers-Joshua*, through the beautiful statement in *Deuteronomy 8:3* quoted by Jesus in his first temptation (Mt 4:4; Lk 4:4), ''Not by bread alone does man live but by every word that comes forth from the mouth of God,'' on through his prophetic word in the so-called *Historical Books* and especially the *Prophets*, for example Isaiah 55:10-11,

> For just as from the heavens
>> the rain and snow come down
> And do not return there
>> till they have watered the earth,
>> making it fertile and fruitful,
> Giving seed to him who sows
>> and bread to him who eats,
> So shall my word be
>> that goes forth from my mouth;
> It shall not return to me void,
>> but shall do my will,
>> achieving the end for which I sent it.

As might be expected, this same emphasis on the intrinsic power of God's word continues unabated in the *Wisdom Literature*, e.g., Psalm 33:6, "By the word of the Lord the heavens were made . . ." and in a beautiful passage which the Church accomodates to the Liturgy of the Christmas Season,[20] "When peaceful stillness compassed everything and the night in its swift course was half spent, your *all-powerful word* from Heaven's royal throne bounded, a fierce warrior, into the doomed land, bearing the sharp sword of your inexorable decree" (Ws 18:14-16).

This same understanding of *word* is found also in the *New Testament*, especially in the *Gospels*, where Jesus shows himself "powerful in word and deed in the eyes of God and all the people" (Lk 24:19), even eliciting from the temple guards the awed declaration, "No man ever spoke like that before!" (Jn 7:46). This is particularly true of his parables, which both instruct and challenge the hearers. For example, in the parable of the sower (Mt 13:4-23, Mk 4:1-20, Lk 8:4-15), "the seed is the word of God" (Lk 8:11) which is *fruitful of itself* and limited only by lack of readiness on the part of the soil, that is, of human hearts. Likewise, we see in the Gospels the extraordinary power of Jesus' words in the performance of his numerous miracles, among which must be included his institution of the

Eucharist (Mt 26, Mk 14, Lk 22, and 1 Cor 11) when by his transforming word he changes common bread and wine into his own body and blood. This same power of the word continues in the *Church*, as is evident in the discourses and miracles of Peter and Paul in *Acts* and confirming statements in the *Epistles* (e.g., 2 Tm 2:9, "There is no chaining the word of God!" and 1 P 1:23, "Your rebirth has come, not from a destructible but from an indestructible seed, through the living and enduring word of God").

In our own time, Thomas Merton has given us a clear and powerful summary of the transforming nature of the Bible in his unforgettable little book, *Opening the Bible:*

> The basic claim made by the Bible for the word of God is not so much that it is to be blindly accepted because of God's authority, but that it is *recognized by its transforming and liberating power*. The "word of God" is recognized in actual experience because it does something to anyone who really "hears" it: it transforms his entire existence. Thus Paul writes to the Thessalonians: "And we also thank God constantly for this, that when you received the word of God which you heard from us, you accepted it not as the word of men but as what it really is, the word of God, which is at work in you believers" (1 Th 2:13). But this "operation" of the word of God penetrating our inmost being is more than a communication of light: it is a *new birth*, the beginning of a *new being*![21]

St. Jerome, the great patron of Sacred Scripture loved to say in his usual blunt fashion, "Ignorance of the Scriptures is ignorance of Christ!"[22] and "We have in this life only this one good thing: to feed upon his flesh and drink his blood, not only at the table of the Sacrament (of the Eucharist) but also at the table of his Word."[23] In apparent allusion to this statement of St. Jerome, the *Constitution on Divine Revelation* of Vatican II begins its climactic final chapter with these incisive words:

The Church has always venerated the divine Scriptures as she venerated the Body of the Lord, in so far as she never ceases, particularly in the sacred liturgy, to partake of the bread of life and to offer it to the faithful from the one table of the *Word of God* and the *Body of Christ*.[24]

Notice the balance between the Eucharist and the Scriptures, a balance emphasized clearly in the *Mass* with its division into Liturgy of the Word and Liturgy of the Eucharist, reflecting the balance of word and sacrifice which had prevailed among the Jews, for example, in the combination of synagogue and temple worship. In fact, this same balanced pattern of the Word and the Eucharist seems to be reflected in the *New Testament*, where Jesus first teaches the crowd before multiplying the loaves and fishes (Mk 6:34-44; Lk 9:10-17), discourses on faith before promising the Eucharist (Jn 6), and instructs his disciples on the way to Emmaus before revealing himself to them ''in the breaking of bread'' (Lk 24:13-35). And this same practice is obviously continued in the early Church, as Luke indicates in his summary statement (Ac 2:42): ''They devoted themselves to the Apostles' instruction and the communal life, to the breaking of bread and the prayers.''

In *summary*, we have seen that the very essence of religion, Christianity, and spirituality or the Spiritual Life is relationship with God and with one another because of God, and further that, in the words of Vatican II, Scripture is the ''pure and lasting fount of the Spiritual Life''[25] because it is not only informative and revealing, communicative and communion-forming, but creative and formative, life-giving and redemptive, as well as profoundly transforming. No wonder St. Paul exhorts the Colossians, ''Let the word of Christ, rich as it is, dwell in you'' (Col 3:16).

Perhaps a fitting *conclusion* to this first chapter might be an account of my own personal experience and consequent conviction regarding the important relationship of Scripture and the Holy Eucharist, mentioned above. Growing up in New Orleans, Louisiana,

I used to pass by the Salem Evangelical Church en route to St. Stephen's Catholic Church for Sunday Mass. As I heard the preaching and singing of hymns emanating from the former, I would think to myself (in that unecumenical time and place), "That sounds beautiful, but how can these people consider themselves fully Christian if they do not truly believe in the Real Presence of Jesus in the Eucharist as we Catholics do?" Later, after growing up and coming to appreciate the importance of the Bible, I could not but turn the question around and ask: "How can we Catholics consider ourselves fully Christian if we do not read the Bible, the very Word of God?"

If we truly appreciate the meaning of religion, Christianity, and the Spiritual Life as consisting essentially of relationship, and if we fully recognize the vital role of God's powerful word in Sacred Scripture in building and perfecting our relationship with him and with one another, then we will wholeheartedly make our own the striking sentiments of the great prophet Jeremiah (15:16),

> When I found your words, I devoured them!
> They became my joy and the happiness of my heart,
> because I bore your name, O Lord, God of hosts.

Are not these the very same sentiments echoed in the New Testament by the two disciples of Emmaus? "Was not our heart *burning* within us while he [the risen Christ] was *speaking* to us on the way as he was *opening* for us the *Scriptures*?" (Lk 24:32, WD).

RECOMMENDED READING LIST

1. Bouyer, Louis. *The Spirituality of the New Testament and the Fathers* (A History of Christian Spirituality, vol. I), trans. Mary P. Ryan, New York, NY: Seabury Press, 1975.
2. Carter, Edward. *Response in Christ* (A Study of the Christian Life), 2nd revised edition, Staten Island, NY: Alba House, 1972.
3. Daughters of St. Paul. *Spiritual Life in the Bible,* Boston, MA: St. Paul Editions, 1980.
4. Kodell, Jerome. *Responding to the Word* (A Biblical Spirituality), Staten Island, NY: Alba House, 1978.
5. Stuhlmueller, Carroll. *Thirsting for the Lord* (Essays in Biblical Spirituality), Staten Island, NY: Alba House, 1977.

POINTS FOR REFLECTION AND DISCUSSION

1. What is our understanding of religion, Christianity, and spirituality? How has it changed during our lifetime, especially as a result of Vatican II?
2. How does our understanding of religion, Christianity, and spirituality make a difference in our lives, individual and communal, in today's world?
3. What is a covenant? How does covenant theology play a crucial role in our understanding of religion, Christianity, and spirituality?
4. What are some of the rich meanings inherent in the expression "Spiritual Life" and what relevance do they have for our lives?
5. How does the very nature of spirituality and of Scripture indicate the basic logical and theological interrelationship between the two?

CHAPTER TWO

THE HUMAN PARTNER OF THE RELATIONSHIP:
"The Three Faces" of Humans

To anyone enamored of Greek history and culture, indeed to anyone appreciative of natural and man-made beauty, the name *Delphi* evokes a panorama which is literally overwhelming. The physical setting alone is enough to take one's breath away! Perched on a series of terraces which cling to a spur of majestic Mt. Parnassos and surrounded by a semi-circular "theater" carpeted with thousands of olive trees, Delphi even today transports tourists back to that period of nearly a thousand years (7th century B.C. to 4th century A.D.) when she was the "navel" (*omphalós*) or center of the world, the mythological meeting place of the divine and the human. Kings and commoners arrived from all over the known world to learn from Apollo through the Pythian priestess (from *punthánomai,* to inquire?) the will of the gods for them. Surprisingly, however, according to *Plato* there once existed at the very heart of this religious complex, on the facade of the great temple of Apollo itself, not a religious but a philosophical inscription, *Know Thyself (gnóthi sautón)*![1]

Surprisingly? Perhaps not, since both religious and philosophical thinkers down through the centuries have agreed that knowledge of God begins with knowledge of ourselves and our human nature. Psalm 139 thanks and praises Yahweh in awestruck, lyrical terms,

> Truly you have formed my inmost being;
>   you knit me in my mother's womb.
> I give you thanks that I am fearfully, wonderfully made;
>   wonderful are your works! (Ps 139:13-14)

And *Paul* (in Rm 1:20) reminds us that, "Since the creation of the world, invisible realities, God's eternal power and divinity, have become visible, recognized through the things he has made," including ourselves.

Closer to our own time, the seventeenth century English religious poet, Francis Quarles, remarks in his popular collection of epigrams called *Hieroglyphics,*

> Man is man's A B C. There is none that can
> Read God aright, unless he first spell Man. [2]

In the same vein, the great neo-classicist poet of the following century, Alexander Pope, in his masterful *Essay on Man* cautions us with words of sober wisdom,

> Know then thyself, presume not God to scan,
> The proper study of mankind is man. [3]

And finally, H. W. Ramsaur, a contemporary American poet and musician, warns us in his *Epitaph, Found Somewhere in Space,*

> In desolation, here a lost world lies.
> All wisdom was its aim: with noble plan,
> It sounded ocean deeps; measured the skies;
> And fathomed every mystery but Man. [4]

Now, if all these reminders of the necessity of self-knowledge deserve our attention on both religious and philosophical grounds, how much more so when we are considering the very essence of religion which, as we have seen, is *relationship*. For there can be no relationship without at least two parties or partners, and certainly no deep and lasting relationship unless the partners really know both themselves and each other. How many times has this been proven true, for example in the case of marital relationships. In much the same way, and even more importantly because of their eternal effect, true religion, Christianity, and spirituality require a thorough practical knowledge on our part of both partners of our covenant relationship, namely God and ourselves.

The study of God is called *theology*; that of human nature, *anthropology*, both terms being derived (like so much of our language) from the Greek words for *god* and *man* respectively. There are many kinds of theology and many kinds of anthropology, depending on one's starting point and methodology. For our purposes, however, we will concentrate on biblical theology and anthropology, which provide us with God's own portrait of himself and of ourselves, albeit somewhat shaped by the culture(s) of the human authors involved. In a synthesis such as this, it will be necessary and even helpful to limit ourselves to certain *basic considerations* of biblical theology and anthropology. We will begin with the latter. Not, of course, that our human nature is more important than God, the creature than the creator, but rather it is somewhat more familiar and, as we have seen, forms a necessary stepping-stone from the "known to the unknown," from the "visible to the invisible" (Rm 1:20). Therefore, we will examine the biblical portrait of our human nature in this chapter, reserving to the next the biblical portrait of God.

How does the *Bible* speak of our human nature? Certainly not philosophically, still less scientifically, but rather religiously, namely according to our relationship with God. The contrast between the two approaches is shown to some extent in their divergent views regarding the seat of thought and knowledge; Greek philosophy perceiving it to be the mind (*noûs*) or brain (*phrén*), Scripture generally identifying it with the heart (Hebrew *lev*, Greek *kardiá*), anticipating by centuries the much-admired aphorism of Pascal in his *Pensées*, "Le Coeur a ses raisons que la raison ne connaît point" (The heart has its reasons which the reason knows nothing of).[5] If there is philosophy here, it is not that of the Greeks, still less that of Descartes which has influenced so much of modern thought, but rather that of such contemporary thinkers as Martin Buber, Gabriel Marcel, Alfred North Whitehead, and Pierre Teilhard de Chardin.

Perhaps even more dramatically, the contrasting approaches of Greek philosophy and biblical thought are delineated in their basic statements about *wisdom*. The sages of Greece enshrined their idea of wisdom (*sophia*), as we have seen, in the famous inscription "Know Thyself," mentioned no less than eight times in the *Dialogues* of Plato.[6] By contrast, the sages of Israel enshrined their idea of wisdom (*hochmah*) in a kind of motto, "Fear of the Lord is the beginning of wisdom," as found variously in the Wisdom Books of the Old Testament, not once but eight times. (Pr 1:7; 9:10; 15:33; Jb 28:28; Si 1:14, 16, 18, 24). Personally, I prefer to translate this cherished saying with words which, I believe, more faithfully reflect the true meaning of the sages, "The *love* of Yahweh is the *height* of wisdom." In any case, principally because of Israel's (and Christianity's) religious view of our human nature, biblical anthropology is fundamentally different from that Greek philosophical portrait of ourselves with which most of us have grown up and which we tend to take for granted, even using it (or rather misusing it) indiscriminately in our understanding of Sacred Scripture.

According to Greek anthropology, especially in Platonism and Neo-Platonism, we humans are composed of two distinct *parts*: body (*sôma*) and soul (*psyché*), united in life and separated at death. Our body is subject to sickness, death, and corruption, while our soul is of its nature immortal and, after death, continues to exist as a separate entity. In traditional Christian belief, our dead body will be raised to life again at the end of time and reunited with our soul for all eternity. This has been for centuries the accepted understanding of our human nature, one that is taken for granted today by most Christians, especially most Catholics.

I am not proposing a rejection of the body-soul concept. After all, we are obviously both physical and spiritual and, at death, this body of ours does stop breathing, our heart stops pumping, our brain stops functioning, and we begin to decay. It is no longer animate; that is, it no longer possesses the principle of life, which is one definition of a soul. Moreover, Scripture itself in both the Old and New Testaments does exhibit a certain amount of Greek influence, as a result of which there are references to body and soul in the commonly understood sense. This is especially true, for example, of the *Book of Wisdom* or *Wisdom of Solomon*, written originally in Greek and probably at Alexandria, Egypt, during the final century before Christ. It quite clearly refers to immortality of the soul, not so much as an intrinsic quality but as a gift of God (Ws 2:23-3:9). Likewise, in the New Testament, *Matthew* has Jesus refer to body *and* soul (Mt 10:28), "Do not continue to fear those who kill the body but cannot kill the soul; rather fear the one who can destroy both soul and body in Gehenna" (WD). And *St. Paul*, as might be expected from his Greek as well as Jewish education, does refer to sexual immorality as a sin against one's own body, which belongs to Christ and is a temple of the Holy Spirit (1 Cor 6:13-20). He also, as is well known, uses the analogy of the human body and its members to inculcate unity in the Church, the "Mystical Body of Christ" (1 Cor 12:12-27; Rm 12:3-7). And in 1 Th 5:23 his final blessing includes, "May he [God] keep whole your spirit (*pneûma*) and soul (*psyché*) and body (*sôma*) blamelessly in the [second] coming of our Lord Jesus Christ" (WD).

Besides the evidence of experience, observation, and the Scriptures just mentioned, we also need to take full advantage of the incredible *marvels of our body and soul,* particularly as discovered by the sophisticated technology of today's sciences, to become ever more aware of our human capacity and potential, but above all of the greatness and goodness of our God, who has made us "little less than the angels" and crowned us "with glory and honor!" (Ps 8:6). Fortunately, we now have available in our quest for this awareness a growing number of extraordinary works which combine accurate science with excellent teaching methods. To summarize even a fraction of their contents would take us far afield, but perhaps it will be helpful if I mention just a few of these books, ones in fact that can be found in my own personal library: *The Body in Question*[7] by Jonathan Miller (1978), *The Natural History of the Mind*[8] by Gordon Rattray Taylor (1979), *Breakthroughs*[9] by Charles Panati (1980), and *Fearfully and Wonderfully Made*[10] by Dr. Paul Brand and Philip Yancy (1982). The final title, of course, is borrowed from the haunting Psalm 139, which should be read in full, and specifically from verse 14, which begs to be repeated since it so perfectly epitomizes the awe, gratitude, and praise we owe God our Creator and Father for our body and soul, "I give you thanks that I am fearfully, wonderfully made; wonderful are your works!"

Yes, our Greek body-soul anthropology has, indeed, served us well through the centuries, at least in general. But, as we have come to realize more and more in recent years, it does have its limitations. It is good so far as it goes, but it is certainly incomplete, most notably in the following particulars:

(1)   It constitutes a *dichotomy*, with a sharp distinction between two entities, body and soul, united only during life — a portrait of human nature which has come increasingly into question because of the findings of biochemistry and other sciences, the philosophies of process and existentialism, and the vision of Teilhard de Chardin.

(2)   It postulates the continuation after death of the *soul* as a distinct, imperishable entity; but the soul by itself is, even by Greek definition, not a person!

(3)   It requires, in Christian belief, the incredible reconstruction and resurrection of billions of *bodies* which have been corrupted or cremated and intermingled for centuries. (Oriental reincarnation is, if anything, even more difficult philosophically and, of course, totally unknown to Sacred Scripture and Christian Tradition.)

(4)   It speaks only of a natural relationship between *body and soul* and is completely silent about any natural relationship with or orientation toward God.

For all these negative reasons and for as many positive ones, which will surface from our treatment, a number of Christian theologians are turning to biblical anthropology, to that portrait of our human nature which is expressed or implied throughout the Bible.

BIBLICAL ANTHROPOLOGY AND ITS IMPLICATIONS, PART I:

We find the basic scriptural anthropology expressed clearly, if somewhat figuratively, in the *Book of Genesis*, especially in the *second chapter*. In the typical anthropomorphic style of the "Yahwist tradition," apparently the oldest of the four traditions underlying the Pentateuch, God is depicted as a potter working with clay, which reflects the most common industry of the ancient world. At a particular time, he takes some clay, shapes it into a figure, then breathes into that figure the "breath of life" and lo and behold! the figure becomes a living being or person (Gn 2:7). This vivid portrayal, of course, was never intended by the human author inspired by God to argue one way or the other between creationism and evolutionism, but more importantly it presents a three-dimensional picture of our human nature which, despite the mythical imagery in which it is framed, is more accurate, complete, and meaningful than the one offered by Greek philosophy.

According to this biblical anthropology, in contrast with the dichotomy of Greek philosophy, we humans are identified as *one entity, one being,* not divided into parts but existing in *three dimensions or aspects.* Briefly, we are three-dimensional beings! We are *flesh* (Hebrew *bashar,* Greek *sárx*), as suggested by our formation from clay. We are *spirit* (Hebrew *ruah,* Greek *pneûma*), as indicated by God's breathing into us the breath of life. (Both *ruah* and *pneûma,* like Latin *spiritus,* can mean breath, wind, or spirit.) And we are a *being or person* (Hebrew *nephesh,* Greek *sôma* or *psychē,* depending on whether emphasis is on body or soul according to Greek anthropology).

Each of these three dimensions of our human nature is full of meaning. *Flesh* describes our human nature as one with the rest of creation and particularly as subject to physical and moral weakness: to sickness, pain, and death as well as to temptation and sin. *Person or (human) being* describes our human nature as distinguished from and superior to the rest of earthly creation, especially because of our imagination, intelligence, and free will. And, most significantly of all, *spirit* describes our human nature as naturally oriented toward God, capable and desirous of existence and perfection beyond the natural powers of imagination, intelligence, and free will; in other words, open to divine grace, virtues, and gifts, to divine relationship, union, possession, and transformation. As Paul says (in Rm 8:16), "The *Spirit* himself gives witness with our *spirit* that we are children of God."

Earlier, I suggested that the Greek *body-soul* anthropology is not so much erroneous as incomplete. It does describe us as a person, albeit as a split person — a dichotomy of body and soul, but it says nothing about our human inclinations to weakness and sin, nothing about our human aspirations to goodness and God. It has served and can continue to serve us well, provided that we view it within the context of the more complete, instructive, and religious anthropology of Sacred Scripture. And this is nowhere more true than when we are reading the Bible itself, for we will constantly distort the meaning of the human authors, who wrote out of a Semitic, Eastern manner of thinking and writing, if we insist on interpreting them according to our Greco-Roman, Western mentality and terminology — a fact that will become evident as we examine some of the more pertinent texts of Sacred Scripture, especially the New Testament.

For example, the word *flesh* in Scripture is normally not to be identified with our word *body*, as we tend to do, still less with sin. When John 1:14 tells us that "The Word became flesh," in no way does this mean that the Word became simply a human body or that the Word became sinful, but rather that he became human in all our human weakness, sin alone excepted. Nor does Paul's emphatic declaration (2 Cor 5:21) contradict this, for in the context the meaning of Paul's paradox is clear. "For our sakes God made him who did not know sin [who was totally sinless] to be sin [to be like one who was sinful], so that in him we [who are sinful] might become the very holiness of God."

And when *Jesus* in Gethsemane (Mt 26:41; Mk 14:38) and *Paul* in his letters to the Galatians and Romans (Gal 5:16-17; Rm 8:1-13) refer to the conflict between *spirit and flesh*, they are not speaking of a war between our soul and our body, but rather between our aspirations to good and God on the one hand and our inclinations to temptations, sin, and Satan on the other. Richard McBrien, in his landmark work *Catholicism*, expresses it well. "The spirit-flesh opposition in Paul is between the whole person as oriented toward the Kingdom of God, and the whole person as oriented away from God in pursuit of selfish interests."[11] Thus, when Paul, referring to the incestuous man, declares (in 1 Cor 5:5), "I hand him over to Satan for the destruction of his flesh, so that his spirit may be saved on the day of the Lord," he is not condemning the man to death as some have incredibly maintained, but rather exercising a form of excommunication for his conversion and salvation.

In confirmation of this important truth, Paul's list of the *"fruits of the flesh"* (Gal 5:19-21) contains mostly sins which do not primarily involve the body, if at all, e.g., "idolatry, sorcery, hostilities, bickering, jealousy, outbursts of rage, selfish rivalries, dissensions, factions, envy. . . ." How many Manichaean or Puritanical aberrations, ancient and modern, inside and outside the Church, which insist on the "evil of the body," might have been avoided through proper understanding of these passages! Conversely, how many opposite reactions of glorification of the body and especially of sexual permissiveness might never have developed!

Likewise, the Hebrew word for *person* in Scripture is not translated by the Greek word for *person (hypóstasis)*, which is entirely too abstract, but sometimes by the Greek word for *face (prósopon)* and more often by the Greek word for *body (sôma)* or *soul (psyché)*, depending on the emphasis implied. Therefore, when reference is made to the "body of Christ," it must be carefully interpreted according to the context; for example, as the (risen) person of Christ, his Eucharistic presence, or the Church as the communal body or community of Christ. By Baptism, we are incorporated into the *body-person* of the risen Christ, thereby also becoming one with all others who are "baptized into Christ" (as the branches of a vine are united with one another because they are all united with the vine, Jn 15), forming with them the *mystical body* of the Church, whose sign and sacrament of unity is the Holy Eucharist, in which we partake of the *body and blood* of Christ. (To appreciate these usages, see Rm 6:3; 7:4; 12:1, 4-5; 1 Cor 10:14-17; 11:23-29; 12:12-27; Ep 1:22-23; Col 1:18, 24).

In the same way, when the Greek word for *soul* (*psyché*) is used, we must try to determine whether it signifies *soul* as distinguished from *body* (Mt 10:28), or *soul* in the sense of *person*, usually translated simply as "I" (Mk 14:34), or *soul* in the sense of *natural life* (Jn 12:25), or sometimes even *soul* as equivalent to *spirit* (Lk 1:46-47). All of these, but especially the middle two, are possible meanings of the Greek word for *soul*.

Above all, the dimension of *spirit* not only contrasts with that of *flesh*, with which it is in conflict (Gal 5:16-17; Rm 8:1-13), the *person* being constantly torn between the two, but it also describes our *natural orientation* to God, to relationship and union with him, much as the heliotrope plant always seeks the sun. [12] Scripture is replete with expressed or implied references to this natural "hunger and thirst" for good and for God, a longing made all the more acute and consuming by grace, for example:

> As the hind·longs for the running waters,
> so my soul longs for you, O God.
> Athirst is my soul for God, the living God.
> When shall I go and behold the face of God? (Ps 42:2-3).
>
> O God, you are my God whom I seek;
> for you my flesh pines and my soul thirsts

like the earth, parched, lifeless and without water (Ps 63:2).

Blest are they who hunger and thirst for holiness;
they shall have their fill [be satiated] (Mt 5:6).

I long to be freed from this life and to be with Christ, for that is
the far better thing . . . (Ph 1:23). I wish to know Christ and the
power flowing from his resurrection. . . . I am racing to grasp the
prize if possible, since I have been grasped by Christ . . . My
entire attention is on the finish line as I run toward the prize to
which God calls me — life on high in Christ Jesus. All of us who
are spiritually mature must have this attitude (Ph 3:10, 12,
14-15).

Hence, the folly and failure of *atheistic movements* such as Communism in their attempts to destroy religion when, in fact, it is an
integral trait of our human nature. Hence also, the phenomenon of
moral philosophies such as Confucianism, Taoism, and Buddhism
which in time have become religions because we are by our very
nature religious. At the same time, the Western World, which prides
itself on its religious freedom and profession, is in danger of self-
destruction because of its failure to practice the religious beliefs that it
professes. Among so many of us in the West, there occurs what
Shakespeare's *Richard III* calls "the winter of our discontent,"[13] a
dark uneasiness or downright unhappiness because, though free from
external coercion, we often frustrate our hunger for God by allowing
ourselves to be enslaved by the "lust of the flesh, and the lust of the
eyes, and the pride of life" (1 Jn 2:16, WD) which, like the thorns in
the seed-parable, tend to choke off the good seed of the Word of God
(Mt 13; Mk 4; Lk 8).

All of this takes on added meaning when we consider the question of life after death. While Greeks, with their body-soul anthropology, naturally thought of an afterlife in terms of immortality of the
soul (Ws 2:23-3:4), Jews, with their three-dimensional body-soul-
person anthropology, came just as naturally in the course of time to

think of afterlife in terms of *bodily resurrection* (Dn 12:1-3). For us Christians, of course, resurrection of the body is a fundamental tenet of our faith (Mt 22:23-33; Jn 11:23-26; Ac 23:6-10; 1 Cor 15, etc.). But *when* and *how* does this resurrection take place? For various reasons which deserve a respectful hearing, based as they are on Sacred Scripture and sound theological reasoning, some biblical scholars and theologians, most notably *Ladislaus Boros,* have suggested the possibility of bodily resurrection, with a new and glorified body, immediately after death.[14] Those desiring a more complete discussion of this important question than would be appropriate here will please refer to *Appendix A* at the conclusion of the book. In the meantime, let us proceed to the second part of our examination of scriptural anthropology and its implications, in which we will concentrate on the first chapter of Genesis, so full of rich and salutary considerations that follow, surprisingly but naturally, the reflections we have just completed on Genesis, chapter two.

BIBLICAL ANTHROPOLOGY AND ITS IMPLICATIONS,   PART   II:

In my general introduction to this entire work, I mentioned that, "In an effort not to 'miss the forest for the trees,' I have tried to paint my portrait of scriptural spirituality with 'broad brush strokes.' " Now, in this chapter on scriptural anthropology, I am forced to apply this rule rigorously. There are so many insights in the Bible which pertain in one way or the other to anthropology that even an entire book, let alone a chapter, could hardly do them justice. To single out just a few, there is the relationship of the sexes, of personal and social responsibility, of individual and corporate personality, of security and change, etc. Some of these, at least, will be touched upon in other chapters, but in this chapter I simply must confine myself to only a pair of topics which I consider especially crucial. One, the three-dimensional makeup of our human nature (from Gn 2), we have already examined. The other, our creation *"in the image and like-ness" of God* (from Gn 1), we will now proceed to consider. Going from the second to the first chapter of Genesis may appear to be a strange retrogression on my part, but such is not the case, for in fact the Yahwist tradition (Gn 2) evidently antedates the Priestly tradition (Gn 1) by several centuries, a fact which I believe is reflected in the very content of the chapters themselves, and specifically of the two matters under consideration.

Genesis 1 was probably written during or right after the Babylonian Captivity of the Jews in the sixth century B.C. In it, God is described as if he were a house-builder, constructing by his almighty Word the "house" of creation in just six days, a time-pattern which is clearly modeled on the days of the week, most probably in order to emphasize the seventh day as the Sabbath or day of rest. (After the Exile, observance of the Sabbath became the hallmark of a good Jew, as we see reflected so often in the New Testament.) The first three days of creation are devoted to "building the house itself," the last three (which parallel the first three) are devoted to "furnishing the house." And the climax of all this "construction" is the creation of humankind, male and female, *"in the image and likeness" of God himself* (Gn 1:26-27).

This sublime, mysterious declaration, which seems to leap out at us from the Sacred Page, has been the object of innumerable theories of interpretation throughout Judeo-Christian history. What does it really mean? The answer to that question is not at all easy. First of all, we must try to determine what the human author, writing centuries before Christianity and millennia before our own time, intended to say. For, what the human author inspired by God meant by his statement is, in the terminology of modern biblical studies, the *literal sense* of Scripture and therefore the first and primary meaning that we need to discover and understand. Then, in the light of further revelation and inspiration, as unfolded especially in later Old Testament and more often in New Testament works, we are warranted in discovering possible *spiritual senses* (or, better still, *Spiritual senses*), that is, meanings intended by the Holy Spirit, the Author of all the Scriptures, beyond the limited knowledge and intention of the human author. Any other approach tends to neglect either the human or the divine authorship of the Bible, as has been pointed out in various Church pronouncements in this century, most notably in the encyclicals *Spiritus Paraclitus*[15] of Pope Benedict XV in 1920 and *Divino Afflante Spiritu*[16] of Pope Pius XII in 1943, as well as in the *Constitution on Divine Revelation* (Dei Verbum)[17] of the Second Vatican Council in 1965. What, then, did the human author intend by his startling declaration?

> Let us make man in our image, after our likeness. Let them have dominion over the fish of the sea, the birds of the air, and the cattle, and over all the wild animals and all the creatures that crawl on the ground.
>
> God created man in his image; in the divine image he created him; male and female he created them (Gn 1:26-27).

First of all, the context itself appears to suggest that *dominion* over the other living creatures is the principal characteristic of our creation in the image and likeness of God. As creator, God has supreme dominion over all his creation, including ourselves, but in his gratuitous generosity he chooses to share his dominion with us, his own creatures. What a staggering statement! But wait! There are implications here which demand our attention. After all, creation is his, not ours. Hence, our "dominion" is one of *stewardship,* not ownership. We have a responsibility to foster and protect created life, imaging the creative and protective love of God himself. If we fail in this, are we not guilty of the same kind of sin as Moses and Aaron, who failed to reflect his loving kindness and patience toward his Chosen People, and as a consequence were prohibited from entering the Promised Land (Nb 20:12)? Are we not like the careless or conniving stewards condemned in Jesus' parables (e.g., Lk 12:45-46 and 16:1-2)? By the same token, if we are created as responsible stewards of creation, are we not by implication intelligent and free human beings, endowed with a mind to know and a will to choose? Rightly, then, we can say with many that our *intelligence and free will* are at least implied as constituting our creation in the image and likeness of God or, in the words of Psalm 8:6, our being made "little less than the angels," and "crowned with glory and honor."

But is there a further implication? Are we made in God's image and likeness, not only in our stewardship of creation, but also in the very *ability to create*? Is this the significance of the words of our text, "male and female he created them" followed by "God blessed them, saying, 'Be fertile and multiply' "? According to Daniel Day Williams in *The Spirit and the Forms of Love*, "Man's creation in the image of God is his call to participate in creativity, in its splendor and its suffering."[18] If this be so, what an encomium on the sacredness of love and sex as the God-given means of cooperating with the Creator in bringing new life into the world! And what a condemnation of the abuse or misuse of this sacred gift of creativity contrary to the will of the Creator himself!

One final remark about the possible meaning or meanings intended by the human author inspired by God. We of the Western world, with our Greco-Roman background, are naturally inclined to attribute only one possible meaning to the human author. For example, if "the image and likeness of God" concerned dominion, then it did not concern the gift of creativity. But that is to apply our own Western way of thinking and writing to the human author, who in fact lived and wrote centuries ago in an Eastern context, whose mentality favored *multiplication rather than division of meanings*. This basic reminder will have even greater application in the New Testament, particularly when we encounter the characteristically pregnant expressions of writers like St. John and St. Paul.

In the meantime, however, let us examine briefly the light cast on our text by *later passages of Sacred Scripture*. Interestingly enough, *Genesis* itself contains some rather pointed references. For example, our human makeup as flesh, person, and above all *spirit* (Gn 2:7), discussed earlier, and our being placed in the "garden of

Eden.''(Gn 2:8 ff.) which so beautifully describes the gift of *grace* (symbolized by abundance of water and growth) and special relationship with God (symbolized by his own walking in the garden, Gn 3:8), do these not reflect our *natural orientation to God*, confirmed and perfected by grace, which seems to be implied somehow in our being created in his image and likeness?

And do not the ''surgical'' formation of Eve from Adam (so described to emphasize love, equality, and marriage, Gn 2:18-25) and the birth of Seth (Gn 5:1,3) reinforce the possibility of *sexual creativity* as a meaning of our text? Notice the wording of Genesis 5:1,3, ''When God created man, he made him in the likeness of God . . . Adam was one hundred and thirty years old when he begot a son in his likeness, after his image. . . .'' In fact, there may be an additional meaning here, namely that, as Seth is Adam's son, begotten in Adam's image and likeness, so Adam, and indeed all of us humans, are, by our very creation, *children of God*, formed in his own image and likeness, as implied in Luke's genealogy of Jesus, ''. . . son of Enos, son of Seth, son of Adam, son of God'' (Lk 3:38; cf. also Jn 1:12-13, Gal 4:4-7, and Rm 8:14-17).

A little further on (in Gn 9:6), the *unique dignity of human life* is forcefully underlined, ''If anyone sheds the blood of man, by man shall his blood be shed; for in the image of God has man been made,'' followed by the command to Noah, ''Be fertile, then, and multiply, abound on earth and subdue it'' (Gn 9:7). Other Old Testament references pertaining to our text are principally those found in the *Book of Wisdom* (notably 2:23, where we have a clear allusion to Gn 1:26-27), this time as a basis for the teaching on the *immortality of the soul*, ''For God formed man to be imperishable; the image of his own nature he made him.'' Likewise, *divine wisdom personified* is described (in Ws 7:26) as ''the refulgence of eternal light, the spotless mirror of the power of God, the image of his goodness.''

In the *New Testament*, the same terminology that has been used to describe the personification of God's creative and guiding wisdom, especially in the Book of Wisdom, is used to portray Jesus Christ the

Son of God as *Incarnate Wisdom*, first in Colossians 1:15, "He is the image of the invisible God, the first-born of all creatures," then in Hebrews 1:3, "This Son is the reflection of the Father's glory, the exact representation of the Father's being. . . ." Is it possible that, in a *Spiritual sense*, Genesis 1:26-27 is looking toward fulfillment in Jesus the Messiah, the very Son of God, who is the perfect image and likeness of the Father? Is it further possible, that, by extension, it also looks toward fulfillment in all of us, as is at least hinted in certain Pauline passages, e.g., Romans 8:29, "Those whom he foreknew he predestined to share the image of his Son," and 2 Corinthians 3:18, "All of us, gazing on the Lord's glory with unveiled faces, are being transformed from glory to glory into his very image by the Lord who is the spirit" (See also Col 3:10 and Ep 4:24).

Finally, in the light of the revelation of the Holy Trinity, is it possible to see a *Trinitarian Spiritual meaning* in our text, especially in the plural forms used, "Then God (*elohim*, a plural noun) said, 'Let *us* make man in *our* image, after *our* likeness' "? And, in this interpretation, is it possible that the "image and likeness of God" is actually the *ability to relate*, to love, to live in the loving relationship of *community* as do the three Persons of the Holy Trinity itself? In the thoughtful expression of *Daniel Day Williams*, "Man, created in God's image, is created for participation in the infinite life of communion within the everlasting creativity of God."[19]

Admittedly, much of the above is speculation, which I have tried to indicate by putting it in the form of questions. For me personally, the "image and likeness of God" is profoundly meaningful, but primarily in the *total context* of *Sacred Scripture*, especially the *New Testament*. Yes, we have been created from the beginning in God's image, but the full meaning, possibility, and actuality thereof had to await the coming of *Jesus Christ*, the perfect image of the Father (Col 1:15; Heb 1:3), into whose image we are called to be transformed (Rm 8:29; 2 Cor 3:18). To put it another way, we are indeed created "in the image and likeness" of God, but this permits of degrees, and the highest degree of this blessed gift can become ours only when, through total self-surrender, we allow Jesus Christ, the perfect image of the Father, to make us his own habitation and possession and to so transform us into himself that he can continue, in and through us, to be present, visible, and tangible, reflecting the Father's love and life to all about us. This is truly *"To Live the Word, Inspired and Incarnate!"*

SUMMARY AND CONCLUSION:

In *summary*, we have seen the importance of *self-knowledge* for our relationship with God. We have also learned how the traditional dualistic portrait of our human nature, drawn from Greek philosophy, has its merits but leaves several problematic questions unanswered; how the *three-dimensional anthropology* described in Genesis and reflected all through the Bible, provides a more satisfactory picture of our human nature and certainly a more appropriate basis for our loving spiritual relationship with God. Finally, we have examined the many rich meanings of our creation *"in the image and likeness"* of God, especially that fullness of meaning which has become possible for us through the coming of Jesus Christ, the perfect image of God, and through our transformation into him. In the incisive words of *St. Irenaeus*, "The glory of God is man fully alive!"[20] or, to quote Irenaeus' beautiful Latin expression in full, together with my own English translation,

> Gloria enim Dei vivens homo;
> Vita autem hominis visio Dei.[21]
>
> Man alive is the glory of God;
> Man's life is a vision of God!

By way of conclusion to this examination of biblical anthropology, let us allow the Word of God, both Inspired and Incarnate, to reveal us to ourselves, for it is certainly true that,

God's word is living and effective, sharper than any two-edged sword. It penetrates and divides soul and spirit, joints and marrow; it judges the reflections and thoughts of the heart. Nothing is concealed from him; all lies bare and exposed to the eyes of him to whom we must render an account (Heb 4:12-13).

Let us listen carefully to the reminder of James 1:21-24:

Humbly welcome the word that has taken root in you, with its power to save you. Act on this word. If all you do is listen to it, you are deceiving yourselves. A man who listens to God's word but does not put it into practice is like a man who looks into a mirror at the face he was born with; he looks at himself, then goes off and promptly forgets what he looked like!

And, finally, let us praise God in the words of the American educator. *William De Witt Hyde*:

> Creation's Lord, we give Thee thanks
> That this Thy world is incomplete;
> That battle calls our marshaled ranks,
> That work awaits our hands and feet;
>
> That Thou hast not yet finished man,
> That we are in the making still,
> As friends who share the Maker's plan,
> As sons who know the Father's will. . . .[22]

RECOMMENDED READING LIST

1. Gelin, Albert. *The Concept of Man in the Bible.* trans. David Murphy, Staten Island, NY: Alba House, 1968.
2. Mork, D. Wulstan. *The Biblical Meaning of Man,* Encino, CA: Glencoe Publishing Co., 1967.
3. Sharkey, Owen. *The Mystery of Man* (An Anthropologic Study), Philadelphia, PA: Franklin Publishing Co., 1975.
4. Verduin, Leonard. *Somewhat Less Than God* (The Biblical View of Man), Grand Rapids, MI: Eerdmans Publishing Co., 1970.
5. Wolff, Hans Walter. *Anthropology of the Old Testament,* trans. Margaret Kohl, Philadelphia, PA: Fortress Press, 1974.

POINTS FOR REFLECTION AND DISCUSSION

1. Why is it important in the Spiritual Life to have a clear knowledge of our basic human nature?
2. What is the biblical picture of our human nature and how does it differ from the familiar picture derived from Greek philosophy?
3. What is the meaning of each of the dimensions of our human nature according to the second chapter of Genesis?
4. What are some of the possible meanings of our being created in the "image and likeness" of God, according to the first chapter of Genesis?
5. What are some of the ways in which the biblical picture of our human nature can help us in our Spiritual Life and growth?

CHAPTER THREE

THE DIVINE PARTNER OF THE RELATIONSHIP:
"The Three Faces" of God

One of the most dramatic episodes in the history of the early Church is that which Luke recounts in Acts 17, namely St. Paul's address to the Athenians at the Areopagus, the Hill of Ares (Mars) overlooking the agora or marketplace of Athens. Paul begins: "Men of Athens, I note that in every respect you are scrupulously religious. As I walked around looking at your shrines, I even discovered an altar inscribed 'To a God Unknown.' Now, what you are thus worshipping in ignorance, I intend to make known to you" (Ac 17:22-23).

We may smile condescendingly at the naive superstition of the Athenians in trying to "touch all the bases" and avoid offending some god who may possibly exist without their knowledge. But the pity is that, even to many in our long monotheistic tradition, which includes at least Jews, Christians, and Moslems, God remains truly an "Unknown God"!

There are various reasons, of course, for this phenomenon. One is our human inclination (of the "flesh") to value knowledge of creation over that of the Creator. Another is our human tendency to *know about* God (Greek *oída* or *epístamai*, Latin *scio*) rather than to *know* God (Greek *ginósko*, Latin *cognosco)* in a personal, even biblical sense, which includes knowledge, love, relationship, and union. It is possible for philosophers, theologians, and Scripture scholars to be experts in knowledge *about* God, yet never to know him personally. Is this not what the *Imitation of Christ* decries, "If you knew the whole Bible by heart, and the sayings of all the philosophers, what would all that profit you without the love of God and his grace?"[1] And, even more tersely, St. Paul declares (1 Cor 13:2), "If I have the gift of prophecy and with full knowledge, comprehend all mysteries . . ., but have not love, I am nothing."

Finally, a third reason lies in the choice of *sources* used in seeking to know God. It is true that nature, science, psychology, philosophy, and philosophical theology can all provide knowledge of God, but what source can surpass that of the Bible, in which God reveals himself to us on every page? Hence, in the need of knowing the divine "partner" of that relationship which we call religion, and especially Christianity and spirituality, we will turn to *Sacred Scripture,* which the Catholic Church calls "the very soul of sacred theology,"[2] that is, of the study and knowledge of God.

Now, entire books have been written on biblical theology, the portrait of God delineated in Sacred Scripture, but the limitations of this synthesis require that we concentrate on only a few *outstanding points* which are more likely to foster true knowledge of and relationship with God. None of us, of course, can paint a total picture of God, however empathetic we may be toward the well-known story of the little girl whose mother tries to dissuade her from attempting such a portrait on the grounds that "No one knows what God looks like," to which the child triumphantly replies, "They'll know now!" What we can do, however, is focus on certain of God's "features" as they shine forth from the pages of his self-revealing Word.

THE BIBLICAL PORTRAIT OF GOD:

First, as all Scripture scholars and theologians agree, *the God of the New Testament is the God of the Old Testament.* It is bordering on blasphemy to speak of the God of Israel as a God of fear and the God of Christianity as a God of love. After all, the dual commandments so basic to Christian living, namely the love of God and neighbor, are inherited from Deuteronomy (6:5) and Leviticus (19:18). And even the title *"Father,"* so prominent in Jesus' discourses and especially in the Lord's Prayer (Mt 6:9; Lk 11:2), is found throughout the Old Testament, e.g., Deuteronomy 32:6, "Is the Lord to be thus repaid by you, O stupid and foolish people? Is he not your father who created you?" (See also the last prophet, Malachi 1:6; 2:10.) In fact, the Old Testament even contains a wealth of *maternal imagery about God,* most of it concerning his unlimited *compassion* (Hebrew *rahamim,* from *rehem,* meaning womb).[3] Note, for example, Yahweh's tender expressions in the book of Isaiah:

> Can a mother forget her infant,
>> be without tenderness for the child of her womb?
> Even should she forget,
>> I will never forget you.
> See, upon the palms of my hands I have written your name . . .
>> (Is 49:15-16).
> As a mother comforts her son,
>> so will I comfort you;
>> in Jerusalem you shall find your comfort (Is 66:13).

This maternal imagery will continue on into the New Testament, especially in Jesus' lament over Jerusalem (Mt 23:37-39 and Lk 13:34-35),

> O Jerusalem, Jerusalem, you slay the prophets and stone those who are sent to you! How often have I wanted to gather your children together as a *mother bird* collects her young under her wings, and you refused me.

And since, as St. John Chrysostom observes, "the heart of Christ was the heart of Paul,"[4] it is not surprising that the same kind of imagery also occurs in the Apostle's own writing, most notably in Galatians 4:19, WD: ". . . my little children, with whom I am *in labor again* until Christ be formed in you!" (See also 1 Th 2:7, 11.)

In addition, the *Old Testament* is replete with many highly descriptive references to God, almost all of them *relational*. These include *proper names* such as "Yahweh" (Ex 3:13-14), meaning "I (alone) am," "I am (present to save)," or possibly "I cause to be" (as Creator); *titles* such as Shepherd (Ps 23:1; 80:1; Is 40:11; Ezk 34), i.e., one who rules and leads with loving care; *substantive attributes* such as God's "face" (Nb 6:25); and *adjective attributes* such as "gracious and merciful" (Jon 4:2). And, in the *New Testament*, God continues to reveal himself in all these ways, but now in and through Jesus Christ (e.g., *"I am"* [Yahweh] in Jn 4:26; 6:20; 8:28,58; 13:19; *Shepherd* in Mt 18:10-14; Lk 15:4-7; Jn 10:11-18, 26-30; 21:15-17; *"face"* in Mt 17:2; Lk 9:29; 2 Cor 3:18; Col 1:15; Heb 1:3; Rv 1:14; *"gracious and merciful"* in Mt 5:7, 21-26, 38-48; 11:28-29; 12:15-21, etc., including the whole Gospel of Luke).

But, in order to appreciate something of God's unbelievable love for us, chronicled in the Old and especially the New Testament, it is not only helpful but indispensable to contemplate his greatness, his *supreme transcendence,* his unlimited "otherness." The apostles and early Jewish Christians had grown up with this sense of Yahweh's transcendence, so much so that out of reverence and awe, they would not even pronounce his sacred name of Yahweh. Hence, their astonishment, gratitude, love, and joy when they realized, at least through the resurrection, ascension, and Pentecost, that Jesus of Nazareth was not only their Messiah but the very Son of God! "My Lord and my God!" exclaimed Thomas for us all (Jn 20:28)!

It is difficult for us Christians today to develop that same attitude of awe, not only because we are heirs of centuries of emphasis on "Emmanuel" ("God with us," Is 7:14; Mt 1:23; 28:20; Jn 1:14; 14:23; Rv 3:20, etc.), but also because we live in a cynical age when "nothing is sacred" except, perhaps, science and technology, and we are taught by the media to worship ourselves and our own accomplishments. Yet science itself, especially the science of *astronomy,* can (when rightly used) be one of our most valuable aids enabling us to appreciate with awe the greatness of God.

First of all, as Robert Jastrow, a renowned and avowedly agnostic astronomer, details in *God and the Astronomers,* the discoveries in this century by astronomers like Slipher, Friedmann, De Sitter, Le Maitre, Hubble and Humason, Penzias and Wilson have established beyond doubt that we live in a huge exploding and rapidly expanding universe which (though continuously in process) began at a definite time, about twenty billion years ago, in what is whimsically called the "Big Bang."[5] To Jastrow and to an increasing number of scientists, this clearly points in the direction of initial creation and a Creator — "an exceedingly strange development, unexpected by all except the theologians."[6] And this may be confirmed even more within the next few years when, with more advanced earth and space telescopes, astronomers will be able to look back, so to speak, to a point in time very close to the "Big Bang" itself.[7]

Perhaps these recent advances may have the effect of converting some atheistic astronomers at least into agnostic astronomers — scientists willing to admit the possibility, perhaps even the probability, of a supreme "intellectual power" or "cosmic force" which is ultimately responsible for the origin of the universe but which is in no way personal, still less loving and caring toward us tiny specks on this ordinary planet (25,000 miles around, 93 million miles from the sun), in this ordinary solar system (some 7.4 billion miles across), in this ordinary galaxy (the Milky Way, some 100,000 light years across, containing billions of stars), only one among billions of other galaxies (each containing billions of stars) so far known to compose the universe.[8] But scientific observation itself may hopefully enable them to go a step further. For, in nature, there is a definite correlation between intelligence, personhood, and the capacity to love. Must we not conclude, then, that whoever or whatever is supremely intelligent must be also supremely personal and supremely loving?

But what has all this astronomy to do with *Scripture*? A great deal indeed! The psalmist, overwhelmed even by his extremely limited view of the night sky, exclaimed, "When I behold your heavens, the work of your fingers, the moon and the stars which you set in place — what is man that you should be mindful of him, or the son of man that you should care for him?'' (Ps 8:4-5). What awe of Yahweh he would have felt if he had possessed the knowledge of the universe which astronomy has given us! What a sense of personal insignificance before the vast dimensions of creation and before the Creator who brought it all into being by his mere will and word! And what gratitude, what desire to return love for love to this supremely intelligent, personal, and loving God who ''dwarfs'' the universe, yet chooses to be born among us as a tiny, helpless baby! In the inspiring words of the 17th century poet *Richard Crashaw*:

> Welcome! all Wonders in one sight!
>   Eternity shut in a span.
> Summer in winter, Day in night,
>   Heaven in earth, and God in man.
> Great little one! whose all-embracing birth
>   Lifts earth to heaven, stoops heav'n to earth![9]

Yes, with the birth of Jesus Christ, and even before that with his conception in the womb of the Virgin Mary, we are challenged to think the unthinkable, to believe the unbelievable, that God, the Creator of this stupendous universe, has chosen to become human like us. Incredible! How could this be? Why should it be? To questions such as these, there can be only one answer: *"Love does such things!"* [10] Unlimited love does unbelievable things! And, as John declares (in 1 Jn 4:16), "God is love," unlimited love! Is it any wonder, then, that "God so loved the world that he gave his only Son . . ." (Jn 3:16), and that "The Word became flesh and made his dwelling among us, and we have seen his glory: the glory of an only Son coming from the Father, filled with enduring love" (Jn 1:14)?

THE BIBLICAL PORTRAIT OF JESUS CHRIST:

At the conclusion of John's Gospel, we are told, "There are still many other things that Jesus did, yet if they were written about in detail, I doubt there would be room enough in the entire world to hold the books to record them'' (Jn 21:25). Perhaps there is some kind of oriental hyperbole here, and yet it certainly is true, as Mark Link, S.J., observes in *He is the Still Point of the Turning World,* that

> Down the corridor of time has travelled a man
> Whose life and spirit have changed men's lives
> And shaped the course of history
> As no other man has ever done.

> Art galleries capture his life in paintings,
> Libraries are lined with books exploring his thought.
> Hospitals and schools are dedicated to his memory.

> He is the focus of controversy, the rallying point of unity,
> The object of love, the subject of debate,
> A basis for hope, and the goal of lives.

> No man interested in the meaning of life
> And its ultimate questions can ignore him.
> He towers above the giants of history.

> To some he is an uneasy feeling in times of silence;
> To others he is a sunrise of hope.
> To all he is a challenge.[11]

How, then, can we possibly do justice to *Jesus Christ* within the limits of a synthesis like this? The answer is obvious: we certainly cannot! But what we can do is contemplate him as he is profiled in the various kinds of literature found in the New Testament. In other words, we can let the inspired Word reveal for us the Incarnate Word!

In the *Gospel literature,* we have four complementary profiles of Jesus, which should never be merged into one (regardless of the temptation to achieve a unified "life" of Our Lord) because then the clarity and effectiveness of each profile would be lost. *Mark's portrait* in his "pioneer" Gospel of Jesus is summarized in his first line, "The beginning of the gospel (good news) of Jesus Christ, the Son of God" (Mk 1:1 WD). In it, Jesus, filled with and driven by the Holy Spirit who (in Mk 1:10) descends "into him" (*eis autón*), reveals himself more by his "mighty deeds" and sufferings than by his words as Son of God but also Son of Man and suffering Servant of Yahweh (Is 53), so human (so "emptied," according to Ph 2:7) that he may have had to live by *faith* in, rather than certain knowledge of, his Messiahship and divinity (Mk 10:18); so human that perhaps he *could* have sinned, "yet never sinned" (Heb 4:15). Incredible? Mysterious? Yes, indeed, but so is the entire mystery of the Incarnation. Formerly, theologians used to emphasize the unity of the divine and human in Jesus and attribute to his human nature every privilege that was not metaphysically impossible. Now, much more in keeping with the evidence of the New Testament (especially Mark) and of the Council of Chalcedon in 451 A.D., the emphasis is rather on the extent to which the Incarnate Word could and did "empty himself" (Ph 2:7) out of love for us in order to be as completely identified with us as he possibly could.[12] Love does such things! This latter approach certainly offers rich food for our contemplation of his profound humility and indescribable love as well as for our *identification* with him in our own personal and communal life. (For deeper reflection on this subject, please see Appendix B.)

To *Matthew*, Jesus is not only the Christ, the *Messiah* predicted by the prophets and eagerly awaited by the Jewish people, but also a new and greater *"Moses"* mediating a new and greater *Covenant* with a new and more perfect *Law*, that of unlimited love (Mt 5-7; 25:31-46) and, above all, establishing a new *"Israel,"* the *Church* (Greek *ekklesía* meaning the people "called out" of all the nations, Mt 16:18; 18:17), the beginning, at least, of the "Kingdom of Heaven" or *"Kingdom of God"* (Mt 13), with a new *leadership*, one with God-given authority (Mt 16:16-19; 18:17-18; 28:18-20) to be exercised with humility, love, patience, and forgiveness (Mt 5-7; 11:25-30; 18:1-4, 10-18, 21-35; 23:8-12) and, finally, with a new and lasting *presence* or dwelling (Hebrew *Emmanuel* meaning "God with us," Mt 1:23; 28:20), as far surpassing the Old Testament presence in the tabernacle and temple as the reality surpasses the symbols, as the light surpasses the shadows! No wonder Matthew's is called the "Ecclesial Gospel," for it is so full of stimuli and guidance for meditation on our personal and communal *relationship* with Christ in his Church.

In the *Gospel of Luke*, Paul's "dear physician" (Col 4:14), Jesus is portrayed as universal *Savior*, the gentle and compassionate healer of all humankind, especially the most rejected and neglected, for example the poor, sick, and sinners; women, Samaritans and Gentiles. Where Matthew's Jesus in his "Sermon on the Mount" (reminiscent of Sinai), challenges us to "be perfect as our heavenly Father is perfect" (Mt 5:48), Luke's Jesus in his "Sermon on the Plain" (humble and accessible) challenges us to "be compassionate as our Father is compassionate" (Lk 6:36). In addition, Luke's is the Gospel of *prayer* (e.g., 10:38-42; 11:1-13), the Gospel of the *Holy Spirit* (e.g., 1:15, 35, 41; 2:26-27), the Gospel of *joy* (e.g., Lk 1:14, 44, 47; 2:10), the Gospel of *peace* (e.g., 1:79; 2:14, 29; 19:38). Interestingly, however, as full of gentleness and compassion, of joy and peace, as is Luke's Gospel, it also is the *most demanding,* especially in terms of *humility* (e.g., 9:46-47; 14:7-11; 17:7-10; 18:9-17; 22:24-27) and *poverty* (e.g., 6:20, 24-25; 12:13-34; 16:1-15, 19-31), which Luke evidently regards as two of the most important virtues in our "followship" of Jesus as he leads us, particularly in Luke's long theological journey (Lk 9:51-19:27) toward (the spiritual, heavenly) Jerusalem. Luke has often been hailed as a "Liberation Theologian" and Luke's Jesus as a "Liberationist,"[13] perhaps with some justification, but one thing is certain: both Jesus and Luke are intent on our liberation from sin and selfishness, from pride and greed, so that we can, indeed, *follow Jesus wholeheartedly* to our spiritual Jerusalem.

Finally, the sublime, spiritual, even mystical *Gospel of John*, the "beloved disciple" or, more accurately, the "disciple whom Jesus loved," (Jn 13:23; 19:26; 20:2; 21:7, 20) portrays Jesus, not only as the Messiah and Son of Man, but preeminently as the *Son of God,* the Light and Life of the world, already *exalted in triumph* throughout his life, even or especially in the midst of persecution and humiliating death, as Jesus himself indicates, "Just as Moses lifted up the serpent in the desert, so must the Son of Man be *lifted up*" (in crucifixion, resurrection, and ascension), "that all who believe may have *eternal life* in him" (Jn 3:14 f, also 8:28; 12:32). With admirable use of "concentric circles," John, in the beginning of his Gospel, presents in the prologue (Jn 1:1-18) *three major themes*: life, light, and love, and in the rest of Chapter One (Jn 1:19-51) *seven major titles of Jesus*: Lamb of God, Son of God (the better reading of Jn 1:34), Rabbi or Teacher, Messiah or Anointed, Prophet (implied in Jn 1:45), King of Israel, and Son of Man; and then proceeds to elucidate both themes and titles by returning to them in various ways throughout the Gospel. In particular, John emphasizes the *intimate union of love* between Jesus and his Father (e.g., Jn 5:19-30; 8:12-30; 10:25-38; 12:23-32; 13:1-17:26), as well as between Jesus and his followers (e.g., Jn 10:11-30; 14:18-24; 15:1-17; 17:1-26), a loving union accomplished through the Holy Spirit (e.g., Jn 7:37-39; 14:16-26) and through the Sacraments: Baptism (Jn 3:3-8), Eucharist (Jn 6:48-58), Reconciliation (Jn 20:21-23), and possibly Matrimony (Jn 2:2-11), Confirmation (Jn 7:37-39), and Holy Orders (Jn 15:16; 17:17-19; 20:21-23; 21:15-19).

In the historical, epistolary, and apocalyptic literature respectively of *Acts,* the *Epistles,* and the *Book of Revelation,* we are offered a portrait, indeed a theology, of *the Risen Christ living in his Church and in individual Christians*: preaching and teaching, serving and suffering, guiding by his Spirit and ultimately triumphing in and through his followers. *St. Paul* in particular, mystical missionary that he is, teaches us to surrender our unique self so completely to the Risen Christ, to be so "possessed" by him (Ph 3:12) that, in a kind of second incarnation or true "reincarnation," he who no longer appears among us as he once did may, through us, continue to live and minister visibly and tangibly to all in need,

> Seeing with our eyes,
> Hearing with our ears,
> Speaking with our tongue,
> Thinking with our mind.

> Loving with our heart,
>> Working with our hands,
>>> Walking with our feet,
>>>> Suffering with our body.

For, "the love of Christ" (especially his love for us) "impels us" (2 Cor 5:14) to "owe no debt to anyone except the debt that binds us to love one another" (Rm 13:8), to "help carry one another's burdens" (Gal 6:2), and to fill up in our own bodies "what is lacking in the sufferings of Christ for the sake of his body, the church" (Col 1:24). See also the even better known Galatians 2:19-20 and Philippians 1:21.

This brief survey of the New Testament has, I trust, helped to answer the questions, first of the apostles, "What sort of man is this?" (Mt 8:27), and then of Jesus himself, "Who do you say that I am?" (Mt 16:15). Above all, I hope that it has enabled us to perceive more clearly the central role Jesus Christ fulfills in that relationship between God and ourselves which is the essence of religion. The distinguished Congregationalist theologian, John Seldon Whale, expresses it cogently in his Cambridge lecture, *Mysterium Christi,*

> The Man Christ Jesus has the decisive place
> In man's ageless relationship with God.
> He is what God means by "Man."
> He is what man means by "God!"[14] (arrangement mine)

Thus, it is through our relationship and union with Jesus Christ that we also enter into the very mystery of the Holy Trinity, which he has revealed to us, as we will see in the following section.

THE BIBLICAL PORTRAIT OF THE TRINITY:

Let us remember that we are in the realm of theology, the study of God himself, and in the New Testament as distinguished from the

Old, God is revealed to us as triune, tri-personal: one Nature (answering the question "what?") existing in three Persons (answering the question "who?"). Small wonder that, when we come to a consideration of *the Holy Trinity,* an interesting thing happens. We immediately bow down in awe before this profound mystery. With *Paul,* we cry out,

> How deep are the riches and the wisdom and the knowledge of God! How inscrutable his judgments, how unsearchable his ways! For 'who has known the mind of the Lord? Or who has been his counselor? Who has given him anything so as to deserve return?' For from him and through him and for him all things are. To him be glory forever. Amen (Rm 11:33-36; cf. Is 40:13; Ws 9:13).

In the Preface of the *Mass of the Holy Trinity,* we exclaim:

> Father, all-powerful and ever-living God, we do well always and everywhere to give you thanks. We joyfully proclaim our faith in the mystery of your Godhead. You have revealed your glory as the glory also of your Son and of the Holy Spirit: three Persons equal in majesty, undivided in splendor, yet one Lord, one God, ever to be adored in your everlasting glory. And so, with all the choirs of angels in heaven, we proclaim your glory and join in their unending hymn of praise. . . .[15]

This attitude of humble awe, admiration, and adoration is perfectly understandable and correct, so far as it goes. The doctrine of three Persons in one God is certainly a *mystery,* impervious to our limited human understanding. Not a contradiction, of course, as would be the belief in three Persons yet only one Person, or three Gods yet only one God. But definitely a mystery! And mysteries about God there must necessarily be; otherwise, we would be God! Even in Heaven, it seems to me, we will never totally comprehend God because we will never become God. Instead, we will spend an eternity, not in restful inactivity as is usually envisioned, but in the most dynamic spiritual activity, always growing in knowledge of God and thereby in love of Him, and never reaching the end of that growth because we can never become God; in fact, ever rejoicing that God is always greater than we can fully comprehend.

Yes, before the mystery of the Holy Trinity, we can only humble ourselves, believe, and adore. All the philosophical and theological attempts by giants like St. Augustine and St. Thomas Aquinas, Matthias Scheeben and Karl Rahner, Michael Schmaus and Bernard Lonergan, to make the Trinity more understandable, are valuable but only in a limited way because they do not and cannot penetrate the mystery itself. Even though they help us to appreciate, adore, and to some extent imitate the Holy Trinity as supremely relational and communitarian from all eternity (a perfect community of love!), they cannot enable us to *relate* to the Trinity as such, for how can we relate to a mystery? How can we relate to something that is beyond our human experience and understanding? Yet, as we have already seen, relationship is essential to religion, especially to Christianity and the Spiritual Life.

Are we then faced with an impossibility? No, not at all! For *Sacred Scripture,* the Word of God himself, invites us to relate, not so much to the Trinity as Trinity, but to *each of the three Persons* of the Trinity. Only in the Trinitarian baptismal formula (in Mt 28:19) and in greetings such as Paul uses at the beginning and end of his letters, do we find the three Persons of the Trinity mentioned together. Elsewhere, reference is made to only one Person or perhaps two, if the relationship between them is being emphasized (e.g., in Mt 11:25-27 and most of Jesus' final discourse in Jn 13-17). And is this not to be expected? Relationships can exist only between persons and, as every theological study of the Trinity points out, relationships within the Trinity itself are only among the three Persons as distinguished from but related to one another.[16] As already seen earlier in this chapter, God is not only infinitely intelligent but infinitely loving and infinitely personal, and each of the three Persons, Father, Son, and Spirit, not only lives in infinitely personal relationships with each other but also desires a personal, spiritual relationship with us.

How, then, do we enter into that personal relationship with each of the Persons of the Holy Trinity? The New Testament provides the answer on almost every page: *through Jesus Christ!* We can relate to him and through him to the Father and the Holy Spirit, not only because he is *human like us,* but also and more importantly because he is risen and still living *with us, among us,* and even *in us!* "No one knows the Father but the Son — and anyone to whom the Son wishes to reveal him" (Mt 11:27); "I am with you always, until the end of the world" (Mt 28:20); "I am the way, and the truth, and the life; no one comes to the Father but through me" (Jn 14:6); "Whoever has seen me has seen the Father" (Jn 14:9); "I am the vine, you are the branches. He who lives in me and I in him, will produce abundantly, for apart from me you can do nothing" (Jn 15:5); "I am Jesus, the one you are persecuting" (Ac 9:5). And the numerous references by Paul to our life in Christ and his in us can be summed up in his pregnant expression, "the mystery of Christ in you, your hope of glory" (Col 1:27). Yes, Jesus Christ is the Mediator both of the revelation of the Trinity and of our relationship with the three Persons of the Trinity. If we are truly one with Jesus Christ, the Son of God, then we experience his Father as truly our Father and his Spirit as truly our Spirit, as we see in John and Paul:

> On that day you will know that I am in my Father, and you in me, and I in you . . . He who loves me will be loved by my Father, I too will love him and reveal myself to him . . . Anyone who loves me will be true to my word, and my Father will love him; we will come to him and make our dwelling place with him . . . The Paraclete, the Holy Spirit whom the Father will send in my name, will instruct you in everything, and remind you of all that I told you (Jn 14:20-21, 23, 26).

> All who are led by the Spirit of God are sons of God. You did not receive a spirit of slavery leading you back into fear, but a spirit

of adoption through which we cry out "Abba" (that is, "Father"). The Spirit himself gives witness with our spirit that we are children of God (Rm 8:14-16).

God sent forth his Son born of a woman, born under the law, to deliver from the law those who were subjected to it, so that we might receive our status as adopted sons. The proof that you are sons is the fact that God has sent forth into our hearts the Spirit of his Son which cries out "Abba!" ("Father!"). You are no longer a slave but a son! And the fact that you are a son makes you an heir, by God's design (Gal 4:4-7).

What makes these quotations especially meaningful is that the Aramaic word, *"Abba,"* seems to have been uniquely favored by Jesus Christ and carries a particularly intimate connotation which is perhaps best translated "Daddy!"[17]

Just as we are able to relate to Jesus Christ as our Savior and Mediator, our Good Shepherd and Divine Physician, our Lord and Master, our Friend and Brother, so we are able to relate to his *Father* as our own Father, partly because we have had the personal experience of relationship with our natural father. And, fortunately or unfortunately, the image we have of our own father, good or bad, kind or cruel, loving or neglectful, present or absent, is normally the image we subconsciously develop of God our Father. But how can we possibly relate to the *Holy Spirit,* since we have no image in our experience with which to associate such a relationship?

The title *"Paraclete"* (Comforter, Strengthener, or Intercessor) is not one with which we are very familiar, and certainly the image of a *"dove"* in the story of Jesus' baptism by John (Mt 3:16; Mk 1:10; Lk 3:22; Jn 1:32) is hardly calculated to foster a relationship, even if we relate it to "peace" (as in Gn 8:11) or "love" as in the Song of Songs (2:14; 5:2; and 6:9). Reading and reflecting on what is said of the Holy Spirit, e.g., in the Gospels of Luke and especially John, and in the letters of Paul, particularly Romans 8, can be very helpful. Perhaps for some, picturing the Holy Spirit as feminine, even as *"Mother"* in much the same way as we speak of God the "Father," may be of help, and does have some biblical justification insofar as the Hebrew word for spirit (*ruah*) is feminine and nurturing characteristics such as gentleness, kindness, patience, comfort, and guidance (along with strength and power, Is 11:2; Ws 7:23; 8:1), attributed to the Holy Spirit in Scripture, are usually associated with women, together with courage and moral strength as we see in the many heroines of the Bible. For others, meditation on the *role* of the Holy Spirit in our lives may provide an avenue of relationship, especially if we realize that the Holy Spirit, the mutual love of the Father and the Son, is given us not only to enlighten us (Jn 14:26) but also to sanctify us, to spiritualize us, particularly by forming Christ in us in somewhat the same way as he formed Christ in the womb of Mary (Mt 1:20; Lk 1:35). Again, reflection on the sanctifying and charismatic *gifts* of the Holy Spirit may help us to relate to him. But, in the final analysis, we relate more truly and completely with the Holy Spirit the more fully we *live the "life of the spirit"* beyond images and even intellectual concepts, united spirit and Holy Spirit, in that serene realm where "the Spirit himself gives witness with our spirit that we are children of God" (Rm 8:16), and where "the Spirit scrutinizes all matters, even the deep things of God" (1 Cor 2:10).

Finally, but I trust helpfully, we may find it easier to relate to the three Persons of the Holy Trinity if we reflect that, as we have seen in the previous chapter, we are as spirit naturally oriented toward God and therefore our relationship with each of the Persons of the Trinity fulfills a very *deep personal need* within ourselves. For example, perhaps our deepest need of all is that of *self-identity*: "Who am I?" Book stores have entire sections of "self-image" works which claim to supply us with surefire means of finding our true identity, building our self-image, and learning to "feel good about ourselves." But ultimately our true identity, our real self-image, is that of *Jesus Christ*, the Son of God, into whom we are called to be transformed. "Those whom he foreknew he predestined to share the image of his Son" (Rm 8:29), and "All of us, gazing on the Lord's glory with unveiled faces, are being transformed from glory to glory into his very image by the Lord who is the Spirit'' (2 Cor 3:18).

A second profound personal need, especially in these times, is that of *security*. With everything around us changing so rapidly, with life becoming ever more complex, with death through war, violence, terrorism, and crime becoming daily more commonplace, and with the economy always so fickle, we cannot but wonder where and how we can possibly find security. We can seek the most stable job, take out as much insurance as we can afford, protect ourselves and our possessions with the most sophisticated alarm systems available, and build up a strong national defense, but ultimately our only security lies in the realization that God, the Creator of this vast universe, God who knows all things and can do all things, is *our own Father!* And he who ''feeds the birds'' and ''clothes the lilies'' ''knows all that we need'' and will certainly ''provide'' for those needs so that we may live in peace and security (Mt 6:25-34; Lk 12:22-31).

A third personal need is that of *direction* in our lives. ''What shall I be, what shall I do, which direction shall I take?'' During the time between Vatican I and Vatican II, we Catholics felt that the Church, and we in the Church, had all the answers to everything. And, if at any time we sensed that we needed direction, we had only to ask the parish priest who, if by some slim chance he did not know the answer, could always ask the bishop, who of course could always ask the pope. Since Vatican II, we are happily much more on our own, or rather we are encouraged to seek the guidance and direction that we need from the indwelling Holy Spirit who, especially through the gift of counsel, enables us (if we are truly attuned to him) to know what to do, what direction to take, in given circumstances. This, of course, does not negate the role of Church authority and that of spiritual direction, but recognizes the action of the Holy Spirit throughout the leadership and membership of the Church. ''The wind blows where it will. You hear the sound it makes but you do not know where it comes from, or where it goes. So it is with everyone begotten of the Spirit'' (Jn 3:8). And in the profound words of Paul (1 Cor 2:10-16):

The Spirit scrutinizes all matters, even the deep things of God. Who, for example, knows a man's innermost self but the man's own spirit within him? Similarly, no one knows what lies at the depths of God but the Spirit of God. The Spirit we have received is not the world's spirit but God's Spirit, helping us to recognize the gifts he has given us. We speak of these, not in words of human wisdom but in words taught by the Spirit, thus interpreting spiritual things in spiritual terms.

The natural man does not accept what is taught by the Spirit of God. For him, that is absurdity. He cannot come to know such teaching because it must be appraised in a spiritual way. The spiritual man, on the other hand, can appraise everything, though he himself can be appraised by no one. For, "Who has known the mind [Hebrew *ruah:* spirit] of the Lord so as to instruct him?" [Is 40:13; cf. Ws 9:13; Rm 11:34]. But we have the mind [spirit] of Christ.

SUMMARY AND CONCLUSION:

By way of *summary,* we have been reflecting on the divine partner of the covenant relationship between God and ourselves. We have stared in wonderment at the grandeur of God revealed through his universe, and knelt in adoration and love before his littleness and weakness in the crib at Bethlehem. We have bowed low in baffled admiration before the mystery of the Trinity, and accepted the invitation to enter into personal relationship with each of the Persons of the Trinity through the perfect mediator, Jesus Christ, the Son of God and our human brother.

By way of *conclusion,* I humbly offer for reflection my own re-writing of the Nicene Creed. It must seem particularly presumptuous of me to undertake such a daring endeavour, but there is, I believe, a justifying reason. In leading the assembled faithful Sunday after Sunday in the recitation of the Nicene Creed at Mass, I finally arrived at the conviction that, by and large, we were just saying

— Hell's Bells - he can justify Luther

Christ's words + N.T. were 1ST Century!

4TH Century things have got to go!

words. Oh, we believed and professed them, all right, but not only were they always the same words; they happened to be formulations of truths by two general councils against heresies of the fourth century! Nothing wrong with that except that, as I have explained in Chapter One, religion, Christianity, and the Spiritual Life consist primarily of relationship, for which truths, morality, and worship exist. After looking around in vain for another creed or another translation of the Nicene Creed in terms of relationship, I felt impelled to try my own hand at producing something suitable, with the help of a great deal of prayer and, I trust, the guidance of the Holy Spirit. The result is my *"Creed of a Christian,"* which many people of all ages and various Christian affiliations have found helpful; yes, even helpful in reciting the Nicene Creed because of the background emphasis on relationship that my Creed provides. May it also be of assistance to you, the reader, in developing more and more that blessed relationship that we are called to have (and enjoy!) with the Father, the Son, the Holy Spirit, and the Church.

Nicene Creed was official dogmatic statement on belief by an Ecumenical Council.

CREED OF A CHRISTIAN *Catholic?*

I believe in God, our kind and loving Father,
Almighty, all-knowing, and always present with us,
Who, out of boundless, personal, creative love,
Brought all things and persons into being, even me;
Who keeps us all in being and with paternal care
Calls us all to share His love and life and happiness.

GoD? I believe in Jesus Christ, our Brother, Master, Lord,
God's only Son, of Virgin Mary born, human like us
In everything but sin, from which He came to save us;
Who by His life and death and rising, made us whole
And gave us true identity as, we in Him and He in us,
We live His life today and carry on His mission.

GoD? I believe in the Holy Spirit, our Blessed Sanctifier,
Gift of love and life to us from the Father and the Son,
Creative and transforming, our guide and inspiration,
Who leads us in our prayer, directs us in our living,
Fills our minds with wisdom, our hearts with courage,
And constitutes our pledge of endless happiness.

I believe in the Church, God's pilgrim People on earth,
So human yet divine, communal Body of the risen Christ,
Saved by Jesus' Blood, consecrated by His Covenant,
Guided by His Spirit and by chosen human leaders,
Serving all with truth and love, word and sacraments,
And leading us, through life and death and rising,
To our eternal home with God, our final End.   Amen.

Catholic?
Communion of Saints

RECOMMENDED READING LIST

1. ON GOD: Bardotin, Edmund. *The Humanity of God*, trans. Matthew O'Connell, Maryknoll, NY: Orbis Books, 1976.
2. ON THE FATHER: Hamerton-Kelly, Robert. *God the Father* (Theology and Patriarchy in the Teaching of Jesus), Philadelphia, PA: Fortress Press, 1979.
3. ON JESUS CHRIST: Lane, Dermot. *The Reality of Jesus* (An Essay in Christology), New York, NY: Paulist Press, 1975.
4. ON THE HOLY SPIRIT: Montague, George. *The Holy Spirit* (Growth of a Biblical Tradition), New York, NY: Paulist Press, 1976.
5. ON THE HOLY TRINITY: Ratzinger, Joseph: *The God of Jesus Christ*, trans. Robert Cunningham, Chicago, IL: Franciscan Herald Press, 1978.

POINTS FOR REFLECTION AND DISCUSSION

1. What is our personal idea of God and how has it tended to change both with the changing times and with our own personal growth?
2. What are the similarities and differences in the revelation of God between the Old and New Testaments, and how do these speak to us?
3. How real is Jesus Christ to us, especially in his divine and human natures? To what extent was he able to "empty himself" to be like us?
4. How real is the Holy Spirit to us? What is his role in our Spiritual Life? In the life of the Church and of the World?
5. What is the significance and relevance of the Holy Trinity for us personally and communally? How can we relate in a meaningful way to this mystery of our faith?

CHAPTER FOUR

THE DIVINE-HUMAN PROCESS OF THE RELATIONSHIP:
The Seven Phases of Initiative and Response

When I was studying *scholastic philosophy* in the seminary during the early forties, certain conclusions left me puzzled and unconvinced. One that I clearly remember was the dictum that we human beings are related to God because we are dependent on him, but God is not related to us because, if he were, then he would somehow be dependent on us, which would involve an imperfection that is impossible in God.[1] I could not, for the life of me, understand how we could relate to God but not he to us. What possible kind of relationship would that be? And does it not contradict Scripture which, from beginning to end, recounts the mutual relationship between God and human beings? I believe that I was able to reconcile myself with this problem only by accepting it as a kind of philosophical or theological mystery which I would perhaps some day come to understand.

Thank God, *Sacred Scripture* and (modern) *process philosophy and theology* have done much to unravel the "mystery" for me by explaining, in the words of *Bernard Meland* and *Norman Pittenger*, that God is not "an impassive sovereign or the Absolute, devoid of relationships"[2] but rather "living, dynamic, energizing . . . related." His perfection "is not that proper to some unmoved mover or absolute essence; it is the perfection of his own identity as being himself, but

that perfection subsists in his identity in and with relationships . . .
Indeed, he may best be defined as perfect love or the perfect lover,
working ceaselessly to express his love and to establish communities
of love."[3] In other words, God's relationship with humankind, so
clear and constant in the Bible, is not at all the imperfection of
dependence but the perfection of love and all that love comprises:
care, concern, communication, correction, compassion, forgiveness,
and always patience. As John expresses it succinctly and experien-
tially, "God is love, and he who abides in love abides in God, and
God in him" (1 Jn 4:16).

It is fitting, then, to entitle this chapter "The Divine-Human
Process of the Relationship" because, as we see in the fundamental
thought of process philosophers and theologians, stemming mainly
from the pioneering theories of *Alfred North Whitehead* and *Pierre
Teilhard de Chardin,* religion, history, and Scripture are all concerned with the dynamic, ongoing, mutual relationship between God
and the human race. In this chapter, we will examine, as through a
prism, the various steps involved in the process or development of this
relationship, taking as our best possible teacher God himself through
his word in Sacred Scripture, where we see the process of relationship
in both Testaments as one of *divine initiative* and *human response.*

From beginning to end of salvation history, as recorded in the
Bible, God himself takes the initiative and calls for a response. Nor
can it possibly be otherwise, for as the *Psalmist* declares, "Salvation
is the Lord's" (Ps 3:9). Correlatively, all religion (above all, revealed
religion) is response. Nowhere is this more evident than in the early
chapters of *Genesis.* "In the beginning," God creates "the heavens
and the earth," then he forms man and woman and from them he
requires a response of gratitude and obedience. Unfortunately, they
fail to render the desired response and thus become estranged from
that intimate relationship with God (symbolized by the garden) for
which he has destined them (Gn 1-3).

Things then go from bad to worse. Sin and violence proliferate
(Gn 4). Even the worldwide deluge (apparently borrowed and sub-

limated from Mesopotamian stories such as the *Epic of Gilgamesh)*[4] fails to achieve the true salvation that is needed (Gn 6-9). In Genesis 11, humans try to take the initiative themselves by constructing the Tower of Babel (''Gate of God'') after the manner of Mesopotamian ziggurats, seeking to build their own way up to heaven ''and so make a name'' for themselves (Gn 11:4). All in vain! The human race cannot save itself, cannot of its own initiative bridge the gap between God and humankind, heaven and earth. But immediately afterward, in Genesis 12, God himself initiates the process of human salvation with the call of Abram, ''Go forth from the land of your kinsfolk and from your father's house to a land that I will show you'' (Gn 12:1). And he continues with promises of extraordinary blessings:

I will make of you a great nation, and I will bless you;
   I will make your name great, so that you will be a blessing.
I will bless those who bless you and curse those who curse you.
   All the communities of the earth shall find blessings in you.

(Gn 12:2-3)

Abram responds in faith and obedience, and thus begins the real story of salvation history — which turns out to comprise a whole series of divine initiatives and human responses.

But before we examine in detail the process of initiative and response characteristic of salvation history, we would do well to consider the rich meaning of certain key words, for example:

Initiate and *initiative,* from the Latin *initium* meaning ''beginning.'' God initiates or takes the initiative in our salvation in the sense that he begins and continues the process. But he also initiates or introduces us into salvation through *initiation rites* such as circumcision in the Old Testament and baptism in the New.

Respond and *response,* from the Latin *respondere* meaning ''to answer.'' However, by dividing the Latin word into its component parts (*re - spondere,* meaning ''to pledge or espouse again''), we find that it also includes the idea of *renewed commitment and consecration,* even of *renewed espousal,* particularly in our covenant relationship with God, which the Prophets Hosea, Isaiah, Jeremiah, and

Ezekiel picture as a spiritual marriage (Ho 1-3; Is 49-54; Jr 1-3; Ezk 16).

Responsibility, from the Latin *responsabilitas* meaning stability, reliability, accountability. But when the word is taken apart, it literally means the ability to respond, the freedom and readiness to respond quickly and totally to God's salvific initiatives. For us humans, *"to be is to respond!"* [5]

Finally, the proper names *Joshua, Hosea,* and *Jesus,* which are all variants of the same Hebrew name meaning "Yahweh is Salvation." How appropriate! For it was Joshua who was God's instrument in leading the Israelites into the Promised Land and saving them from their surrounding enemies. It was Hosea who first compared Israel's covenant with Yahweh to a marriage union, of which his own ill-fated marriage was a living symbol. And, of course, Jesus is *the* Savior of all humankind from the slavery of sin and *the* mediator of a new and eternal covenant.

The Bible, particularly the Old Testament, is replete with examples of divine initiative and human response, e.g. in the stories of Adam, Noah, Abram, Jacob, Joseph, Moses, Joshua; the Judges, especially Gideon, Samson, and Samuel; David; the Prophets, principally Elijah, Isaiah, Jeremiah, and Ezekiel; not to mention such pseudo-historical figures as Tobit, Judith, and Esther. For our purposes, however, it will suffice to concentrate on Moses and the Israelites in the Old Testament and on the Apostles and the Church in the New Testament. By means of these examples, we will be in a better position to *apply to ourselves today* what we have learned from Scripture about the initiative-and-response process in our relationship with God.

A careful study of all the examples just listed, and most notably those which we are about to feature, leads to the discovery that there are *normally seven steps* (the perfect biblical number!) in the initiative-and-response process of our relationship with God and others. At first sight, the delineation of these steps may seem to complicate rather than clarify the process, but this is only apparent, for this analysis will serve to reveal the riches of the relationship just as a *prism* or a *rainbow* (Gn 9:8-17) reveals the richness of light.

The seven steps of *God's initiative* toward us are: (1) his presence, (2) his self-revelation, (3) his vocation or call, (4) his salvation or liberation, (5) his covenant, (6) his consecration, and (7) his adoption or filiation. The seven steps of our *human response* to God's initiative are: (1) awareness of his presence, (2) attention to his revelation, (3) acceptance of his call through faith and obedience, (4) humble gratitude for his salvation, (5) faithful, patient, and persevering love because of his covenant, (6) purity, and prayerfulness, commitment and sacrifice because of his consecration and (7) child-like trust, hope, and obedience because of his adoption. Now let us apply these steps to the examples we have chosen in the two Testaments.

OLD TESTAMENT INITIATIVE AND RESPONSE:

In the story of *Moses and Israel,* as we find it principally in Exodus and Numbers, we see the above seven steps dramatically fulfilled:

(1)   God manifests his *presence* to Moses in a special way (through an angel?) in (or as?) a burning bush. Moses is "surprised to see that the bush, though on fire" is "not consumed," so he decides to "go over to look at this remarkable sight," whereupon God directs him to "remove the sandals" from his feet because he is standing on holy ground (Ex 3:2-5).

(2)   God then *reveals* himself to Moses as "the God of Abraham, the God of Isaac, the God of Jacob," who has "come down to rescue them [the Israelites] from the hands of the Egyptians and lead them out of that land into a good and spacious land, a land flowing with milk and honey." Moses, for his part, "hides his face," for he is "afraid to look at God" (Ex 3:6-9).

(3)   God *calls* Moses with these words, "Come now! I will send you to Pharaoh to lead my people, the Israelites, out of Egypt."

But Moses' response is, "Who am I that I should go to Pharaoh and lead the Israelites out of Egypt?" Thereupon, a dialogue ensues in which God, to calm Moses' fears, promises to be with him, reveals his personal name of *Yahweh*, meaning "I am (who am)," unlike the pagan "no gods" (2 K 19:18; Ps 96:5; Jr 2:11; 5:7; 16:20), instructs Moses how to persuade the Israelites to follow him, and foretells the "wondrous deeds" (the ten plagues) that he will perform to persuade Pharaoh and the Egyptians to let Israel go (Ex 3:10-4:17). Only then does Moses respond in faith and obedience.

Thus, through Moses — and Aaron, his brother, whom Yahweh appoints as Moses' "prophet" or spokesman (Ex 4:10-16; 7:1) and later as the first Israelite priest (Ex 28:1) — God also calls *Israel* as a people out of Egypt to a covenant relationship at Mount Sinai and to the promised land of Canaan. Appropriately, then, the Septuagint Greek translation of the Hebrew word *qahal* (assembly) for the Israelite Community, especially in the desert, is *ekklēsia* (from Greek *ek* meaning "out of" and *kaleō* meaning "to call") which designates those called out of Egypt to be God's Covenant People. The very same word *ekklēsia* is used in the Greek New Testament for the *Church*, which is a community of people called, not just out of slavery in Egypt, but out of the slavery of sin and from all the nations of the earth. In the same tradition, the Greek word *ekklēsia* was simply transliterated into Latin as *ecclesia*, from which we have the Italian *chiesa*, the Spanish *iglesia*, the French *église*, and of course the English adjectival forms *ecclesial* and *ecclesiastical*.

(4)   Then Yahweh, against humanly impossible odds, *frees or saves* his people with "wondrous deeds" from bondage under the most powerful nation on earth, Egypt (Ex 5-14), and institutes a special sacrificial rite called the *Passover* (Ex 12), whereby Israel might for all time and in every generation celebrate annually with gratitude and joy Yahweh's great mercy and love in saving his people. According to the great Dominican scholar, Roland De Vaux, in his book *Ancient Israel*,[6] the *Feast of Passover* or *Pasch* (perhaps originally a nomadic or semi-nomadic pastoral rite, a "Feast of the

Flocks'') and the *Feast of Unleavened Bread* or *Massoth* or *Azymes* (perhaps originally an agricultural rite, a ''Feast of First Fruits'') were celebrated to commemorate: (a) the misery (Massoth) of slavery under Egypt, (b) a ''passing over'' of the Hebrew first-born by the ''angel of death'' who destroyed the Egyptian first-born in the tenth plague, (c) the ''passing over of Israel'' from Egypt to the Sinai desert, made possible by the miraculous crossing of the Reed Sea (later identified with the Red Sea), and (d) the unleavened bread (Azymes) eaten through necessity by the Israelites upon and after their departure from Egypt. In addition, Moses and the Israelites sing a special song of thanksgiving, known as the Song of Moses, while Miriam his sister leads the Israelite women in song and (sacred) dance (Ex 15). Feast, song, and dance, these constitute Israel's response of gratitude.

(5) Arriving at *Mount Sinai,* which is traditionally identified with *Jebl Musa* (''Mountain of Moses'') but may perhaps have been *Jebl Serbal,* the ''Giant of the Peninsula,''[7] overlooking the great Oasis of Feiran the ''Pearl of the Sinai'' and ''Paradise of the Bedouin,''[8] the Israelites encamp there for approximately a year, during which time Yahweh enters into a *sacred covenant* with them. In a formula reminiscent of Hittite suzerainty treaties,[9] he first reminds them of his past favors and promises his special care and protection, then he lays down the conditions which they must fulfill in order to preserve the covenant, conditions which we know as the Ten Commandments (Ex 19:1-6; 20:1-17). The people respond by accepting the covenant, ''Everything the Lord has said, we will do'' (Ex 19:8), and the conditions of the covenant (as well as the ''Book of the Covenant''?), ''We will do everything that the Lord has told us'' (Ex 24:3, 7). Meanwhile, Moses ratifies the covenant with a ceremony which includes sprinkling an altar and the people with the blood of young bulls, adding, ''This is the blood of the covenant which the Lord has made with you in accordance with all these words of his'' (Ex 24:4-6, 8). This may also have included a sacred (sacrificial) meal (Ex 24:11).

Centuries later, the *Feast of Weeks* (originally an agricultural feast celebrating the end of the wheat harvest seven weeks after the *Feast of First Fruits* which marked the beginning of the barley harvest) became a thanksgiving feast both for the harvest and for the Covenant and Law given through Moses at Mount Sinai.[10] Besides the name *Feast of Weeks,* it also came to be called *Pentecost,* Greek for "Fifty Days" (seven times seven plus one). There is, then, a correlation between the central Jewish feasts of *Passover* and *Pentecost* and the central Christian feasts of *Easter* and *Pentecost.* In addition, a beautiful book called *Deuteronomy* ("Second Law") was written to clarify beyond doubt the *relationship of love* to which Yahweh and Israel had committed themselves, e.g., in the beloved *Shema* ("Hear!"), Israel's profession of faith: "Hear, O Israel! The Lord is our God, the Lord alone! Therefore, you shall love the Lord, your God, with all your heart, and with all your soul, and with all your strength" (Dt 6:4-5; Mt 22:37; Mk 12:29-30; Lk 10:27).

(6)   No sooner has the covenant thus been ratified than Yahweh immediately gives directives about the building of the *Ark of the Covenant,* the construction of the tabernacle or *Tent of Dwelling,* and the *institution of the Aaronic priesthood* (Ex 25-31). Why? Because, as Yahweh had promised the Israelites on their arrival at Sinai, they have become by reason of the covenant, not only his "special possession," but also a "kingdom of priests, a holy nation" (Ex 19:5-6). Yes, Israel is now *consecrated* to Yahweh. The word "consecration" is extremely rich in meaning, including as it does the ideas of real or figurative anointing, separation from profane usage and setting aside for sacred use alone, total dedication and commitment to the sacred, internal and external purity as befits such dedication, and even sacrifice or immolation. And, just as the Book of Deuteronomy exhorts Israel to respond to the love-relationship inherent in the covenant by living true to Yahweh, so the Book of *Leviticus,* written even later than Deuteronomy, emphasizes the sacredness of all the people (Lv 20:26), especially the priests (Lv 21), and the consequent obligation of *holiness* undertaken by the people and, above all, the priests, in

response to their consecration by covenant. This obligation is summed up (Lv 19:1-2), "The Lord said to Moses, 'Speak to the whole Israelite community and tell them: Be holy, for I, the Lord your God, am holy!' "

It is noteworthy that, in the story of Israel's wanderings in the desert, there are many *doublets,* basically the same things happening before and after Sinai, e.g., complaints about lack of food and water. And Yahweh responds in the same way before and after Sinai, but with one important difference: before Sinai, he grants their requests yet never punishes them; after Sinai, he still grants their requests, but always punishes them. Why the difference? Because after Sinai Israel is *consecrated by covenant* to Yahweh and should no longer be acting like a petulant child. *Noblesse oblige!* Yahweh's punishments are a salutary reminder to Israel to live worthy of her covenant consecration.

Elsewhere in the *Old Testament,* there are many examples of the importance of consecration. To mention only a few, *Samson* was invincible as long as he remained faithful to his consecration as a Nazirite, symbolized by his uncut hair (Jg 13-16); *David* would not touch King Saul, "the Lord's anointed" even though the latter, in pursuing David, had fallen into his hands (1 S 24, 26); and in the Book of Daniel, King *Belshazzar* beheld the fateful "handwriting on the wall" precisely at the moment when he, his courtiers, his wives, and "entertainers" were defiling the consecrated vessels from the temple in Jerusalem (Dn 5).

(7) Finally, by reason of the covenant, the people of Israel have become God's *adopted people,* his *adopted children* (Ex 19:5). Even before the covenant, Yahweh refers to Israel as his "firstborn," his "son" (Ex 4:22-23) in anticipation of the Covenant of Sinai, either by the Lord himself or, more probably, by the inspired author writing centuries later. Afterwards, of course, Yahweh will refer to David's royal decendants, notably Solomon, as his own sons (2 S 7:14 and probably Ps 2:7), an expression applied to all the people in the prophets (e.g., Ho 11:1-2; Is 1:2; Jr 3:4, 19-22; 31:9, 20), and

even in the wisdom literature (e.g., Pr 3:12; Ws 2:13-18). As Yahweh's adopted people, Israel owes him a *response* of respect, reverence, and obedience. Sadly, this response, due in justice and love, becomes more and more noteworthy for its absence, forcing Yahweh to complain in Isaiah 1:2-4,

> Hear, O heavens, and listen, O earth, for the Lord speaks:
> *Sons* have I raised and reared, but they have disowned me!
> An ox knows its owner, and an ass, its master's manger;
> But Israel does not know; *my people* have not understood.
> Ah! sinful nation, people laden with wickedness,
> Evil race, *corrupt children!* They have forsaken the Lord,
> Spurned the Holy One of Israel, apostatized!

Only exile in a distant land would suffice, as it had for their ancestor Jacob (Gn 27-35), and as it would for the prodigal son of Jesus' parable (Lk 15), to bring about their *metanoia,* their change of heart, their conversion — at least for a time (Ml 1:6).

NEW TESTAMENT INITIATIVE AND RESPONSE:

In the *New Testament,* the seven steps in the process of relationship between Jesus Christ and his Church, especially his Apostles, are often in parallel with those which we have just studied in the Old Testament.

(1) God, of course, was *present* in a unique way in his Son, Jesus Christ, "the reflection of the Father's glory, the exact representation of the Father's being" (Heb 1:3), "the image of the invisible God" (Col 1:15), in whom "the fullness of deity resides in bodily form" (Col 2:9). It is evident, however, that this unique presence, though alluded to in the Infancy Gospel (Mt 1:23; Lk 1:35, 43-44, cf. 2 S 6:9, 14) and mentioned in John's prologue (Jn 1:14), was not manifest until the beginning of Jesus' public ministry, specifically with the baptism and witness by John the Baptist and the declaration of the Father, "You are my beloved Son. On you my favor rests" (Mk

1:11 and parallels; Ps 2:7; Is 42:1), and the descent of the Holy Spirit "into him" (Mark's Greek 1:10), "upon him" elsewhere. This is the beginning of the *kerygma*, the Church's public proclamation about Jesus Christ in all four Gospels and in the discourses of Acts. As God's personal presence on earth, Jesus is the *living temple of God*, especially in John's Gospel: "The Word became flesh and made his dwelling [pitched his tent!] among us" (Jn 1:14); "I solemnly assure you, you shall see the sky opened and the angels of God ascending and descending on the Son of Man," an allusion to Jacob's vision at Bethel ("House of God") in Genesis 28:10-19 (Jn 1:51); and "destroy this temple . . . and in three days I will raise it up" (Jn 2:19), to which John adds that "Actually he was talking about the temple of his body" (Jn 2:21). And all the references to his "glory" throughout John's Gospel (especially in 1:14; 2:11; 12:28; and 17:1, 5) seem to be allusions to the *shekinah* ("overshadowing"), the *kavod Yahweh* ("glory of Yahweh"), the luminous cloud that covered and filled the Tent of Dwelling in the desert (Ex 40:34-35) and the Temple of Yahweh at Jerusalem (1 K 8:10-13; Is 6:3-4).

(2)   Jesus' *self-revelation* is recorded in different ways in the various Gospels, e.g., his preaching of the *kingdom* in Matthew 4:17 and Mark 1:15, his self-identification as *Messiah* at the synagogue of Nazareth in Luke 4:16-21, followed by his exorcism of a demoniac at Capernaum in Luke 4:33-41 as well as the miraculous catch of fish in Luke 5:1-7 (corresponding to Jn 21:1-14?), and, of course, his touching self-revelation in Matthew 11:25-30 and Luke 10:21-22, and in a unique way his *transfiguration* in Matthew 17, Mark 9, Luke 9. In *John's Gospel*, Jesus reveals himself throughout his public ministry as the Messiah and Son of God. We must bear in mind, however, that John has anticipated in every part of his Gospel that self-revelation of Jesus and faith of his followers which apparently occurred only with his glorious resurrection (Jn 20:28; Rm 1:4, etc.) or, at the earliest, with the limited resurrection of Lazarus (Jn 11). Thus, John portrays Jesus as revealing himself, not only as the *Messiah* (Jn 4:25-26), but also as the *Son of God* (Jn 5:16-38), and even as *identified with*

Yahweh himself, "I solemnly declare it: before Abraham came to be, I AM!" (Jn 8:58, see also Jn 13:19; 14:9). And just as being the personal presence of God made Jesus a living temple, as we have seen above, so his being the personal revelation of God made him the *"light of the world"* (Lk 2:32; Jn 1:4-9; 8:12; 9:5; 12:35-36). In addition, every chapter of John's Gospel features a self-revelation of Jesus, often in *symbolism,* e.g.,the Bread of Life (6), the Living Water (4 and 7), the Good Shepherd (10), and the True Vine (15).

The *response* of the Apostles and the Church to Jesus' presence and self-revelation was, of course, awareness of the former and attention to the latter, but even more significantly, *identification* with Jesus as a living temple (1 Cor 3:16-17; 6:19; 2 Cor 6:16; Ep 2:20-22) and as the light of the world (Mt 5:14-16; Ep 5:8-14). Nor is this surprising, for Jesus formed and commissioned us his Church on the foundation of his Apostles (Mt 16:18; 18:17-18; Ep 2:20), not only to preach, teach, and baptize, but in a very true sense to continue his own life and ministry on earth until the end of time (Mt 10:40; 28:18-20; Lk 10:16; Jn 13:20; 15:4-7; 17:20-26; Ac 9:5), as exemplified in *Paul,* "a light to the nations" (Ac 13:47) and lyrically described by him in 2 Corinthians 4:6, "For God, who said, 'Let light shine out of darkness,' has shone in our hearts that we in turn might make known the glory of God shining on the face of Christ." What a privilege, what a responsibility is ours: to be the presence and revelation of Christ in the world today!

(3)   Jesus' *call* of his disciples is quite clear in all the Gospels, taking place at or near the Sea of Galilee in the Synoptics (Mt 4:22; 9:9-13; Mk 1:16-20; 2:13-17; Lk 5:1-11, 27-32), but mostly in Judea in John 1:35-51. It is interesting and instructive to note the *occupations* or *titles,* stated or implied, in the context of these calls. In the *Synoptics,* fishermen such as Peter and Andrew, James and John, are invited to follow Jesus and become *"Fishers of men,"* an obvious reference to their former occupation and future vocation. In the call of Matthew, Jesus takes the opportunity to identify himself as a spiritual *physician.* In John's Gospel, there is such a profusion of incredible

titles, at least *seven* in all, accorded Jesus by his first disciples at the very beginning of his public ministry that, as I indicated in the previous chapter, we are certainly justified in regarding them as a preview of titles to be developed in the course of the Gospel.

In all these cases, the *response* is the same, namely immediate acceptance of the call and "followship" of Jesus. Dietrich Bonhoeffer, in his challenging work, *The Cost of Discipleship,* draws attention to the fact that the disciples first obeyed and then believed, concluding that, "The road to faith passes through obedience to the call of Jesus."[11] Was it not the same with Abram and with Moses? Is it not always the same? Does not Jesus continue to reveal his presence and extend his invitation to us in the beautiful words of Revelation 3:20, "Here I stand, *knocking* at the door. If anyone hears me calling and *opens* the door, I will enter his house and have supper with him, and he with me"?

(4)   The *liberation and salvation* of human beings by Jesus Christ can be seen as occurring throughout the three years of his public ministry of preaching, teaching, healing, and exorcising, but the beneficiaries were somewhat limited in number. It was principally at the end of his ministry that, through his love and obedience, he effected salvation for all humankind of all time by means of his sufferings, death, and glorious resurrection. What an incredible turnabout in salvation history! He who had declined Abraham's sacrifice of his son, accepting an animal sacrifice instead (Gn 22), now chooses to sacrifice his own divine Son, in lieu of all animal sacrifices, for the salvation of the world! He who had saved his chosen people from Egyptian slavery through his "wondrous deeds" now saves the entire human race from the slavery of sin and self-indulgence, not by "wondrous deeds" but by the public degradation of death by crucifixion and the hidden exaltation of glorious resurrection! For, Jesus "was handed over to death for our sins and raised up for our justification" (Rm 4:25). Because of his union with us in our human nature and our reciprocal union with him through faith and baptism, his death has become our death to sin; his resurrection, our

rising to new life, his own life! "For our sakes God made him who did not know sin to be sin, so that in him we might become the very holiness of God" (2 Cor 5:21; see also 1 P 2:24).

Nor is that all! He himself has provided the very means of our *response!* He bestows the gift of *faith,* by which we are justified (Rm 3:28; Gal 3:24-26). He has instituted the Sacrament of *Baptism,* whereby "through baptism into his death we were buried with him, so that, just as Christ was raised from the dead by the glory of the Father, we too might live a new life" (Rm 6:4). And, "before the feast of Passover, Jesus who "realized that the hour had come for him to *pass* [*over*] from this world to the Father" and who "had loved his own in this world . . ., would show his love for them to the end" (Jn 13:1). This he did, not only by washing his disciples' feet and discoursing with them (Jn 13-16) but (as is clear from the Synoptics and Paul) by instituting the Holy *Eucharist* as our Passover celebration, our sacramental sacrifice of thanksgiving (from Greek *eucharisteo,* to thank, be thankful) for the Paschal or Passover Mystery of our salvation, since *"Christ our Passover* has been sacrificed" (1 Cor 5:7), and even as the incredible means by which we too can offer ourselves and participate personally in his saving death and resurrection, for our own growing union with and transformation into Christ and for the ongoing redemption of the world. This we will penetrate more deeply later on, when we reflect of the Holy Eucharist.

(5)   While the word *covenant* is not all that explicit in the New Testament, nevertheless, without it one can hardly hope to understand Christ and Christianity. The very word (Old or New) *Testament* (Greek *diatheke*) happens to be the Septuagint translation of the Hebrew word for *Covenant (berith).* Jesus' Sermon on the Mount in Matthew 5-7 is in obvious parallel with the Mosaic Covenant and Law given at Sinai. The Holy Eucharist is instituted as a covenant sacrifice ("the blood of the covenant" in Mt 26:28 and Mk 14:24, "the new covenant in my blood" in Lk 22:20 and 1 Cor 11:25). And various references are made to Christ the Bridegroom (Mt 9:15; 25:1, 5-6; Mk 2:19-20; Lk 5:34-35; Jn 3:29), to the Messianic Wedding Feast (Mt

22:1-14; Jn 2:1-11; Rv 19:9), and to our "spiritual marriage" with
Christ (Rm 7:4; 1 Cor 6:17; 2 Cor 6:14-15; 11:2; Ep 5:25-32). All of
these passages implicitly speak of the New Covenant, while others do
so explicitly (e.g., Rm 11:27; 2 Cor 3:6; Gal 4:24; and especially Heb
8-13).

As with salvation, so with the New Covenant, Jesus not only
requires but even provides the necessary *response,* a response primarily of love — faithful, patient, and persevering love. With the Sacrament of *Baptism,* he enables us to enter into the covenant relationship
with him and with his Church. With that of the *Eucharist,* he enables
us to grow in that covenant relationship by regular renewal of our
covenant commitment and the transforming action of our covenant
sacrifice. And the very love which he seeks for himself, for the
Father, for the Spirit, for the Church, and, indeed, for all humankind,
he himself provides as a gift. When he gives us his "new commandment" (Jn 13:34; 15:12, 17), "Love one another as I have loved
you," he is referring not only to imitation but to identification,
implying, "Love one another with the very love with which I have
loved you!" Thus, Paul can claim that "the love of Christ [his love in
us] impels us . . ." (2 Cor 5:14).

(6)   Like covenant, *consecration,* in any or all of its varied
meanings (previously mentioned) plays an important role in the New
Testament. First, Jesus himself is "consecrated" or anointed as the
Messiah or Christ (*Anointed One*) and "sent into the world" (Jn
10:36), his symbolic "anointing" apparently taking place at the time
of his baptism by John when the Holy Spirit comes upon or into him.
He himself refers to this anointing by the Spirit in his "Messianic
address" in the synagogue at Nazareth in Luke 4:16-22, "The spirit
of the Lord is upon me; therefore, he has anointed me . . ." (cf. Is
61:1-2). Of course, the word *Messiah* or *Christ* implies an anointed
king, a "Son of David," as shown especially at his triumphant entry
into Jerusalem (Mt 21; Mk 11; Lk 19; Jn 12), at his trial before Pilate
(Jn 18), at his crucifixion (Mt 27:37; Mk 15:26; Lk 23:38; Jn 19:19)
and, above all, after his resurrection (1 Tm 1:17; Rv 1:5; 11:15; 17:14;

19:16). But, at the same time, these very instances show that his is not a kingdom of power but the "Kingdom of God" who is love, dwelling within us and among us (Lk 17:21), hence a kingdom of love, for Jesus is truly the king of hearts! Secondly, Jesus is consecrated or "anointed" as the living *temple* of God's presence (already examined), as the great and eternal *high priest* (so celebrated in the Epistle to the Hebrews, especially Heb 4:14-8:6), and even as the *sacrifice*, set apart and immolated for God's glory and our salvation (Heb 9-10).

In Jesus' so-called *"priestly prayer"* which climaxes his final discourse in John's Gospel, he prays for his followers, particularly his apostles, "Consecrate them by means of truth — your word is truth . . . I consecrate myself for their sakes now, that they may be consecrated in truth" (Jn 17:17-19). Thus, through his union with us and ours with him, he shares his *consecration*, his anointing, his sacredness with us as "a royal priesthood, a holy nation" (1 P 2:9), "a royal nation of priests in the service of his God and Father" (Rv 1:6), "a kingdom of priests to serve our God" and to "reign on the earth" (Rv 5:10). This he does especially through the Sacraments of Baptism (Mt 28:19) and Confirmation (Ac 8:17), in which we are consecrated to him and, through him, to the Father and the Spirit by the anointing with holy chrism or, in the stirring words of 1 Peter 1:1-2, "chosen according to the foreknowledge of God the Father, consecrated by the Spirit to a life of obedience to Jesus Christ and purification with his blood."

Our *response*, then, as Christians (anointed people) individually and communally consecrated to God, must be characterized by *purity* and *prayerfulness*, by total *commitment* and willingness to *sacrifice* ourselves and be sacrificed. If we are consecrated temples of his presence and holiness, then we need to heed the words of Jesus, " 'My house shall be called a house of prayer,' but you are turning it into a den of thieves" (Mt 21:13; cf. Is 56:7), and of Paul, "Let us purify ourselves from every defilement of flesh and spirit, and in the fear of God strive to fulfill our consecration perfectly" (2 Cor 7:1). If we are, with Jesus, consecrated as priests and victims, committed to service and sacrifice, then we must listen and respond to these revealing words of Jesus, "The Son of Man has not come to be served but to serve — to give his life in ransom for the many" (Mk 10:45) and "Whoever wishes to be my follower must deny his very self, take up his cross each day, and follow in my steps" (Lk 9:23), as well as these challenging words of Paul, "Offer your bodies as a living sacrifice holy and acceptable to God, your spiritual worship" (Rm 12:1) and "Follow the way of love, even as Christ loved you. He gave himself for us as an offering to God, a gift of pleasing fragrance" (Ep 5:2).

(7)   Last, but far from least, Yahweh's *adoption* by covenant of the Hebrews as his people (Ex 19:5), his children (Ho 11:1), great and irrevocable gift that it is (Rm 11:29), pales before the natural sonship of Jesus Christ and, in him, the adoption of his followers. In the parallel theophanies of Jesus' baptism by John and his transfiguration (in Mt 3:17; 17:5; Mk 1:11; 9:7; Lk 3:22; 9:35; and Jn 1:34; 12:27-28 — the final reference being John's equivalent of both the agony in the garden and the transfiguration in the Synoptics), and indeed in the entire Gospel of John (especially 5:16-47; 8:16, 58; 10:22-38, and the final discourse in Jn 13-17) particularly such expressions as "Whoever has seen me has seen the Father" (Jn 14:9, ff.) and "Yet I can never be alone; the Father is with me" (Jn 16:32), Jesus is revealed clearly and convincingly as God's Son. But, wonder of wonders!, what he is by nature we are called to be by adoption, "Go to my brothers and tell them, 'I am ascending to my Father and your Father, to my God and your God' " (Jn 20:17), with all the gratuitous privileges of intimacy, trust, inheritance, and freedom that flow therefrom, as Paul describes,

All who are led by the Spirit of God are *sons of God*. You did not receive a spirit of slavery leading you back into fear, but a spirit of *adoption* through which we cry out, *"Abba!"* (that is, "Father!"). The Spirit himself gives witness with our spirit that we are *children of God*. But if we are children, we are *heirs* as well: heirs of God, heirs with Christ, if only we *suffer* with him so as to be glorified with him (Rm 8:14-17).

Brothers, as long as a designated *heir* is not of age his condition is no different from that of a slave, even though in name he is master of all his possessions . . . but when the designated time had come, God sent forth his Son born of a woman, born under the law, to deliver from the law those who were subjected to it, so that we might receive our status as *adopted sons*. The proof that you are sons is the fact that God has sent forth into our hearts the spirit of his Son which cries out, "*Abba!*" ("Father!"). You are no longer a slave but a son! And the fact that you are a son makes you an *heir,* by God's design (Gal 4:1, 4-7).

The unique nature of this adoption becomes even more evident when we consider this important fact: in human adoption, the parents cannot communicate to the adopted child their own nature, whereas in this divine adoption God makes us by grace "sharers of the divine nature" (2 P 1:4). Hence, we are truly a "new creation" (2 Cor 5:17), "begotten not by blood, nor by carnal desire, nor by man's willing it, but by God" (Jn 1:13). Understandably, then, both Peter and Paul, in parallel *"berakoth"* or *"blessing prayers"* typical of synagogue services, praise and thank God for our new birth through baptism, as follows:

PETER	PAUL
Praised be the God and Father of our Lord Jesus Christ, he who in his great mercy gave us new birth:	Praised be the God and Father of our Lord Jesus Christ, who has bestowed on us in Christ every spiritual blessing in the heavens.
A birth unto hope which draws its life from the resurrection of Jesus Christ from the dead	God chose us in him before the world began to be holy and blameless in his sight, to be full of love;

A birth to an imperishable inheritance, incapable of fading or defilement, which is kept in heaven for you,	He likewise predestined us through Christ Jesus to be his adopted sons, — such was his will and pleasure — that all might praise the glorious favor he has bestowed on us in his beloved.
Who are guarded with God's power through faith; A birth to a salvation which stands ready to be revealed in the last days (1 P 1:3-5).	It is in Christ and through his blood that we have been redeemed and our sins forgiven, so immeasurably generous is God's favor to us. . . . (Ep 1:3-8)

As a consequence of our adoption as children of God, our *response* should naturally be one of childlike trust, hope, and obedience, as so beautifully inculcated by Jesus, in a passage which may well have been used by the early Church and Mark to confirm the practice of infant baptism,

"Let the children come to me and do not hinder them. It is to just such as these that the kingdom of God belongs. I assure you that whoever does not accept the reign of God like a little child shall not take part in it." Then he embraced them and blessed them . . . (Mk 10:14-16).

But Paul adds two important *cautions,*

(1) "Brothers, do not be childish in your outlook. Be like children so far as evil is concerned, but in mind be mature" (1 Cor 14:20).

(2) "My brothers, remember that you have been called to live in freedom — but not a freedom that gives free rein to the flesh. Out of love, place yourselves at one another's service. . . . My point is that you should live in accord with the spirit and you will not yield to the cravings of the flesh" (Gal 5:13, 16).

SUMMARY AND CONCLUSION:

We have now completed our reflection on the seven steps which, according to Scripture and our own personal experience, seem to constitute the process of initiative and response in the development of our relationship with God. In so doing, we have come full circle. We began with the consideration of God's presence with us, among us, and within us, and we finished with the consideration of our adoption as children of God. There is a vital connection between the two. Among other things, to live as children of God means, with *Gerard Manley Hopkins,* to be "all lost in wonder,"[12] for "the world is charged with the grandeur of God."[13] It is to possess the mystic conviction of *Pierre Teilhard de Chardin* that,

> . . . the real is charged with a *divine presence* in the entirety of its tangible layers. As the mystics knew and felt, everything becomes physically and literally lovable in God; and, conversely, God can be possessed and loved in everything around us. . . . What can this mean except that every action, as soon as it is oriented towards him, takes on, without any change in itself, the psychic character of a center to center relationship, that is to say, of an act of love.[14]

Yes, to live as a child of God is to be, in the words of the *Desiderata,* a "child of the universe,"[15] playing and praising in our "Daddy's" house where, again with *Teilhard,* "Nothing . . . is profane for those who know how to see. On the contrary, everything is sacred!"[16] For, in the haunting insight of *Elizabeth Barrett Browning* which forms a kind of commentary on the burning bush of Moses in Exodus 3,

> Earth's crammed with heaven,
> And every common bush afire with God.
> But only he who sees, takes off his shoes;
> The rest sit round it and pluck blackberries. . . .[17]

Each of us is sought out and "wooed" by him whom *Francis Thompson* calls "this tremendous lover,"[18] our God who is love itself (1 Jn 4:16); perhaps not confronted in spectacular ways like burning bushes or miraculous catches of fish, but in ways just as real and unmistakable, if we are but alert and open to his invitation. It may come in the ordinary events of our lives, in the words and actions of a relative or a friend, in a passage of Scripture as with *St. Augustine,*[19] or in the lives of the Saints as in the case of *St. Ignatius of Loyola.*[20] In whatever way it comes, he stands "knocking at the door" (Rv 3:20; Sg 5:2), a door which can be opened only from the inside! He never breaks down the door. He does not even demand its opening. Rather, like the gentle "whispering sound" of his call to Elijah in 1 Kings 19:12, he pleads, "My child, give me your heart" (Pr 23:26). To which every consideration of gratitude, love, and even enlightened self-interest urges us to respond, "My heart is ready, O God, my heart is ready!" (Ps 57:7; 108:1 JB). And if we are willing to "still and quiet our soul like a weaned child" (Ps 131:2), then we will learn with *Paul* (after Isaiah) that,

> Eye has not seen, ear has not heard,
> Nor has it so much as dawned on man
> What God has prepared for those who love him!
>
> (1 Cor 2:9; Is 64:3)

With *St. Augustine,* we will "confess" with our whole being,

> Late have I loved you, O Beauty ever ancient, ever new, late have I loved you! . . . You were with me, but I was not with you. . . . You called, you shouted, and you broke through my deafness. You flashed, you shone, and you dispelled my blindness. You breathed your fragrance on me; I drew in breath and now I pant for you. I have tasted you, now I hunger and thirst for more. You touched me, and I burned for your peace.[21]

And, in particular, we will be so attuned to our real "self," Jesus our beloved Savior and Bridegroom, that ours perhaps will be the spiritual experience so touchingly described by *Joseph Mary Plunkett,*

I see His blood upon the rose
And in the stars the glory of His eyes,
His body gleans amid eternal snows,
His tears fall from the skies.

I see His face in every flower;
The thunder and the singing of the birds
Are but His voice — and carven by His power
Rocks are His written words.

All pathways by His feet are worn,
His strong heart stirs the ever-beating sea,
His crown of thorns is twined with every thorn,
His cross is every tree.[22]

RECOMMENDED READING LIST

1. Cousins, Edward H., ed. *Process Theology: Basic Writings,* New York, NY: Paulist Press, 1971.
2. Fleming, David A., ed. *The Fire and the Cloud* (An Anthology of Catholic Spirituality), New York, NY: Paulist Press, 1978.
3. Goulet, Yvonne. *To Live God's Word,* Chicago, IL: Thomas More Press, 1979.
4. McNamara, William. *Mystical Passion* (Spirituality for a Bored Society), New York, NY: Paulist Press, 1977.
5. Pittenger, W. Norman. *The Lure of Divine Love,* New York, NY: Pilgrim Press, 1979.

QUESTIONS FOR REFLECTION AND DISCUSSION

1. What is the meaning of initiative and response in our relationship with God?
2. What are the seven steps of God's initiative toward us in Sacred Scripture? What is the meaning and example of each of these important steps?
3. What are the seven steps of our response toward God in Sacred Scripture? What is the meaning and example of each of these important steps?
4. How are these seven steps of God's initiative and our response exemplified in our personal and communal lives?
5. What conclusions can we draw from these considerations for our personal and communal spirituality?

CHAPTER FIVE

THE GREATEST OBSTACLES TO THE RELATIONSHIP:
"Whatever Became of Sin?"

Every now and then, I recall with a smile the first impromptu sermon I ever had to give. It occurred during my seminary days. Our regular professor of speech and homiletics being ill, the seminary rector himself decided to take his place and proceeded to assign Scripture texts for five-minute sermons to be preached in that very class! Who was the first person chosen to preach? "Yours truly!" And what was my assigned text? Believe it or not, it was the question which the three women were anxiously pondering as they hurried to Jesus' tomb on the morning of his resurrection, "Who will roll back the stone for us from the entrance to the tomb?" (Mk 16:3). Good grief! How does one preach on a text like that, especially with only a ten minute preparation?

Well, thanks surely to the mercy of God on this erstwhile stutterer, I managed to muddle through a five-minute reflection on *three basic spiritual truths*: (1) that, in the life of each of us, there are various kinds of "stones," that is, *obstacles* to our union with God, specifically our union with Jesus Christ who is our way to the Father (Jn 14:6); (2) that it is imperative for us to discover, not only what these obstacles are, but also what we can do (with God's grace) to *remove* them; and (3) that ultimately only *God* himself, with our desire and cooperation, can "roll back the stone for us" as he did for the three women of the Gospel (Mk 16:4). Since then, especially when that same Gospel selection is read at the Easter Vigil of Holy Saturday Mass, I invariably recall that first traumatic sermon and realize anew that God is still trying to tell me something, for such obstacles remain and will continue to remain, despite my struggles, until he himself (with my desire and cooperation) removes them, as he alone can!

Unfortunately, we human beings seem to spend more of our energy and our lives in collecting our "stone obstacles" than in trying to remove them. Or, like *Augustine* before his conversion, we beg God to remove them — "But not yet!"[1] We are like the "brazen girl possessed of seven devils" who, in a kind of parable by *A. J. Langguth,* "was brought before Jesus to be cured. 'I am going to cast out those seven devils from you,' he said. 'May I ask you a favor? . . .' 'What is it?' 'Cast out six!' "[2] Yet, if we are at all serious about the Spiritual Life, which consists essentially in our relationship with God, then we must also be "dead serious" about removing and letting him remove the obstacles to that relationship. The expression, "dead serious" is most appropriate here because "death to self" is the correlative condition to being "alive for God in Christ Jesus our Lord" (Rm 6:11). Does not Jesus himself warn us, "Whoever would save his life will lose it, but whoever loses his life for my sake will find it" (Mt 16:25)? Does not *Paul* remind us,

> Are you not aware that we who were baptized into Christ Jesus were baptized into his death? Through baptism into his death we were buried with him, so that, just as Christ was raised from the dead by the glory of the Father, we too might live a new life (Rm 6:3-4).

And, along the same lines,

> Since you have been raised up in company with Christ, set your heart on what pertains to higher realms where Christ is seated at God's right hand. Be intent on things above rather than on things

of earth. After all, you have died! Your life is hidden now with Christ in God. When Christ our life appears, then you shall appear with him in glory. Put to death whatever in your nature is rooted in earth . . . (Col 3:1-5).

Yes, *freedom*, the freedom to live in intimate loving relationship with God, necessitates the removal of our "stone obstacles" in a salutary death to self. But, to remove them, or to allow God himself to remove them, ordinarily requires that we recognize them, that we know them as they are. Not that knowledge alone is capable of removing them, as psychology and psychiatry often infer, for, in the words of *Richard Emrich,* "if evil is due to ignorance, then all professors should be saints!"[3] But knowledge is the first step. In any endeavor, be it business, sports, or life itself, it is important, even necessary, to know the obstacles to success in order to overcome them. This is even more true in the Spiritual Life, in which it is essential, but far from easy because of self-deception, to recognize the obstacles to our relationship with God and with others.

In our reflections on these obstacles, we will consider: (1) the great obstacle of *sin,* especially as seen in the Bible, (2) the *effects* of sin, not only for ourselves but also for others, including the Church and society generally, and (3) *other* obstacles, which can also lead to sin, e.g., temptations, occasions of sin, attachments, and imperfections. Our treatment of this vital subject will unavoidably be rather lengthy, both because of its intrinsic importance and because of its general neglect in recent years.

THE GREAT OBSTACLE OF SIN AND SINFULNESS:

"Whatever became of sin?" is the question asked by many concerned Christians today, especially in reference to the virtually total about-face in preaching and teaching over the past couple of decades. As is so often the case with our human nature, we have moved from one extreme to the other, from an admitted overemphasis on sin and the penalties for sin to an eclipse of the subject so total that many today seem to exclaim in triumph, "Sin is dead!"

It is this loss of a sense of sin that constituted a principal focus of the 1983 Synod of Bishops in Rome. *Cardinal Bernardin* of Chicago commented before the Synod,

> While various explanations — psychological, sociological, and political — are given for the hostilities, disorders, and unjust structures in the world today, the root cause is sinfulness. If we are honest with ourselves, we know this to be true. And we therefore know our need for repentance and forgiveness. We crave to be made whole again. We want to be reconciled with God and one another. The good news of the Gospel is that God offers us reconciliation in Christ Jesus. Encouraging and helping people to respond to it is the Church's mission.
>
> But an obstacle to it is that many people have lost any sense of sin. The term has virtually disappeared, but it remains a fact of the human condition and must be recognized to cope with it. . . . It may be popular to pooh-pooh sin, but deep down we know better — we know we are weak and sinful. If we deny this, we create problems for ourselves and begin to suffer from nameless anxieties and guilty feelings.[4]

When I was ordained to the priesthood in 1945, most of my sermons were centered around God's love for us, partly at least to counteract the fearsome image of a punitive God that was being constantly thundered at the Sunday congregations of that time. Later, however, while I never ceased to preach love as my central theme, I began to introduce more than previously the problem of sin, to compensate for the growing neglect of the subject. The reason is simple and compelling. How can we possibly speak of the loving relationship between God and ourselves without also calling attention to sin, the supreme obstacle to that bond of love? *To sin is to sunder* (or strain) the divine-human relationship which is the very essence of religion!

"Whatever Became of Sin?" is not only a concerned question, as we have just seen, but also the title of a very timely book written, not by a clergyman or religious, but by the most famous psychiatrist in this country, *Dr. Karl Menninger,* M.D.[5] In this widely read book, he directs the attention of people generally and of his fellow psychiatrists in particular, but especially of the clergy, to the fact of sin, and attempts to provide an antidote to the dangerous poison of ignorance and denial in its regard. The authorship is significant, for there is a certain appropriateness, a kind of "poetic justice," to a crusade on the part of a psychiatrist to return an awareness of sin to our collective consciousness. Why? Because, even more than the limited influence of preachers and teachers in putting sin "on a back burner," has been the pervasive influence of psychiatrists and psychologists, as well as sociologists, and the media affected by them, in suppressing a sense of sin among a large proportion of the population.

This is not, of course, a condemnation of psychiatry, psychology, or sociology as such. Far from it, since the contributions of these *behavioral sciences* in the understanding of human nature, collectively and individually, especially regarding the Spiritual Life, have been incalculable. It is not even an attempt to blame these sciences exclusively for the current disregard of sin, since the causes are manifold. But it is a recognition, even a condemnation, of that irresponsible use of these sciences in such a way as to explain away all sin and consequent guilt as the fault of parents, society, environment, education, or even religion. Granted that all of these factors exert an influence on our lives, nevertheless, as good behavioral scientists agree, we still have free will and, despite all influences to the contrary, we can and must take *responsibility* for our own attitudes and decisions, our own voluntary thoughts, words, actions, and omissions.

Sin is a fact of life. If we are honest with ourselves, our own experience and observation are proof enough. But perhaps nowhere is this more vividly confirmed than in the pages of Sacred Scripture, which always "tells it like it is!" The so-called *"original sin"* of

MODERNISM /
POLYGENISIS

Page #44

Adam and Eve in Genesis 3 is a kind of primeval parable, a masterful, mythical expose of human sin as a universal phenomenon and clearly the result, not of divine creation as in many other ancient religions, but of human willfulness. The Hebrew word *Adam* (from *adamah* meaning "earth" or "ground," cf. Gn 2:7) simply means "man" in a generic sense ("everyman"), while his partner is called "woman" (Hebrew *ishah*) in Genesis 2:23 because she is taken from her "man" or "husband" (Hebrew *ish*) and *Eve* (Hebrew *evah* meaning "living") in Genesis 3:20 because "she became the mother of all the living." In other words, Adam and Eve are symbolic and corporate personalities representing *all humankind,* male and female, and the so-called "original sin" is simply a beautiful way of describing the sinfulness of the human race and its own collective responsibility for it.[6]

Quite possibly, the story of the "Fall of Man" in Genesis 3, like that of the "Deluge" in Genesis 7-8, was borrowed from the Mesopotamian legend of *Gilgamesh,*[7] King of Uruk, who tries to obtain the secret of immortality from Utnapishtim "The Faraway," the sole survivor of the "Great Flood" caused by the caprice of some of the gods. Utnapishtim tells Gilgamesh that his best hope for immortality, or at least rejuvenation, lies in finding and retrieving from the sea a certain thorny "plant of life" called "Man Becomes Young in Old Age." With the help of Urshanabi the boatman, Gilgamesh retrieves the coveted "plant of life" and is taking it back to Uruk when, hot and tired from his long journey, he decides to refresh himself in a cool spring-fed pool, depositing his "plant of life" nearby. Sadly for Gilgamesh, while he is enjoying his dip, a serpent comes up from the water and carries off the plant, which rejuvenates it by enabling it to slough its skin. Note the similarities to the Genesis story in the references to a "plant of life" and to a "serpent," but note also, as always in these appropriations from pagan literature, the complete absence of any moral in the Gilgamesh account, unless it be, "Before you go swimming, be sure to check your valuables!"

By contrast, the biblical account in *Genesis 3* is true to life religiously, morally, and even psychologically. The serpent, symbol of evil and later of Satan (Rv 12:9; 20:2), either because of its naturally deceptive habits or because it was worshipped as a fertility symbol in Canaanite religion,[8] tempts Eve, who in turn tempts Adam, to eat the "forbidden fruit." God then confronts Adam, who blames Eve, who in turn blames the serpent. Finally, God metes out punishments, beginning with the serpent, then Eve, and then Adam, the punishments being well-known characteristics of the ones punished (serpents slither; women suffer the pains of childbirth; men till the soil, often fruitlessly) and saying nothing about the state of serpents and humans before the Fall. All that is taught, and taught very effectively, is that the universal phenomenon of sin is the result of the misuse of free will, perhaps occasioned by diabolical temptation. And Paul's inspired contrast in Romans 5:12-19 between universal sinfulness and death as originating with Adam's disobedience, and universal justification and life as originating with Jesus' obedience, no more requires the historicity of the Genesis myth than does Jesus' own reference to the parable of Jonah's sojourn in the great fish (Mt 12:40) compel us to accept the historicity of that fascinating "fish story." Divine inspiration is quite compatible with any legitimate form of literature, including myths and fables.

After being introduced in the third chapter of Genesis, sin becomes a central theme throughout the Bible, both the Old and the New Testaments, as is clear for example in the Psalms, particularly Psalms 14, 32, 38, 51, and many more. But perhaps nothing underlines the biblical preoccupation with sin, especially in the *Old Testament,* more than a brief examination of the *terminology* used. It is most instructive that Greek, though a word-rich language, possesses only the one basic word for sin, namely *"hamartía"* and *"hamártēma"* from the verb *"hamartánō"* meaning "to miss the mark, to err, to make a mistake, to go astray," reflecting generally the Greek emphasis on the intellectual. On the other hand, Hebrew, though a word-poor language, employs a number of terms for sin, each specifying a particular aspect of this evil. *Gottfried Quell,* in

Kittel's *Theological Dictionary of the New Testament*, describes the situation thus:

> The concept of sin is linguistically expressed in many ways in the Old Testament. Indeed, justice is hardly done to this variety either in the [Greek] Septuagint with its summary use of *hamartia* (sin, error), *adikia* (injustice, unrighteousness), *anomia* (lawlessness), *asebeia* (godlessness), *kakia* (evil) and their derivatives, nor by our modern translations, which neither express the richness of the original nor even catch the decisive point in some cases.[9]

Time does not permit an examination of all the Old Testament expressions for sin, but it may be helpful to note the *principal roots* which underlie most of the various words employed.

These are all richly exemplified in Psalm 32:1, 5 which, if we were to translate according to the *connotations* contained therein, might look something like this,

> v.1.   Happy is he whose transgression (*pesha'*) is taken away,
> whose estrangement (*hattah*) is covered (or buried).
> Happy the man to whom the Lord imputes no guilt (*a'won*),
> in whose spirit there is no guile (*r'miyah*). . . .
> v.5.   Then I acknowledged my straying (*hattah*) to you,
> my guilt (*a'won*) I covered not.
> I said, "I confess my rebellion (*pesha'*) to the Lord,"
> and you took away the guilt (*a'won*) of my sin (*hattah*).[10]

In the thought and history of Israel, then, as reflected in the inspired writers, sin is so prominent a concern that one might say with *St. John Chrysostom* that "There is only one calamity — sin!"[11] And yet, one can detect a subtle change in the theology of sin after the exile, and especially in the time immediately preceding and during the ministry of Jesus, namely a change from the view of sin as primarily a personal offense against God, a breach of his Covenant, a straying from his love, to the view of sin as primarily an offense against the Law, with a corresponding shift of emphasis from God's punishment of sin, e.g., in David (2 S 11-20 and 24) and Ahab (1 K 21-22; 2 K 9-10), to man's punishment of sin according to the Law, as reflected time and again in the attitude of the Scribes, Pharisees, and Sadducees in the New Testament. In fact, this proved to be one of the principal areas of conflict between Judaism on the one hand and Christ and Christianity on the other.

The *New Testament,* on the whole, reverts back to Israel's earlier and more personal theology of sin, with special emphasis on the concept of sin as (1) primarily *interior,* in the heart (e.g., Mt 5:21-30; Mk 7:1-23); (2) an *attitude,* state, or condition more than an act (e.g., Rm 1:18-2:20; 1 Jn 3:4-10); (3) an attitude or act of *omission* more than commission (e.g., Mt 25; Lk 16:19-31; Jm 4:17; 1 Jn 3:17); and (4) a *power* in itself (e.g., Rm 7:13-25). But, most notably of all, the New Testament presents Jesus Christ as the universal *Savior from sin,* called "Jesus" from the womb specifically "because he will save his people from their sins" (Mt 1:21), the sacrificial "Lamb of God who takes away the sin of the world" (Jn 1:29, 36; cf. Is 52:13-53:12), winning salvation from sin by his death and resurrection (Mk 10:45; Rm 3:21-26; 4:25; 5:12-19; 6:1-14), calling all humankind to repentance (Greek *metánoia,* meaning a change of heart or conversion) and forgiveness (Greek *áphesis,* meaning a sending or taking away of sin, e.g., in Mt 4:17; 9:12-13; Mk 1:15; Ep 1:7; Col 1:14; 1 Jn 1:8-9), and reconciling us to the Father (*katallagé,* meaning reconciliation, i.e., with another) through atonement (which was originally at-*one*-ment, making one,[12] e.g., 2 Cor 5:14-21; Ep 1:9-10; 2:11-22).

Without a clear consciousness of sin, especially our own, we cannot possibly understand Christ and Christianity, we cannot possibly relate to Jesus in the primary way in which he came among us, namely as our Savior from sin. This consciousness, however, must not be a morbid or fearful preoccupation, but a gateway to closer relationship. In the person of *Jesus Christ*, we have at one and the same time the most graphic picture of the *horror of sin* (for which he suffered the most shocking of deaths) and the most touching picture of the *compassion of God* toward sinners. The first becomes most evident from a careful reading of the passion account in all four Gospels coupled, if possible, with a knowledge of the inhuman cruelty and degradation inflicted on Jesus by the scourging, the crowning with thorns, the carrying of the cross, the nailing to the cross, and the terrible agony of three to six hours until his death. For this knowledge, there is revealing information from history and archaeology[13] (except for the crowning), and also from the *Holy Shroud of Turin*, the authenticity of which seems to be more and more corroborated from a multitude of scientific tests.[14]

But all of this, of course, takes on an incredible dimension when we let it soak into our consciousness that this pitiable figure, subjected as a public criminal to such monstrous torture, is also the all-wise, all-loving, and all-powerful Creator of this tremendous universe of ours! What a colossal evil must sin be, to have caused God himself to pay such a price for our salvation! But that is far too general. What a colossal evil must *my* sin be, to have caused such a tragedy! It is so easy to blame the murderous expedience of the high-priest Caiaphas, the ambitious greed of Judas Iscariot, the deplorable fickleness of the Passover crowd, the pitiable weakness of Pontius Pilate, but in the final analysis, as we know from faith it was *all* sin, *our* sin, *my* sin that took the life of the Son of God!

The Saints fully realized this, as exemplified in St. Paul's "confession" to Timothy, "Christ Jesus came into the world to save sinners. Of course I myself am the worst" (1 Tm 1:15). And the reason is obvious. If sin is the death or at least the corrosion of our loving relationship with God, and particularly if by sin we are guilty of "crucifying the Son of God . . . and holding him up to contempt" (Heb 6:6), then the more conscious we are of God's unlimited love for us and the more intimately we are united with him, especially in the person of Jesus Christ, the more clearly we are able to discern the enormity of our sinfulness and the more personally those dramatic words of Nathan to David strike home to each of us, "You are the man!" (2 S 12:7). It is precisely when Isaiah is favored with the awesome vision of God that he is most aware of his own sinfulness and that of his people (Is 6:1-7). And it is especially the intimate friendship accorded Judas as an Apostle that renders his betrayal of Jesus so heinous (Jn 13:18; cf. Ps 41:10; 55:13-15) as to seem unforgivable (Mt 27:3-5). Is not then our own spirituality suspect if we "feel" singularly close to God but continue to "drink down sin like water" (Jb 15:16), seeing no connection between religion and morality, or even trading on our emotional enthusiasm to presume that God's love for us will tolerate whatever we do? If we lack a sense of sin, is it because we lack a genuine sense of God?

On the other hand, as I have indicated, in the person of Jesus Christ we also have the most touching picture of the *compassion* of God toward sinners. This is so striking that both ancient and modern "Pharisees" have accused Jesus of being "soft on sin." It is true that the Synoptic Gospels in particular contain relatively few condemnations of sin by Our Lord, but the explanation is not difficult to discover. He himself was (and is, of course) totally free of sin (Jn 8:46; 2 Cor 5:21; Heb 7:26; 1 P 2:22). In fact, he is the absolute conqueror of sin (Mt 9:2; Mk 2:5; Lk 5:20; Jn 1:29). Nevertheless, "God did not send the Son into the world to condemn the world but that the world might be saved through him" (Jn 3:17). The time for the condemnation of sinners will be at the end of the ages, when Jesus will come as Supreme Judge (Mt 25; Jn 5:22, 27-30) or even at death, for "It is appointed that men die once, and after death be judged" (Heb 9:27).

In the meantime, he is with us as our Savior, bringing redemption and forgiveness. He clearly does condemn sin (Mt 5:17-18; Mk 10:19; Lk 13:1-9; Jn 5:14; 8:11), but he is far more intent, as Savior, Physician, and Shepherd, on calling sinners to repentance and readily forgiving them (Lk 15). "The bruised reed he will not crush; the smoldering wick he will not quench" (Mt 12:20). "The healthy do not need a doctor; sick people do. I have not come to invite the self-righteous to a change of heart, but sinners" (Lk 5:31-32). He is the Divine Shepherd who leaves the ninety-nine sheep in an uninhabited area (not a desert!) in order to find the one lost sheep (Lk 15:1-7), for "The Son of Man has come to search out and save what is lost" (Lk 19:10). And this is nowhere more vividly and accurately expressed than in the parable of the prodigal son or, more accurately, the merciful father (Lk 15:11-32), which we will examine in detail later on when we consider (the Sacrament of) reconciliation. *Gerhard Kittel* provides us with an excellent brief summary with which we can close this section, "In Christ we have both the holiness of God's judgment on sin and the love of God's saving of the sinner."[15]

THE PRINCIPAL EFFECTS OF SIN:

If such be the root, what shall be the fruit? What evils, as from Pandora's Box, does sin unleash upon ourselves and upon our world? Whether *physical evils* such as sickness, pain, and death are caused by sin or are the natural conditions of our limited human nature can be argued. Science favors the latter view, as summarized by Leslie Weatherhead in *Psychology, Religion, and Healing,*

> Disease was rife on this planet before man came into existence, and it has continued ever since. Students of the remains of prehistoric animals tell us quite definitely that those remains leave indubitable evidence of the early existence of painful disease. It is quite false to suppose that disease only appeared with man and is wholly attributable, as some suppose, to man's sin.[16]

Scripture seems to confirm the former view, but when it names sin as the cause of death among humans (e.g., in Gn 2:17; 3:19; Rm 5:12), is it not speaking etiologically and rhetorically rather than theologically? If there were no sin in the world, would we, by a kind of preternatural gift, be immune from these physical evils? That would be very difficult to establish from Scripture, but one thing is certain, as has been shown at length above, namely that sin has indeed caused or at least occasioned the death of the Son of God himself. It therefore can be rightly called the greatest of evils, even though, as we must never forget, God used it as a *"felix culpa"* (happy fault)[17] to bring about the greatest of goods: our salvation and reconciliation with him. "For our sakes God made him who did not know sin to be sin, so that in him we might become the very holiness of God" (2 Cor 5:21). For, as F. X. Durrwell has called to our attention in his pioneering work *The Resurrection,* the death of Jesus was the necessary condition of his resurrection (Lk 24:26; Ph 2:5-11), without which we would not be saved (Rm 4:25; 1 Cor 15:17)[18]

In addition, modern studies of the interrelationship among our body, mind, and soul (roughly corresponding to our makeup as "flesh, person, and spirit" discussed in Chapter Two) have produced convincing evidence of their mutual influence, most notably of physical illness and even death resulting from moral guilt and despair. Hence, in recent years, physicians, psychiatrists, and clergy have happily learned to cooperate extensively with one another in working for the physical, mental, and spiritual health or wholeness of their clients. The very words *health* and *healing* derive from Old English "hal" (hale) meaning whole, just as *illness* comes from an Old Norse word "illr" meaning evil, and *disease* (dis-ease) connotes a lack, not only of physical comfort, but of peace of mind and soul. "A joyful heart is the health of the body, but a depressed spirit dries up the bones" (Pr 17:22).

But what about *moral evils?* Here the evidence of Scripture, especially in the prophets and psalms, is dramatically clear. Sin is a *moral disease* (often symbolized by leprosy, e.g., Nb 12:10; 2 K 5:27; 2 Ch 26:16-23) which, if left to grow unchecked, tends to ravage the entire person, as the Psalmist describes so graphically in Psalm 38, e.g. vv. 4 and 6,

There is no health in my flesh because of your indignation;
There is no wholeness in my bones because of my sin . . . .
Noisome and festering are my sores because of my folly.

And *Process Theology*, far from downplaying sin and its effects, actually provides us with powerful assistance in appreciating them, as we see in this quotation from *Daniel Day Williams*,[19]

> This thesis that the *imago dei* is the form of creation for life fulfilled in love gives us our basis for the interpretation of sin. The root of sin is failure to realize life in love. The cleft in man which results from sin is more than the loss of a supernatural endowment. It is disorder in the roots of his being. It is the disaster resulting from twisted, impotent or perverted love.
>
> Sin infects the whole man. It does not at once destroy the reasoning powers, though in extremity it may do even that. It does not completely take away conscience, though the loss of love may finally result in the disappearance of conscience. It does not eliminate creativity from man's life, though it may turn that creativity into demonic self-destructiveness. It does not leave man without any sense of God or knowledge of the holy, though it may distort this sense, turning man's worship into idolatry and leaving him without hope and seemingly without God.

But perhaps nowhere in all of secular literature do we find a more unforgettable portrait of the effects of sin than in the haunting novel by Oscar Wilde, *The Picture of Dorian Gray*.[20] In it, the handsome Dorian remains ever young, irresistible, and conscienceless, while his portrait (which is really his conscience) shows through the years the aging and ugliness of his sins. Would that we could all view the effects of our sins as clearly as could Dorian, but without the spiritual blindness which caused him to continue his depravity to the ultimate disaster!

In another favorite analogy, the Bible describes one of the effects of sin as a painful *deprivation of freedom*, whether through *paralysis* (Mt 9:1-7; Mk 2:1-12; Lk 5:17-26; Jn 5:1-14), *imprisonment* (Mt 5:25-26; 18:21-35; Lk 12:58-59), *darkness* (Mt 8:12; 22:13; 25:30; Jn 8:12), or *slavery* (Jn 8:34; Rm 6). This is a most appropriate analogy, for habitual sin does indeed blind our mind, our conscience, our moral sense, and bind our will, imprison our spirit, and enslave our whole being. Freedom is a precious treasure which, unfortunately, those of us who possess it do not fully appreciate, while those who do not are often willing to die in order to obtain it. But is it not ironic that, while enjoying the blessings of political, social, economic, and religious freedom, we so readily allow ourselves to be enslaved, imprisoned, paralyzed by our own attachment to sin?

Another important consequence of sin, as is well known, is a *sense of guilt*. Adam and Eve "hid themselves from the Lord God among the trees of the garden" because they were "naked" (Gn 3:7-11). David, according to ancient tradition, was moved by Nathan's revelation of his guilt to compose the soulful penitential prayer which we know as Psalm 51. The collective guilt of Judah was acknowledged and lamented in the masterful alphabetic dirges known as the *Lamentations*, once attributed to Jeremiah but now generally considered anonymous, and in the humble prayers of the three young men and of Daniel himself in Daniel 3 and 9 respectively. And world literature, both ancient and modern, is replete with dramatic portrayals of guilt, e.g., Sophocles' *Oedipus Rex*, Shakespeare's *Macbeth*, Dostoyevsky's *Crime and Punishment*, and Poe's *The Telltale Heart*, to mention only a few.

In one sense, *guilt* is indeed a moral evil, constituting a built-in torment and punishment for sin, but in another sense it is a salutary good because it tends to lead us to repentance for our sins. The true moral evil in this regard is *"hardness of heart"* or lack of any sense of guilt, such as we find attributed to Pharaoh during the plagues (Ex 7-10); to Saul in his persecution of David (1 S 18-28); to the leadership and membership of Israel and Judah before the exile, as reflected in the pre-exilic Prophets; to the leadership of Israel in the time of Jesus, as mirrored in the Gospels; to the pagans generally of Paul's time, whom he so emphatically condemns in Romans 1; and to the "backsliders" (described in Heb 6:4-8; Jude, vv. 5-19; and 2 P 2:10-22). Perhaps it is best summed up scripturally in Psalm 14, "The fool says in his heart, 'There is no god, etc.' " and literarily in Oscar Wilde's *The Picture of Dorian Gray*. And closely related to this moral "hardness of heart" is that psychological "Fool's Paradise" which results when some therapists insist on treating all guilt, deserved or otherwise, as irrational and unworthy of "normal" human beings.

Essentially, however, the principal consequence of sin is its effect on our *relationship with God*. The traditional division of sins into "mortal" and "venial" is basically a distinction between sin, or more often a state of sinfulness, which completely *sunders* our relationship with God (hence the term mortal or deadly) and sin or sinfulness that does not sunder but *strains,* wounds, corrodes, cools that relationship (hence the term venial or easily forgivable). In more recent years, theologians have begun to suggest a threefold division of sin into *mortal* (a fundamental rejection or turning of one's back on God, 1 Jn 5:16-17), *serious or grave* (not a fundamental rejection but a deliberate offense against God and others in a grave or serious matter, e.g., adultery, murder, etc., 1 Jn 3:4-10; 5:18), and *venial or light* (either a less than deliberate offense in a serious matter or a deliberate offense in a less than serious matter, e.g., vanity, "white" lies, small thefts, etc., 1 Jn 1:8-10). Personally, I favor the threefold distinction as being both more scriptural and more realistic, but I do not intend to pursue the question further, primarily because this is not a book about Moral Theology but about the Spiritual Life.

To one who is serious about the Spiritual Life, the distinction between mortal and venial sin is not a priority. Mortal sin in the sense of deliberate rejection of God is unthinkable; serious sin in the sense of a willfully grave transgression, highly unlikely. What is of special concern is *venial sin,* not so much in a quantitative as in a qualitative sense. Just as in a loving marriage, the partners do not speculate how far they can go without rejecting or seriously offending each other, but are rather concerned about the quality of their love and with avoiding anything that might offend each other, so it is with the human partner in a loving relationship with God. To him or her, what is of prime concern is the *quality* of love and fidelity, especially the avoidance of any *deliberate* offense against God, even in matters of (objectively) lesser importance.

Actually, to a genuinely Spiritual person, no sin (especially no deliberate sin) can be considered light or insignificant, regardless of theological categories. After all, the gravity of an offense is measured by: (1) the dignity of the One offended, (2) the debt of gratitude owed the One offended for his love and blessings, and (3) the closeness of relationship or union with the One offended; to which we might append, (4) the degree of knowledge and volition involved as a result of the above. And, in addition, viewed in the context of relationships (especially the covenant relationship described in the previous chapter), every sin is not only significant but comprises also, to one degree or another, infidelity, sacrilege, and rebellion: *infidelity* because of our covenant relationship with God which constitutes a spiritual union or "marriage" (1 Cor 6:17), *sacrilege* or abuse of a sacred thing or person since we are personally consecrated by covenant and anointed with the Spirit (1 P 1:2), and *rebellion* because by covenant we are adopted as children of God, our heavenly Father (Rm 8:15). Sin there will be, as indicated in 1 John 1:8-10, because of human weakness, but it will be humbly repented and readily forgiven, even contributing to our growth in humility, loving dependence, and great holiness. It is *deliberate sin*, mortal or venial, which is avoided at all cost as *the* great obstacle to our relationship, our intimate union, with Christ and, through him, with the Father and the Holy Spirit.

As the reader must have noticed by now, I have said nothing about *rewards and punishments* in this context of the results of sin. Perhaps this is because, like so many others before Vatican II, I heard too much about rewards and punishments, especially in heaven and hell, as *the* great motive for doing good and avoiding evil — the old "pie in the sky" or, more often, the old "fire and brimstone" approach. My underplaying of these "last things" stems not from denial or doubt of their existence, so clear from the New Testament (e.g., Mt 25), nor even from their uselessness as motivation for, as the *Imitation of Christ* so realistically expresses the matter, "If love cannot recall you from evil, it is good that the fear of hell at least should restrain you."[21] A fortiori, for one who truly loves God above all things, the eternal possession of him in heaven or the eternal estrangement from him in hell are powerful motives indeed. Yet I do not stress this motivation for the simple reason that, in the Spiritual Life, it is not and should not be paramount. Rather, the operative consideration is and should be that union with God in love is already heaven begun here on earth, as emphasized in John's Gospel and in the famous saying of *St. Catherine of Siena,* "All the way to heaven is heaven!"[22] To which we can rightly add the correlative conviction, "All the way to hell is hell!"

But our treatment of sin would be conspicuously incomplete if we failed to consider another dimension which we have so far adverted to only indirectly. We have been concentrating on the significance of sin in our personal relationship with God, but that personal relationship cannot be divorced from our *communal relationship with others in God.* Sin is just as social as our covenant is communal. Not only are most sins committed against another human being as well as against God, but in addition every sin (especially every deliberate sin) has an adverse effect on the Church, the covenant People of God and Bride-Body of Christ, and even on human society as a whole. Each of us is a kind of "corporate personality," contributing by the quality of our life to the advancement or retreat of the Church and the human race; to the perfection, hominization or humanization, and Christification or, conversely, to the degradation, animalization, even Satanization of the human species. Many have written eloquently on this important point, e.g., *John Donne* and *Teilhard de Chardin,* but perhaps the succint statement of *George Crespy* expresses it best,

. . . what is biblical is the idea of the solidarity of the group —

what *Wheeler Robinson* has called the idea of *"corporate personality."* According to this idea, the individual represents the whole group in space and in time, and reciprocally the entire group is responsible for the individual. In other words, no human act whether bad or good is the isolated act of an individual only. Every act involves the group and at the limit all mankind, because of the interrelationship between groups. . . . The more the world contracts, the more the influence of isolated, individual acts whether good or bad expands and strengthens itself.[23]

OTHER OBSTACLES TO THE RELATIONSHIP:

It is not by accident that the Lord's Prayer follows the petition for forgiveness with the petition "And lead us not into temptation (or trial), but deliver us from evil (or the evil one)" (Mt 6:13), for *temptation* is intimately connected with sin as cause or occasion to possible effect. Yet, strangely enough, the connection is not particularly understood among many people, including a good number of Christians. Some well-meaning Christians long for the day when they can be completely free of temptations; others foolishly conclude that they have already reached that point. Some blame all their temptations on Satan; others deny in practice that he even exists or has any interest in us. Some tend to regard all temptations as sins or at least confess them "just to be on the safe side"; others have accepted the popular slogan of "doing what comes naturally" and agree with the remark of Oscar Wilde's Lord Henry to *Dorian Gray* that, "the only way to get rid of a temptation is to yield to it."[24] We could go on and on, but limitations of time and space dictate that we confine ourselves to some pertinent passages of the Bible and to some common-sense observations.

As we have already seen in Genesis 3, temptation is portrayed as existing from the very beginning of the human race. Whether that is true or not, it certainly has been a fact of life throughout *recorded history* and, all in all, humankind has had a rather poor record of resisting temptations. Witness *Abram* weakly protecting himself by passing off his wife Sarai as his sister (Gn 12:13; 20:5), *Jacob* deceptively fulfilling his desire for the birthright (Gn 27), *Moses and Aaron* giving in to their impatience and anger with their petulant people (Nb 20:3-13), even *David,* a man after God's own heart, failing to resist temptations to adultery, murder, and pride (2 S 11, 24). This is so true that examples of obedience to God's will and resistance to temptation stand out as rare exceptions, e.g., Abraham's willingness to sacrifice Isaac (Gn 22), Joseph's resistance to the blandishments of Putiphar's wife (Gn 39), Moses' courage in confronting Pharaoh (Ex 5-11), David's rejection of the natural desire to rid himself of his enemy, Saul (1 S 24, 26). In the *New Testament,* the record is hardly better, especially as exemplified in the betrayal by *Judas* (Mt 26:14-16, etc.), the denial by *Peter* (Mt 26:69-75, etc.), the ambition of *James and John* (Mk 10:37), the weakness of all the Apostles (Mt 25:56, etc.), in spite of Jesus' clear warning to his favored three, "Be on guard and pray that you may not be put to the test. The spirit is willing but nature (the flesh) is weak" (Mk 14:38). Even after the resurrection and the outpouring of the Holy Spirit, the record is not much improved, as we see in the deception of *Ananias and Sapphira* (Ac 5:1-11), the "simony" of *Simon Magus* (Ac 8:18-19), the weakness of *John Mark* (Ac 13:13), the estrangement of *Paul and Barnabas* (Ac 15:36-41), the "de facto" discrimination of *Peter* (Gal 2:11-14), and the obstinacy of the *Jerusalem faction* (Ac 14:1, etc.).

By contrast, we have the dramatic portrayal of *Jesus'* resistance to temptation from beginning to end of his life. *Mark* summarizes the "opening round" of temptation thus, "He stayed in the wasteland forty days, put to the test there by Satan" (Mk 1:13), but later provides us with the most powerful account of Jesus' agonizing struggle in the garden (Mk 14:32-42). *Matthew and Luke,* reflecting their common source called "Q," dramatize the temptations of Jesus by depicting him in a "three-round bout" with Satan, primarily over what kind of Messiah and Savior he would be, the kind decreed by his Father or the kind expected by the Jewish people and offered by Satan (Mt 4:1-11; Lk 4:1-13). That this is a dramatization, it seems to me, is evident from common sense, simply because there were no witnesses but Satan and Jesus. Satan, like the Egyptian Pharaohs, would not talk about his defeat, and one can hardly visualize Jesus, one night while sitting around the campfire, saying to his Apostles, "Did I ever tell you about my temptations?" But there is a value in this dramatization because of the lessons found therein, not the least of which are contained in the masterful quotations from Deuteronomy, the Old Testament book of divine love. Finally, *John,* who has already implicitly referred to Jesus' temptations with the expression, "The word became flesh" (Jn 1:14) sprinkles those temptations throughout his life. Three in particular correspond to the three dramatized by Matthew and Luke but seem to be much more according to factual history in the life of Jesus, namely the Jews' demand for "miraculous bread" in John 6:25-35, their prior attempt to "carry him off and make him king" (Jn 6:15), and his own relatives' enticement to work miracles in Jerusalem in order to "display" himself "to the world at large" (Jn 7:2-19).[25]

In the *epistolary literature,* the author of *Hebrews* holds up the example of Jesus' temptations as an encouragement to us all,

> Since, then, we have a great high priest who has passed through the heavens, Jesus, the Son of God, let us hold fast to our profession of faith. For we do not have a high priest who is unable to sympathize with our weakness, but one who was *tempted* in every way that we are, yet *never sinned.* So let us confidently approach the throne of grace to receive mercy and favor and to find help in time of need (Heb 4:14-16).

Paul, on the other hand, gives us a frank but enigmatic account of what seems to have been an exceptionally difficult kind of temptation, perhaps involving also an illness or opposition of some sort.

As to the extraordinary revelations, in order that I might not become conceited I was given a thorn in the flesh, an angel of Satan to beat me and keep me from getting proud. Three times I begged the Lord that this might leave me. He said to me, "My grace is enough for you, for in weakness power reaches perfection." And so I willingly boast of my weaknesses instead, that the power of Christ may rest upon me (2 Cor 12:7-9).

And *James,* in his usual manner of practical wisdom, provides us with some common sense advice about temptations,

Happy the man who holds out to the end through trial! Once he has been proved, he will receive the crown of life the Lord has promised to those who love him. No one who is tempted is free to say, "I am tempted by God." Surely God, who is beyond the grasp of evil, tempts no one. Rather, the tug and lure of his own passion tempt every man. Once passion has conceived it gives birth to sin, and when sin reaches maturity it begets death (Jm 1:12-15).

It behooves us to have a very *common-sense attitude* about temptations. As we have seen in abundance from Sacred Scripture and as we know so well from our own experience and observation, temptations are a fact of life. Why? For as many reasons as there are *factors* that combine to make us what we are as "flesh": (1) our basic instincts of self-preservation and preservation of the race, (2) our hereditary characteristics, (3) the influence of environment: especially our parents, family, friends, education, and life experiences, and (4) the cumulative aftereffects of our own thoughts, imaginations, acts, and habits. All of these factors unite to engender in us attitudes, impulses, and drives which can at times seem utterly overwhelming! With Paul we cry out, "Who will free me from the body of this death?" (Rm 7:24, WD). To which the answer comes immediately, "Thanks be to God [or: The Grace of God] through Jesus Christ our Lord!" (Rm 7:25, WD). For, as Paul had learned when tormented by his famous "thorn for the flesh," his buffeting "angel of Satan" (2 Cor 12:7, WD), "My [Christ's] grace is enough for you, for power is perfected in weakness!" (2 Cor 12:9, WD). The more we surrender to Jesus Christ, the more perfectly we are related to and united with him, so much the more completely does he himself combat and overcome our temptations in us and for us, or at least empower us to avoid surrendering to them.

Not that temptations ever disappear completely in this life. There is an old saying, sometimes attributed to *St. Francis de Sales* but probably anonymous, that our selfishness dies some fifteen minutes after we are in the grave! Rather than receding, temptations tend to assume different forms according to our level of age and spirituality, and at each level we must, with the author of the *Imitation of Christ,* "be solicitous about our temptations,"[26] for "we must undergo many trials if we are to enter into the reign of God" (Ac 14:22; cf. Si 2:1).

Part of the process, however, is the avoidance of unnecessary *occasions of sin,* which constitute another obstacle to our relationship with God. To pretend that we are serious about union with Christ and therefore about conquering our temptations and growing in holiness, and yet to indulge our curiosity, our sense appetites, our imagination, in preoccupations with things, places, or persons which we know are likely to cause serious temptations, is simply to "carry dust into the wind." This does not mean, of course, that we are to live a life of fear and scrupulosity; still less that we are to condemn for ourselves and others legitimate recreation and relaxation of mind and body. We are certainly not to go around with a face "like a great Amen!" But we are to recognize that, in our particular age and culture, we are much like the early Christians in Corinth — surrounded by occasions of sin. The atmosphere reeks with pollution, not only the physical kind, but the far more dangerous moral kind with which we are daily assaulted, especially through the media of movies, television, plays, novels and magazines.

We need, then, in Christ and under the guidance of the Spirit, to calmly avoid, resist, and overcome this onslaught on our moral and

Spiritual Life with appropriate and prudent measures. It does no good to wish, like Edwin Arlington Robinson's *Miniver Cheevy*,[27] that we had been born in an earlier period when things were different. We are children of this age with its unparalleled dangers, but God never fails to provide the help necessary to combat the unique dangers of each age and each situation. Jesus prayed to his Father for his Apostles and for us, "I do not ask you to take them out of the world, but to guard them from the evil one" (Jn 17:15). In fact, God raises up in every age holy men and women to be signs of "contradiction" (Lk 2:34) to their age; witnesses who, in the challenging words of *Cardinal Suhard*, "so live that their lives would not make sense if God did not exist!"[28] Could we not, by the grace of God, be the witnesses to this age, the saints of this century? After all, as Leon Bloy observes in the final line of his inspiring book, *The Woman Who Was Poor*, "There is only one misery, and that is — not to be saints!"[29]

But sometimes our temptations arise from or are symptomatic of two other obstacles to our relationship with God, namely our *inordinate attachments* and our *moral and spiritual imperfections*. As "flesh," we can so easily and so completely center our lives around persons, places, and things, around occupations, recreations, reputations, and pleasures, that there is little room or time left for God and his loving service in our lives. An exaggerated but trenchant illustration is the story of the man whose wife did not realize he was dead in front of the television set until after the Super Bowl! Jesus' words still challenge us today, perhaps more than ever, "Remember, where your treasure is, there your heart will likewise be" (Mt 6:21). *St. John of the Cross*, the great teacher of detachment, reminds us that, "whether a bird be held by a slender cord or by a stout one . . ., it will not attain to the liberty of divine union."[30] Hence we need to examine ourselves on a regular basis to see if we are unduly attached to something or someone, and to determine how we might free ourselves from this attachment or at least render it less of a problem or occasion of temptation. We will pursue this more fully in the following chapter.

By *imperfections* we mean deliberate choices of less perfect actions when we could choose and, indeed, feel called to choose a more perfect action (or suffering) for God and for others. A good example might be that of the "rich young man" in Mark 10:17-22. Not that these imperfect choices are sins, but rather that they tend to cool our love, to turn our will, little by little, toward other choices which might be venial sins and perhaps later serious ones. Above all, they act like "stone" obstacles, preventing our loving Savior, Jesus Christ, from living in us and working through us as perfectly and effectively as he desires. And, in fact, they can lead to the kind of tepidity or *lukewarmness* which has been immortalized in Christ's letter through John to the Church of *Laodicea,*

> I know your deeds; I know you are neither hot nor cold. How I wish you were one or the other — hot or cold! But because you are lukewarm, neither hot nor cold, I am about to spew you out of my mouth! (Rv 3:15-16).

The solution, of course, is suggested by Jesus himself in the very same letter,

> Here I stand, knocking at the door.
> If anyone hears me calling and opens the door,
> I will enter his house and have supper with him . . . (Rv 3:20).

SUMMARY AND CONCLUSION:

By way of *summary,* let me quote from the opening paragraph of Lyonnet's excellent article on sin in Leon-Dufour's *Dictionary of Biblical Theology,*

> The Bible speaks often, almost on every page, of the reality that we commonly call *sin.* The terms the Old Testament uses to designate it are numerous and ordinarily borrowed from *human relations*: omission, iniquity, rebellion, injustice, etc. . . . It is particularly through the whole sweep of Bible history that the

true nature of sin appears with all its malice and in all its dimensions. Here we also learn that this revelation about man is at the same time a revelation about God; about his love to which sin is opposed, about his mercy which he exercises in regard to sin; for the *history of salvation* is nothing other than the tirelessly repeated attempts of God the Creator to draw man away from his sin.[31]

By way of *conclusion,* I can do no better than to quote some key verses from *Psalm 51,* which has so much to say to us about sin, about guilt, and above all about the remedy for both:

3. Have mercy on me, O God, in your goodness;
   in the greatness of your compassion,
   wipe out my offense.

4. Thoroughly wash me from my guilt
   and of my sin cleanse me.

5. For I acknowledge my offense,
   and my sin is before me always . . . .

9. Cleanse me of sin with hyssop,
   that I may be purified; wash me
   and I shall be whiter than snow.

10. Let me hear the sounds of joy and gladness;
    the bones you have crushed shall rejoice.

11. Turn away your face from my sins,
    and blot out all my guilt.

12. A clean heart create for me, O God,
    and a steadfast spirit renew within me.

13. Cast me not out from your presence,
    and your holy spirit take not from me.

14. Give me back the joy of your salvation,
    and a willing spirit sustain in me . . . .

19. My sacrifice, O God, is a contrite spirit;
    a heart contrite and humbled, O God,
    you will not spurn.

RECOMMENDED READING LIST

1. Durham, Charles. *Temptation: Help for Struggling Christians,* Downer's Grove, IL: Inter-Varsity Press, 1982.
2. Lyonnet-Sabourin. *Sin, Redemption, and Sacrifice*: A Biblical and Patristic Study, Chicago, IL: Loyola University Press, 1971.
3. Menninger, Karl. *Whatever Became of Sin?,* New York, NY: Bantam Books, 1978.
4. Pittenger, W. Norman. *Cosmic Love and Human Wrong*: The Meaning of Sin and Process Thinking, New York, NY: Paulist Press, 1978.
5. Taylor, Michael, ed. *The Mystery of Sin and Forgiveness,* Staten Island, NY: Alba House, 1971.

QUESTIONS FOR REFLECTION AND DISCUSSION

1. From Scripture and experience, what are the importance and nature of obstacles to our relationship with God?
2. What are the importance and nature of sin, especially in terms of relationship between ourselves and God and between ourselves and others?
3. What is the meaning of "Original Sin" according to modern biblical and theological studies?
4. What are some of the principal effects of sin in ourselves and in others?
5. What are the meaning and importance of other obstacles, e.g., temptations, occasions of sins, inordinate attachments, imperfections, lukewarmness?

SECTION TWO:
THE FEATURES OF THE SPIRITUAL LIFE

CHAPTER SIX

THE QUALITIES OF THE RELATIONSHIP,   PART I:
The Three "Virtues of Letting Go"

In today's world, there is an admirable concern about *quality,* for example: the quality of the air that we breathe, the food that we eat, and the water that we drink; the quality of life that we live and bequeath to those who follow us, the quality of goods that we produce for competitive markets at home and abroad. The same and even greater concern should be applied to our *Spiritual Life.* "The sons of this world are wiser than the sons of the light!" (Lk 16:8). But here, since it is so difficult to assess the quality of our relationship with God and with others in God, we must be more specific and examine the *qualities,* the characteristics, the conditions, the authentic signs of that relationship, namely the *virtues* that we need to practice in our Spiritual Life.

The word *virtue* is one which reflects the long and ever-changing history of civilization. The Hebrew word *hayil,* the Greek *aretē,* and the Latin *virtus* all exhibit a singularly masculine connotation, comprising such ideas as strength, valor, and virility. For example, the Latin word *vir* underlying *virtus* signifies man, male, or husband. Even when applied to woman, as in Proverbs 31:10-31, the masculine flavor of the expression is evidenced in the traditional title, "The Valiant Woman." In other words, whether described as a gift of God in Scripture or as the achievement of intellectual or moral self-development in philosophy, virtue in the ancient world definitely projected a "macho" image.

It was only later, especially in Christian times, that the word *virtue* tended to lose its male overtones in favor of a more balanced meaning of goodness, holiness, and spiritual perfection. In fact, it became in time even more closely identified with women than with men, e.g. in such an expression as "losing one's virtue." Finally, in our own "emancipated," permissive society of media-created anti-heroes, virtue has often become the object of cynical scorn or condescending pity, as exemplified in the anonymous modern versions of an ancient axiom, "Virtue is its own (and only) reward!"[1] and "While virtue is its own reward, most people are looking for a better offer!"[2]

Even in spiritual circles, there has been a fundamental and understandable shift of emphasis regarding virtue. When I was fulfilling my Novitiate in 1937-1939, our very first required spiritual reading was a three-volume work by a Spanish Jesuit Novice Master, the English translation of which was entitled, "The Practice of Perfection and Christian Virtues."[3] Each individual virtue was proposed as if it were the most important, and the clear impression was given that, if one were to acquire all the virtues mentioned, he would certainly reach perfection. In contrast with this rather Stoic approach is the reality, already noted in Chapter One, that perfection is not a pursuit of virtues, like a hunter filling his game bag; it is not even a pursuit of Christ, but rather his pursuit of us and our surrender to him. For, Christian perfection is not a collection to be made but a *Life to be lived*; not a pursuit of something but a personal relationship with Someone, namely with Jesus Christ and, through him, with the Father and the Holy Spirit.

But herein lurks a hidden danger. Yes, loving relationship is the essence, but it is not arrived at, nor grown in, nor truly genuine and authentic, without certain basic qualities, *certain virtues* which form the indispensable prerequisites and ongoing conditions of loving union with God. This is abundantly clear from Sacred Scripture.

Recall, for example, the haunting pleas of Yahweh in Micah 6:8,

> You have been told, O man, what is good,
> and what the Lord requires of you:
> Only to do right and to love goodness,
> and to walk humbly with your God.

Even more familiar are the many collective proposals of virtues in the New Testament, beginning with Jesus' open-ended challenges called the *Beatitudes* (Mt 5:3-12) through Paul's descriptions of the qualities of Christian love (1 Cor 13) and the fruits of the Spirit (Gal 5:22) to his sweeping recommendation in Philippians 4:8,

> Finally, my brothers, your thoughts should be directed to all
> that is true, all that deserves respect, all that is honest, pure,
> admirable, decent, virtuous, or worthy of praise.

This too is the lesson of *all the Saints* throughout the centuries, who reflect for us by word and example the virtues of Jesus Christ himself in the varied circumstances of different times, places, cultures, and problems. And, in fine, this is also the conclusion derived from the very nature of the Spiritual Life as essentially one of our relationship with God and others in God.

According to a very ancient Latin axiom, *"In medio stat virtus,"* that is, "In the middle stands virtue." Traditionally and quite correctly, this famous saying epitomizes the truth of experience and observation that genuine virtue avoids the two extremes of excess and defect, of too much and too little. But, in the context of the Spiritual Life, it takes on (at least, for me) an additional meaning, namely that Christian virtue "stands in the middle" between God's gratuitous gift and our cooperative effort. On the one hand, the virtues characteristic of our union with God are and can only be the free gift of God, as gratuitous as grace itself. Hence, they are often called "infused virtues," though I must admit that I dislike the term "infused" because it gives me a mental picture of virtues (like grace and the Holy Spirit himself) being literally "poured into" us like water or gasoline. To me, this is hardly the language of relationships. I much prefer to emphasize "Uncreated Grace," namely God himself dwelling in us and empowering us to live in relationship with him. Thus, any and all "infused virtues" we may have are actually the *virtues of Jesus Christ himself* living in us and continuing his virtuous life and ministry in and through us today.

On the other hand, virtues are at the same time *habits,* good habits as opposed to vices or bad habits. And habits grow through practice, whether they be physical, emotional, mental, or spiritual. Gifts of God and virtues of Christ though they certainly are, they exist and operate within us weak, fragmented, and earthbound human beings. Only gradually, in the beautiful words of John the Baptist, do we become "less and less" while he becomes "more and more" (Jn 3:30). And only gradually, with responsive effort on our part, do the virtues of Christ really become *our virtues,* practiced easily and, as it were, automatically, to the point where we can truly say with St. Paul, "I live, now not I, but Christ lives in me" (Gal 2:20), "To me, to live is Christ" (Ph 1:21), and "Imitate me as I imitate Christ" (1 Cor 11:1)!

But in this important matter of practicing the virtues of Christ, or rather of allowing him to practice his virtues in us, even the example of St. Paul, the other Apostles, and all the other Saints, pales before the shining example of *Mary of Nazareth,* the chosen mother of Jesus Christ, Our Lord and God, whom the great Protestant poet, William Wordsworth, did not hesitate to praise as "our tainted nature's solitary boast!"[4] Her profound humility (Lk 1:29, 48), her angelic purity (Lk 1:34), her incomparable faith, trust, and obedient love (Lk 1:38-39, 45), her patient acceptance of suffering (Lk 2:35; Jn 19:25), all these and more suffice to remind us that, if we desire to practice the virtues of Christ living in us, Mary is our model and our mother, given us by Jesus himself, "Woman, there is your son . . . There is your mother" (Jn 19:26-27).

In the touching words of St. Paul to the back-sliding Galatians, but with far greater right and God-given spiritual power, Mary can say to us, "You are my children, and you put me back in labor pains until Christ is formed in you" (Gal 4:19). Even the very term "woman," which seems at first blush to be a pejorative expression on the lips of Jesus (Jn 2:4 and 19:26) turns out to be, on closer inspection, quite the opposite, for (given John's love of symbolism and allusion) it clearly recalls that first "woman," *Eve,* the "mother of all the living" (Gn 2:23; 3:20). Mary is indeed the "mother of all the living," that is, of all the redeemed who live, not simply the life of *psyché* (natural life) but the life of *zoé* (spiritual, supernatural, eternal life) won for us and shared with us by her Divine Son.

Virtues are traditionally divided into *theological,* that is, those which are directly concerned with our relationship with God, and *moral,* that is, those which are concerned with our relationship with others. The theological virtues are three, namely faith, hope, and love or charity, as attested in many places of Scripture, especially the New Testament, e.g., "There are in the end three things that last: faith, hope, and love, and the greatest of these is love" (1 Cor 13:13). Moral virtues, of their very nature, are much more numerous and varied, as already indicated. Of these, the so-called "Cardinal Virtues" comprise four which are considered the "hinges" (from Latin *cardo*) for all the other moral virtues. Their listing, interestingly enough, is derived from Wisdom 8:7, "For she [Wisdom] teaches moderation [temperance] and prudence, justice and fortitude, and nothing in life is more useful for men than these."

In this and the following chapter, I propose to consider the virtues somewhat differently, concentrating on what I perceive from Scripture and other sources to be the six virtues that are most basic and characteristic in our relationship with God. The first three are what I like to call the *"Virtues of Letting Go,"* for they enable us to free ourselves from the three principal obstacles to union with God, obstacles which St. John identifies as "the lust of the flesh, the lust of the eyes, and the pride of life" (1 Jn 2:16). In our reflection, therefore, we will devote this chapter to an examination of humility, purity, and poverty. In the following chapter, we will concentrate on those three virtues which we have already called the Theological Virtues of faith, hope and love, but which I like to identify by the more graphic designation of the *"Virtues of Holding On,"* for they enable us to cling to God in personal, lasting relationship despite all obstacles and adversities.

Since time and space do not permit more than a summary treatment of each of these important virtues, we will focus on those considerations which promise to be the most fruitful in our Spiritual Life. Primary attention will be given, of course, to the testimony of the Word of God, both in Sacred Scripture and in the person of Jesus Christ, but the word and example of others, especially Mary and the other Saints, will likewise be invoked, along with other sources that offer outstanding help in this regard.

THE VIRTUES OF LETTING GO:

As we begin our consideration of the *"Virtues of Letting Go,"* I am reminded of a challenging modern-day parable which I first discovered in the form of a cartoon of unknown origin. It is the story of a man who, while walking along a precipice, happens to fall over the edge, but is fortunate enough to grasp a branch on his way down. As he clings precariously to the branch, he cries out in desperation toward the cliff above, "Help! Help! Can anyone up there help me?" An unearthly voice replies at once, "Of course, I can help you." Encouraged, the man pleads, "Then help me, please!" Calmly the voice directs him, *"Let go the branch!"* There is a long pause, then the man calls out even more desperately, "Can anyone else up there help me?"

The point of the parable should be clear. We are like the man who has fallen over the cliff, is clinging desperately, and crying for help. God longs to help us, but insists that we "let go the branch" in complete faith and trust. Can we "let go the branch"? Each of us clings as desperately to the "branch" of our pride, pleasure, and possessions as if our very life depended on it. These constitute our "Linus blanket" of personal security which prevents us from reaching spiritual maturity. As long as we continue to cling to them, we cannot be free to climb to God. Unless we consent to be emptied of them, we cannot hope to be filled with God. Until we are willing to die to them, we cannot expect to live in God and have the risen Christ live in us.

Remember the beautiful parable of Jesus about the *sower and the seed* (Mt 13:4-23)? The sower, of course, is God himself or Jesus Christ or his missionaries. The seed, as Jesus himself explains, is the Word of God, which is effective of itself, its fruitfulness being limited only by the lack of preparation of the soil. In our pride, we are like the trodden wayside or the shallow soil, totally lacking the life-giving root of humility. In our attachment to our pleasures, comforts, conveniences, and possessions, we are like the soil among thorns, where the precious seed of God's life in us never reaches maturity because it is simply choked off by the thorns of our sensuality and acquisitiveness.

Not, however, that many of us are capable, even with God's grace, of once-and-for-all "death to self" in order to live for God. In the first place, we become aware only gradually of the hydra-headed nature of our internal enemies. And secondly, even when we become acutely conscious of the "spiritual surgery" required of us, we may need much reflection and humble prayer to be able to "let go the branch." It is not so much a case of "digging out and laying the foundation," as spiritual writers often describe the process, but rather of constantly tilling and weeding the soil, or of continually bailing out the boat while we row or sail to our destination of union with God. Even the realization that we are not talking about "our" virtues of "letting go" but of Christ's virtues in us does not contradict the fact that transformation into Christ is a *gradual, lifelong process,* not for lack of power on his part but for excess of obstacles on ours and imperfect cooperation with him in removing them. We ourselves, even more than others, need the gentle reminder, "Please be patient. God isn't finished with me yet!"

In other words *self-control or self-discipline* is required, especially in the beginning but even throughout the Spiritual Life. This is what has traditionally been known as asceticism, from the Greek word *áskēsis* meaning (athletic) exercise or training. Far from conjuring up frightening pictures of hair shirts and scourges common to an earlier age, asceticism should rather remind us of the importance, in fact the necessity, of spiritual as well as physical *fitness*. Hence, St. Paul, who uses athletic imagery in many of his writings (e.g. Ph 3:12-16; 2 Tm 4:7-8), declares,

> You know that while all the runners in the stadium take part in the race, the award goes to one man. In that case, run so as to win! Athletes *deny themselves* all sorts of things. They do this to win a crown of leaves that withers, but we a crown that is imperishable.
>
> I do not run like a man who loses sight of the finish line. I do not fight as if I were shadowboxing. What I do is *discipline* my own body and master it, for fear that after having preached to others I myself should be rejected (1 Cor 9:24-26).

In our own day, when physical fitness through diet and exercise has become a national, even a worldwide obsession, and when athletes of all kinds train so long and hard in order to excel in their particular sports or Olympic events, can we afford to do less in the eternally important Life of the Spirit? As Paul reminds his beloved Timothy (1 Tm 4:1-8), *"Train yourself* for the life of piety, for while physical training is to some extent valuable, the *discipline of religion* is incalculably more so, with its promise of life here and hereafter!" Has not Jesus himself laid down the clear conditions of his "followship"? "Whoever wishes to be my follower must *deny his very self,* take up his cross each day, and follow in my steps" (Lk 9:23; Mk 8:34; Mt 16:24).

Has Christianity in our day "gone soft"? Have we Christians so adopted the ways of the world that we are indistinguishable as Christians? Here, as always, a *"via media"* is necessary. On the one hand, self-discipline and self-control are more difficult and perhaps more meritorious in our consumer society, but on the other hand this offers only a meager excuse because we do have the example of so many today, especially athletes, who are willing to "pay the price" in order to compete and triumph.

THE VIRTUE OF HUMILITY:

The first of our virtues of "letting go" is and must be that of *humility*. On this, the *Sacred Authors* and the *Saints* all agree. For example, virtually the same categorical warning appears in Job 22:29, Proverbs 3:34, Matthew 23:12, James 4:6, and finally in 1 Peter 5:5, "God opposes the proud but gives grace to the humble" (NIV). Aptly, then, does *St. Vincent de Paul*, that great model of humility, conclude: "Let us not deceive ourselves; if we have not humility, we have nothing!"[5] The reason for this agreement should be obvious. If, as we discussed at length in Chapter Four, the process of the Spiritual Life is basically one of God's initiative and our response, then it clearly follows that the more truly humble we are the more completely God is free to exercise his initiative. Again, *St. Vincent* declares, "As soon as we are emptied of ourselves, God fills us with himself because he cannot endure a void!"[6]

Humility is so basic to the relationship of Yahweh and Israel in the *Old Testament* that Hebrew, which is normally a word-poor language, uses no less than seven different verbal roots to express this attitude. And, hardly by accident, one of the principal roots used, *'anah*, also happens to be the normal expression for *response*! Throughout the Old Testament, this basic response of humility before God is required of everyone (Mi 6:8), but notably of kings (e.g., Ahab in 1 K 21:27-29), while the sin of pride is categorically condemned even in so-called "ideal" kings such as David (2 S 24) and Hezekiah (2 K 20:12-17). The damnable pride of foreign kings is singled out in Psalm 2, Isaiah 13-23, etc., and epitomized in the haughty, even ludicrous, expression of Pharaoh, "The river [Nile] is mine; I made it [for] myself!" (Ezk 29:3, 9).

On the positive side, besides many other expressions regarding humility, particularly in the Wisdom Literature (e.g., Si 3:17-24), the touching little Psalm 131 captures the right attitude of childlike humility:

> O Lord, my heart is not proud,
>   nor are my eyes haughty;
> I busy not myself with great things,
>   nor with things too sublime for me.
>
> Nay rather, I have stilled and quieted
>   my soul like a weaned child.
>
> Like a weaned child on its mother's lap,
>   so is my soul within me. . . .

In the *New Testament,* because of the example and teaching of Jesus himself as well as his mother, Mary, and his faithful followers, humility is inculcated as even more essential, if that is possible, than in the Old Testament. *John and Paul,* in particular, share with us the results of their lifelong contemplation of the Word Incarnate, especially in the former's *Gospel Prologue* and in the latter's *Philippian Hymn.* After insisting that "the Word was God" (Jn 1:1) and that "Through him all things came into being, and apart from him nothing came to be " (Jn 1:3), John then proceeds to "drop his bombshell" with those history-making words, *"The Word became flesh!"* (Jn 1:14), that is, completely human in all our human weakness, including the most real and virulent temptations, to which however he never gave the slightest consent (Heb 4:15). Even before John's masterful description, Paul had presented Jesus as the perfect model of humility to his beloved Philippians in a magnificent hymn, either original or borrowed, which has deserved to be known simply as *"Carmen Christi,"* the *"Hymn of Christ"*:

Never act out of rivalry or conceit; rather, let all parties think *humbly* of others as superior to themselves, each of you looking to others' interests rather than to his own. Your attitude must be that of Christ:

> Though he was in the form of God,
>   he did not deem equality with God
>   something to be grasped at.
>
> Rather, he *emptied himself*
>   and took the form of a *slave,*
>   being born in the likeness of men.
>
> He was known to be of human estate,
>   and it was thus that he *humbled himself,*
>   obediently accepting even death,
>   *death on a cross!*
>
> Because of this,
>   God highly exalted him
>   and bestowed on him the name
>   above every other name.
>
> So that at Jesus' name
>   every knee must bend
>   in the heavens, on the earth,
>   and under the earth,
>
>   and every tongue proclaim
>   to the glory of God the Father:
>   Jesus Christ is Lord! (Ph 2:3-11).

As mentioned in Chapter Three, some theologians used to attribute to the human nature of Jesus, because of its "hypostatic" union with his Divine Person, everything that was not metaphysically impossible, including the Beatific Vision, all infused knowledge, and freedom even from the possibility of sinning. Today, however, many Scripture scholars and theologians tend to interpret expressions like "became flesh" (Jn 1:14) and "emptied himself" (Ph 2:7) in all their fullness, including limitations on Jesus' human knowledge, e.g., of his divinity (Mk 10:18) and of the future (Mk 13:32), as well as the possibility, but not the actuality, of sinning (Heb 4:15).

This not only seems to agree more with the New Testament itself but also enables us to appreciate, imitate, and identify with the depth of Jesus' humility, trust, and love. "For our sakes God made him who did not know sin to be sin, so that in him we might become the very holiness of God" (2 Cor 5:21). And, in the unforgettable words which *Charles de Foucauld* adopted from his spiritual director, the *Abbe Huvelin,* "Our Lord took the last place in such a way that nobody can ever rob him of it!"[7] After all, he started from the highest possible position, that of God himself, and abased himself to the lowest possible position, not only becoming like us a fetus in Mary's womb, a helpless baby at her breast, and "subject" to Mary and Joseph at Nazareth (Lk 2:51), but incredibly "a worm, not a man" (Ps 22:7), "one smitten by God and afflicted" (Is 53:4), "smitten for the sin of his people" (Is 53:8), namely all of us. And we have not even said a word yet about his final self-abasement as our very food and drink in the Sacrifice and Sacrament of the Holy Eucharist. "Having loved his own in this world, he loved them to the very end" (Jn 13:1). No wonder *St. Ignatius of Antioch* can assure the Magnesians, "I know that you are not inflated with pride, for you have Jesus Christ within you."[8]

Who, therefore, has a better right than Jesus to challenge us to absolute humility? "Learn from me, for I am gentle and humble of heart" (Mt 11:29). "If I washed your feet — I who am Teacher and Lord — then you must wash each other's feet" (Jn 13:14). "Unless you change and become like little children, you will not enter the kingdom of God" (Mt 18:3). But even apart from the irrefutable example and teaching of Jesus, echoed through the centuries by all the *Saints,* our own common sense and our faith in general should teach us the need of humility. Are we not "like grasshoppers" (Is 40:22), tiny specks bound by gravity to this little planet, Earth, in a solar system almost lost in our vast universe? The related words *human* and *humble* (both from Latin *humus* meaning ground) bespeak our earthly origins and limitations (Gn 2:7). We are not fully human unless we are truly humble. And, even granted that we may possibly be the only intelligent life in this great universe, cannot Paul challenge us as he does his factious Corinthians, "Who confers any distinction on you? Name something you have that you have not received. If, then, you have received it, why are you boasting as if it were your own?" (1 Cor 4:7). Name something? Yes, we can name something we have not received from God — our sins! They and they alone come solely from us and not from God. But can we possibly be so hardened in pride that we will even boast of our sins?

Given the above examples and teachings, it would seem comparatively easy to lay a solid groundwork of humility which would be proof against all temptations to pride. But such is not the case, for three important reasons. First, our most basic human instinct is that of *self-preservation,* which providentially enables us to preserve our lives but also, unless properly controlled by humility, emboldens us to promote our selves. We are all born with congenital "I trouble" and plagued with it throughout our lives — an endless source of increasingly subtle temptations, especially when pride wears the mask of humility itself. Humility, therefore, is (like Jesus himself) the *"alpha* and the *omega,* the first and the last, the beginning and the end" (Rv 22:13), for it is the first and most basic virtue needed in the Spiritual Life and, along with love, the final virtue needed in our lifelong struggle against the parasite of pride.

Secondly, we live in an age of epidemic "I trouble," an atmosphere of rampant *narcissism* or self-centeredness. Whatever the causes, and they are manifold, we are being literally deluged with "self-help prescriptions," from the so-called philosophy of "Objectivism" of the late Ayn Rand to the self-serving pragmatism of Robert Ringer's *Looking out for #1,* from Silva Mind Control to Biofeedback, from EST to Esalen, from Psycho-Cybernetics to Psycho-Hypnosis, from Transactional Analysis to Jungian Dream

Analysis. And so it goes, this far from complete list, each new faddish panacea succeeding its predecessor like clockwork. Not that they lack value, but unfortunately these cure-alls never seem to rise above the natural level and therefore promote the illusion that we humans can somehow "pull ourselves up by our own bootstraps."

Thirdly, even if we recognize and acknowledge the truth of our total dependence on God, certainly a great victory over our human pride, we still find it extremely difficult to practice genuine humility toward our *fellow human beings*. It is so tempting to compare ourselves favorably with others, like the Pharisee with the Publican (Lk 18:9-14), so easy to use a double standard between ourselves and others, to build ourselves up by putting others down, to excuse ourselves while judging and condemning others, to nourish resentments when we find or imagine ourselves to be ignored and unappreciated. The following reflection, which I have adapted and expanded from an anonymous one,[9] exemplifies our notorious double standard and forms an effective examination of conscience:

> When others "act that way," they're ugly and boorish;
>   when we do it, we just blame it on our nerves.
>
> When they're true to their ways, they're plain obstinate;
>   when we're set in ours, we're courageous and firm.
>
> When they don't like our friends, they're clearly prejudiced;
>   when we don't like theirs, we're showing good judgment.
>
> When they discover flaws, they're being unduly critical;
>   when we find fault, we're unusually perceptive.
>
> When they're accomodating, they're "polishing the apple";
>   when we do the same, we're prudent and tactful.
>
> When they take time to do things, they're painfully slow;
>   when we take ages, we're only being deliberate.
>
> When they're "being themselves," why don't they ever try
>   to change?
>
> When we're "being ourselves," why don't they accept us as
>   we are?

Especially in the early days of our spiritual conversion, when we are making great demands on ourselves in our efforts toward *perfection,* it is difficult to avoid making equal or greater demands on others. I like the definition I once saw of a perfectionist as "one who takes infinite pains — and gives them to others." Here again, Jesus shows us the way in one of his sternest warnings, "Do not judge, and you will not be judged. Do not condemn, and you will not be condemned" (Lk 6:37). Why? Because, while we can to some extent know ourselves, our virtues and our vices, our motives and our temptations, we simply cannot know others in the same way. We must, therefore, regardless of outward appearances, refrain from judging and condemning others. We should be far quicker to excuse others than to excuse ourselves. With St. Paul, we need to "think humbly of others as superior" to ourselves (Ph 2:3), adding that "Christ Jesus came into the world to save sinners. Of these I myself am the worst" (1 Tm 1:15).

Humility, however, does not require the denigration of *God's gifts* to us, whether natural or supernatural. Quite the opposite! Humility is self-knowledge and truth. It therefore encourages and enables us to recognize God's gifts in us and to appreciate them precisely as gifts. In the words of Mary's canticle, "God who is mighty has done great things for me!" (Lk 1:49). All we are, all we have, all we can be, are God's gracious gifts to us — not as owners but as stewards. What we become with his help, how we develop and use our endowments of nature and grace, are our gifts to God. The thought-provoking parable of the talents (in Mt 25:14-30 and Lk 19:11-27) applies not only to spiritual gifts but to all the gifts of our three-dimensional makeup. The whole development of our body and mind, our emotions and personality, our will and character, far from being opposed to the Spiritual Life, should actually constitute an integral part of it because it is directly opposed to that sloth, self-indulgence, and narcissistic pride which Scripture refers to as "the flesh." In the words of St. Thomas Aquinas, *"Gratia perficit naturam."*[10] Grace perfects nature. Holiness, etymologically, psychologically, and theologically, derives from *wholeness!*[11]

Further, humility helps us to know ourselves as individual persons and to accept ourselves as we are. We cannot launch out into spiritual orbit from someone else's launching pad. We can only start from where we are. We must, in the words of a popular saying, "bloom where we are planted." Each of us must recognize and learn to love ourselves as the *unique individuals* we are, the sum total of what we have received from God's creation and salvation, from our ancestry, from our environment and interaction with others, from our own efforts aided by grace, and from our education and life experience. It is so tempting to envy someone else's endowments, to go through life always wishing, "If only. . . ." But that is an exercise in frustration and stagnation. Any time we feel that we have been short-changed in comparison with others, we need only remember those consoling, paradoxical words of St. Paul, "God chose those whom the world considers absurd to shame the wise; he singled out the weak of this world to shame the strong" (1 Cor 1:27).

To accept ourselves as we are, however, is not an excuse for complacency, still less for a dogged determination to cling to the status quo, as if we cannot and should not *change*. To live is to grow, and to grow is to change! The great Cardinal *Newman* recognized this over a hundred years ago, at a time when the Church as a whole was much more inclined to avoid change, "In a higher world it is otherwise; but here below to live is to change, and to be perfect is to have changed often."[12] And, more succinctly, "Growth is the only evidence of life!"[13] Since we are imperfect people in an imperfect world, growth and change are necessities of life, both for ourselves personally and for the world around us. Injustices need to be corrected, human dignity guaranteed, peace and security achieved, a healthful environment established. But it all begins with us. In the words of a Chinese proverb,

> If there is right in the soul, there will be beauty in the person;
> If there is beauty in the person, there will be harmony in the home;

If there is harmony in the home, there will be order in the nation;
If there is order in the nation, there will be peace in the world. [14]

THE VIRTUES OF PURITY AND POVERTY:

After our necessarily long reflection on the basic virtue of humility, the virtue of our humanness, I would like to consider *together* the two other virtues of "letting go," namely purity and poverty. The reason is simple enough: they have so much in common. Just as humility is concerned with our basic instinct of self-preservation and self-aggrandizement, so purity and poverty are concerned respectively with our basic instincts of preservation of the human race and acquisition of the things necessary for our self-preservation. Just as pride tends inwardly, so lust and greed tend outwardly. Yet, in a very true sense, all three are but different forms of *theft*, of taking what does not really belong to us. All three are reducible to *misguided self-love*, the root of it all, because they constitute our selfish desire for personal praise, pleasure, and possessions.

Perhaps that is why, particularly in Mark's Gospel, Jesus seems to link these three aberrations together, treating first the prideful tendencies of ambition and envy (9:33-37); then (after some general remarks) the issue of divorce and remarriage, so crucial for the proper preservation of the human race and the People of God (10:2-12); then again the danger of attachment to riches in the story of the rich young man (10:17-31); and finally (after Jesus' third prediction of his passion and resurrection) back to the dangers of prideful ambition and envy in the episode of the requests of James and John (10:35-44), climaxed with that key declaration of Jesus, "The Son of Man has not come to be served but to serve — and to give his life in ransom for the many" (10:45).

PURITY:

As we have already seen with regard to sin in general, so also in particular with regard to *sexual impurity*, there has been a drastic *about-face* in society at large during the past several decades. From an earlier period of what might be called Puritan or Victorian mores, there has been a wholesale but not wholesome swing in Western society to the opposite extreme of unbridled permissiveness or what is commonly designated as the "sexual revolution." This so-called "New Morality" is unfortunately neither new nor moral. The causes are manifold, but possibly the three greatest (which need no commentary) are: the increased emphasis on personalism and unlimited individual freedom ("doing one's own thing"), the pervasive influence of the mass media, especially the "graduation" of "sexploitation" films, television shows, and pornography to the status of technical and artistic perfection, and finally the legalization, availability, and effectiveness of modern, inexpensive methods of birth control and abortion.

In the Church too there has been a widespread and generally healthy abandonment of the former overemphasis on sexual morality as if it were the most (or even the only) important morality, to the current unhealthy fear of ever mentioning the subject lest one be considered prudish or old-fashioned, narrowminded or just plain "hung up on sex." It was a tremendous advance when, first Scripture scholars and theologians, then the Church at large became newly aware of the primacy of love and, correlatively, of the heinousness of sins against love and justice, for example in the form of racial discrimination or neglect of the needy, but (human nature being what it is) the whole important issue of sexual morality has largely been "lost in the shuffle." We have tragically "thrown out the baby with the bath-water"! The truth of the matter is that we cannot really practice a religion of love, which Christianity certainly is, still less can we pretend to live a Spiritual Life, if we allow ourselves to be enslaved by sexual desires and habits. As St. James so tersely expresses it, "Religion pure and unstained before our God and Father is this: to look after *orphans and widows* in their suffering and to keep oneself *unspotted* by the world" (1:27, WD).

In contrast with the current "hush-hush" policy of permissiveness regarding sexual morality that pervades society and much of the Church today, *Sacred Scripture* provides us with a clear, balanced, and wholesome approach to the subject. From the very beginning, God made humankind "male and female" in his (creative?) "image and likeness" (Gn 1:27) and, blessing them, directed them to "increase and multiply" (Gn 1:28). In the Yahwist account of chapter two, after the formation in Genesis 2:27 of Adam (man) from *adamah* (earth), Eve (living) is described as "surgically" formed from Adam because, according to their nature, men and women are to be united again in monogamous marriage, whereby they become "two in one flesh" (Gn 2:21-25). Some Scripture scholars and theologians theorize that the basic temptation of Adam and Eve (the human race), so imaginatively described in the third chapter of Genesis, is the same temptation which plagues humankind today, namely the *desire to decide our own morality,* notably in sexual matters. Lending credence to their opinion, they cite references to the forbidden "tree of the knowledge of good and evil" (Gn 2:17; 3:3; 11, 22); the temptation by the "serpent" (Gn 3:1, ff.), a common phallic symbol, especially in Canaanite religion; the enticement of Adam by Eve (Gn 3:6); and the resulting consciousness of nakedness and concupiscence (Gn 3:7).[15]

But why should sexual morality be accorded such a prominent place in the Bible, even from the very beginning? The reason, as we have seen in Chapter Two, is quite simple and compelling: sex is that creative drive of our human nature which is concerned with the two most basic and sacred dimensions of creation, namely *love and life* — the loving relationship between husband and wife and the providential creation of new life resulting therefrom. Sex is divinely regulated, not because it is "dirty," but because it is sacred! And, by the same token, to indulge in sex simply according to our own desire or selfish purpose, contrary to God's clear regulations regarding this sacred gift, is to commit *sacrilege* — the abuse of a sacred thing. And this quality of *"sacred sex"* becomes even more evident when, because of the Covenant at Sinai, Israel is consecrated as the sacred People of

God, "a kingdom of priests, a holy nation!" Hence, while the basic covenant virtue expected of Israel is love of God (Dt 6:5) and consequent love of neighbor (Lv 19:18), there is also a corresponding emphasis on the purity required of Israel, God's sacred partner in the Covenant. We see this, of course, in the commandment, "You shall not commit adultery" (Ex 20:14; Dt 5:18), but also and especially in the "book of holiness," *Leviticus,* where the reminder to "be holy as I your God am holy" is repeated over and over again (e.g. Lv 11:44-45; 19:2, etc.) and sexual holiness is particularly insisted on in Leviticus 18:20-24.

If such is true of the Old Covenant, how much more is it true of the New, in which even greater holiness, including sexual holiness, is required (Mt 5:6, 8, 20, 27-30, 48). In this matter, of course, we have the perfect example of *Jesus* himself, the paragon of purity. Not only did he practice lifelong celibacy, free from any accusation in this regard even from his worst enemies but, while he readily pardoned sexual sinners and regarded their sin as less offensive than the pride and hypocrisy of some of the religious leaders (Mt 21:31), he always insisted that they renounce their sinfulness (Jn 8:10 and, by implication, Lk 7:47-50). Then there is the immaculate example of "our tainted nature's solitary boast,"[16] Jesus' virgin-mother *Mary,* who was so emptied of self by her profound humility and spotless purity that she, by God's grace, was a worthy receptacle for the very Son of God himself!

But perhaps nowhere else in the New Testament is the importance of sexual morality more evident than in St. Paul's letters to and from the city of *Corinth* in Southern Greece. Corinth was one of the most interesting and appalling cities of the first century A.D. Incredibly, it was at the same time a political center as the seat of Roman government in Achaia (the lower half of Greece, including Athens, the cultural heart of the world); a commercial center, enjoying the booming trade of its two ports, especially in the sale of its world-famous Corinthian pottery; an athletic center where, every two years, the Isthmian Games were held; and, above all, a religious center, being the principal site for the worship of *Aphrodite* or Venus, the goddess of (sexual) love. It is estimated that, in the great temple of Aphrodite at Acrocorinth (the acropolis or high city of Corinth), some one thousand hierodules or sacred prostitutes enabled the goddess' devotees from near and far to practice her cult by sexually and symbolically "uniting themselves with the goddess." In short, the religion of Corinth was sex. Perhaps one might even say that the life of Corinth was sex, for the conjunction of the cult of Aphrodite and the permissiveness of two ports created such an atmosphere of licentiousness at Corinth that, in the Greek language, prostitutes everywhere came to be known as "Corinthian girls."[17]

Into this sex-saturated cosmopolis came St. Paul on his second missionary journey, understandably disappointed, even depressed (1 Cor 2:3), by the failure of his great address at the Areopagus (Hill of Mars) to the intellectuals of Athens (Ac 17) and determined henceforth to avoid philosophical presentations in favor of preaching "Jesus Christ and him crucified" (1 Cor 2:2). Imagine his astonishment and delight when great numbers of Corinthians, probably sick of the notorious Corinthian lifestyle, enthusiastically embraced Christianity. By and by, however, problems began to surface and, prominently among them, the almost insuperable difficulty of trying to live a chaste Christian life amidst the polluted atmosphere of Corinth. The plight of the Corinthian Christians was not unlike that of so many Christians today, surrounded and assaulted as they feel by sexual permissiveness on all sides. But what was Paul's solution? Accomodate Christian morality to the circumstances, as many advocates of Situation Ethics might favor today? Not at all! Have recourse to the Sixth Commandment? This might have helped to some extent, but it did not go deeply enough. No, Paul went right to the heart of the matter — the individual Christian's call and consecration to spiritual union with Christ! And so he insists,

> *The body is not for immorality, it is for the Lord,* and the Lord is for the body. God, who raised up the Lord, will raise us also by

his power. Do you not see that your bodies are *members of Christ?* Would you have me take Christ's members and make them the members of a prostitute? God forbid! Can you not see that the man who is joined to a prostitute becomes one body with her? Scripture says, "The two shall become one flesh." But whoever is joined to the Lord becomes *one spirit* with him.

Shun lewd conduct. Every other sin a man commits is outside his body, but the fornicator sins against his own body. You know that your body is a *temple of the Holy Spirit,* who is within — the Spirit you have received from God. You are not your own. You have been purchased, and at a price! So glorify God in your body (1 Cor 6:13-20).

I have a feeling that Paul, confronted today with the same problem of Christians trying to live a moral life in the midst of sexual permissiveness, would respond in exactly the same way, adding other expressions of his, for example from 1 Thessalonians and Romans, both of which he wrote *from Corinth*:

It is God's will that you grow in holiness: that you abstain from immorality, each of you guarding his members in sanctity and honor, not in passionate desire as do the Gentiles who know not God . . . God has not called us to immorality but to holiness . . . (1 Th 4:3-5, 7).

Just as formerly you enslaved your bodies to impurity and licentiousness for their degradation, make them now the servants of justice for their sanctification (Rm 6:19).

And now, brothers, I beg you through the mercy of God to offer your bodies as a living sacrifice, holy and acceptable to God, your spiritual worship. Do not conform yourselves to this age but be transformed by the renewal of your mind, so that you may judge what is God's will, what is good, pleasing, and perfect (Rm 12:1-2).

And, in a reminder that purification (so necessary to our growth in the Spiritual Life) is a lifelong process, Paul urges us, "Beloved, let us purify ourselves from every defilement of flesh and spirit, and in the fear of God strive to fulfill our *consecration* perfectly" (2 Cor 7:1).

POVERTY:

Outside of Palestine itself, perhaps no place in the world conveys the spirit of Jesus Christ so tangibly as does the little town of Assisi in the Umbrian Hills of Italy. There, when one visits the tiny chapel of the Portiuncula, the convent of San Damiano, the hermitage high up in the hills, and the tomb of "Il Poverello" (the little poor man), one cannot but feel the presence of "everybody's saint," *Francis of Assisi,* the most famous imitator of the poor man of Nazareth, Jesus himself. Born into a family, a country, a time which had become enamored of material things, particularly the exotic imports from the East, Francis felt called to be "a sign of contradiction" to this spirit of affluence and a sign of witness to the *spirit of poverty* which Jesus Christ both lived and taught. He learned, as we must learn, that to follow Jesus, to be one with him in loving relationship, is to "travel light" (Mt 10; Mk 6; Lk 9-10), free from the idolatry of material possessions (Col 3:5), our heart attached to him alone as our treasure (Mt 6:21). It is to let him live his poverty again in us who for our sake "made himself poor though he was rich, so that we might become rich by his poverty" (2 Cor 8:9).

On first consideration, one would think that detachment from material goods is not all that difficult, certainly not as difficult as the detachment involved in the virtues of humility and purity. Yet experience, observation, history, and the clear evidence of Sacred Scripture combine to teach us otherwise. So many wars have been fought, so many crimes committed out of greed that St. Paul's remark to Timothy, "The love of money is the *root of all evil!"* (1 Tm 6:10) may not be as hyperbolic as it seems. In fact, if we read the context of that remark, we are forced to look deeply into ourselves, because Paul is talking precisely about the temptation to "value religion only as a means to personal gain" (1 Tm 6:5). Apart from the common phenomenon today of religious preachers, teachers, and gurus of various kinds whose spiritual and material "success" seem to be interchangeable, there is the natural and often nurtured tendency in all of us to expect *material rewards* for our spiritual faithfulness.

Ultimately, of course, this attitude of so-called "Positive Thinking," that is, of expecting temporal rewards of fame and fortune through religion, goes back to our basic instinct of self-preservation and the *insecurity* stemming therefrom, constantly reinforced by the advertisements and commercials of our consumer society. But perhaps *immaturity* even more than insecurity is the operative consideration. For example, it was when the *Israelites* were immature in their practice of Yahwism that the *Deuteronomic theology* of "prosperity and posterity" as the reward of religious fidelity was most in vogue. Only later, in such *questioning works* as Job, Qoheleth or Ecclesiastes, and Wisdom, do we find this simplistic expectation definitely put on trial. Yet even before then (e.g., in such passage as Ex 23:6, 11; Dt 15:7-11; 24:14, and 1 S 2:8 as well as in many of the Prophets and Psalms), special *compassion* is evidenced toward the poor and needy (in Hebrew, the *anawim*), who are particularly dear to Yahweh because they have no one else to depend on but him and his covenant people.

In the *New Testament,* from beginning to end, there is not only the predilection for the *anawim* ("Blessed are the poor in spirit" in Mt 5:3, "Blessed are you poor" in Lk 6:20), but at every turn there are warnings against greed and reminders of the need for Christian poverty. Nowhere is this more evident than in the *Gospel of Luke,* sometimes called the Gospel of the Poor or the Gospel of Christian Poverty. Mary echoes Hannah's Canticle about the poor in Luke 1:46-55. Jesus is born in a stable and revealed first to poor shepherds (2:7-17). The offering for his presentation in the temple is that of the poor (2:24). His "Messianic Manifesto" at Nazareth features the evangelization of the poor (4:18). He chooses to be homeless, traveling about with "nowhere to lay his head" (9:58). He dies stripped of everything, hanging on a cross between criminals (23:32-49) and is buried in a borrowed tomb (23:50-53). In addition, Luke's Gospel contains those timeless warnings about the danger of riches in the Parable of the Rich Farmer and its context (12:13-34), the Parable of the Rich Man and Lazarus (16:19-31), and (along with Mark and Matthew) the episode of the Rich Young Man (18:25), of which the final verse contains that dramatic hyperbole, "It is easier for a camel to go through a needle's eye than for a rich man to enter the kingdom of heaven!"

Luke's emphasis on detachment in general and poverty in particular was apparently intended as an antidote to the loss of pristine fervor among Christians, once they realized (especially after the destruction of Jerusalem) that the *"éschaton"* or end-time was not imminent. And, human nature being what it is, that same kind of antidote has been needed ever since. It is nothing short of amazing that, generation after generation, we Christians can manage to fall back into the same old trap. Is there any difference between the so-called Deuteronomic theology mentioned earlier and the *"theology" of material rewards* promised by today's popular preachers? Not long ago, I chanced upon a typical book in the religious section of a national bookstore entitled, "Pray and get rich!" What a prostitution of religion! And what a contradiction to the example and word of Jesus Christ, whom we Christians claim to follow! No wonder the great English poet, William Wordsworth, in his *Miscellaneous Sonnets,* No. XXXIII, begins:

> The world is too much with us; late and soon,
> Getting and spending, we lay waste our powers:
> Little we see in Nature that is ours;
> We have given our hearts away, a sordid boon![18]

And, if such is true of nature, how much more so of the supernatural, the Spiritual! It is impossible to find God within if our whole being is absorbed by things without. Nor is this true only of the wealthy and perhaps the middle class. I used to wonder why Jesus, addressing himself to *poor people,* began his Sermon on the Mount (Mt 5-7) *with a challenge to poverty,* "Blessed are the poor in spirit, for theirs is the kingdom of heaven!" Then I went to a small town in *China* as a missionary and saw with my own eyes how desperately attached poor people could be to the few things they possessed: a sleeping mat, a rice bowl, a water jug, a few scraps of clothing. But this need not have surprised me, for I should have remembered how preoccupied most of us were with material concerns during the *Great Depression,* a preoccupation which many of us may still subconsciously retain even today. I distinctly remember when, as a boy, I came into possession of a fifty-cent piece. To me, that was a small fortune, and I proceeded to hide it or, worse still, hoard it. Then, suddenly, it disappeared. I was heart-broken! To this day, I do not know whether it was stolen or somehow lost, but for me the lesson was unforgettable! "Vanity of vanities! All things are vanity!" (Ec 1:2, also the first verse of the *Imitation of Christ*).[19] And, more fully in Jesus' own words,

> Do not store up for yourselves treasures on earth, where moth and rust destroy, and where thieves break in and steal. But store up for yourselves treasures in heaven, where moth and rust do not destroy, and where thieves do not break in and steal. For where your treasure is, there your heart will be also (Mt 6:19-21, NIV).

> No one can serve two masters. Either he will hate the one and love the other, or he will be devoted to the one and despise the other. You cannot serve both God and Money (Mt 6:24, NIV).

Then follow those magnificent passages against *anxiety and worry* about material things, using as examples God our Father's care of the birds of the air and the lilies of the field, climaxed in the injunction, "Seek first his kingdom and his righteousness, and all these things will be given to you as well" (Mt 6:33, NIV). Or, in the words of St. Peter, "Cast all your cares on him because he cares for you" (1 P

5:7). But let us leave further consideration of this until the treatment on trust in the next chapter.

Finally, not only is attachment to material things directly opposed to trust in God, but also to the basic Christian virtue of *love*. For, if we regard ourselves as owners rather than stewards of our so-called "possessions," as having an absolute right to whatever we can amass as long as we do so legally, then we will certainly fail in the fundamental Christian duty of love, even of social and distributive justice, toward the "least" of Christ's brothers and sisters (Mt 25). John spells it out for us in 1 John 3:17-18,

> I ask you, how can God's *love* survive in a man who has enough of this world's *goods* yet closes his heart to his brother when he sees him in need? Little children, let us love in *deed* and in *truth* and not merely talk about it!

To live is to love and to love is to give — to share what God has given us, both material and spiritual. As Jesus insisted with his disciples and all of us, "Freely you have received, freely give" (Mt 10:8, NIV). And, more fully in Luke 16:9-11,

> What I say to you is this: Make friends for yourselves through your *use of this world's goods,* so that when they fail you, a lasting reception will be yours. If you can trust a man in little things, you can also trust him in greater; while anyone unjust in a slight matter is also unjust in greater. If you cannot be trusted with *elusive wealth,* who will trust you with lasting?

This, too, will be examined more closely in the following chapter.

SUMMARY AND CONCLUSION:

In this chapter, we have been considering the three virtues of "letting go" the "branches" of our pride, sensuality, and greed —

namely humility, purity, and poverty. *In summary,* our challenge is simple: we cannot be filled with Christ, we cannot enable him to continue his life and ministry through us in the world today, if we are already filled up with attachments to self, sex, and possessions. We must "let go these branches"! But that is neither easy nor instantaneous. We first have to realize the *need* to "let go," then develop the *desire* to "let go," but above all we must pray for the *courage* to "let go"! For only God himself can supply the realization, the desire, and the courage. We might well make our own that popular prayer attributed to Reinhold Niebuhr,

> God grant me the serenity
> To accept the things I cannot change,
> The courage to change the things I can,
> And the wisdom to know the difference! [20]

This beautiful prayer has been a marvelous source of consolation and strength for many people who are addicted to alcohol or other drugs; but do not our attachments to pride, pleasure, and possessions also deserve to be called *addictions*? We need to think about that, don't we?

In conclusion, let us learn the lesson of the *butterfly,* one of the symbols of the resurrection. As long as we remain attached to "carnal allurements, enticements for the eyes and the life of empty show" (1 Jn 2:16), we are like a caterpillar, completely bound to the earth and the things of the earth. We cannot even dream of flying! But if we are willing to undergo a complete *transformation* like the caterpillar, then we will be free to fly like the butterfly. It is not coincidental that Paul associates freedom and transformation,

> The Lord is the Spirit, and where the Spirit of the Lord is, there is *freedom.* All of us, gazing on the Lord's glory with unveiled faces, are being *transformed* from glory to glory into his very image by the Lord who is the Spirit (2 Cor 3:17-18).

In the same way, Jesus associates freedom and union with himself in word and in life, "If you remain in my *word,* you will be my disciples, and you will know the truth, and the truth will set you *free* . . . If, then, the *Son* will set you free, you will be free indeed!" (Jn 8:31-32, 36, WD).

Our freedom and transformation are nothing less than our "death and resurrection" with Christ, which is the ultimate purpose of Baptism and the Holy Eucharist. And our death and resurrection are our only avenue to *true happiness,* the treasure we were mistakenly seeking in self-glorification and self-gratification. In a thoughtful statement akin to our own reflection above, *Nathaniel Hawthorne* reminds us that, "Happiness is a butterfly which, when pursued, is always just beyond your grasp, but which, if you will sit down quietly, may alight upon you!"[21]

RECOMMENDED READING LIST

1. Crosby, Michael. *Spirituality of the Beatitudes*, Maryknoll, NY: Orbis Books, 1980.
2. Daughters of St. Paul. *The Practice of Humility*, Boston, MA: D.S.P. Press, 1978.
3. Derrick, Christopher. *Sex and Sacredness*, San Francisco, CA: Ignatius Press, 1982.
4. Guinan, Michael, tr. *Gospel Poverty: Essays in Biblical Theology*, Chicago, IL: Franciscan Herald Press, 1977.
5. Kehl, D.G. *Control Yourself!*, Grand Rapids, MI: Zondervan Publishing House, 1982.

POINTS FOR REFLECTION AND DISCUSSION

1. What are the nature and importance of virtues and beatitudes in our Spiritual Life?
2. What are the nature and importance of self-control, self-discipline, or asceticism in Sacred Scripture and our Spiritual Life?
3. What is the relationship between the "virtues of letting go" and our spiritual freedom, authenticity, and transformation into Christ?
4. What is the key role that humility plays in our Spiritual Life according to the evidence of Sacred Scripture, especially in the life and teaching of Jesus Christ?
5. What important role is played by the virtues of purity and poverty in our relationship with Jesus Christ, especially in the context of today's world and lifestyle?

CHAPTER SEVEN

THE QUALITIES OF THE RELATIONSHIP, PART II:
The Three "Virtues of Holding On"

In every relationship, there is an essential need of *faith, hope and love*. This is true of friendship, and even more true of that closest of human relationships, marriage. Without love, marriage is but an empty shell; without faith and hope, love is a hollow sham! And if this be true of human relationships, how much more so of that relationship with God which we call religion, especially Christianity. For, in both Old and New Testaments, love is the very essence of relationship with God, as Jesus insisted by first recalling for his contemporaries the dual commandments of the love of God and neighbor in Deuteronomy 6:4-5 and Leviticus 19:18 respectively (Mt 22:34-40; Mk 12:28-34; Lk 10:25-37), and then adding his own new commandment: "Love one another *as I have loved you*" (Jn 13:34; 15:12).

But this love is inconceivable without faith and hope. How can we possibly love someone (especially someone whom we have never seen!) if we deny or doubt that he even exists or, if we admit his existence, but have no faith and hope that he loves us as he says? On the other hand, with faith and hope, our love for God, especially in the person of Jesus Christ, can far surpass the love we have for any and all human beings, no matter how close. Why? Because in himself and in his relationship with us he is free from those limitations and failings which put such a strain on every human relationship. We can love Jesus Christ with our entire human being because we hope and trust that he loves us with his entire divine-human being! As Paul reminds Timothy, "If we are unfaithful he [Jesus Christ] will still remain faithful, for he cannot deny himself" (2 Tm 2:13).

It is no wonder then that, both in Scripture and tradition, faith, hope and love are so frequently linked together and have come to be known as the three *theological virtues,* that is, the virtues which directly concern our relationship with God. For example, a reflective reading of Jesus' discourse in John 13-17 reveals how tenderly he inculcates faith, hope, and love in his dismayed and utterly fearful apostles. And in Paul's writings, which constitute the first Christian theology, these same three virtues are united, not only in the familiar "There are in the end three things that last: faith, hope, and love, and the greatest of these is love" (1 Cor 13:13), but in several less known passages as well, e.g., Romans 5:1-5, Colossians 1:4, and even at the very beginning of Paul's (and the New Testament's) first writing: ". . . We constantly are mindful before our God and Father of the way you are proving your *faith,* and laboring in *love,* and showing constancy of *hope* in our Lord Jesus Christ" (1 Th 1:3).

In fact, such is our familiarity with these three virtues from our earliest childhood, that there is an understandable tendency to dismiss or at least ignore them as "old hat" and hardly worth consideration in our sophisticated age of behavioral sciences. Partly for this reason, but principally to emphasize the essential nature of these three indispensable qualities of our Spiritual Life, I have chosen to describe them as the fundamental *"Virtues of Holding On."* For, it is through faith, hope, and love that, in spite of inevitable human weaknesses, worldly pressures, and ongoing purifications (dark nights or deserts), we cling to God, we remain united with Jesus Christ our Spiritual Spouse, we continue to let him transform us into an instrument of his life and love and ministry in the world today. And, partly because our long familiarity with these virtues tends to lull us into the assurance that we know all about them, I have attempted to focus on the hidden depths of meaning revealed in them by the bright light of Sacred Scripture and the insights of prayerful reflection.

THE VIRTUE OF FAITH:

As humility is the most basic and indispensable of the "Virtues of Letting Go," so faith is the *most basic and indispensable* of the "Virtues of Holding On." For, without faith, there can be neither hope (including trust and confidence), nor love. Faith provides the light, even the very eyes, by which the invisible becomes visible, the unknowable knowable, the unreachable reachable! Hence, in the Old Testament, the *"Prophets of Faith,"* notably Isaiah and Habakkuk, declare, "If you do not stand firm in your faith, you will not stand at all" (Is 7:9, NIV), and "The righteous will live by his faith" (Hab 2:4, NIV; cf. also Rm 1:17; Gal 3:11; Heb 10:38). Hence also, in the New Testament, the *"Preachers of Faith,"* especially Paul and the anonymous author of Hebrews insist, "All depends on faith, everything is grace" (Rm 4:16), "All of you are children of God because of your faith in Christ Jesus" (Gal 3:26, WD), and "Without faith, it is impossible to please God" (Heb 11:6).

In the same vein, the *Church Fathers* also describe faith as the beginning, the basic condition of our Christian Life. For example, *St. Ignatius of Antioch* wrote around 110 A.D. to the Church at Ephesus,

> None of this escapes your notice if you have perfect faith and love toward Jesus Christ; these are the beginning and end of life, for the *beginning is faith* and the end is love. When the two exist in unity, it is God, and everything else related to goodness is the result. [1]

And, more succinctly, *St. Ambrose* wrote in the fourth century, "Faith is the firm foundation of all the virtues!" [2]

But just *what is faith,* this indispensable condition of revealed religion? Perhaps it would be better to examine, first of all, what faith is not, and then what it actually is. To begin with, *faith is not feeling.* This realization is very important, especially in our "Age of Feeling," when we are constantly urged by popular psychiatrists and psychologists to "get in touch with our feelings." In itself, that is good advice because feelings are part of our makeup but, like so many good things, our age has largely taken it to silly and even dangerous extremes, as evidenced in the various "touchy-feely" movements, the cults of enthusiasm, and the general tendency to do "what comes naturally," regardless of commandments or consequences. Feelings or emotions are indeed an integral dimension of our human nature, but hardly superior to our intelligence and free will, and certainly not to our spiritual potential. After all, even the animals have feelings, though not to the same degree as humans.

In the *Spiritual Life,* feelings can play a most helpful role, particularly in the beginning of our spiritual conversion and commitment. Like booster rockets for space travel, they provide a strong initial thrust in our journey toward union with God. This period is sometimes referred to as our "spiritual honeymoon" for, in its emotional intensity, it is not unlike the honeymoon and early months of marriage. But, sooner or later, the time will come when "the honeymoon is over" and feelings level off; indeed, when we may seem to feel nothing at all. Everything becomes darkness and desert! Yet all is not lost. This is only the necessary purification through which we must pass in order to live our Spiritual Life, not on the level of feelings which ebb and flow like the waves of the sea, but on the level of faith, of the will strengthened by grace, and especially on the level of spirit, like the calm, serene depths of the sea. "Blessed are those who have not seen" (or who no longer see and feel) "and yet believe!" (Jn 20:29, WD).

Moreover, *faith is not knowledge,* at least not knowledge in the ordinary sense of the word. This too is most important, particularly in the midst of our vaunted "knowledge explosion." It is commonly asserted that the human race has acquired more knowledge in the past ten years than in its entire previous existence. Whether that is true or not, there is no question that our computer society can indeed acquire more information more quickly than ever before. But does this kind of knowledge qualify as wisdom? Is it knowledge about things that really matter in the history of the human race, in the light of eternity and, above all, in our relationship with God? Hardly! Some of the most brilliant scientists have testified in this regard. *Blaise Pascal,* precocious seventeenth century mathematician, inventor, and philosopher, cherished above all his mystical experience of November 23, 1654, an account of which was found sewn in his clothes when he died in 1663 and is quoted here in part:

> Fire! God of Abraham, God of Isaac, God of Jacob,
> not the God of philosophers and scholars.
>
> Certainty, joy, peace! God of Jesus Christ!
> He is only found along the ways taught in the gospel.
>
> Tears of joy! I had parted from him.
> Let me never be separated from him!
> Surrender to Jesus Christ![3]

And the great *Louis Pasteur,* who pioneered so many breakthroughs in the fields of chemistry and biology, used to say that he wished he had "the faith of a Breton peasant or, better still, the faith of a Breton peasant woman!"[4]

This is not, of course, to deny the *importance of knowledge*. One of the great spiritual masters, *Hugh of St. Victor,* urged his disciples, "Learn everything you possibly can, and you will discover later that none of it was superfluous!"[5] But knowledge not translated into wisdom and love and service leads only to conceit. "Knowledge puffs up, but love builds up!" (1 Cor 8:1, RSV). And even wisdom, if it is only the natural wisdom of the philosophers, will not suffice in the Spiritual Life. Paul makes this abundantly clear to his immature Corinthians,

> Has not God turned the wisdom of this world into folly? Since in God's wisdom the world did not come to know him through "wisdom," it pleased God to save those who believe through the absurdity of the preaching of the gospel. Yes, Jews demand

"signs" and Greeks look for "wisdom," but we preach Christ crucified — a stumbling block to Jews, and an absurdity to Gentiles; but to those who are called, Jews and Gentiles alike, Christ the power of God and the wisdom of God . . . (1 Cor 1:20-24).

There is, to be sure, a certain wisdom which we express among the spiritually mature. It is not a wisdom of this age. . . . No, what we utter is God's wisdom, a mysterious, a hidden wisdom. . . . Of this wisdom it is written: "Eye has not seen, ear has not heard, nor has it so much as dawned on man what God has prepared for those who love him" [Is 64:3]. Yet God has revealed this wisdom to us through the Spirit. The Spirit scrutinizes all matters, even the deep things of God. . . . For, "Who has known the mind of the Lord so as to instruct him?" [Is 40:13] But we have the mind of Christ! (1 Cor 2:6-7, 9-10, 16).

The great difference between natural knowledge and wisdom on the one hand and the supernatural knowledge and wisdom of faith on the other is that the latter begins where the former leaves off. Faith is participation in God's own knowledge! For, faith is like a powerful telescope or microscope enabling us to see and to know the spiritual, supernatural macrocosm and microcosm which lie beyond our natural vision. It empowers us to penetrate the dark *"Cloud of Unknowing"*[6] and "see" God himself! As *Abbot John Chapman* describes it in one of his *Letters,* "Faith is the door through which we enter the supernatural order. It opens into heaven. It tells us: 'We have not here a lasting city, but we seek one that is to come!' "[7] (Heb 13:14). And *St. Augustine,* in his lyrical Latin style asks, "What is faith (*fides*) but to believe what you do not see (*vides*)? And the reward of faith is to see what you believe!"[8]

As we have observed, faith does not consist of natural feelings or knowledge, for it transcends both. *What, then, is faith?* For a biblical definition or at least description of faith, we can hardly surpass that of the great *Epistle to the Hebrews,* written not by Paul but by an anonymous author, possibly Paul's friend and fellow missionary, Apollos (Ac 18:24-19:1; 1 Cor 1:12; 3:4-6, 21-23). Anxious to strengthen the Jewish Christians against the temptation to abandon Christianity and return to Judaism, the author first establishes the superiority of Jesus Christ to Moses and even the angels, and the superiority of Christ's covenant, priesthood, and sacrifice to those of Israel. Then he proceeds to focus on faith and fidelity as the key to salvation, invoking the examples of heroic Jews throughout the history of Israel, from Abraham to the Maccabees. As a kind of preface to these examples, he describes the "what" and the "why" of faith itself in profound statements which Christianity, and especially the Catholic Church in the *First Vatican Council,*[9] have accepted as normative,

> Faith is the substance of things to be hoped for, the evidence of things that appear not . . . (Heb 11:1).

> Without faith it is impossible to please God, for anyone who comes to God must believe that he exists and that he rewards those who seek him (Heb 11:6).

These statements from Hebrews, appropriately rendered from the Vulgate of St. Jerome, which was the official version used by the First Vatican Council, are extremely rich in their Greek original and therefore capable of various nuances that are reflected in today's many translations. For example, the word *hypóstasis* (literally: "standing under") can mean substance as in the citation above, or foundation, being, nature, courage, confidence, or conviction; while the word *élenchos* (from *elénchō*: to show, convince, convict) can mean evidence as in the quotation above or proof, conviction, verification, refutation, or correction. In the light of these rich possibilities, I would like to present for the reader's personal reflection a couple of different translations of Hebrews 11:1 which occur to me:

(1) Faith substantiates what is hopeful,
And verifies what is invisible!

(2) Faith is the basis of things still awaited,
Evidence plain of things that remain unseen!

But most rewarding of all is an examination of the *meaning of the word faith* itself in Greek (the language of the New Testament) and Hebrew (the principal language of the Old Testament). The Greek word for faith, *pistis*, derives from the verb *pisteuo* (to persuade) and, in keeping with the typical Greek emphasis on the mind, tends to focus on an intellectual (and voluntary) acceptance of what is spoken, taught, or promised. By contrast, the principal Hebrew word for faith, *emunah*, is from the root verb *aman* (to stand, to be stable, from which we obtain our common word "Amen") and, in keeping with typical Semitic emphasis on the whole person, includes the notions of intellectual and voluntary belief, total trust, and confidence, trustworthiness and fidelity, but above all personal acceptance, submission, self-surrender, and relationship. In brief, it means saying "Yes" to God! As Edward Carter, S.J. observes in his landmark work, *Response in Christ,*

> Contemporary theology emphasizes that faith is not merely an intellectual assent to a body of doctrine, but primarily a *personal commitment* to God who reveals these truths. For too long theology seemed to invert the order, but it is interesting to note that St. Thomas was not one of those theologians who gave the wrong emphasis. His words are in the mainstream of current thought on faith: "Now, whoever believes, assents to someone's words; so that, in every form of belief, the person to whose words assent is given seems to hold the chief place and to be the end as it were; while the things by holding which one assents to that person hold a secondary place."
>
> By faith, through the order of knowledge, we enter into an intimate personal relationship with the Trinity. Because faith is

thus fundamentally a personal dialogue between God and the Christian, it has a deep, personalizing efficacy. If I respond properly to God revealing, I achieve in graced freedom my greatest potential as a person. I become the person I should become.[10]

To this I can only add a remarkably rich and often overlooked description of faith by St. Thomas at the beginning of his explanation of the *Creed* in a priceless little work entitled *The Three Greatest Prayers,* "Faith *unites the soul to God*: because by faith the Christian soul is in a sense *wedded to God*: 'I will espouse thee to myself in faith (Ho 2:22)' "[11] But, if there is any doubt in the matter, all we need do is refer to *the Creed itself,* either the so-called *Apostles' Creed* or the longer *Nicene Creed,* in which we do not say, "We believe God" but rather "We believe *in* God . . . *in* Jesus Christ . . . *in* the Holy Spirit. . . ." Yes, clearly from *Sacred Scripture* and even from *St. Thomas Aquinas,* faith is not so much a belief in something (e.g., a revelation, a promise, etc.) as a *belief in Someone,* namely God, and a *total submission* to him in *personal relationship!*

Such is the current direction among Protestant, Catholic, and some Jewish scholars about the meaning of faith in the Holy Bible. Unfortunately, this enlightened relational consensus has, to a larger extent, not yet reached the rank and file among Christians and Jews. As a result, *Jewish believers* tend to understand faith as primarily faithfulness or *fidelity,* above all fidelity to the Mosaic Law as the essential means of justification and salvation. *Protestant Christians,* at least those who adhere to the original teaching of the Reformers, especially Martin Luther, generally view faith as trust (*fiducia*), namely *trust* in the justification and salvation wrought by Jesus Christ on our behalf. *Catholic Christians,* influenced for so many centuries by emphasis on philosophical theology, tend to stress the intellectual dimension of faith as the *belief* in all that God has revealed and the Church teaches. The time has come, however, to inculcate among Jews and Christians at large, not just one dimension of faith, but faith in its holistic entirety as total surrender, *total gift of self to God in loving relationship*. Then and only then, will we begin to see the long-awaited convergence of Christians among themselves and Christians with Jews in genuine, lasting reunion. Indeed, there are already some hopeful signs, such as the recent declaration of Lutheran and Catholic theologians expressing unity of belief about faith, justification, and salvation.[12] For a fuller treatment of this sensitive issue, the reader is invited to refer to *Appendix C* at the end of the book.

Meanwhile, we must carefully reflect on the necessity of *growth in faith*. For faith, in all its dimensions and especially as surrender to our loving God, is not a once-for-all act that we make but a *habit,* a *virtue,* an *attitude,* even a *way of life,* in which we can and must grow. Faith is indeed a gift of God but, as we see in the *Parable of the Talents* (Mt 25:14-30 and Lk 19:12-27), God expects his gifts to grow. This is crucial for our entire Spiritual Life, since our love and life and service will be no greater than our faith which supports them. Faith is not like the lifeless foundation of a building, established once and for all, but like a living root system whose growth enables a tree to stretch its trunk and limbs upward and outward, and to luxuriate in leaves, blossoms, and fruit. Or, in the analogy which we have already used, faith is the eyes of our Spiritual Life, eyes which (unlike our natural vision) are capable of indefinite improvement until death, when faith gives way to the Beatific Vision. The eyes of faith are the "windows of the soul," not only in the sense of revealing our spiritual interior, but also in the sense of providing a clear and true outlook on God and on all persons and things in their relationship to God. Perhaps this is one of the meanings contained in that enigmatic statement of Jesus in Matthew 6:22 and, slightly longer, in Luke 11:34-36, JB:

> The lamp of your body is your eye. When your eye is sound, your whole body is filled with light; but when it is diseased your body too will be all darkness. See to it then that the light inside you is not darkness. If, therefore, your whole body is filled with light, and no trace of darkness, it will be light entirely, as when the lamp shines on you with its rays.

But *how does faith grow* in us? Through *preaching and teaching*? Yes, for "faith comes through hearing, and what is heard is the word of Christ!" (Rm 10:17). Through *reading the Word of God*? Certainly, for "the Sacred Scriptures [are] the source of the wisdom which through faith in Jesus Christ leads to salvation" (2 Tm 3:15). Through the *Sacraments*? By all means, for the Sacraments are "mysteries of faith." But there are other means as well, which I would like to reflect on, at least briefly.

First, as we have mentioned above, faith is a *good habit or virtue,* and habits are strengthened by repeated acts. Just as our eyesight and other senses, our musculature and other parts of our anatomy, our memory and other intellectual powers all improve with proper use, both in actual effectiveness and in potential for future growth, so it is with faith. Acts of faith, but especially *acting on the basis of faith,* contribute greatly to our growth in living faith, as James insists in his very practical Epistle (Jm 2:14-17):

> What good is it to profess faith without practicing it? Such faith has no power to save one, has it? If a brother or sister has nothing to wear and no food for the day, and you say to them, "Goodbye and good luck! Keep warm and well fed," but do not meet their bodily needs, what good is that? So it is with the faith that does nothing in practice. It is thoroughly lifeless. . . . Be assured that faith without works is as dead as a body without breath!

Secondly, as a good habit or virtue, faith grows and is strengthened not only by practice but also by the *testing* that we may have to undergo at the hands of others or in the adverse circumstances of life. Thus, *St. Peter* assures us,

> You may for a time have to suffer the distress of many *trials*: but this is so that your *faith,* which is more precious than the passing splendor of fire-tried gold, may by its genuineness lead to praise, glory, and honor when Jesus Christ appears. Although

you have never seen him, you love him, and without seeing you now *believe* in him, and rejoice with inexpressible joy touched with glory because you are achieving *faith's goal,* your salvation (1 P 1:6-9).

We must realize, however, that growth in faith requires, not only practice on our part, but continuing help (grace) on God's part. And grace comes normally through prayer and the sacraments. Confining our consideration at this time to prayer, we need to imitate the *humble petition* of the possessed boy's father (Mk 9:24, JB), "I do have faith. Help the little faith I have!" And that of the Apostles (Lk 17:5), "Lord, increase our faith!" Also, mindful that sight is a biblical symbol of faith and blindness of unbelief, we can make our own the plaintive prayer of blind Bartimaeus at Jericho, "Master, help me to see!" (Mk 10:51, WD). And both by deed in this instance and by word in the following chapter of Mark, Jesus assures us that he will never turn a deaf ear to such a humble and especially persevering prayer, "Therefore, I declare to you: everything you ask for in prayer, believe that you will receive [or: have received] it, and it will be yours" (Mk 11:24).

Contemplative prayer in particular, as we will see in the next chapter, not only requires a living faith but also contributes greatly to the growth of that faith. And growth comes, not so much through the bright light of special insights and experiences, as through the dark light of the dark nights through which we must pass on our journey to union with God. Of course, our basic instinct of self-preservation causes us to fear and shun the dark, but one kind of light must be extinguished before we can see by another. Except at night and away from city lights, we cannot observe the beauty of the stars. In fact, the darker the night, the brighter the stars! So it is in our prayer life. Only if we are willing to forego the "bright lights" of imagination, feelings, reasoning, and even intuitive insights, are we able to "see" by the "dark light" of pure faith characteristic of life in the Spirit. The poignant prayer of *John Henry (later Cardinal) Newman,* which has become one of the world's most beloved poems and hymns, describes this situation admirably,

> Lead, kindly Light, amid the encircling gloom;
>   Lead thou me on!
> The night is dark, and I am far from home;
>   Lead thou me on!
> Keep thou my feet: I do not ask to see
> The distant scene; one step enough for me.[13]

Of course, in our effort to live and grow in faith, we are not alone. We have the *powerful example* of so many who have walked the same path through the centuries. The great *Epistle to the Hebrews* has already reviewed for us the heroic faith of various Old Testament figures. In the New Testament and in the history of Christianity, examples of outstanding faith are without number. *The Saints,* in particular, have demonstrated by their lives even more than by their words and writings what it means to live by faith. But far surpassing the example of all other Saints is that of *Mary,* the faith-filled and faithful Mother of Jesus.

At one time, some Mariologists so emphasized the privileges of Mary because of her virginal motherhood of Jesus that they attributed to her, as to Jesus, the lifelong enjoyment of the Beatific Vision and of vast infused knowledge. But that is certainly not the picture of Mary in the New Testament. Privileged, yes, for she gave birth to Jesus Christ, the Incarnate Word and Son of God, whence she deserves by God's favor to be called *theótokos* (Mother of God) according to the declaration of the Council of Ephesus in 431.[14] (One gives birth to a person, not just a nature, and Jesus is a divine person!) But it is quite evident that, at the Annunciation, she was startled and confused (Lk 1:29). At the birth of Jesus and the adoration of the shepherds, as well as at the presentation and finding in the temple, she "kept all these things, pondering them in her heart" (Lk 2:19, 51, RSV). And the reason is obvious: she had to live by sheer faith, as was attested so sublimely by her cousin Elizabeth at the time of the visitation, "Bless-ed is she who has believed that what the Lord has said to her will be accomplished!" (Lk 1:45, NIV).

But ultimately our life of faith is nothing less than that of *Jesus Christ* himself living in us. As we have already seen in Chapter Three, there was a time when Christian theologians tended to attribute to the human nature of Jesus everything that was not metaphysically impos-sible. Now, more healthily and accurately, the tendency is to consider how completely Jesus may have "emptied himself" (Ph 2:7) in order to be as fully human as possible. In former times, as I well recall from my seminary studies, we were taught that two virtues in particular could not be attributed to Jesus, namely faith and penance: faith, because he enjoyed the Beatific Vision and all infused knowledge throughout his life; and penance, because he did not and indeed could not sin. Now, however, a growing number of Scripture scholars and theologians are inclined to believe that *Jesus may have had to live by faith* just as we do. And, in a challenging sense, he can continue his life of faith only in and through us. With Paul, then, we can say, "I live, no longer I, but Christ lives in me. And the life I now live in the flesh, *I live in the faith of the Son of God,* who loved me and delivered himself for me" (Gal 2:20, WD). What is the meaning of those words? Does Paul want to say, "I live by faith in the Son of God"? That is the traditional interpretation, but it does not fit very well with the grammar employed, as is clear from my exact translation above. Might it not mean that "I live in the Son of God's faith," that is, that the Son of God continues to live by faith in me?

This latter interpretation may be startling, but it certainly fits the grammar better and therefore should be considered at least as a possibility. Not that the risen Christ, the glorified Word Incarnate, can possibly live by faith within himself, any more than he can now suffer within himself. After all, he is risen and is in all his glory "at the right hand of the Father" as we profess in the Creed, after Psalm 11:1, Matthew 22:44, etc. Yet, if Paul can say, "In my own flesh, I fill up what is lacking in the sufferings of Christ for the sake of his body, the Church'' (Col 1:24), and if Scripture scholars and theologians can understand this in terms of Christ mystically living and suffering in Paul and the other members of his Church, then why cannot we understand our text in the same way *as Christ mystically continuing his life of faith in and through us?* And cannot we hear Paul exhorting us as he did the Colossians (2:6-7, WD), "As then you have received Christ Jesus the Lord, continue to walk [i.e. live] in him, [constantly] being rooted and built up in him and strengthened by faith just as you have been taught, abounding more and more in thanksgiving''? What a challenge, what a calling is ours: to let Jesus Christ be enfleshed again in us, so that through us he can continue to live by faith, serve by love, and suffer by fidelity, even to the cross and a joyous resurrection!

THE VIRTUE OF HOPE:

Closely related to faith, indeed clearly stemming from faith, is the second of our "Virtues of Holding On," namely *hope.* It has been well observed that "Hope is putting faith to work when doubting would be easier,"[15] and "Hope is faith holding out its hand in the dark."[16] For this reason, what has been said about faith is largely applicable also to hope and, as a result, we will not have to reflect as long on the latter as we did on the former. However, we certainly cannot afford to neglect this precious virtue, for it is singularly characteristic of what it means to be a Christian or, for that matter, a human being. *We simply cannot live without hope!* According to *Emil Brunner,* "What oxygen is to the lungs, such is hope for the meaning of life."[17] *Viktor Frankl* has vividly portrayed what a crucial difference meaning and hope made in the concentration camps of the Nazi holocaust.[18] And *Alexander Pope,* in his usual incisive fashion, has left us a couplet in his *Essay on Man* which has become nothing less than proverbial,

> Hope springs eternal in the human breast:
> Man never is, but always to be blest![19]

Like love, hope is a "many splendored thing," for it includes the synonymous virtues of trust, confidence, and abandonment to Divine Providence. *Hope,* strictly speaking, always contains a future note. In fact, the common Greek word for hope, namely *elpis,* is related to the Latin *velle,* which means "to wish." It is faith in the future tense, both for this life and the next. As Paul explains in Romans 8:25, "Hoping for what we cannot see means awaiting it with patience." Or, in the thoughtful words of *Simone Weil,* "The virtue of hope is an orientation of the soul towards a transformation after which it will be wholly and exclusively love!"[20] Hope, then, is always forward-looking, as we hear echoed in Don Quixote's wisdom according to *The Man From La Mancha,*

> Love not what you are,
> > but only what you may become . . .
> Look always forward:
> > in last year's nest,
> > there are no birds this year![21]

Trust, on the other hand, is concerned primarily with the present, the here and now, as exemplified in Psalm 91:1,

> You who dwell in the shelter of the Most High,
> > who abide in the shadow of the Almighty,
> Say to the Lord, "My refuge and my fortress,
> > my God, in whom I trust."

Further, trust generally carries with it the connotation of confidence in the midst of *difficulties.* With this connotation in mind, the famous preacher, *Charles H. Spurgeon* urges: "Be it ours, when we cannot see the face of God, to trust under the shadow of his wings!"[22]

Confidence is used in two related ways: (1) as an exact synonym for trust, but derived from a Latin rather than an Anglo-Saxon root, e.g., "We have this confidence in God: that he hears us whenever we ask for anything according to his will" (1 Jn 5:14), and (2) as a subjective attitude which results from faith, hope, and love, as Paul manifests in 2 Corinthians 5:8, "We are full of confidence and would much rather be away from the body and at home with the Lord." In a remarkable statement, the great spiritual writer, *Frederick William Faber,* does not hesitate to assert that "Confidence is the only worship!"[23]

Abandonment to Divine Providence presupposes faith, hope, trust, and confidence but goes even further, including as well the attitude of total self-surrender to the loving will of God and therefore of total acceptance, without fear or anxiety, of whatever must be done or suffered according to his will. It is the disposition of *Mary* at the annunciation, "I am the servant of the Lord. Let it be done to me as you say" (Lk 1:38), and especially of *Jesus* himself at Gethsemane, "Father, if it is your will, take this cup from me; yet not my will but yours be done!" (Lk 22:42) and on the cross, "Father, into your hands I commit my spirit!" (Lk 23:46, JB; Ps 31:6).

The virtue of hope, with all its synonyms, has a prominent place throughout the Bible, particularly in the *Prophets,* the *Psalms,* and the *Letters of St. Paul.* And no wonder! The Israelite people, in spite of (or because of) all their adversities, lived personally and communally according to their hope in the fulfillment of God's promises initially given to Abram at the beginning of Salvation History, "I will make of you a great nation. . . . All the communities of the earth shall find blessing in you" (Gn 12:2-3). And, even when all seemed totally lost in the Babylonian Captivity, there emerged the shining hope of a Messiah, an anointed one, whose future coming would be the salvation not only of the Jews but also of the Gentiles, for "he shall bring forth justice to the nations" (Is 42:1) and "in his name the Gentiles will find hope!" (Mt 12:21).

St. Paul and his fellow Christians, Jewish and Gentile alike, have two great reasons for hope. First, they are *heirs of the hope of Israel,* as Paul remarks in Ephesians 2:11-14,

You men of Gentile stock . . . remember that, in former times, you had no part in Christ and were excluded from the community of Israel. You were strangers to the covenant and the promise; you were without hope and without God in the world. But now in Christ Jesus you who once were far off have been brought near through the blood of Christ. It is he who is our peace, and who made the two of us one by breaking down the barrier of hostility that kept us apart.

Secondly, and more importantly, *Jesus has come as the world's hope,* has sacrificed himself for our sins, and has risen again in order to be, not only the means of our own justification, but also the earnest of our own resurrection. What ground for unlimited hope! To his disciple, Titus, Paul writes:

> The grace of God has appeared, offering *salvation* to all men. It trains us to reject godless ways and worldly desires, and live temperately, justly, and devoutly in this age as we await *our blessed hope,* the appearing of the glory of the great God and of our Savior Christ Jesus (Tt 2:11-13).

> When the kindness and love of God our savior appeared, he saved us; not because of any righteous deeds we had done, but because of his mercy. He saved us through the baptism of new birth and renewal by the Holy Spirit. This Spirit he lavished on us through Jesus Christ our Savior, that we might be justified by his grace and become *heirs, in hope, of eternal life* (Tt 3:4-7).

The foregoing passages clearly indicate that Jesus Christ is the center of our hope, but they also infer that, for a complete understanding of hope and its synonyms, we need to reflect on *our relationship* with each of the three Persons of the *Holy Trinity.* First, through our baptism into Christ and his risen life in us, we become "children of the resurrection" (Lk 20:36, NIV), full of hope, trust and confidence. Hence, St. Paul reminds the Colossians of "the mystery of *Christ in you, your hope of glory!"* (Col 1:27). To which, Alfred Wikenhauser, in his magnificent work, *Pauline Mysticism: Christ in the Mystical Teaching of St. Paul,* adds:

> What dwells in the faithful is not the image of Christ on earth, but the Lord who was raised up by God. . . . Christ is not merely an ideal which stands before Paul's eyes: he is a reality which operates in Paul. Paul is certainly not using metaphor. His words mean that Christ who died and who rose again from the dead, is *present as a living person* in those who believe in him![24]

Secondly, as we reflected in Chapter Three, if we are really one with Christ, then his Father is literally *our Father* and we as his children can place all our hope, trust, and confidence in him. For, he who feeds the birds of the air and clothes the lilies of the field (Mt 6:26-30) knows all things, can do all things, and loves us with an unlimited, everlasting love (Jr 31:3)! And finally, as the indescribable gift of their love for us, the Father and the Son, Jesus Christ, have given us the *Holy Spirit* to dwell with us, to guide us aright, and to transform us into Christ. He is the seal and "pledge of our inheritance" (2 Cor 5:5; Ep 1:13-14) in which we can hope, the "proof" that we are God's children with the right, like Jesus himself, to call him "Abba" (Gal 4:6; Rm 8:14-16) and therefore to trust him as our very own "Daddy"!

All of this we know by faith, but just as soon as a *real crisis* occurs in our life, our heart trembles "as the trees of the forest tremble in the wind" (Is 7:2). Our beautiful thoughts and fervent intentions desert us like an outnumbered army (1 M 9:6). In spite of so many graces through Christ, we cannot even begin to imitate Old Testament Abram who "hoped against hope" (Rm 4:18), and Job who declared, "Though he slay me, yet will I hope in him!" (Jb 13:15). Why is this? Basically, because of a deadly combination of a world that has lost its roots and our own instinct of self-preservation which tends to keep us in a state of insecurity, beset by nameless fears, anxieties, and

scruples that beget sadness, discouragement, and depression bordering on despair. With Paul, we cry out, "Who will rescue me from this
body of death?" (Rm 7:24). Who? Like Job, we are immediately
surrounded by a "support group" of so-called "friends" — doctors
with their tranquilizers, psychologists and psychiatrists with their
various kinds of psychotherapy, but especially *"image-builders"*
(including some religious "positive thinkers") who assure us with
their Pollyannish smiles that we *can* heal ourselves and become
whatever we want to be if only we try "every day in every way to be
better and better!"

Let me repeat my earlier *disclaimers,* namely that I do not intend
to downplay in any way the great good that can be done by physicians
and psychologists, but only to indicate that, in a situation of this kind,
spiritual solutions should be included (along with natural ones, if
necessary) as the most profound, salutary, and lasting. The worse the
situation in which we find ourselves, the more we need *"a bridge over
troubled waters,"* [25] and that bridge consists of the virtue of hope and
its allied virtues. In many instances, it may not be so much a case of
either-or but of both-and, the different healing disciplines (medical,
psychological, and spiritual) cooperating with one another for a
holistic solution. But here, let me leave the realm of theory for that of
personal experience.

When I was about nineteen, just out of a two-year Vincentian
Novitiate, committed to God and the Community by perpetual vows,
and beginning a long six-year preparation in philosophy, theology,
and various other studies for the Catholic priesthood, I suddenly
realized that I was beginning to suffer terrible eyestrain. Perhaps, I
thought, it was due to eagerness in reading a lot of additional books
(which we could not read in the Novitiate) in an effort to acquire a
so-called general culture. So I began to cut down on my reading, but
that did not seem to help. The situation grew worse and worse, to the
point where I could not read more than fifteen minutes at a time
without my eyes feeling as if they were about to fall out of my head.
How could I possibly manage six years of difficult study in this

condition? Naturally, I sought medical help. As a matter of fact, over the next six years I went to no fewer than six different eye doctors, with discouraging results. Nothing helped! Even prayer, which we did plenty of, did not seem to bring a solution, at least not immediately.

Meanwhile, being a natural born worrier, I was almost going out of my mind! Would I ever be able to become a priest? Should I interpret this condition as a sign that, after all, I did not really have a vocation to the priesthood? I was not only perplexed; I was utterly paralyzed with anxiety! Then, providentially, I happened upon a little book called *Abandonment to Divine Providence* by Jean-Pierre de Caussade, with such refreshing advice as the following,

> If we do not concentrate entirely on doing the will of God, we shall find neither happiness nor holiness, no matter what pious practices we adopt, however excellent they may be. If you are not satisfied with what God chooses for you, what else can please you?
>
> If we wish to live according to the Gospel, we must *abandon* ourselves simply and completely to the action of God. Jesus Christ is its source. He "is the same today as he was yesterday and as he will be forever" (Heb 13:8). What he has done is finished, what remains to be done is being carried on every moment. . . . To let God act and obey his demands on us: that is the Gospel and the whole Scripture and the law. This, then, is the straight road to holiness and perfection. This is the great, unique *secret of self-abandonment*, although it is a secret that is no secret and an art without art. . . .
>
> If we have abandoned ourselves, there is only one rule for us: the duty of the *present moment*. The soul is as light as a feather, as fluid as water, simple as a child and as lively as a ball in responding to all the impulses of grace. . . . We must offer ourselves to God like a clean, smooth canvas and not worry ourselves about what God may choose to paint on it, for we have

perfect trust in him, have abandoned ourselves to him, and are so busy doing our duty that we forget ourselves and all our needs.[26]

In reading it, I felt as if it were written for me personally, as if Jesus were saying to me: "Trust me! Abandon yourself to me without reserve! Nothing happens by chance, including your mysterious eye problems. Humanly speaking, there is no way that you can reach your goal of the priesthood, but I have called you to it and I can make it possible! Do not worry at all! 'Cast all your cares' on my Father and yours, 'because he cares for you' (1 P 5:7). Do what you can at each moment and leave the rest to me: the past, the future, your health, everything!''

At his gentle invitation and by his powerful grace, I was able to abandon myself to "this tremendous lover,"[27] and immediately my whole being was flooded with peace. My eyes were not healed until several years later, just before my ordination to the priesthood; but my worries were gone, my "paralysis" healed (Mk 2:3-12), and I was able to continue my preparation for the priesthood in complete tranquility. Those six years of apparent "handicap," of my own "thorn in the flesh" (2 Cor 12:7), became for me an unforgettable "blessing in disguise" which I would cherish for the rest of my life. My temporary "blindness" was a small price to pay in order to "see" what really mattered and to "follow him [Christ] on the road" (Mk 10:52). My temporary "paralysis" had given way to the joy of the cured beggar, "walking, jumping about, and praising God" (Ac 3:8). My abandonment to Christ had freed me to live for him with the energy, the enthusiasm, the *abandon* of a child. And since then, no amount of work, no weight of responsibilities, no army of adversities, not even life under Communism in China, have ever succeeded in plunging me back into my former paralytic state of anxiety.

These days, much is being spoken and written, especially by psychologists, about *stress* and so-called *"burnout,"* particularly among people in roles of service. I do not question that psychology can play a very helpful role in this problem, but I submit that precisely in the area of Christian ministry, the remedy should be sought primarily in the realm of the *spiritual*. If we are really committed and consecrated to Christ, if our service to others is actually his ministry continued in and through us, if we are channeling our energies into work rather than worry, if we are constantly being renewed and transformed by the Holy Spirit, then there is very little chance of "ministerial burnout." Even the psychological solutions which are usually suggested, such as working within our limitations, learning to say "No!" gently but firmly whenever necessary, trusting others through cooperation and delegation, all of these and more are actually spiritual in essence, for they are all reducible to the virtues of humility and confidence. But, if we would only "let go and let God," it is amazing what he can accomplish through us, even in spite of us!

> They that hope in the Lord will renew their strength,
>   they will soar as with eagles' wings;
> They will run and not grow weary,
>   walk and not grow faint (Is 40:31).

With St. Paul, we can declare in all humility and confidence, "When I am powerless, it is then that I am strong!" (2 Cor 12:10), and "I can do all things in him who strengthens me!" (Ph 4:13).

To conclude this brief but very important treatment of hope and its synonyms, let me suggest certain passages, in Scripture and otherwise, for prayerful reflection:

(1) *From Sacred Scripture,* everybody's favorite Psalm 23, "The Lord is my shepherd," then Jesus' identification of himself as "The Good Shepherd" (Jn 10:14-18, 27-30), and the so-called "Johannine" section of Matthew, "Come to me, all you who are weary and find life burdensome, and I will refresh you . . ." (Mt 11:28-30), finally St. Paul's lyrical encouragement, "We know that God makes all things work together for the good of those who have been called according to his decree" . . . (Rm 8:28-39).

(2) *From other sources*, the following:

St. Teresa's Bookmark	*G.K. Chesterton*
Let nothing disturb you,	If seeds
Let nothing trouble you;	in the black earth
All things pass away,	can turn into beautiful roses,
God alone remains.	what might not
Patience overcomes everything,	the heart of man become
He who has God has everything;	in its long journey
God alone suffices.[28]	to the stars?[29]

Victor Hugo

Let us be like a bird for a moment perched
   On a frail branch while he sings;
Though he feels it bend, yet he sings his song,
   Knowing that he has wings.[30]

THE VIRTUE OF LOVE:

The word *love* may well be the most common four-letter word in the English language. Especially in the Western World, an endless stream of songs, movies, television shows, books, stories, and articles keep the word and idea ever at the forefront of our consciousness. "Love," indeed, "makes the world go round!" This evident truth is lyrically expressed in the familiar little poem of *Francis W. Bourdillon,*

The night has a thousand eyes,
   And the day but one;
Yet the light of the bright world dies
   With the dying sun.

The mind has a thousand eyes,
   And the heart but one;

> Yet the light of a whole life dies
> When love is done.[31]

So important is love in everyone's life that, according to a growing mass of evidence, children can be affected for life, not only emotionally but even physically, by lack of love. No wonder President *Harry S. Truman,* known to history for his toughmindedness in making difficult decisions, could nevertheless declare, "In love alone — the love of God and the love of man — will be found the solution of all the ills which afflict the world today!"[32] In the same vein, former Congresswoman *Barbara Jordan* explains, "When love will have more attention than hate, then peace will prevail over war, justice over injustice, sanity over insanity."[33] And this is confirmed by the great psychiatrist, *Dr. Karl A. Menninger,* "Love is the key to the entire therapeutic program of the modern psychiatric hospital!"[34]

The reason for love's preeminence is not hard to find: love is an essential trait of human nature itself! The beloved Catalan mystic, *Ramon Lull* said it seven centuries ago, "He who loves not, lives not!"[35] Yes, *to live is to love!* And *Ernesto Cardenal,* in an inspired little book by that title, explains more fully,

> God is love. And man, too, is love, because man was made in God's image and likeness. God is love. And since He is an infinitely simple Being, if He is love, He can be nothing more and nothing less than love. . . . And man, made in the image of God, is likewise nothing but love. . . . The unadulterated substance of our being is love. Ontologically we are love![36]

Thus, *Thomas Merton,* in his highly supportive Introduction to Cardenal's book, states categorically, "Love is the only reality!"[37] And is this not substantially what we read in the *Song of Songs*?

> Deep waters cannot quench love,
>   nor floods sweep it away.
> Were one to offer all he owns to purchase love,
>   he would be roundly mocked (8:7).

Hence, our *Spiritual Life,* even more than our natural life, is nothing at all unless it is, above all, a life of love! *St. Paul* makes this crystal clear at the beginning of his famous *"Song of Love,"*

> If I speak with human tongues and angelic as well, but do not have love, I am a noisy gong, a clanging cymbal. If I have the gift of prophecy and, with full knowledge, comprehend all mysteries, if I have faith great enough to move mountains, but have not love, I am nothing. If I give everything I have to feed the poor and hand over my body to be burned, but have not love, I gain nothing (1 Cor 13:1-3).

Such is the essential importance of love in life and especially in the Spiritual Life. But *what is love?* A virtue? Yes, and that is why we are treating it here, but it is also more than *a* virtue. It is *the* virtue par excellence! It is the very queen of the virtues, the very bond of perfection, "Over all these virtues put on love, which binds the rest together and makes them perfect" (Col 3:14). For that reason, *Thomas Merton* writes in his Introduction to Ernesto Cardenal's book,

> For the moralist human life is a complex system of virtues and vices, and love is assigned a definite place in the system; it is one of the several virtues. However, the mystic knows of no such complex system; for him love is the one and the all. For him the virtues are different aspects of love, and he holds that the same is true of the vices. The virtues are manifestations of a love that is alive and hale. And the vices are symptoms of an enfeebled love, of a love which refuses to be what it is in essence. Actually, there is nothing else but love![38]

But here, our English language proves so ambiguous. For example, the *one word "love"* calls attention to the fact that, in a sense, all love is one because all love is from God and, in one way or another, reflects God who is love (1 Jn 4:8, 16). At the same time, however, the one word "love" fails to emphasize the richness of love by not distinguishing among the various kinds of love. In this, as in many similar instances, the Greek language is far superior, because it distinguishes three kinds of love in particular: *erōs*, passionate love, especially the emotional and physical love between men and women; *philĭa*, fond affection, particularly the love of friendship, with the connotation of some kind of equality between the friends; and *agápe*, spiritual love, above all the love of God himself shared with humankind and the love we are called and commanded to have for God and for one another because of God.

Now, while Classical Greek favored the use of the first two terms, in Biblical Greek it is the other way around. *Erōs*, in the form of noun, adjective, or verb, is rarely used in the Septuagint (Greek) translation of the Old Testament (not even in the Song of Songs!), and never used in the New Testament. *Philĭa*, in its various forms, is only moderately used in the Greek translation of the Old Testament, and only somewhat more so in the New Testament, largely because some authors, e.g. John, tend to employ *philĭa* and *agápe* interchangeably. But by far the chosen word for love in both Testaments is *agápe*, even in the Song of Songs (which many, if not most, Scripture scholars today interpret as a collection of erotic songs extolling human love) and in the description of Jonathan's love for David (1 S 18:1, 3 and 20:17), which most interpret as friendship and some even as a homoerotic relationship.

What are we to conclude from this phenomenon? Either that *agápe* was utilized as a generic term for love of all kinds; or that love, like wisdom, goodness, and everything else worthwhile, was regarded in both Testaments as belonging to God who, out of his loving-kindness, shares it with us humans. I, for one, certainly favor the latter conclusion as far more in keeping, both with the Greek precision in the use of words, and with the Jewish and early Christian preference for attributing everything good to God (Mk 10:18). At any rate, in our own reflection on love in the Spiritual Life, we will quite logically confine ourselve to *agápe*, which is spiritual or divine love shared with humankind.

The thread of *agápē* love, like fine gold, is woven throughout the fabric of both Testaments. However, in the interest of time and space, we shall limit our examination of this beautiful virtue to certain books which give it special prominence. The *first* of these, in the order of the biblical books, is that of *Deuteronomy,* God's book of love in the Pentateuch. Written under prophetic influence around the time of the Babylonian Captivity in the sixth century B.C., this challenging book (whose Greek name means "Second Law") contains a sermon or series of sermons purportedly addressed to the Israelites by Moses just before their entry into Canaan after the Exodus and wanderings in the desert of Sinai. From beginning to end, it reminds God's People of his loving, gratuitous choice of them and the many privileges bestowed on them, in return for which all he asked for (in vain) was their love and loyalty. Particularly moving are the following sections: 4:32-40; 6:4-9 (containing the *"Shema"* or love commandment); 11:10-21; and especially 32:10-12:

> He [Yahweh] found them [Israel] in a wilderness,
> a wasteland of howling desert.
> He shielded them and cared for them,
> guarding them as the apple of his eye.
> As an eagle incites its nestlings forth
> by hovering over its brood,
> So he spread his wings to receive them
> and bore them up on his pinions.
> The Lord alone was their leader,
> no strange god was with him.

The *second* book of love, but probably the first in chronological order, was that of the *Prophet Hosea* (around 800 B.C.), who introduced the idea of the Covenant as a love and marriage relationship between Yahweh and Israel. It contains the poignant story of how Hosea was directed to marry a "harlot wife" who turned out to be blatantly unfaithful, cruelly breaking the prophet's heart. Yet he was told to take her back again and forgive her, if only she would return. This was a prophetic "parable in action," followed later (at least in word) by Jeremiah, Ezekiel, and Second Isaiah, depicting the love of Yahweh for Israel, his beloved spouse through the Covenant of Sinai, her gross infidelity (her idolatry constituting a spiritual adultery), and his willingness to receive her back with forgiveness if she would only return to him. The two most meaningful passages portray Yahweh as a forgiving husband (2:16-17, 20-23) and as a nurturing father (11:1-4):

Yahweh — Forgiving Husband:

So I will allure her;
  I will lead her into the desert
  and speak to her heart. . .
She shall respond there
  as in the days of her youth,
  when she came up
  from the land of Egypt. . .
I will make a covenant for them
  on that day. . .
I will espouse you to me forever;
I will espouse you in right and justice,
  in love and in mercy;
I will espouse you in fidelity,
  and you shall know the Lord.

Yahweh — Nurturing Father:

When Israel was a child I loved him,
  out of Egypt I called my son.
The more I called them,
  the farther they went from me. . .
Yet it was I who taught Ephraim to walk
  who took them in my arms;
I drew them with human cords,
  with bands of love;
I fostered them like one
  who raises an infant to his cheeks;
Yet though I stooped to feed my child,
  they did not know
  that I was their healer.

The *third Old Testament book of love* is the famous *Song of Songs*. Reams have been written about the purpose, content, and form of this passionate and puzzling book. As mentioned previously, it is commonly regarded now among Scripture scholars as a collection of love songs or marriage songs (*epithalámia*) extolling the sublimity of *human love*. This is certainly a legitimate interpretation and may well represent the literal meaning intended by the human author, but so many factors urge a deeper, more *spiritual meaning* as well: (1) the *marriage analogy* just treated in prophetic literature, (2) the use of the word *agápē* for love throughout the book, and (3) the centuries-old Judeo-Christian *tradition* interpreting it as a love song celebrating the union of Yahweh and Israel, Christ and the Church. And, while the division into *seven love songs* appears well founded and is widely accepted, I believe that a sound case can be made for a development in *three widening concentric circles,* each featuring the three stages of love, loss, and reunion, and each ending with the beautiful expression:

> I adjure you, daughters of Jerusalem,
> > by the gazelles and hinds of the field,
> Do not arouse, do not stir up love
> > before its own time (Sg 2:7; 3:5; 7:4).

In the *New Testament,* the most notable books of love are those of *John and Paul.* The entire *Gospel of the "Beloved Disciple"* is a love story, yet even so the farewell discourse and prayer of Jesus (Jn 13-17) stand out from the rest because of their tender expression of love, e.g., the new commandment of love (Jn 13:34-35 and 15:12, 17) as well as the promise of loving manifestation and presence (Jn 14:21, 23). But probably the clearest and most persuasive teaching on love is found in *John's First Epistle,* especially 4:7-21, which insists on love among ourselves because God, who is Love itself, has shown his love for us particularly in the gift of his Son and his Spirit. The following arrangement, which I have made of the *Jerusalem Bible* translation, may assist the reader in recognizing more clearly the profound development of thought in this section of John's letter:

1.	2."
My dear people	*God's love for us was revealed*
let us love one another	when God sent . . .*his only Son*
since love comes from God	so that we could have *life through him;*
and everyone who loves	this is the love I mean;
is begotten by God and knows God.	*not our love for God,*
Anyone who fails to love	*but God's love for us*
can never have known God,	when he sent his Son to be the Sacrifice
because *God is love.*	that takes our sins away.

3.

My dear people,
since God has loved us so much,
we too should love one another.
No one has ever seen God;
but *as long as we love one another*
God will live in us
and his love will be complete in us.
We can know that we are living in him
and he is living in us
because *he lets us share his Spirit.*

4.

We ourselves saw and we testify
that the Father sent his Son
as saviour of the world.
If anyone acknowledges
that Jesus is the Son of God,
God lives in him,
and he in God.
We ourselves have known
and put our faith in
God's love towards ourselves.

5.

God is love
and anyone who lives in love
lives in God, and God lives in him.
Love will come to perfection in us
when we can face the day of Judgment
without fear;
because even in this world
we have become as he is.
In love there can be no fear,
but fear is driven out by perfect love;
because to fear is to expect punishment,
and anyone who is afraid
is still imperfect in love.

6.

We are to love, then,
because he loved us first.
Anyone who says, "I love God,"
and hates his brother,
is a liar,
since the man who does not love
the brother that he can see
cannot love God,
whom he has never seen.
So that is the *commandment*
that he has given us,
that *anyone who loves God*
must also love his brother.

Finally, St. Paul can truly be described as a "man of love," for love constantly surfaces throughout his life and his writings. To mention only a few passages,

And this hope will not leave us disappointed, because the *love of God* has been poured out in our hearts through the Holy Spirit who has been given to us. . . . It is precisely in this that God proves his love for us: that while we were still sinners, Christ died for us (Rm 5:5, 8).

Who will separate us from *the love of Christ?* . . . "For your sake we are being slain all the day long. . . ." Yet, in all this we are more than conquerors because of him who loved us. For I am

certain that neither death nor life, neither angels nor principali-
ties, neither the present nor the future, nor powers, neither
height nor depth nor any other creature will be able to separate us
from the love of God that comes to us in Christ Jesus, our Lord
(Rm 8:35-39).

Your love must be sincere. . . . Love one another with the
affection of brothers (Rm 12:9-10). Owe no debt to anyone
except the debt that binds us to love one another. He who loves
his neighbor has fulfilled the law. . . . Love never wrongs the
neighbor, hence love is the fulfillment of the law (Rm 13:8, 10;
cf. also 1 Cor 13:1-13; 1 Th 4:9).

May Christ dwell in your hearts through faith, and may charity
be the root and foundation of your life. Thus you will be able to
grasp fully, with all the holy ones, the breadth and length and
height and depth of *Christ's love,* and experience this love which
surpasses all knowledge, so that you may attain to the fullness of
God himself (Ep 3:17-19).

Be imitators of God as his dear children. Follow *the way of love,*
even as Christ loved you. He gave himself for us as an offering
to God, a gift of pleasing fragrance (Ep 5:1-2).

From this sampling of the Old and New Testaments, it is clear
that the Bible is not only a love story but a whole *library of love!* And
not surprisingly, for it has God, who is love itself, as its principal
author! To learn more and more about love, then, all we need to do is
read his *"love letters"* in the Holy Scriptures and prayerfully reflect
on them, perhaps with the help of others who have been given special
insights. Let us attempt, as succinctly as possible, to examine various
important aspects of this central virtue of love.

First, what is the *meaning of love?* As *Edward Carter, S.J.* states
it on the very first page of *Everyday and its Possibilities,* "Love in any
of its forms is a gift of self to promote the authentic goodness and
happiness of the other."[39] How much more is this true of genuine

agápē love! Not only is it incomparably *beyond liking,* which is a natural, spontaneous attraction and affection based on a variety of human factors, but it is also far superior to *érōs* and *philía,* for it is centered in the will influenced by grace or, better still, it is centered in the spirit, where Christ himself loves in and through us. Hence, it is above all *selfless,* not seeking or requiring (as other loves do) any return of love whatsoever. "Love is not jealous. . . . It is not self-seeking . . . neither does it brood over injuries" (1 Cor 13:4-5). This will be clearer as we consider some other characteristics of *agápē* love.

Secondly, what is the *measure,* what are the *dimensions,* of love? *Deuteronomy 6:4-9,* often repeated by Jesus, prescribes, "You shall love the Lord, our God, with all your *heart,* and with all your *soul,* and with all your *strength."* St. Paul, in his masterful description of *agápē* love (1 Cor 13:7, RSV), tells us, "Love *bears* all things, *believes* all things, *hopes* all things, *endures* all things!" And Jesus himself commands us to "love one another *as I have loved you!"* (Jn 13:34-35; 15:12, 17). How has he loved us? "Having loved his own who were in the world, he loved them *to the end!"* (Jn 13:1). *Limitless love!* Or, as *John Powell, S.J.* entitles it in his book, *"Unconditional Love!"*[40] But *St. Bernard's* declaration has been even better known for centuries, "The measure of loving God is to love him without measure."[41] However, *St. Vincent de Paul,* the Apostle of Love (especially for the poor), reminds us that even love must be regulated by prudence.[42] And *Lewis B. Smedes,* in his thoughtful work, *Love Within Limits,*[43] points out different ways in which Paul's description of love in 1 Corinthians 13 must not be misinterpreted to justify what cannot be condoned. Jesus' love did not condone sin (Jn 8:11) nor hypocrisy (Mt 23), nor the desecration of the temple (Mt 21:12-13 and parallels). In modern parlance, love at times must be "tough love!"[44]

Thirdly, what are the *qualities* or *conditions* of love? Here, Paul certainly comes to our aid, "Love is patient and kind; love is not jealous or boastful; it is not arrogant or rude. Love does not insist on its own way; it is not irritable or resentful; it does not rejoice at wrong, but rejoices in the right" (1 Cor 13:4-6, RSV). Now we have enough food for thought to last us a lifetime! As Smedes points out, these qualities represent the *ideal* for which we are to strive. In fact, with this description of love, as with the Beatitudes in Matthew 5:3-12, we must humbly admit that Jesus himself, along with his holy mother, Mary, alone have lived the ideal perfectly. The rest of us are but pilgrims and strivers toward the ideal. And in our striving, we would do well to emphasize the qualities of love in the same order that Paul lists them, "Love is *patient* and *kind!*" Those two qualities alone are as difficult to acquire as they are essential to have. Anyone can be a "saint for a day" or maybe even a week, but only real *agápe* love can enable us to be patient day in and day out over a long period of time. And kindness? I do not recall who said it (though it sounds most like St. Francis de Sales), but I have remembered this advice for over forty years, "Be kind, be kind, and you will be saints!"[45] And, somewhat facetiously, the interesting little prayer, "Lord, make all the bad people good, and all the good people nice!"

Of course, patience and kindness involve, above all, loving other human beings, that is, our neighbors, as commanded in Leviticus 19:18 and interpreted by Jesus to include *everyone,* even our *enemies* (Mt 5:43-48; Lk 6:35; 10:30-37). But very importantly, "love begins at home" and includes, first of all, our married partner, our family, our friends. Yes, it begins at home, but it does not end there, for "love is a fire" and, like a fire, will soon go out if it does not spread. Whether at home or elsewhere, *agápe* love requires *creative kindness,* which strives to recognize and foster the potential good in others, even to discern and minister to *Christ himself* disguised, so to speak, in the person of everyone we meet. "I assure you, as often as you did it (or neglected to do it) for one of my least brothers, you did it (or neglected to do it) for me!" (Mt 25:40, 45). Or, as *St. John of the Cross* summarizes it, "In the evening of life, we will be judged on love!"[46]

Likewise, loving others with *agápe* love means loving *generously, compassionately,* and *forgivingly* because, in my own favorite expression,

> To live is to love,
>   To love is to give;
>   To love deeply is
>   To forgive completely!

Did not Jesus exhort, even command, us: "Be compassionate as your heavenly Father is compassionate" (Lk 6:36)? Did not St. Paul remind his readers that "God loves a cheerful giver" (2 Cor 9:7) and, in a saying which he attributes to Jesus himself even though it is in none of the Gospels, "It is more blessed to give than to receive" (Ac 20:35, RSV)? Finally, loving others with *agápe* love means *transcending our natural feelings* of insecurity, fear, distrust, discrimination, rash judgment, perhaps even contempt when we encounter others who are different from us, particularly in race, color, language, culture, religion, or anything else. We tend to be such slaves of our feelings that, while we think we are living in *agápe* love, we often find, if we are honest with ourselves, that we are ruled more by our likes and dislikes. It has been well said that, "We like someone because. We love someone although."[47] And another challenging statement, which I remember reading years ago, has rattled around my memory and conscience ever since, "We love God only as much as we love the one whom we love the least!"

Love, then, is a really "tough" proposition. And commanded at that! *How can we possibly fulfill such a command?* By ourselves, of course, we simply cannot. Only God who is love can enable us to love with *agápe*, his own kind of love. But is this not exactly what he desires and has made possible? In his love, he has given us his own Son, *Incarnate Love,* and his own Spirit, the very *Spirit of Love,* to transform us and enable us to love with his love. Is this not the fulfillment of his promise, "I will give them a new heart and put a new spirit within them; I will remove the stony heart from their bodies, and replace it with a natural heart" (Ezk 11:19; 36:26; cf. Jr 31:33)? What does Jesus mean when he says, "Love one another *as I have loved you*" (Jn 13:34-35; 15:12, 17)? "In imitation of my selfless, limitless love"? Yes, of course! But also *"with the very love* with which I have loved you."* No wonder this is a new commandment, for both the extent and the means are new! Seen in this light, St. Paul's inspired expressions take on deeper meaning, "The love of Christ [not only our love of him, but also his love in us] impels us . . ." (2 Cor 5:14) and, "Walk in love, as Christ loved us and gave himself up for us . . ." (Ep 5:2, RSV).

What excuse have we, then? None whatever! He himself gives us in full measure the very love with which we are to love him and others. All we need to do is open ourselves to it, particularly through humility, purity, and a spirit of poverty, and exercise it on every occasion so that it will grow in us and transform us into him. No wonder this love "covers a multitude of sins!" (1 P 4:8, RSV; cf. also Lk 7:47). But let us never forget that this love, being that of Jesus Christ himself and of his Holy Spirit (Rm 5:5), is not general, or generic, but deeply *personal.* We are not God, of course, and therefore we cannot, even with his love, have the same knowledge and loving-kindness toward every human being that he has. But we can and we should love Jesus Christ and, through him, the Father and the Holy Spirit, with a truly personal love and, by the same token, we can apply the same personal love to others, especially those closest to us and those in most need. It is not enough or even possible to just "love people." We are so made and so empowered that we can and must love individual persons, and especially one individual person. For the married, that person under God must be one's partner in life. For the celibate, especially the consecrated Christian celibate, that person is to be Jesus Christ himself! He must be the very center of our life, the "treasure where our heart is" (Mt 6:21). He longs to be our love, our life, our all! And, far more perfectly and uninterruptedly than in human marriage, he can so live in us, so take possession of us, so transform us into himself, that he can indeed be the very love and life of our life! But to describe this "indescribable gift" (2 Cor 9:15), I feel totally inadequate. Therefore, let me call upon the author of the *Imitation of Christ* to do it for me:

A great thing is love, a great good every way; which alone lightens every burden and bears equally every inequality. . . The noble love of Jesus impels one to do great things, and even excites him to desire that which is more perfect. . .

Nothing is sweeter than love, nothing stronger, nothing higher, nothing wider, nothing more pleasant, nothing fuller or better in heaven or on earth; for love is born of God and cannot rest but in God, above all created things.

The lover flies, runs, and rejoices; he is free and is not bound. He gives all for all, and has all in all; because he rests above all created things in the one Sovereign Being, from whom flows and proceeds everything that is good. . .

Love feels no burden, thinks lightly of labors, aims beyond its strength, complains not of impossibility; for it conceives that all things are possible to it, and all things are free.[48]

Love has often been compared to a *fire,* and justly so. For, like a fire, it is able to destroy whatever is unworthy, purify whatever needs cleansing, and transform one into Another. Like a fire, it provides light for our understanding, warmth for our will, and energy for our whole being. And finally, like a fire, it must be fanned and helped to grow within and spread without; otherwise, it will shortly flicker and go out. We Christians need to remember always those challenging words of Jesus, "I have come to light a fire on the earth. How I wish the blaze were ignited!" (Lk 12:49). Let us listen to two great thinkers of our time using the same analogy of love as a fire:

Teilhard de Chardin	*Dom Bede Griffiths*
Someday,	The love of God
after mastering	is not a mild benevolence.
the winds, the waves,	It is a consuming fire!
the tides, and gravity,	To those who resist it,
we shall harness for God	it becomes an eternal torment.
the energies of love,	To those who are willing
	to face its demands,

and then,   it becomes a fire
for the second time   that cleanses and purifies.
in the history of the world,   Those whom it has once penetrated,
man will discover fire![49]   it transforms into itself![50]

SUMMARY AND CONCLUSION:

In this chapter, which is somewhat longer than usual, we have
been reflecting on the very important *"Virtues of Holding On,"*
namely faith, hope and love. We have seen that *faith*, biblically
speaking, is not simply an acceptance of truths to believe and live by,
but a total surrender to a Triune God who desires to live with and in us.
We have come to realize also that the virtue of *hope* contains several
allied virtues (trust, confidence, abandonment to Divine Providence),
which enable us to carry on our quest, our otherwise "impossible
dream,"[51] of transforming union with God through Jesus Christ.
And, finally, we have come to appreciate something of the riches of
spiritual, transforming, *agápe* love, the queen of the virtues, the
indescribable gift of our loving God.

By way of *summary* of this reflection on the theological virtues,
let me quote briefly from the great Protestant Theologian, *Reinhold
Niebuhr*:

> Nothing true or beautiful makes complete sense
>   in any context of history,
>   therefore we must be saved by *faith*.
>
> Nothing worth doing is completed
>   in our lifetime,
>   therefore we must be saved by *hope*.
>
> Nothing we do, no matter how virtuous,
>   can be accomplished alone,
>   therefore we are saved by *love*.[52]

And, by way of *conclusion*, I offer a *song of love* which I composed many years ago, during the period of my "spiritual honeymoon,"

> Some may live only for riches,
> Some may live only for fame;
> My life is given to Someone,
> And Love is his Name . . .

> Love, how can I sing the rapture of your charms,
>   your tenderness, your fond caress.
> Love, how dare I e'er escape your circling arms?
>   The more I flee, the less I'm free!

> Once I dreamed that I would love another,
> Now I know there's only one for me;
> Unlike any ordinary lover,
> You'll be true to me right through eternity!

> Now, though bitterness may come, I'll see it through,
>   for at your feet, the bitter's sweet!
> And, though weary, sick, and blind, I'll cling to you;
>   You'll be my light, my very sight!

> Ah Love! You're life and breath and everything divine,
> And just to think! You're mine, all mine!

RECOMMENDED READING LIST

1. Alberione, James. *A Time for Faith,* Boston, MA: Daughters of St. Paul, 1978.
2. Macquarrie, John. *Christian Hope,* New York, NY: Seabury Press, 1978.
3. De Caussade, J.-P. *Abandonment to Divine Providence,* Garden City, NY: Doubleday and Co., 1975.
4. Goergen, Donald. *The Power of Love,* Chicago, IL: Thomas More Press, 1979.
5. Tavard, George. *A Way of Love,* Maryknoll, NY: Orbis Books, 1977.

POINTS FOR REFLECTION AND DISCUSSION

1. What are the general importance and application of the theological virtues in our life today?
2. What is biblical faith and how does it differ from traditional theological faith?
3. What is the importance of hope and its synonymous virtues in our Spiritual Life, especially in the world today?
4. What kind of love is emphasized in the Bible, and what is its role in our Spiritual Life?
5. What are the principal qualities of this love and what is their application in everyday Christian living?

CHAPTER EIGHT

THE INNER DIMENSIONS OF THE RELATIONSHIP:
The Prayerful Life of the Spirit

Webster's Ninth New Collegiate Dictionary defines *dimensions,* first in terms of *measurements* and then as *"one of the elements or factors making up a complete personality or entity."*[1] Initially, I chose the word in the second meaning as the most appropriate for this and the following chapter, in which I will consider the inner and outer elements or factors of our relationship with God, which basically constitutes our Spiritual Life. And this takes on added meaning when we realize that the "complete personality" we are referring to is especially that of *Jesus Christ* continuing his life and ministry in and through us. However, further reflection has shown me a fullness and uncanny aptness in the first meaning as well.

It is surprising and revealing how often the Scriptures use the term *measurement* or simply *measure* in regard to God and our own life in relationship with him. For example, God and God alone is the *"Great Measurer"* of: (1) *The earth,* "Where were you when I founded the earth? . . . Who determined its *size,* do you know? Who stretched out the *measuring line* for it?" (Jb 38:4-5); (2) *Peoples,* "From one, he made every nation of humans to dwell on the face of the earth, having *determined* their *designated* times and the *boundaries* of their habitation" (Ac 17:26, WD); (3) *Individuals,* "O Lord, my allotted portion and my cup, you it is who hold fast my lot. For me the *measuring lines* have fallen on pleasant sites; fair to me is my inheritance'' (Ps 16:5-6).

Not only is God the ''Great Measurer,'' but he is *loving and generous beyond all measure* and he desires that we be also, as we see in the following quotations: (1) ''Give and it shall be given to you. *Good measure* pressed down, shaken together, running over, will they pour into the fold of your garment. For the *measure* you *measure* with will be *measured* back to you'' (Lk 6:38); (2) ''He whom God has sent utters the words of God, for it is *not by measure* that he gives the *Spirit''* (Jn 3:34); (3) ''He had loved his own in this world, and would show his love for them *to the end''* (Jn 13:1); (4) ''This hope will not leave us disappointed, because the love of God has been *poured out* in our hearts through the *Holy Spirit* who has been given to us'' (Rm 5:5).

In keeping with God's limitless love for us, *St. Bernard* (as we have seen in the previous chapter) can declare, ''The *measure* of loving God is to love him *without measure!''*[2] And the *Imitation of Christ* follows suit, ''Love often knows *no measure,* but grows fervent *beyond all measure,''*[3] adding an inspiring paean of love for Jesus:

> My God and my Love! Thou art all mine, and I am all Thine.
> *Enlarge me in love,* that I may learn to taste with the inward palate of my heart how sweet it is to love, and to melt and bathe in love. Let me be possessed by love and *mount above myself* from the very fervour and ecstasy of love. Let me sing Love's song; let me follow Thee, my Beloved, *to the heights*; let my soul quite lose itself in Thy praises, rejoicing exceedingly in love. Let me love Thee more than myself, and myself only for Thee. And in Thee *let me love all* who truly love Thee, as is commanded by the law of love which shines forth from Thee.[4]

In the following reflections on the dimensions of our relationship with God in the Spiritual Life, we will consider in the course of this chapter what I refer to as the *inner dimensions,* particularly that of prayer and then, more generally but very importantly, other characteristics of Life in the Spirit. In the following chapter, we will take up the *outer dimensions* of service or ministry, witnessing, and suffering or sacrifice. Because of the crucial importance of these chapters, especially this one on "The Prayerful Life of the Spirit," they will tend to be somewhat longer than usual, but I hope not too long for the reader's patience.

PRAYER:

In one sense, prayer might well be treated in the final section of this work, when we will discuss the *special means* of the Spiritual Life but, in another sense, prayer is so *essential* to and so *characteristic* of our relationship with God that it would be inexcusable of me not to consider it as the very first among the inner dimensions of the Spiritual Life. This is well expressed by Mark Link, S.J. in his *Still Point,*

> Prayer should not be thought of as a means to an end. True, it serves the noble purpose of motivating us to live for God. But it is also an end in itself — loving God. Prayer is an expression of love — complete and total in itself.[5]

With this statement, I fully agree, but I become somewhat uneasy with the current tendency to completely identify *prayer and the Spiritual Life,* as if the two were totally coextensive, as if learning to pray were all we need to know and do in order to be spiritual persons, even saints! Just a cursory overview of the vast literature on prayer that is flooding the market naturally leads one to this conclusion, which in turn can easily produce a generation of "quietists" or of "prayer sharers" who labor under the delusion that they are well on the road to spiritual perfection. But this is where, as is so often the case, *the Bible* provides us with the proper corrective. Jesus is quite clear and emphatic, "Not everyone who says to me, 'Lord, Lord,' shall enter the kingdom of heaven, but he who *does the will of my*

Father who is in heaven'' (Mt 7:21, RSV). And again (quoting Is 29:13), Jesus declares, "This people pays me lip service but their heart is far from me" (Mt 15:8; Mk 7:6). And finally, what is the basis of our judgment in Matthew 25:31-46? Is it the quality of our prayer-life? No, as the great Master of Prayer, *St. John of the Cross* insists, "In the evening of life, we will be judged on love"[6] — and practical love at that!

On the other hand, as I have already indicated, while prayer is not the totality of spirituality, it certainly holds a *central place*, and for a very simple reason. The essence of the Spiritual Life is *relationship*, particularly our loving relationship with God and others in God. But *relationship is impossible without communication*, as is daily so evident in the human relationships of marriage, family life, and friendship. And, in our relationship with God, that *indispensable* communication is called *prayer!* To this, we have the attestation of many saints and sages, e.g.:

St. Augustine, "As our body cannot live without nourishment, so our soul cannot spiritually be kept alive without prayer."[7] *Bl. Robert Southwell*, "As the soul life to the body gives, so prayer revives the soul, by prayer it lives!"[8] *St. Vincent de Paul*, "Give me a man of prayer; he will be able to do all things!"[9] *St. John Eudes*,

> The air which we breathe, the bread which we eat, the heart which throbs in our bosoms, are not more necessary for man that he may live as a human being, than is prayer for the Christian that he may live as a Christian.[10]

Finally, in our own day, *P.T. Forsyth* declares, "We pray because we were made for prayer, and God draws us out by breathing himself in."[11]

As always, however, our very best witness is not that of the saints and sages, but that of *the Son of God himself*, in the example of his life and the authority of his words reflected in the New Testament. The great German Scripture scholar, *Joachim Jeremias*, has lucidly explained, both in *The Prayers of Jesus* and in his *New Testament Theology* that Jesus was not only a praying Jew (that is, a fervent member of a praying people, the people of the Psalms!), but a *uniquely praying Jew*! He alone, it appears, was wont to address Yahweh as *"Abba,"* that is, father in such a familiar sense that it is best translated "Daddy" (Mk 14:36; Gal 4:6; Rm 8:15).[12] His prayers in the New Testament are masterpieces of humility, confidence, and love, e.g., the *Lord's Prayer* (Mt 6:9-13 and Lk 11:2-4); the "Thanksgiving or *Blessing Prayer"* (Mt 11:25-26 and Lk 10:21); the *Johannine prayers* (Jn 11:41-42 and 17:1-26); the agonized prayer in he Garden of *Gethsemane* (Mk 14:36; Mt 26:39, 42, 44; Lk 22:42; and John's equivalent in Jn 12:27-28); and the final prayers on *Calvary* (Mk 15:34; Mt 27:46; and Lk 23:34, 46). In addition to these explicit prayers, we have the testimony that Jesus prayed alone in the early morning (Mk 1:35), on a mountain (Mt 14:23; Mk 6:46; Lk 6:12), in lonely or deserted places (Mk 1:35; Lk 5:16), that he spent whole nights in prayer (Lk 6:12), that he prayed on the principal occasions of his life, e.g., at his baptism (Lk 3:21), the choice of his Apostles (Lk 6:12), his transfiguration (Lk 9:29), and his support of Peter at the last supper (Lk 22:31-32). Also, we know that Jesus carefully *taught the necessity and qualities of prayer,* notably in his Sermon on the Mount (Mt 6:5-15; 7:7-11) and especially in Luke's "Gospel of Prayer," e.g. in the story of Martha and Mary (Lk 10:38-42) and his famous parables of prayer (Lk 5-13 and 18:1-14). Finally, the *Epistle to the Hebrews* reminds us that Jesus "in the days when he was in the flesh, offered prayers and supplications with loud cries and tears to God, who was able to save him from death, and he was heard because of his reverence" (Heb 5:7) and that, even in Heaven, "He is always able to save those who approach God through him, since he forever lives to make intercession for them" (Heb 7:25; cf. also 1 Jn 2:1).

Why was prayer so terribly *important to Jesus*? Because he was human in all our human weakness and needs! If, for example, his human mind had enjoyed the Beatific Vision and all infused knowledge throughout his life, and if his human will had been absolutely immune from sin and even genuine temptation, what need would he have had for prayer? No, it was precisely *because he was so human* that he felt such a vital need for prayer. We cannot possibly imagine the depth of that need: his real human need for divine strength in his tiredness, temptations, and trials and, at the same time, his real human need for divine communication and communion in his otherness and aloneness. No wonder he spent whole nights in prayer!

The great Lebanese poet, Kahlil Gibran is particularly insightful in his work, *Jesus, the Son of God,*

> Jesus was not a phantom,
>   nor a conception of poets.
> He was a man like
>   yourself and myself.
>
> He saw visions we did not see,
>   and heard voices we did not hear.
> He was upon the earth
>   yet he was of the sky.
>
> And only in our aloneness
>   may we visit the land
>   of his aloneness. [13]

Perhaps I myself was experiencing something of his need when, years ago in the minor or high school seminary, I used to feel so helpless under the cruel persecution of one of my classmates, who was slightly younger but much stronger than I, that I spent hours alone in the chapel. Only there did I feel safe, understood, and loved. From hindsight, I realize that it was all a blessing in disguise, for my traumatic experience had the effect of introducing me to a regular and meaningful prayer life. Whether Jesus felt anything like this, it is hard to say, but I do not find it difficult to visualize him feeling all the weakness of his humanity both in himself and in his being surrounded by powerful, intimidating human and diabolical forces. I particularly like to picture him gazing up to that gorgeous galaxy of stars, which

always seems so close and almost touchable in the Middle East, and
glorifying his Father in the profound words of Psalm 8:1-6,

> O Lord, our Lord, how glorious is your name over all the earth!
>   You have exalted your majesty above the heavens.
> Out of the mouths of babes and sucklings
>   you have fashioned praise because of your foes,
>   to silence the hostile and the vengeful.
>
> When I behold your heavens, the work of your fingers,
>   the moon and the stars which you set in place —
> What is man that you should be mindful of him,
>   or the son of man that you should care for him?
>
> You have made him little less than the angels,
>   and crowned him with glory and honor!

Thus, he could rejoice in God's greatness and his own weakness,
God's transcendence and his own human limitations, God's omni-
presence and his own human aloneness. And all the while he was
being prepared for that night in the Garden of Gethsemane! With such
an incredible example of prayer before us, how can we possibly
neglect this all-important dimension of our Spiritual Life? How can
we refuse to let Jesus, the very model of prayer, continue to pray and
petition, to praise and glorify his Father in and through us today?
Robert Hugh Benson assures us, in his Preface to *Bands of Love,* that
"It is Christ who prays in every soul in whom he lives!"[14]

But now it is time to go beyond the reasons and models of prayer
and attempt to understand just *what is prayer* and how do we personally and communally practice it. There are many definitions of
prayer. The one that I have already used, and that I believe is the most
basic and appropriate in this treatment on our relationship with God as
the heart of the Spiritual Life, is simply that *prayer is communication
with God.* And with this simple definition, most of the great Saints
and spiritual writers agree, both those of the early ages of the Church
and those of more recent centuries.

In the *early ages,* for example, we find these definitions of prayer: Clement of Alexandria, "Prayer is conversation with God,"[15] Sts. Gregory of Nyssa, Augustine, and Jerome, "Prayer is speaking with God,"[16] and St. John Climacus, "Prayer considered in its essence is a conversation and union between God and man."[17]

And in *more recent centuries,* though the definitions or descriptions become somewhat longer, they remain essentially the same, for example: St. Teresa of Avila, "Prayer is conversation with God who loves us,"[18] St. Francis de Sales, "The chief exercise of prayer is to speak to God and to hear God speak in the bottom of our heart,"[19] St. Vincent de Paul, "Prayer is an interview of the soul with God, a mutual communication wherein God speaks to the soul what he wishes it to know and accomplish,"[20] and our own beloved St. Elizabeth Ann Seton, "Prayer is a habit of lifting up the heart to God in a constant communication with him."[21]

From the various definitions above, it is evident that prayer is *communication, conversation, dialogue* between ourselves and God. But how is this possible? It is one thing to speak *to* God, maybe even to speak *with* God, but quite another to "hear" God reply. So what are we talking about? How does God reply to our prayers? The answer is, of course, in a variety of ways, depending largely on the kind of prayer we use: petition, or meditation, or contemplation, etc. Let us, then, examine briefly the various *kinds* of prayer, their *conditions* and the *ways* in which God usually *responds* to them.

PETITION:

The first and most natural form of prayer is that of *petition* in any of a variety of forms: *liturgical* petition, for example in the Eucharist or the Liturgy of the Hours; *communal* but non-liturgical petitions, for instance in novenas, litanies, or other formal prayers outside the liturgy; and finally *personal* or individual petitions, either vocal or mental. Obviously, we do not have time or space to enter deeply into all of these, but we do need to consider the whole subject of petition as such.

I distinctly remember that, just a few years after ordination to the Catholic priesthood, I began (almost unconsciously) to downgrade the importance and usefulness of petition in favor of praise, adoration, and thanksgiving. To me, petition appeared so self-centered and self-serving that I could not help viewing it as a "child's prayer," a "second class prayer," unworthy of committed Christians. Wow! Was I wrong! By and by, a combination of reading the Scriptures and discussion with one of my fellow priests succeeded in opening my eyes to the truth. Far from being unworthy of committed Christians, prayer of petition was practiced and taught by Jesus Christ himself, e.g., in his final discourse (Jn 17) and agony in the Garden (Mk 14:36 and parallels), in the Lord's Prayer (Mt 6:9-13; Lk 11:2-4), and in his many exhortations, even pleadings, to pray regularly and perseveringly for whatever we need, both spiritual and material (Mk 14:38 and parallels; Lk 11:5-13; 18:1-8 and partial parallels).

At first, I still could not fully appreciate the reason for Jesus' insistence on prayer of petition. Did he not seem to be encouraging a "gimme" attitude in his followers? Then it finally dawned on me! True prayer of petition contains elements which are at the very heart of a proper relationship with God: humility and dependence (Mt 6:5-8), faith and confidence (Mt 7:7-11; 17:20; 21:21-22; Mk 11:22-24; Lk 17:5-6), perseverance and resignation (Lk 11:5-13; 18:1-8; Mt 26:39 ff.; Mk 14:36; Lk 22:42), as well as love and charity if we pray *for* others, even our enemies (Mt 5:44; Lk 6:28), and fraternal communion if we pray *with* others, especially our fellow Christians (Mt 18:20).

And from earliest times, *Christians* have prayed, often in common, not only for themselves, but for the whole Church and indeed the whole world, even for enemies and persecutors (e.g. Ac 1:24; 2:42; *4:24-30;* 6:6, *7:59-60; 12:5;* 13:3; 16:25; 20:36; Rm 1:9; *10:1;* 12:12; 15:30-32; Ep 6:19-20; Ph 1:3-5; 4:6; Col 1:3-4; 4:2-4; 1 Th 1:2; 5:17, 25; 2 Th 1:11; *1 Tm 2:1-4, 8;* 2 Tm 1:3; Phm 4, 22; *Heb 13:18-21;* Jm 1:5-7; *5:13-18; 1 Jn 5:14-16.* Note that more important texts are in italics.)

Putting the matter into terms of *human relationships,* what father and mother would consider themselves honored if their children never asked them for anything? Would they not rather feel unnecessary, perhaps even unwanted? And besides, the heart of our prayers of petition is and should be our desire that *God's holy will* be done, for we know that he loves us, knows all things, and can do all things. Prayer of petition is not intended to change God's mind to our way of thinking, but rather to change ours to his way of thinking. And this is precisely where the whole thorny question of God's response to our petitions enters in.

God's response to prayers of petition, which are really our response to his initiative of grace, normally consists in the granting of the petition. And that God does answer our prayers of petition is abundantly clear from Sacred Scripture as well as other sources. In the *Old Testament,* a sharp distinction is made, namely that God hears and answers the prayers of the good, but rejects those of the evil. This belief is clearly summarized in Proverbs 15:8, 29:

> The sacrifice of the wicked is an abomination to the Lord,
>> but the prayer of the upright is his delight.
> The Lord is far from the wicked,
>> but the prayer of the just he hears.

In the *New Testament,* this same thought is echoed in the Epistle of James which, in so many ways, reflects Jewish wisdom, "You ask and you do not receive because you ask wrongly, with a view to squandering what you receive on your pleasures" (Jm 4:3; cf. also 1 Jn 3:21-22). But, both in the Old and New Testaments, it is quite clear that God does hear and answer petitions made in a *spirit of faith.* For the sake of brevity, let us content ourselves with a typical statement (Mt 21:22), "You will receive all that you pray for, provided you have faith" (cf. also Mk 11:24 and Lk 11:9-13). But James 1:5 is, perhaps, the most graphic of all on this point,

If any of you is without wisdom, let him ask it from the God who gives generously and ungrudgingly to all, and it will be given him. Yet he must ask in faith, never doubting, for the doubter is like the surf tossed and driven by the wind. A man of this sort, devious and erratic in all that he does, must not expect to receive anything from the Lord.

However, there are *conditions,* not only the ones already mentioned above, namely humility, confidence, and perseverance, but also and in particular four others: (1) that we be *forgiving* toward others, "When you stand to pray, forgive anyone against whom you have a grievance, so that your heavenly Father may in turn forgive you your faults" (Mk 11:25; cf. also Mt 6:14; 18:35), (2) that we pray in the *Spirit,* "for we do not know how to pray as we ought; but the Spirit himself makes intercession for us" (Rm 8:26), (3) that we be *thankful* (1 Th 5:17-18; Ep 5:20; Col 3:17, etc.), and (4) that we ask in the name of and in union with Jesus, "I give you my assurance, whatever you ask the Father, he will give you in my name" (Jn 16:23) and "If you live in me and my words stay part of you, you may ask what you will — it will be done for you" (Jn 15:7; cf. also Jn 14:13-14). Does this exclude our directing our petitions through the intercession of *Mary and the Saints?* Not at all, if we realize that (as we have been stressing all along) we are actually directing our petitions through *Christ himself* who lives in them.

Non-biblical sources also give strong witness to the power of petition. For example, Tennyson, in his *Idylls of the King,* has the dying King Arthur beg for prayers, adding "More things are wrought by prayer than this world dreams of!"[22] And the saintly *Mahatma Gandhi* used to state categorically, "Prayer from the heart can achieve what nothing else can in the world."[23] Even in my own life and ministry, I not only can witness to the extraordinary power of prayer manifested in dramatic ways (which I do not have time and space to recount), but have also learned the basic everyday truth about the effect of petition from an important physical lesson following a back injury,

> To lift a heavy weight of care,
> We've just to bend our knees in prayer!

Nevertheless, in this matter of petition, we must be careful to *avoid extremes*. For example, there is a school of thought today, mostly among some charismatic and pentecostal Christians, that if we do not receive whatever we specifically pray for, it is clearly because we lack sufficient faith and confidence. That bothers me, as it tends to bother many sincere people, because it lays such a burden of self-accusation and guilt on them. Nor is it in keeping with the evidence of Sacred Scripture. For example, *Jesus* himself did not receive what he initially prayed for in the Garden of Gethsemane, namely that his Father would let the cup of suffering pass from him (Mk 14:35 and parallels). Was his faith too weak? And what about *Paul* and his famous "thorn in the flesh"?

> Three times I begged the Lord that this might leave me. He said to me, "My grace is enough for you, for in weakness power reaches perfection." And so I willingly boast of my weaknesses instead, that the power of Christ may rest upon me (2 Cor 12:8-9).

If God were to respond to all our petitions just as we voice them; for instance, if he kept us all in perfect health and cured all our illnesses, how would anyone ever die and "go home" to him? How indeed would anyone ever be able to suffer in union with Jesus Christ for the ongoing redemption of the world? How would St. Paul be able to say, "In my own flesh I fill up what is lacking in the suffering of Christ for the sake of his body, the Church" (Col 1:24)? No, this is clearly not in accord with the evidence of *Scripture*, with the *nature of God*, or with the real *needs of humankind*. God does answer our prayers, but not necessarily in the way in which we ask and expect. He knows our real needs far better than we do, and therefore he replies to our requests in the way which is truly better for us, whether we realize it or not. *William Culbertson* sagely advises, "Keep praying, but be thankful that God's answers are wiser than your prayer!"[24] However, the classic commentary on our prayers and God's replies is that contained in the following anonymous gem, sometimes ascribed to an unknown Confederate soldier,

> I asked God for strength that I might achieve,
> I was made weak that I might learn humbly to obey.
>
> I asked for health that I might do greater things,
> I was given infirmity that I might do better things.
>
> I asked for riches that I might be happy,
> I was given poverty that I might be wise.
>
> I asked for power that I might have the praise of men,
> I was given weakness that I might feel the need of God.
>
> I asked for all things that I might enjoy life,
> I was given life that I might enjoy all things.
>
> I got nothing that I asked for —
>   but almost everything I had hoped for.
> Almost despite myself,
>   my unspoken prayers were answered.
> I am, among all men, most richly blessed![25]

Yes, prayer of petition is important and necessary, not only at the beginning but all through our Spiritual Life, especially petition to be able to "let go the branches" of our self-love, and petition for an increase of the theological virtues and the sanctifying gifts of the Holy Spirit (Lk 11:13), particularly the gift of Wisdom (Jm 1:5). However, it is primarily in the area of so-called *"mental prayer"* that we can and should look for that communication and even communion which are so essential in our relationship, our union with God. The term itself leaves much to be desired, not only because it seems to suggest a "mental state," but also because it misplaces the emphasis on the mind rather than the heart, and especially the spirit. However, long and traditional usage, plus the problem of finding a suitable substitute, force me to employ the term, at least in quotation marks.

As is well known in spiritual circles, there are *various forms or kinds* of "mental prayer" which are used, either according to one's state in life and particular circumstances or, more often, according to one's progress in prayer. Thus, the most common form, especially for beginners, is that of *meditation*. As the word itself implies, this prayer begins in the intellect or imagination and focuses on spiritual ideas or images in an effort to arrive at understanding, appreciation, and conviction about the subject, which in turn leads to appropriate affections and resolutions. To achieve any real success in meditation, of course, certain *conditions* are necessary, the principal ones being a true and renewed *desire* for success and growth in this form of prayer, a *determination* to avoid preoccupations and distractions in favor of concentration on our prayer life, the regular use of stimulating *material* to provide "food" for our meditation, and an effective *method* for "translating" that material into useful thoughts and images leading to affections and resolutions.

As a source of stimulating *subject-matter,* I can recommend nothing better than the *Holy Bible,* God's own Word, which not only has the unction to stir the mind and the heart but also provides the shortest and straightest path to higher forms of prayer such as contemplation. George Maloney, S.J. states categorically in *The Breath of the Mystic,* "The Bible is the only place to begin, because here we meet the Living Word that has come down from the Father to teach us about Him."[26] There are various translations and arrangements of the Bible for use in meditation, but from experience I would like to suggest in particular the shorter or longer arrangements of the *Liturgy of the Hours.* Unfortunately, some have allowed the obligation of "reciting the Divine Office," which is incumbent on deacons and priests as well as some Religious, to hide the profound riches of this excellent source of meditation. I myself must confess that, during the early years of my life in the priesthood, the Office was indeed more of a special duty than a spiritual help, partly because the "Breviary" (as it was called) was anything but brief, and partly because it was all in Latin. More recently, however, the amount of daily reading has been greatly reduced and, of course, it is entirely in English. Back in the first chapter of this book, I quoted the *Constitution on Divine Revelation* of Vatican II, which in turn was quoting *St. Ambrose,* to the effect that when we pray we speak to God, and when we read the Scriptures he speaks to us.[27] In the Liturgy of the Hours, this is fulfilled in an admirable fashion. In the *Psalms,* we not only have God speaking in his Word but we also have the perfect resource for our speaking to him. And, in the *Office of Readings,* we have God speaking to us in the various other books of the Bible, plus the bonus of carefully chosen texts from the Fathers of the Church, the documents of Popes and Councils, and the lives and writings of the Saints. What a rich treasure of stimuli for meditation! But I do not mean to discourage the use of other material, even this book for example, if it helps toward effective meditation. Outstanding among such ''other material,'' especially among Catholics, are the *Stations of the Cross* and the *Rosary,* both of which are basically devotions of biblical meditation.

The question of *method* in our meditation can be a difficult one, if only because there are so many different methods and techniques being suggested. Should we even use a method at all? *St. Jane Frances de Chantal* recommends, ''The great method of prayer is to have none at all. If one can form in oneself a pure capacity for receiving the spirit of God, that will suffice for all method.''[28] And *St. Anthony of the Desert* says much the same thing centuries earlier, ''He prays best who does not know that he is praying.''[29] Excellent advice, but perhaps a little advanced for the person who may be just setting out on the road of meditation, and therefore may need some road signs to avoid going in circles or tangents and getting nowhere. To me, the most practical advice is simply this: to use *whatever method works best for oneself.* I personally admit to a preference for two in particular, which can happily be combined into one.

The first method is an ancient one called *''Lectio Divina''* or *''Divine Reading.''* It consists of reading the Bible slowly and reflectively, pausing to meditate further when a passage that is especially compelling strikes the mind and imagination or the heart. Then, when the riches are extracted from that passage (which may take some time), one continues reading and reflecting on another passage, and so on, much like the bee and the hummingbird in their quest for nectar. This has the great advantage of being directly involved with the Word of God itself and using it as the basis of dialogue with him, as well as "setting the stage" for higher (or deeper) forms of prayer, such as contemplation. The great French spiritual writer, *Louis Bouyer*, of the Congregation of the Oratory, gives an excellent description of this method in his masterful *Introduction to Spirituality*, from which I will attempt to extract the gist of his thought:

> The *Lectio Divina* is the prime concern of the reflections and counsels of ancient spiritual literature. . . . Here it appears as being the basic food (and we might almost say the basic element) of all spirituality. Such reading must always have the *Divine Word* as its object. Yet the material does not necessarily have to be provided by the very letter of Scripture; it can equally well be a liturgical text or any other spiritual text of Catholic tradition. It is essential, however, that the text proceed from Scripture and lead back to it. . . .
>
> The idea here is that of reading in order to read — not what we usually do: read in order to have read. . . . The proper sense of the Latin *meditari,* from which our word meditation is derived, is vocal rumination — obviously much better adapted to the purpose of impregnating us with what we read than is our kind of reading, the mere running of the eyes across the printed page. . .
>
> But the concentration, the special quality of attentiveness, required by *Lectio Divina* must take on a sacred motivation. What is said to us is the Word of God: in fact, it is *God Who speaks to us,* Who never ceases to speak to us in these words. . . . He is always present to address Himself to us through them, as if they were at this instant pronounced for the first time.
>
> Our reading should, then, be engaged in, pursued, and ceaselessly renewed, as an *act of faith* in this God Who speaks to

us, faith in His actual presence, faith in the present reality of what He says to us and of the way in which He says it. While reading, we should be all adherence, all abandonment, all self-donation, in this faith, to what we hear and to Him Whom we hear behind the words being read or reread. But this presupposes also that we give, together with this faith in the divine presence behind the text, *our own presence,* the presence of our whole selves, before Him Who is present to us. . . .

As the exegete *Bengel* said, ''Apply yourself wholly to the text, and apply its matter wholly to yourself.''. . . Every divine word summons us beyond both commandments and promises. And even in the commandments and the promises, something more than themselves draws us and moves us. . . . This something more, the seed of which is also at the basis of everything, is what we might call the *simple contemplation* of the divine Word, of the revelation of Himself that God is making to us herein. In every Word of God, what matters most is God's opening His own Heart to us in it, and it is by this that our heart should be touched, changed from top to bottom.[30]

The second method is that which is commonly called the *Sulpician Method,* from the Congregation of St. Sulpice, founded by *Jean Jacques Olier,* a contemporary and friend of St. Vincent de Paul in seventeenth century France. The Sulpician Method comprises the same three general points characteristic of most meditation methods (considerations, affections, resolutions), but centers them on Jesus Christ himself in these terms: *''Jesus in my eyes, Jesus in my heart, Jesus in my hands.''*[31] This simple method has the special advantage of focusing our mind and heart on Christ himself, our Model and our Master. As I mentioned above, this and the previous method can be combined very effectively by reading, for example, from the Gospels and then reflecting on that reading in the Sulpician terms of ''Jesus in my eyes (consideration and imagination), Jesus in my heart (affections), Jesus in my hands (resolutions).'' As a matter of fact, would this not help to fulfill from the very outset the dual title and focus of this work: *"To Live the Word, Inspired and Incarnate"*? (For further explanation of the Sulpician and other methods, see Cardinal Lercaro's thorough analysis in his *Methods of Mental Prayer*.[32])

How does God *respond* to us in the prayer of meditation? Normally, in quite *ordinary ways*, namely by enlightening our mind, warming our heart, and firming our will so that we may give ourselves more and more to him. Sometimes, on the other hand, he answers us in a veritable flood of thoughts and inspirations, of affections and resolutions. These occur most easily in the context of *retreats, days of recollection,* and similar times of special openness to grace. Or they may happen in connection with *special events* in our lives, whether positive such as a new role in life or ministry, or negative such as an illness or the loss of someone close. The important thing, of course, is to be attentive and ready for whatever way God chooses for his response to our meditative prayer, always remembering that our own meditation is but our response to his initiative.

Meditation, however, while it is never abandoned, constitutes but the first stage of progress in "mental prayer." *Other stages* include those of "affective prayer," the "prayer of simplicity," and contemplation. To beginners, this may all seem extremely confusing and unnecessary, but to those who have persevered in their prayer life, it is relatively simple, understandable, and completely consonant with *growth in relationships*. Let me use an *analogy* for clarification. When a young man and woman first meet and find themselves attracted to each other, they are very anxious to get to know each other better. Assuming for the sake of my analogy that they avoid the Hollywood scenario of immediate sexual relations (which enable them to know each other in only a physical, and therefore very limited and impersonal, manner), they converse a lot, perhaps they write letters to each other, they arrange to experience things together, all so that they can not only come to know each other, but also discover what they have in common and whether the initial attraction will develop into something deeper and more lasting. Little by little, the sharing of ideas and convictions leads to the sharing of affections of various kinds (admiration, respect, delight, etc.), which merge into the one affection of love. So it is in the life of active prayer. Meditation, with its emphasis on the use of the mind, leads to *affective prayer,* which uses the emotions and will more than the mind (e.g. the affections of admiration, adoration, gratitude, confidence, etc.), and gradually these multiple affections merge into the one great affection of *agápē* love. This is the *prayer of simplicity,* which some call "active or acquired contemplation."

How does God respond to us according to these two stages of "mental prayer"? Normally and very "naturally" (though we must never forget that this whole process is supernatural and due to God's initiative), by *revealing himself* more and more to us and enabling us, by grace, to *know* him more fully and therefore to *love* him more deeply. Again, as with meditation but much more profoundly and unforgettably, he sometimes fills our hearts with such overwhelming emotions of peace, joy, gratitude, humility, and particularly love, that our whole being seems in the process of being consumed and, while we tend to take fewer resolutions, our one *resolution,* that of determination to give ourselves more and more to Christ, becomes all encompassing. But with "affective prayer" and the "prayer of simplicity," we are still largely in the realm of affections, emotions, or feelings, which are superficial compared with the depths of contemplation and mysticism to which God will lead us in prayer if we follow the guidance of the Holy Spirit faithfully.

CONTEMPLATION:

Even with the "prayer of simplicity," we are not yet in the prayer of contemplation, at least not *passive contemplation*. At most, we are in the realm of "active contemplation." The difference is simply one of "our doing the work," or of "God's doing the work." This, of course, is a manner of speaking, because God is always the principal "worker," but in "active or acquired contemplation" (which St. Teresa of Avila refers to as "active recollection"), we have to make a greater effort, while in passive or infused contemplation (which is contemplation properly so-called), we are able by his overwhelming grace to "let go and let God." Some are of the opinion that "active contemplation" pertains to those who are serving God in the active life and ministry, while passive contemplation characterizes those who live a purely contemplative life. Nothing could be further from the truth!

Granted that a contemplative way of life is certainly more conducive to passive contemplation than an active life, nevertheless contemplation, including passive contemplation, is not only possible for those in active life and ministry, it is in fact the proper and destined state of prayer for Christians generally, who are called to be "other Christs" by allowing him to continue his life and ministry in and through them. When we look at Scripture and Church History, must we not say that *Jesus* himself, active as he was in his public life and ministry, was the greatest contemplative of all? And was not *Mary*, his mother and ours, "the model and archetype for all Christians who aspire to become contemplatives"?[33] *The most active Saints* in history have, I am sure, been great passive contemplatives, for instance: St. Paul, St. Augustine, St. Francis of Assisi, St. Catherine of Siena, St. Teresa of Avila, St. Ignatius Loyola, St. Vincent de Paul, to name only a few. As a matter of fact, it was precisely their life of passive contemplation that enabled them, filled with Jesus Christ, to continue his life and ministry so actively in their own time and place. For, passive contemplation is nothing more and nothing less than loving surrender to Jesus Christ and transformation into him, so that he can take full possession of our whole being: living, loving, praying, and serving in and through us! "I live, no longer I, but Christ lives in me!" (Gal 2:20, WD).

If, however, we are to progress from meditation to affective prayer, from the prayer of simplicity to contemplative prayer, we must be willing to *surrender* ourselves to Christ. This is not at all as easy as it sounds. In fact, only God can really bring it about. Our role, especially as we become accustomed to the prayer of simplicity, is primarily to allow him to do so in us, no matter how painful it may seem to be. As we have already seen when discussing the ''Virtues of Letting Go,'' we cling as desperately to our own thoughts and emotions, our own pride, pleasure, and possessions, as if our very life depended on them, when the truth is that our real life (*zoe,* eternal life, the life of Christ himself) depends on our letting them go! ''Whoever wishes to be my follower must deny his very self, take up his cross each day, and follow in my steps'' (Lk 9:23). Oh, we may with God's help be quite willing to deny ourselves, to ''let go'' in the more external and obvious ways, but the greater progress we make the more *subtle* become our ways of clinging, and only gradually can God enlighten and strengthen us to recognize them and let them go as well. We are very much like little children desperately grasping a piece of candy or a toy, and ''forcing'' God our Father to loosen the grip of our fingers, one by one, until we let go. This is the work that he does through the well-known ''dark nights'' or ''deserts.''

What in the world are these so-called *''dark nights''* or *''deserts,''* and why do they occur in our prayer life? One answer, of course, is that we may not always be faithful to God's call, so that ''dark nights'' and ''deserts'' happen to us as a means of bringing us to our senses and revealing to us that we have ''turned aside from'' our ''early love'' (Rv 2:4) and have become ''lukewarm'' (Rv 3:16.) But, assuming that this is not the case, the ''dark nights'' or ''deserts'' occur as part of the *necessary process* of drawing us to higher or deeper levels of prayer and relationship with God.

The expressions ''dark nights''and ''deserts'' are actually two analogous attempts to describe the very *same thing,* the difference being that the term ''nights'' focuses on the intellect's state of ''unknowing,'' while that of ''deserts'' focuses on the will's state of ''unfeeling'' or apparent ''unloving.'' As I mentioned in the previous chapter when discussing faith,

Growth comes, not so much through the bright light of special insights and experiences, as through the dark light of the dark nights through which we must pass on our journey to union with God . . . , for one kind of light must be extinguished before we can see by another. Except at night and away from city lights, we cannot observe the beauty of the stars.

Since all of this is analogous terminology, let me use *other analogies* in an attempt to describe the reality involved. If we enter a dark room and cannot find the light switch, we see at first nothing at all but darkness. However, if we wait and allow our eyes to adjust themselves to the darkness, then little by little we become aware of many if not most of the objects in the room. Or, if we find ourselves in a desert, at first we tend to see nothing at all but sandy waste, but if we are patient and let the desert "grow on us," we will discover that it is very much alive, even fertile, in flora and fauna which at first had completely escaped our notice. Finally, to borrow an analogy from current astronomy, "dark nights" are somewhat like the "black holes" of the universe, through which (according to some theories) one can pass into another universe. So it is with the "dark nights." They enable us to pass from one spiritual "universe" to another in our journey to complete and lasting union with the cosmic Christ, the very Lord of the Universe (Jn 1:3; Col 1:15-16; Heb 1:1-4).

What is important for us is *not to cling* to the "branch" of any particular state or phase of prayer along the way, but rather to have the attitude of the "Athletic Apostle," St. Paul:

Those things I used to consider gain I have now reappraised as loss in the *light of Christ*. . . . For his sake I have forfeited everything; I have accounted all else rubbish so that Christ may be my wealth and *I may be in him*. . . . I wish to *know Christ* and the power flowing from his resurrection; likewise to know how to share in his sufferings by being formed into the pattern of his *death*. Thus do I hope that I may arrive at *resurrection* from the dead.

It is not that I have reached it yet, or have already finished my course; but I am racing to grasp the prize if possible, since I have been *grasped by Christ Jesus*. I do not think of myself as having reached the finish line. I give no thought to what lies *behind* but push on to what is *ahead*. My entire attention is on the finish line as I run toward the prize to which God calls me — *life on high in Christ Jesus!* (Ph 3:7-14).

In our progress in prayer and in our Spiritual Life generally, we can expect to encounter many "dark nights" and "deserts." However, from time immemorial, particularly from that of *Evagrius Ponticus* in the fourth century and *Pseudo-Dionysius* in the sixth century, the Spiritual Life came to be envisioned in three ways, ages, or stages. Later on, *St. Teresa of Avila* and especially *St. John of the Cross* in the sixteenth century came to speak of one or two "dark nights" or "deserts." Then, in more modern times, mystical theologians such as *Reginald Garrigou-Lagrange* and *Eugene Boylan, Louis Bouyer* and *Thomas Merton,* to mention only a few, have attempted with some success to coordinate the "dark nights" or "deserts" with the three ages or stages.[34] Unfortunately, there is no absolute agreement in this correlation. In my own treatment of this important subject, I will try to provide an integrated overview based on the mystical writings of others as well as my own experience and reflections on Sacred Scripture. If it is faulty or confusing, as it may well be, I ask the reader's patience and kindness in advance.

The three stages, as I prefer to call them, are commonly known as the purgative, illuminative, and unitive ways. In the *purgative* way, according to the name itself, we are primarily concerned with purifying ourselves from sin and major attachments (Ps 51:4, 9, 12; 2 Cor 7:1; 1 Jn 3:3), while growing in virtues and in mental prayer from meditation through affective prayer to the prayer of simplicity. This is all done through grace, of course, but with our active cooperation. Then suddenly or, more often, gradually we find that we can no longer meditate, or conjure up affections, or even center our one great affection of love on Christ. We are in the *"dark night of the senses"* which, if we remain faithful to Christ in prayer, will draw us away from dependence on our reasoning and feelings to a deeper way of knowing and loving Christ. As in the analogy of the dark room, we gradually become aware of the presence, the knowledge, the love of Christ, in a newer, calmer, more profound, and more lasting manner.

We are now in the so-called *illuminative way,* which is the first stage of passive contemplation and in which we come to know Christ, not discursively but intuitively, and all things and persons intuitively in relation to Christ. It is *another whole universe,* possibly best described by St. Paul in that magnificent section (1 Cor 2:6-16), which I will not repeat again because I have already quoted it twice. According to St. John of the Cross in *The Dark Night of the Soul,* "Contemplation is nothing else but a secret, peaceful, and loving infusion of God, which, if admitted, will set the soul on fire with the Spirit of Love."[35] In this stage, the *seven gifts of the Holy Spirit,* which I like to call "sanctifying" to distinguish them from the charismatic gifts, become more and more operative within us. As is clear from Scripture and as I indicate in my *New Catholic Encyclopedia* article on *Charism in the Bible,*[36] the so-called charismatic gifts do not make us any holier, but rather are "given for the common good" (1 Cor 12:7), "to build up the body of Christ," the Church (Ep 4:12), whereas the sevenfold gifts are marvelously transforming and sanctifying. In fact, they are a sharing in the very *gifts of Christ* himself, as foretold in Isaiah 11:1-3,

> A shoot shall sprout from the stump of Jesse,
>   and from his roots a bud shall blossom.
> The spirit of the Lord shall rest upon him:
>   a spirit of *wisdom* and *understanding,*
> A spirit of *counsel* and of *strength,*
>   a spirit of *knowledge* and of *fear of the Lord,*
>   and his delight shall be the *fear of the Lord.*
> (N.B. The first "fear" became *"piety"* in the Septuagint.)

Whereas, in the purgative way, we had to work hard, not only to remove vices but to develop the three theological and the moral virtues, now we can do much more and do it more easily through the use of the sanctifying gifts. It is like the difference between rowing and sailing, between the regular gears of a car and overdrive, between driving and flying. And, in addition, the *fruits of the Spirit* become more evident, as Paul lists them, at least partially, in Galatians 5:22-23, WD: "charity, joy, peace, patience, kindness, generosity, faith, mildness, and chastity." But we are not yet in the full state of union with Christ, before which we must experience another "dark night" or "desert."

Many, after St. John of the Cross, call this second "desert" the "dark night of the spirit" which unites with the prior "dark night of the senses" to form the one "dark night of the soul." I personally prefer to distinguish three "dark nights," namely those "of the senses, of the soul, and of the spirit." The reason for my threefold division of "dark nights" is that it corresponds more completely with the biblical *three-dimensional description of human nature* which we examined from Genesis 2:7 in Chapter Two: flesh, person, and spirit. In the *purgative* way, we are engaged in putting aside the life of the flesh (Ps 51; Gal 5:16-21), then through the "dark night of the senses" we enter upon the *illuminative* way (Ps 36:10; Jn 8:12; 14:21; 1Jn 1:5, 7), in which our mind is enlightened and our will enflamed by grace and the gifts to experience God in ways that go far beyond our mere human capacity and energy, even strengthened by grace.

But to enter into the third and final stage, the *unitive* way, we must undergo another dark night or desert, the "dark night of the soul," in which even our intuitive knowledge and love of Christ seem to disappear and become lost. Faith, hope, love, and patience, however, will see us through this night and into the incredible stage of *transforming union,* where our primary occupation is neither with purification from vices and practice of virtues together with active growth in prayer as in the purgative way, nor with passive enlightening of our intellect and inflaming of our will as in the illuminative way, but with the purest, calmest, quietest awareness of being one with Christ and he with us, "My beloved to me and I to him!" (Sg 2:16, WD; Jn 14:21, 23). In this stage, he takes full possession of our whole existence and, through his Holy Spirit, transforms us more and more into himself. Being ever more one with him, we experience him not only as our "tremendous *Lover*" and spiritual *Spouse* (Rm 7:4; 1 Cor 6:17) but even as our true *"identity,"* our very *"self"* (Rm 8:29; 2 Cor 3:18), and we experience his Father as *our own Father* or "Daddy" (*Abba*, Mk 14:36; Gal 4:6; Rm 8:14-17), and his Spirit as *our own Spirit* (Jn 4:23-24; 14:16-17, 26; Rm 5:5; 8:9-11, 14-17, 26-27).

This is the *unitive* way, but it is still life in this "earthly tent" (2 Cor 5:1) and, to be perfectly ready for immediate entry into Heaven, where "we shall be like him for we shall see him as he is" (1 Jn 3:2), we may need one final "dark night" or "desert," that *of the spirit,* when even this beautiful and rarified knowledge and love of God seem to be taken away and we have to cling to God with the highest point of our spirit. This, to me, was the state of Jesus himself on the cross when he cried out from the depths of his being, "My God, my God, why have you forsaken me?" (Ps 22:2; Mk 15:34; Mt 27:46). Not that he needed purification but, while allowing himself to experience the feeling of total abandonment by his heavenly Father, he made the ultimate act of love, "Father, into your hands I commend my spirit!" (Lk 23:46).

For the sake of clarity, I like to describe our prayer during the three stages of the Spiritual Life as follows. In the *purgative* way, we are busy *speaking* to and with God in meditation, affective prayer, and the prayer of simplicity. After the "dark night of the senses," we enter the *illuminative* way, in which we are mostly *listening* to God and perceiving him intuitively, especially with the help of the sanctifying Gifts of the Spirit. Then, through the "dark night of the soul," we reach the *unitive* way, where our prayer consists largely of just *being*: being with, being one with, being transformed into Christ in the highest (or deepest) level of our nature, that of spirit, where alone we can be fully united with God.

Finally, before proceeding to examine mysticism, I feel that I need to make some *additional remarks* which I believe are of some importance:

(1) The traditional three stages of the Spiritual Life are only *approximations*; that is, they are not so clear-cut and naturally exclusive that there is no *overlapping* among them and no *return* (at least temporarily) to former stages for further purification and illumination. As Mark Link, S.J. expresses it so well in *Still Point,* "Prayer normally takes three forms: meditation, contemplation, and direct address. Often these three forms occur intertwined in one and the same prayer — like strands of wire coiled together in one and the same cable."[37]

(2) The "dark nights" or "deserts" occur in the Spiritual Life of different people according to their individual *life situation*: for those living a purely contemplative life, entirely or almost entirely in the area of their prayer life; for those living an active or an active-contemplative life, through a combination of prayer life and exterior circumstances, for example the trauma of being misinterpreted, misunderstood, perhaps even judged and condemned by one's spouse, relatives, friends, community, and especially religious or ecclesial superiors. For both, of course, physical, emotional, or mental trauma may be closely connected with a "dark night" or "desert."

(3) The stages of illumination and union are not at all inimical to *activity*; but on occasion activity may have to give way to solitude and silence, so that it may continue and even increase, but on a different and more perfect level. We will have more to say about this in the following section, as we consider the idea of Mysticism.

(4) One of the truths most strongly insisted upon by *St. Teresa of Avila* in her *Autobiography*[38] (because it was explicitly taught her in a vision) is that we cannot arrive at contemplation of and union with the Father or the Holy Trinity except through the sacred *humanity of*

Jesus Christ, who clearly tells us, "I am the way, the truth, and the life; no one comes to the Father but through me" (Jn 14:6).

(5)   Finally and most importantly, it is imperative that we use the foregoing, *not as a yardstick* to measure our progress, but simply as a general aid to encourage and guide us. Contemplation must always be *centered on Christ,* not on ourselves! "All of us, gazing on the Lord's glory with unveiled faces, are being transformed from glory to glory into his very image by the Lord who is the Spirit" (2 Cor 3:18).

MYSTICISM:

One of the most unforgettable views in all of Israel is that of *Mt. Tabor,* the traditional site of the *transfiguration* of Jesus before the eyes of Peter, James, and John (Mt 17:1-8; Mk 9:2-8; Lk 9:28-36; cf. also Jn 12:27-32; 2 P 1:16-18; Rv 1:12-16). The mountain itself is quite impressive, rising as it does in a lofty, perfect dome above the great Valley of Esdraelon in Galilee. But if we have the opportunity of ascending the mountain and visiting the beautiful basilica of the transfiguration, especially when the evening sun is shining through the front door onto the great golden mosaic above the high altar, the actual transfiguration event appears to be unfolding once again, right before our startled eyes. The effect is overwhelming, and it is easy for us to identify with the stunned reaction of the three Apostles and the stammering declaration of Peter, "Lord ["Rabbi" in Mark, "Master" in Luke], it is good for us to be here!" (Mt 17:4, WD).

The moving quotation from St. Paul, with which we closed the preceding segment on contemplation, always reminds me of Mt. Tabor and the transfiguration, "All of us, gazing on the Lord's *glory* with *unveiled* faces, are being *transformed* from glory to glory into his very image by the Lord who is the Spirit" (2 Cor 3:18). Whether Paul had the transfiguration in mind or not, it is easy to notice several connections. First, it refers to the Lord's *glory,* which of course shone forth in his transfiguration as a preview of the lasting glory of his coming resurrection. Secondly, it highlights *transformation,* which of itself recalls Jesus' own transfiguration. Thirdly, it is in contrast with the "veiled" *Moses* at Mt. Sinai (Ex 34:29-35; 2 Cor 3:7-17) who, with *Elijah,* appears with Jesus on Mt. Tabor.

To the majority of interpreters, Moses and Elijah represent the Law and the Prophets or the mediation and preservation of the Covenant and Law, above all of which Jesus is exalted by the Father, "This is my beloved Son, with whom I am well pleased; *listen to him!"* (Mt 17:5, RSV). To me, however, they recall in addition the mystical experiences of God enjoyed by those two great Old Testament figures at Mt. Sinai or Horeb (Ex 33:18-23 and 1 K 19:11-13). These mystical experiences of Moses and Elijah, together with the transfiguration experience of the three Apostles and, of course the post-resurrection appearances of the risen Christ (including Paul's conversion in Acts 9:3-6) enable us to form some idea of mysticism itself, at least in the sense of a *personal, overwhelming encounter with God,* particularly in the person of the *risen Christ.* But here we must exercise a great deal of caution, for two reasons: (1) We cannot remain on Mt. Sinai (Horeb) or Mt. Tabor any more than could Moses, Elijah, the three Apostles, and Jesus himself, because experiences of this kind are rare and temporary, and (2) Mystical phenomena of this kind, while accorded to some and useful to all at least as symbols, are neither usual nor necessary.

In the minds of most people, the word *mysticism* conjures up all kinds of *strange ideas,* e.g. ideas of ecstasies, visions, divine locutions, etc. This is very unfortunate because, in a profound sense, *we are all called to be mystics.* What? Yes, we are all called and predestined, as Paul expresses it in Romans 8:29, RSV, "to be conformed to the image of his [God's] Son," and the only way in which this can transpire is through our letting God accomplish it by his Holy Spirit transforming us into Christ. This "letting go and letting God" transform us into Christ is the *essence of mysticism.* All the so-called mystical phenomena mentioned above and elsewhere are only so many experiences which may or may not occur. They are not at all essential or even integral to true mysticism. Father Louis Bouyer, in his *Introduction to Spirituality*, states categorically,

> Christian mysticism is something entirely different from an extraordinary psychological experience. Neither visions, nor ecstasies, nor raptures, nor anything of the kind constitute an integral part of this mysticism. We should not even think that they are its necessary accompaniments. It is true that they may appear in the course of a Christian mystical life. But, in this case, they should be recognized as being nothing other and nothing more than repercussions of an experience that transcends us: more or less inharmonious reactions of human weakness under the pressure of a grace to which it is not yet fully adapted.

> Without completely rejecting the possibility that visions or interior words may play a providential role in the progress of certain souls . . ., the greatest mystical writers, such as St. Teresa and St. John of the Cross, are unanimous in stating that such experiences betoken a state in the mystical life which is only *embryonic*. In fact, the masters of mysticism tell us, as a general rule, nothing of the sort any longer takes place in the "spiritual marriage," on the earthly heights of union with God.[39]

And, along the same lines, Thomas Merton is just as clear and straightforward in *The Living Bread* when he states,

> The simplicity of the Gospels, if kept in mind, makes false mysticism impossible. Christ has delivered us forever from the esoteric and the strange. He has brought the light of God to our own level to transfigure our ordinary existence.[40]

What, then, is the relationship of mysticism to prayer and to asceticism? Very often, *prayer* (especially contemplative prayer) is identified with mysticism. This is not quite accurate. Granted that it is primarily through prayer, and mainly contemplative prayer, that we can become mystics, the meaning of mysticism goes beyond that of prayer and constitutes a whole way of life, the *mystical life*. Perhaps the only way in which prayer and mysticism can be identified coextensively is in the sense that, in the illuminative and still more in the unitive way, our prayer and our life become so interwoven as to be virtually indistinguishable, thus fulfilling St. Paul's directive to "pray without pause" (1 Th 5:17, WD). In other words, contemplation refers to prayer; mysticism refers to every facet of life, but in practice the two are virtually one. The relationship of mysticism to asceticism is much easier to delineate. *Asceticism* constitutes that active training or purification that is necessary to enter into and live a mystical life (1 Cor 9:27; Rm 8:13; 1 Tm 4:7-8, etc.), while mysticism refers to what God alone can do spiritually in us with our cooperation. Briefly put, asceticism is our work; mysticism is God's work in us.

What, therefore, is mysticism or the mystical life in itself? It is, above all, the day-by-day living in close union with Christ, attentive to his abiding presence, surrendered to his possessing love, and being transformed into him by the Holy Spirit. In the words of *St. Irenaeus,* "The Spirit comes to seize us and give us to the Son and the Son gives us to the Father."⁴¹ What an "indescribable gift!" (2 Cor 9:15). Mysticism is indeed a "buried treasure" (Mt 13:44), a "pearl of great price" (Mt 13:46), a "hundredfold" even in this life (Mk 10:30), which is well worth all the sacrifices, all the "dark nights" or "deserts" that we may have to endure.

Like love itself, which is its core, mysticism is a "many splendored thing" that *varies* from time to time according to the different ways in which we experience God: for example, as a loving *Father* (Mt 11:25-27; Mk 14:36; Lk 10:21-22; Jn 5:16-47, etc.; Gal 4:6; Rm 8:15, etc.), as a beloved *Spouse* (Song of Songs; Rm 7:4; 1 Cor 6:17; Ep 5:22 ff.), as a faithful *Friend* (Lk 10:38-42; Jn 11:3-5; 15:15), as a patient *Teacher* (Mt 11:1; 23:8, 10; Mk 4:1-2; 6:2, 34; 8:31; Jn 1:38; 3:2; 13:13; Ac 1:1), as the *Lord of the Universe* (Jn

1:1-3; 20:28; Ph 2:9-11; Col 1:15-20; Ep 1:20-23; Heb 1:1-4; Rv 1:5, 8; 17:14; 19:16), as the *indwelling Spirit* (Jn 14:16-17, 26; 15:26; 16:13-14; Ac 2:4, 33, 38 ff.; Rm 5:5; 8:9, 14-16, 26-27; 1 Cor 3:16-17; 6:19, etc.). If "variety is the spice of (natural) life," how much more is it the spice of supernatural life, not by our own initiative but by that of God. In order, however, to be fine-tuned to this ever changing yet always the same intimate relationship with our God, we need to observe the necessary *preconditions* and *conditions* of a healthy prayer life, which can also be called the normal *characteristics* of the mystical life.

The principal *preconditions* are usually listed as two, namely *solitude* and *silence,* to which I would like to add a third, *slowness.* Each of these is vitally important in the Spiritual, and especially the mystical, Life. But we must understand them properly. For example, *solitude* is not at all the same as isolation. In isolation, we cut ourselves off from everyone and are wrapped up within ourselves like an autistic child, whereas in solitude we step aside from the busy world to commune with God, with ourselves, with other "pilgrims," so that we can return actually or figuratively to win the world for God. Joseph Roux, in his *Meditations of a Parish Priest,* observes that "Solitude vivifies; isolation kills!"[42]

But solitude is *not at all easy* for us. The fear of being alone is one of life's greatest anxieties, particularly in the Western World. Why? Perhaps because, in our technological age, we feel depersonalized and, if we find ourselves all alone, we tend to draw the conclusion in our insecurity that we are neglected and rejected, and therefore we must be unattractive and unlovable. Nonsense! The solution, especially in our technological society, is to deliberately *choose* solitude, where we will find God (and ourselves) far more easily than when we are lost in a crowd. W.S. Landor, in his *Imaginary Conversations,* calls solitude "the audience chamber of God."[43] And the great French playwright, Eugene Ionesco, in his own *Conversations,* declares:

Life has to be thoroughly impregnated with solitude in order to be livable. Everyone needs a *personal space* to live in. . . . My characters are simply people who don't know how to be alone, . . . and this is why they *are* alone — alone in a different way. . . . Look at crowds, they're depersonalized, people don't have faces in a crowd . . . or if they have a face, it's a collective face and monstrous. . . Every one has the same face in a crowd, whether it is uniform or formless.[44]

As always, the *Sacred Scriptures* provide us with both example and instruction regarding solitude. In the *Old Testament,* all the great figures: patriarchs and prophets, mediators, judges, and kings, normally receive their call from God when they are alone. And the Psalmist (55:7) cries out, "Had I but wings like a dove, I would fly away and be at rest!" The *New Testament* not only continues the tradition but perfects it. *John the Baptist* prepares for his heralding mission by living "in the desert until the day when he made his public appearance in Israel" (Lk 1:80). *Jesus,* like Moses of old (Ex 24:18), spends forty days and forty nights (on Mt. Qarantal?) alone (Mt 4:1-2; Mk 1:12-13; Lk 4:1-2), and moreover (as we have already seen under PRAYER) he steals away to pray alone at every opportunity, though he is never alone because the Father is always with him (Jn 8:16; 16:32). In fact, he also invites his disciples to do the same, "Come by yourselves to an out-of-the-way place and rest a little" (Mk 6:31). *Mary* is alone when she receives the annunciation of the Messiah (Lk 1:26 ff.). *Peter* is alone on a rooftop when he receives the threefold vision (Ac 10:9-23), and *Paul,* though not alone at the time of his encounter with Christ, does go off into desert solitude immediately after his reception into the Church (Gal 1:16-17).

And that same tradition of solitude has remained strong throughout the history of the Church, from the Fathers of the Desert, through the medieval monks and solitaries such as *St. Bernard* ("One is never less alone than when alone!")[45] and *St. Catherine of Siena* (with her interior cell of solitude),[46] to the great Doctors of Prayer, Sts. Teresa of Avila and John of the Cross, and up to our own time, when there is an impressive number of monasteries and hermitages flourishing all over the world, and notably in the United States. One of the leaders in the proliferation of monasticism in America, *Thomas Merton,* provides us in his *New Seeds of Contemplation* with a well-balanced view of solitude that will serve admirably as our conclusion to this brief treatment of the subject,

> The only justification for a life of deliberate solitude is the conviction that it will help you to love not only God but also other men. Otherwise, if you go into the desert merely to get away from crowds of people you dislike, you will not find peace or solitude either, you will only isolate yourself with a tribe of devils. Go into the desert not to escape other men but in order to find them in God. . . . There is no true solitude except interior solitude.[47]

What we have said about solitude is also largely applicable to the *second precondition, silence,* for presumably where there is solitude there is also silence. But this is not usually true of aloneness; in fact, the tendency in our culture is to do all we can to avoid silence lest we feel all alone in our aloneness. For example, when we are driving a car alone, we absolutely *must* have the radio on, ostensibly to catch the news or to soothe our nerves in traffic. Are we not really avoiding the feeling of being all alone? When we are in our house or room alone, we *must* play the radio, stereo, or television. Are we not missing a golden opportunity to be alone with God? Perhaps this tendency to avoid solitude and silence is most marked in the younger generation, who feel impelled to play their music so loud that some degree of deafness has become epidemic among them. Yet silence is every bit as important for a healthy prayer life as is solitude, perhaps even more so. We may not often have physical solitude, but if we can achieve *inner silence,* then we can be at peace and open to God. Unfortunately, we complain that God never speaks to us, when in fact we are rarely quiet enough to listen to him when he does. "Be still, and know that I am God!" (Ps 46:10, RSV).

Here again, however, we must be clear about the *meaning* of this silence. It is certainly not just the absence of noise, though that would be a blessed relief. No, it is above all the kind of purified silence that George Maloney, S.J. speaks of in *The Breath of the Mystic* when he says of the Desert Fathers, "They knew that, unless the heart is silenced from the demands of self-love, God could not communicate His living Word to them."[48] It is the spiritual silence of which the *Imitation of Christ* speaks when it declares, "In silence and quiet, the devout soul goes forward and learns the hidden things of Scripture."[49] It is the mystical silence referred to by *St. John of the Cross* when he asserts, "The Father uttered one Word; that Word is the Son, and he utters him forever in everlasting silence; and in silence the soul has to hear it."[50]

The allusion in this last quotation is, of course, to the beautiful *Book of Wisdom,* where (in a passage adapted to the Church's liturgy on Christmas Day) we read, "When peaceful silence lay over all, and the night had run the half of her swift course, down from the heavens, from the royal throne, leapt your all-powerful Word . . ." (Ws 18:14-15, JB). But this is only one of many passages in *Scripture* which make special note of silence, e.g., the silence of *Job* (Jb 40:4-5), of the *Psalmist* (Ps 39:2-3, 10), of the suffering *Servant of Yahweh* (Is 53:7), of *Ezekiel* (Ezk 3:26), of *Jesus* during his Passion (Mt 26:63; 27:12-14; Mk 14:61; 15:5; Lk 23:9; Jn 19:9; 1 P 2:21-23), of the Book of *Revelation* (Rv 8:1). And, in the statements of some of our *ancient and modern sages* about silence, we can find teaching that, understood in a spiritual sense, is absolutely inspiring, e.g., the Greek poet and playwright *Menander,* "In silence God brings all things to pass,"[51] *William Penn* to his children, "True silence is the rest of the mind; and it is to the spirit what sleep is to the body: nourishment and refreshment,"[52] and finally Thomas Carlyle in *Sartor Resartus,* "Speech is of time, silence is of eternity!"[53]

This brings us, then, to the *third precondition* of the Spiritual, and especially the mystical, Life: *slowness*. Until modern times, slowness was simply not a consideration with regard to prayer life, except in the sense of patient waiting on God to transform us in his own way and time. Sloth was a greater concern than speed (Pr 6:6-11; 24:30-34; 2 Th 3:6-13). In fact, as we all know, *sloth* is listed among the "capital sins." Today, however, *speed* has become such an obsession, particularly in the Western World, that a reminder about slowness is an absolute must. We have *instant everything*: instant communication and transportation, instant coffee and cooking, instant copying and computing, even "fast-speak" commercials! How can God possibly accomplish anything in us when we are always in such a hurry to be somewhere else or to do something else? No wonder we are so subject to stress burnout! It is well said that, "If we are too busy to pray, we are too busy, period!"

Even in our natural life, the futurist Alvin Toffler in his landmark book, *Future Shock*,[54] warns that everything is accelerating so rapidly that our human system, which is not made for such speed, is just not able to adjust, with the direst emotional, mental, and even physical, consequences. Hence, we need "future shock absorbers" including oases of rest which enable us to slow down and relax, so that we can enjoy life rather than have the "rat race" of a pseudo-life destroy us. Applying the same ideas to the life of the Spirit, *Andrew Greeley* observes that, "Contemplation is a casualty of the American way of life. We simply do not have time for it. We read poetry as we would a detective story. . . . We visit art museums as we would tour the Grand Canyon."[55] But most beautifully of all, the beloved *Richard Cardinal Cushing* of blessed memory has a touching prayer called "Slow Me Down, Lord,"[56] which we might well ponder when the pace of our lives becomes dangerously fast:

> Give me, amid the confusion of the day,
> the calmness of the everlasting hills.
> Break the tensions

of my nerves and muscles with the soothing music
of the singing streams that live in my memory.
Help me to know the magical,
restoring power of sleep.
Teach me the art of taking minute vacations —
of slowing down to look at a flower,
to chat with a friend, to pat a dog,
to read a few lines from a good book.

Remind me each day
of the fable of the hare and the tortoise,
that I may know
that the race is not always to the swift —
there is more to life than increasing its speed.
Let me look upward
into the branches of the towering oak and know
that it grew great and strong
because it grew slowly and well.

Slow me down, Lord, and inspire me to send
my roots deep into the soil of life's enduring values
that I may grow toward the stars of my greater destiny.

A common saying these days is, *"Speed kills!"* Of course, the reference is to stimulating drugs or the danger of fast and reckless driving, but to me there is a deeper meaning: *speed kills the spirit!* Granted that *time* is one of God's greatest gifts and therefore we should "make the most" of this precious commodity (Ep 5:16, RSV), the real value of time lies in what we do with it. If we hurry up in order to get our work done, and then have to spend all our spare time at the health club or watching television to overcome stress, what have we accomplished? Where is our time for God? Or for ourselves? I have always loved Jesus' tiny parable (Mk 4:26-29) about the seed growing of itself, because it reminds us so clearly that we can produce a harvest for God (or rather he for us) only through patience and moderation. Is this not also the meaning of Luke 8:15, RSV, "fruit with patience," as well as James 5:7-8?

Look at the life of *Jesus* himself. Can we imagine that anyone in our days who desires to change the world would wait until he was "about thirty years of age" (Lk 3:23)? Today, one is considered "over the hill" at thirty! In those times and especially in "God's time," one was not considered mature and adult until he was at least thirty. But need we look any further than at *Salvation History* itself? Why did God wait so many centuries before sending the Redeemer? And why is he waiting so long for that Redeemer to return? Because "God is love" (1 Jn 4:8, 16), and "love is patient" (1 Cor 13:4). In his universe, which is some twenty billion years old and will last who knows how many more billions of years, what are a few centuries? As we read in 2 Peter 3:8-9 (alluding to Ps 90:4),

> In the Lord's eyes, one day is as a thousand years and a thousand years are as a day. The Lord does not delay in keeping his promise — though some consider it "delay." Rather, he shows you generous patience, since he wants none to perish but all to come to repentance.

Having looked briefly at the three preconditions of solitude, silence, and slowness, let us now (also briefly) consider the *conditions* of the Spiritual, and especially the mystical, Life. These could be listed as many, but I would like to single out just two, namely *recollection* and *direction*. Recollection, of course, embraces several things, but two in particular: *custody of the heart* in not allowing free rein to our runaway steeds of curiosity and imagination, and *attention to the presence of God* in all its manifestations inside and outside of ourselves: his presence in the created universe, especially in nature all around us, his presence in all the events of history and our own experience, his presence in all humankind, his presence in his Church, his presence in his Inspired Word, his presence in his Incarnate Word (especially in the Church, the Scriptures, and the Eucharist) and, in a special way, his presence by grace and mystical awareness with us and within us.

Scripture is replete with references to the presence of God and to the need of living in his presence (e.g. Gn 17:1; Pss 116:9; 139:7; Jn 14:22; Rv 3:20). And, to remind us of God's presence in *nature* as well as in *people*, we have not only such graphic depictions as found in *Psalms 19, 29 and 104,* but also the statements of some of our most sensitive writers, e.g., Walt Whitman in his *Song of Myself,*[57]

> In the faces of men and women I see God,
>   and in my own face in the glass,
> I find letters from God dropt in the street,
>   and every one is signed by God's name,
> And I leave them where they are,
>   for I know that wheresoe'er I go,
> Others will punctually come for ever and ever.

And, somewhat more briefly but just as richly, *Abraham Heschel,* "To meet a human being is an opportunity to sense the image of God, the presence of God."[58] Further, *Teilhard de Chardin* penetrates the mystery of nature itself, "Jesus Christ is shining diaphanously through the whole world for those who have the eyes to see!"[59] Did Teilhard, perhaps, derive his vision of creation evolving toward an "omega point" of "Christification," not so much from science as from Romans 8:19, 21, "The whole created world eagerly awaits the revelation of the sons of God . . . because the world itself will be freed from its slavery to corruption and share in the glorious freedom of the children of God"?

But to me the symbol that provides the most meaningful common denominator for all the manifestations of God's presence is that of his *temple.* In *Sacred Scripture,* all of creation, especially the heavens, is the temple of God and sings his praises (Pss 11:4; 18:7; 29:9; Rv 11:19). In the *Old Testament,* Yahweh manifests his presence in a particular though symbolic way in the desert tabernacle or tent (Ex 40:34-38) and in the Jerusalem temple (1 K 8:10-13; Is 6:1-4, etc.). In the *New Testament,* Jesus himself is the "House of God" (Hebrew *Bethel,* Gn 28:10-19; Jn 1:51), the "Holy Place" (Greek, *to hágion,* Ex 26:33; Lk 1:35; Heb 9:12), the living "Temple of God" (Jn

2:18-22; Rv 21:22). And he continues his presence in the *Church at large,* which is his temple (Mt 28:20; Jn 15:1-8; Ac 9:5; Ep 2:19-22; 1 P 2:5; Rv 1:12-16; 21:1-3), in the local church or congregation (Mt 18:19-20; 1 Cor 3:16-17; 2 Cor 11:2), and in each of us humans (Mt 25:31-46), especially his *followers* (Jn 14:22; 1 Cor 6:17-20; 2 Cor 6:14-16).

When, in his holy zeal, he cleanses the temple at Jerusalem, declaring: "My house is meant for a house of prayer, but you have made it a den of thieves!" (Lk 19:46 and parallels; cf. Is 56:7; Jr 7:11), he is speaking not only to the Jews of his time, but to all of us. As his temple, we are to see to it that "nothing profane shall enter it" (Rv 21:27), hence the need of custody of the senses and of the heart. As his temple, we are to be houses of prayer, especially of praise, thanksgiving, and adoration; hence our need of attending to his presence and of becoming (with *Blessed Elizabeth of the Trinity, O.C.D.*) "the praise of his glory"[60] (Ep 1:6, 12, 14). As a matter of fact, the Church itself reminds us of this whenever she celebrates a feast or memorial of the *dedication of a church,*[61] for example one of the four great basilicas in Rome or a local church anywhere in the world. In the liturgy for such a dedication, what is really being celebrated is the temple which we are individually and communally, as is clear from the liturgical prayers.

The Saints, particularly such teachers of prayer as *St. Teresa of Avila* and *St. John of the Cross,* have always been strong in their recommendation of *constant recollection* or attention to God, so far as possible, regardless of our occupation. The benefits of such recollection are incalculable. Not only can we continue to live spiritually for a time on recollection alone in the event that charity or some other duty forces us to "leave God for God,"[62] in St. Vincent de Paul's expression, but also such recollection enables our regular prayer times to be both possible and fruitful. In this regard, Thomas Merton in his *New Seeds of Contemplation* wisely remarks,

People who only know how to think about God during certain

fixed periods of the day will never get very far in the Spiritual Life. In fact, they will not even think of Him in the moments they have religiously marked off for "mental prayer."[63]

Of course, there will be a marked *difference* in our recollection, depending on what phase of prayer life we are in: meditation, or affective prayer, or prayer of simplicity, or passive contemplation. Obviously, recollection in the earlier phases requires more effort on our part, while it is almost connatural to us if we are in the stage of passive contemplation or mysticism. A tremendous help in this regard is the possibility of regular visits with *Jesus in the Blessed Sacrament,* for example in the chapels of monasteries, seminaries, or houses of religious, or in a quiet parish church, because the very physical habit of stopping in for a visit whenever possible goes a long way toward establishing and maintaining a healthy habit of recollection through-out the entire day. But let us never forget *St. Vincent's* assurance to *St. Louise,* his partner in charity, that "doing the Will of God is more important than feeling his Presence!"[64]

Under the heading of *direction,* I would like to stress two things in particular: the need of *union with the Church* and the need of *personal spiritual direction.* Both are necessary, particularly when we give ourselves wholeheartedly to the interior life, the life of prayer. It is so easy to become subjective, to mistake our own imaginations for the operations of the Holy Spirit, our own en-thusiasms (in Greek, literally "God within") for the love of Christ impelling us (2 Cor 5:14), our own natural energy for "that energy of his which is so powerful a force" (Col 1:29). As Robert Hugh Benson points out in his spiritual classic, *The Friendship of Christ* (now sadly out of print),

Impulses and desires rise within the soul, which seem to bear every mark of a Divine origin; it is only when they are obeyed or gratified that we discover that often, after all, they have risen from self — from association, or memory, or education, or even from hidden pride and self-interest — and lead to spiritual disaster. It needs a very pure intention as well as great spiritual discernment always to recognize the Divine Voice; always to penetrate the disguise of one who, in the higher stages of spiritual progress, so often presents himself as an "Angel of Light" (2 Cor 11:14). . . . There is no obstinacy like religious obstinacy; for the spiritual man encourages himself in his wrong course, by a conviction that he is following Divine guidance. He is not, to his own knowledge, willful or perverse; on the contrary, he is persuaded that he is an obedient follower of a Divine interior monitor. There is no fanatic so extravagant as a religious fanatic.[65]

Was it *St. Bernard* who used to declare without equivocation, "Anyone who directs himself has a fool for a director"?[66] Is this not what Jesus calls the blind leading the blind — into the pit (Mt 15:14)? The great problem is that of finding an experienced and prudent spiritual director. Fortunately, there are now training places for spiritual directors, some excellent books on spiritual direction, and even, in the event of a complete lack of suitable spiritual directors, a helpful work by Adrian van Kamm entitled, *The Dynamics of Spiritual Self-Direction*.[67] The need of spiritual direction can vary considerably. For example, serious beginners in a life of prayer need spiritual direction because everything is so new and unfamiliar, and because it is so easy to be overly impressed by one's own imagination and emotions. Later on, spiritual direction may not be so essential because of a developed sense of discernment. However, as *Robert Hugh Benson* has pointed out, sometimes it is the most proficient in prayer who stand in greater need of spiritual direction[68] because Satan and one's own subtle pride are working overtime to "lead astray, if possible, even the elect" (Mt 24:24).

   One final note on something which has been characteristic of many who have lived an interior life, yet has not been found necessary by others who have also committed themselves to a life of prayer. I speak of a *spiritual journal*. Personally, I have found journal keeping very helpful, particularly during the early years of my spiritual journey. In fact, I started keeping my first spiritual journal when I was only twelve years old, my first year in the minor or high school seminary. No one suggested it to me. I did not even have a spiritual director in the proper sense of the word. I just felt (under the guidance of the Holy Spirit, I trust) that it would be of assistance in objectifying what seemed to be happening within. In it I kept notes, not only of thoughts, inspirations, resolutions, etc. that occurred to me, particularly during my times of retreat and days of recollection, but also inspiring poems and sayings which, as the reader is well aware, I still find helpful. However, I have not preserved all my journals, both because there were so many over the years, and because I felt no great need of keeping them indefinitely. For whom would I be preserving these notebooks, for myself or for others? So, periodically, I would destroy the ones I had compiled so far and, in a sense, start over. In more recent years, I have written less but have tended to keep the journals of the past few years in order to review them, gain new or renewed insights and inspirations, and have some general idea of where I am and whether I seem to be following the right road.

Recently, *intensive journals*[69] have become popular and, I trust, have been found useful for many, especially beginners in the Spiritual Life. Nevertheless, it is my impression that, for many others, they can be somewhat too complicated and soul-searching, with too much input from Jungian Psychology. This is not at all intended as a condemnation, but simply a caution and a reassurance to those to whom such a journal holds no special appeal. Sometimes, it is a great temptation to feel that one must adopt every new suggestion that comes along, whether it be personally helpful or not. In other words, I do strongly recommend the keeping of a spiritual journal, particularly in the beginning of one's Spiritual Life, but it does not have to be an "intensive journal." Let it be simply whatever kind of journal is found to be personally the most useful.

SUMMARY AND CONCLUSION:

In this unusually lengthy chapter (which is still far more brief than the whole volumes of many writers on this crucial material), we have considered so many topics that it is extremely *difficult to summarize* them. We can, however, at least recapitulate them under the heading of prayer of various kinds, life in the Spirit, and the mystical life. Under the heading of *Prayer,* we have focused on Petition, "Mental Prayer" (including Meditation, Affective Prayer, and the Prayer of Simplicity), and Contemplation, with special attention to the so-called "dark nights" or "deserts." Under *Life in the Spirit,* we concentrated rather briefly on the Sanctifying Gifts and the Fruits of the transforming Holy Spirit. And in the treatment of *Mysticism,* we examined what it is not and what it is, with special attention to its preconditions, plus a final "postscript" on journals.

By way of appropriate *conclusion,* I would like to quote the inspiring *Song of the Mystic*[70] by the poet priest of the South, Father Abram J. Ryan, C.M.

SONG OF THE MYSTIC

I walk down the Valley of Silence —
　　Down the dim voiceless valley — alone!
And I hear not the fall of a footstep
　　Around me, save God's and my own;
And the hush of my heart is as holy
　　As hovers where angels have flown!

Long ago was I weary of voices
　　Whose music my heart could not win;
Long ago was I weary of noises
　　That fretted my soul with their din;
Long ago was I weary of places
　　Where I met but the human — and sin.

I walked in the world with the worldly;
　　I craved what the world never gave;

And I said: "In the world each Ideal,
    That shines like a star on life's wave,
Is wrecked on the shores of the Real,
    And sleeps like a dream in a grave."

And still did I pine for the Perfect,
    And still found the False with the True;
I sought 'mid the Human for Heaven,
    But caught a mere glimpse of its Blue;
And I wept when the clouds of the Mortal
    Veiled even that glimpse from my view.

And I toiled on, heart-tired of the Human,
    And I moaned 'mid the mazes of men,
Till I knelt, long ago, at an altar
    And I heard a voice call me. Since then
I walk down the Valley of Silence
    That lies far beyond mortal ken.

Do you ask what I found in the Valley?
    'Tis my trysting Place with the Divine.
And I fell at the feet of the Holy,
    And above me a voice said: "Be mine."
And there rose from the depths of my spirit
    An echo — "My heart shall be Thine."

Do you ask how I live in the Valley?
    I weep — and I dream — and I pray.
But my tears are as sweet as the dewdrops
    That fall on the roses in May;
And my prayer, like a perfume from censers,
    Ascendeth to God night and day.

In the hush of the Valley of Silence
    I dream all the songs that I sing;
And the music floats down the dim Valley,
    Till each finds a word for a wing,
That to hearts, like the Dove of the Deluge,
    A message of Peace they may bring.

But far on the deep there are billows
　　That never shall break on the beach;
And I have heard songs in the Silence
　　That never shall float into speech;
And I have had dreams in the Valley
　　Too lofty for language to reach.

And I have seen Thoughts in the Valley —
　　Ah! me, how my spirit was stirred!
And they wear holy veils on their faces,
　　Their footsteps can scarcely be heard;
They pass through the Valley like virgins,
　　Too pure for the touch of a word!

Do you ask me the place of the Valley,
　　Ye hearts that are harrowed by Care?
It lieth afar between mountains,
　　And God and His angels are there;
And one is the dark mount of Sorrow,
　　And one the bright mountain of Prayer.

RECOMMENDED READING LIST

1. ON PRAYER: Harrington, Wilfrid. *The Bible's Ways of Prayer*, Wilmington, DE: Michael Glazier, 1982.
2. ON MEDITATION: Leen, Edward. *Progress Through Mental Prayer*, Waldwick, NJ: Arena Lettres, 1978. (Reprint of a modern Spiritual Classic)
3. ON CONTEMPLATION: Maloney, George. *Journey into Contemplation*, Locust Valley, NY: Living Flame Press, 1978.
4. ON MYSTICISM: Egan, Harvey. *Christian Mysticism*, New York, NY: Pueblo Publishing Co., 1983.
5. ON SPIRITUAL DIRECTION: Edwards, Tilden. *Spiritual Friend*, New York, NY: Paulist Press, 1980.

QUESTIONS FOR REFLECTION AND DISCUSSION

1. What are the importance and the role of prayer in the context of today's active life and ministry?
2. What life experiences have you had of prayers answered and of prayers apparently not answered?
3. What is the special value in the Spiritual Life of so-called "Mental Prayer," and what, if any, method have you found helpful?
4. What are the meaning and feasibility of Contemplation and Mysticism for a Christian in today's world?
5. What are the need and the possibility of a personal Spiritual Director in today's Church?

CHAPTER NINE

THE OUTER DIMENSIONS OF THE RELATIONSHIP
The Challenging Life of Sharing

All Christians and many non-Christians are familiar with the *parables of Jesus*. Not that he invented the parable form, for it can be found in many literatures. In fact, it was characteristic of rabbinical teaching before and after the time of Jesus. But no one in the history of the world seems to have been so adept in the use of parables as Jesus. The sheer number of his parables, the ease with which he told them, their vividness of detail and, above all, the dramatic impact of their message, all combine to mark Jesus as the parable teller par excellence.

And yet, there is one magnificent parable emanating from Palestine, the land of Jesus, which he himself never mentioned. And no wonder! For it is a silent parable, a geographical parable, left in the very land itself from time immemorial. I like to call it *"A Tale of Two Seas"* or *"The Parable of Palestine."* Not that I discovered it. No, that credit belongs to someone else, perhaps to the famous American Baptist preacher, *Harry Emerson Fosdick,*[1] to whom I first saw it attributed. At any rate, I cannot help feeling that, in a providential way, God himself left us this beautiful and challenging parable in his land, the land of his Chosen People, and especially the land of his Son.

In the geography of Palestine then and now, the most prominent feature is the great Rift Valley (or *"Ghor"* in Arabic) stretching from

North to South and including the Sea of Galilee, the River Jordan, and the Dead Sea. Herein lies the parable. To the North, the *Sea of Galilee* is alive and beautiful, with an abundance of fish (especially the famous "St. Peter's Fish") to delight the tongue, as well as fauna and flora to delight the eye. To the South, on the other hand, the *Dead Sea* is just that — dead! Though far larger than the Sea of Galilee, it boasts no fish, and no fauna and flora except where fresh water springs occasionally dot its shore, for example at *Ain Feshka* and *Ain Geddi* (En-Geddi). Why such a sharp contrast between these two bodies of water only sixty-five miles apart?

The answer is simple. The heart-shaped Sea of Galilee receives an abundance of water from the great *Beka* or *Big'a* Valley of Lebanon but, even though it is almost seven hundred feet below sea level, it does not keep that water to itself. It passes it on to the Jordan River and the Dead Sea. But the kidney-shaped Dead Sea, some thirteen hundred feet below sea level, has *no outlet*. Though it receives the same abundance of water from the Sea of Galilee and the Jordan River, it does not pass it on. It does not share its blessings, but hoards them to itself. As a result, the water tends to evaporate, leaving salt and chemicals in which nothing lives.

The lesson of the parable is clear and challenging. Water is the biblical *symbol of life,* especially the supernatural life of grace, as we see, for example, in the first seven chapters of John's Gospel. Like the Sea of Galilee and the Dead Sea, we receive an abundance of *grace and gifts* from God. If we try to hoard them to ourselves, we become like the Dead Sea, utterly lifeless. Only if, like the heart-shaped Sea of Galilee, we generously pass them on by *sharing them with others,* do we become and remain truly alive. For, as I stressed in the previous chapter, "To live is to love, to love is to give, and to love deeply is to forgive completely!" Or, to express it another way,

> To live is to love,
> To love is to care,
> To care is to share!

Does not Jesus make this crystal clear in his injunction to his apostles, ''Freely you have received, freely give!'' (Mt 10:8, NIV), in his sharp warning, ''From everyone who has been given much, much will be demanded'' (Lk 12:48, NIV), and in his reminder found only in Paul's address to the presbyters at Miletus, ''It is more blessed to give than to receive'' (Ac 20:35)? Is this not also the teaching of the Saints, as epitomized in that beloved prayer and hymn attributed to *St. Francis of Assisi*?[2]

> Lord, make me an instrument of your peace.
> Where there is hatred, let me sow love;
> Where there is injury, pardon;
> Where there is doubt, faith;
> Where there is despair, hope;
> Where there is darkness, light;
> And where there is sadness, joy.
>
> Divine Master, grant that
> I may not so much seek
> To be consoled as to console;
> To be understood as to understand;
> To be loved as to love.
>
> For it is in giving that we receive;
> It is in pardoning that we are pardoned;
> It is in dying that we are born to eternal life!

In this chapter, we will consider *some of the ways* in which we can and ought to share with others the abundance of grace and gifts which our loving Father has showered on us. To me, these are principally the ways of witnessing, serving, and sacrificing. What must be borne in mind, however, is the deep spiritual truth that, when we share with others, we are sharing not only our gifts, not only ourselves, but above all the utterly ''indescribable gift'' (2 Cor 9:15) of Jesus Christ, our true ''self,'' who is our ''wisdom and also our justice, our sanctification, and our redemption'' (1 Cor 1:30). What a privilege is ours! But also what a challenge and responsibility! Jesus Christ, "who was handed over to death for our sins and raised up for our justification" (Rm 4:25), lives on in glory with his Father and by grace in us, not only to fill us with the peace and joy of his loving presence, but also to continue through us his loving witness to, service of, and sacrifice for our fellow human beings!

At the same time, however, that we are sharing Christ with others, we are also called to *serve Christ in others*. This may present a psychological and spiritual problem to some of us who find difficulty in *St. Augustine's* expression of "Christ loving himself."[3] I submit, however, that it is unnecessary to keep both approaches in mind at the same time. Rather, one or the other can be emphasized, not only according to circumstances, but even according to personalities. For example, those of a more introverted and mystical temperament may be more inclined to share Christ with others. Those of a more extroverted and practical temperament may be more inclined to serve Christ in others. Jesus was present to both Mary the listener and Martha the server. The important thing is not to cling to one approach at the expense of the other. "In the evening of life," *St. John of the Cross* reminds us, "we will be judged on love,"[4] both our openness to the "love of Christ" in us which "impels us" (2 Cor 5:14) to share him with others, and our loving service of Christ in the hungry and thirsty, the homeless and naked, the ill and imprisoned (Mt 25:31-40).

WITNESSING:

The first kind of sharing for our reflection is that of witnessing, a concept which is highly biblical, beginning with the *Old Testament*, where it is used many times in various ways. For example, God himself is the principal witness in covenants and oaths, promises and threats (Gn 31:44, 50; Jg 11:10). God's natural creation (especially the heavenly bodies), and Israel's human creations (mainly stone mounds and altars) are also cited as witnesses in the same circumstances (Dt 4:26; 30:19; 31:28; Ps 89:38; Gn 31:48, 52; Jos 22:26-27,

34; 24:27.) The tables of the Law, as well as the Ark and the Tabernacle housing them, are revered as a witness or testimony to Israel (Ex 25:16, 21; 27:21; 38:21, NIV), though this is not all that clear in the New American Bible. The prophets, of course, are special witnesses against Israel and Judah (2 Ch 25:15; Ne 9:26; Jr 42:19; Am 3:13). Finally, Israel itself is to be God's witness to the nations, a role which we would do well to examine more closely.

After almost two thousand years of missionary Christianity, it is difficult for us to realize that Israel, by contrast, was not and is *not a missionary religion.* God did not send the Israelites, or even their prophets, to other lands in order to proselytize and convert them. Jonah, of course, seems to be an outstanding exception until we realize that it is not actually a book of prophecy but an extended parable. On the other hand, God did call Israel to be his *witness to the nations,* so that through her all might come to the knowledge of Yahweh (Is 43:9-12; 44:8) though sometimes the expression used is that of ensign or standard, signal or sign (Is 11:10, 12; 49:22; 66:19). To me, it is interesting and perhaps more than coincidental that one of the principal Hebrew words for *witness* or *testimony* (*'edah*) also happens to mean *congregation* or *assembly* and is often used of Israel in the Old Testament (see also Heb 12:1).

In the *New Testament,* the concept of witnessing takes on a deeper and fuller meaning. For example, God the Father is the witness to the validity of Jesus' claims (Jn 5:32, 37; 8:18), as are also the Scriptures (Jn 5:39), John the Baptist (Jn 1:7-8, 15; 3:26; 5:33) and the (miraculous) works performed by Jesus (Jn 5:36; 10:25). In the Book of Revelation, Christ himself is called "the faithful witness" (Rv 1:5; 3:14). But more to our purpose, the Apostles and indeed all of the followers of Jesus Christ are called and sent as his witnesses to the whole world (Mt 24:14; Lk 24:48; Jn 15:27; Ac 1:8, 22; 4:33; 22:15; 23:11; 1 Cor 15:15), not in a passive sense as with Israel, but in the active sense of *evangelization,* of making disciples of all the nations (Mt 28:18-20; Mk 16:15-20; Lk 24:46-48; Rm 10:11-15).

What, then, does witnessing mean? How are we called to witness in this *twentieth century?* Well, how did Jesus himself and the Apostles witness? In three ways: by their lives, by their words, and by their deaths. Let us look at each of these in turn, concentrating especially on the first at this time.

In our language, as in most languages of the world, there are a number of proverbs to the effect that we must "practice what we preach,"[5] that "our deeds must match our words."[6] The great Archbishop of Paris, *Cardinal Suhard,* expressed it vividly when he said that "to witness means to live in such a way" that our "lives would not make sense if God did not exist!"[7] But Jesus, in typical Eastern fashion, proclaimed it even more graphically when, early in his great *Sermon on the Mount,* right after the Beatitudes, he challenged us with these incisive words,

> You are the *salt of the earth.* But what if salt goes flat? How can you restore its flavor? Then it is good for nothing but to be thrown out and trampled underfoot.
>
> You are the *light of the world.* A city set on a hill cannot be hidden. Men do not light a lamp and then put it under a bushel basket. They set it on a stand where it gives light to all in the house. In the same way, your light must shine before men so that they may see goodness in your acts and give praise to your heavenly Father (Mt 5:13-16).

The two metaphors used here have one thing in common: they both refer to *essential needs* of the ancient world. In our technological society, with various salt substitutes as well as many other spices, and with inexpensive artificial light, it is understandably hard for us to appreciate the powerful impact of these symbols on their initial hearers and readers. Salt of the earth! Light of the world! No more effective way could Jesus have chosen to impress on his nondescript band of disciples that they had an indispensable mission in life, that they could and would "make all the difference in the world!"

So essential a commodity in ancient times was *salt* that Roman soldiers were given a salt allowance as part of their pay, hence the word *salary*. Wars were fought, e.g. between Romans and the Etruscan Veii, over control of salt beds. And the famous Roman road, *Via Salaria*, was so named because it was the salt route of the Eternal City. The same was true the world over, including Palestine. According to Sirach 39:26, salt is listed among the "chief of all needs for human life." Why? Because of its use as a *condiment* in making food palatable? Yes, certainly, as Job adverts (Jb 6:6, NIV), "Is tasteless food eaten without salt?" But in the ancient world, and especially in Israel, salt had a number of other important uses, for example: as an *antiseptic* in water (2 K 2:19-22) and on newborn babies (Ezk 16:4), and as a *preservative* of foods (particularly meat, in the absence of refrigeration), hence also of covenants (Nb 18:19, NIV; 2 Ch 13:5) and sacrifices (Lv 2:13; Ezk 43:24; see also Mk 9:49-50). To people of ancient times, therefore, and especially to Jesus' hearers, salt would have meant an essential ingredient of life, indispensable for purification and preservation. What a challenge then and now! Would anyone dare to claim that our role as "the salt of the earth" is any less crucial in today's world than it was in the time of Jesus?

Important as salt was in the ancient world, both as commodity and as symbol, *light* was even more so. This is crystal clear in Scripture. From the initial creation of light (in Gn 1:3-5) to the uncreated light of the Heavenly Jerusalem (in Rv 21:23-25), references to light hold a prominent place in the Bible. *Yahweh* himself, for example, lights the way for the wandering Israelites with a "pillar of fire by night" (Ex 13:21-22, NIV; Ps 78:14; 105:39). In fact, God himself is a light to all who seek him, as we note especially in the Psalms: "The Lord is my light and my salvation" (Ps 27:1), "In your light we see light" (Ps 36:10), "Send forth your light and your fidelity" (Ps 43:3), "The light of your countenance . . ." (Ps 44:4), ". . . robed in light as with a cloak" (Ps 104:2). And this is particularly true of his Word, "Your word is a lamp to my feet and a light for my path" (Ps 119:105, NIV).

In the *Old Testament*, however, as later on in the New, the symbolism of light is not confined to God, but is used also of the *just or righteous,* of Israel as a whole, and of the Messiah in particular. Thus, "the path of the just is like shining light, that grows in brilliance every day" (Pr 4:18). And of *Israel,* or more properly Judah, Isaiah 58:10 serves to epitomize the entire chapter,

> If you bestow your bread on the hungry
>> and satisfy the afflicted;
> Then light shall rise for you in the darkness,
>> and the gloom shall become for you like midday.

But it is especially through the *Messiah,* the Servant of Yahweh, that light will shine both on Israel and on all the nations:

> The people who walked in darkness
>> have seen a great light . . .
> For a child is born to us, a son is given to us;
>> upon his shoulder dominion rests . . . (Is 9:1, 5).

> Here is my servant whom I uphold,
>> my chosen one with whom I am pleased . . .
> I formed you, and set you
>> as a covenant of the people,
>> a light for the nations . . . (Is 42:1, 6).

> It is too little, he says, for you to be my servant,
>> to raise up the tribes of Jacob . . .
> I will make you a light to the nations,
>> that my salvation may reach to the ends
>> of the earth (Is 49:6).

Finally, through the Messiah, the Servant of Yahweh, a New *Jerusalem* or Zion will be established as a "City of Light" illuminated by Yahweh himself for all the nations,

> Rise up in splendor! Your light has come,
>> the glory of the Lord shines upon you . . .

Nations shall walk by your light,
    and kings by your shining radiance. . . .

They shall call you "City of the Lord,"
    "Zion of the Holy One of Israel". . . .

No longer shall the sun be your light by day,
    Nor the brightness of the moon shine upon you at night,
The Lord shall be your light forever,
    your God shall be your glory (Is 60:1, 3, 14, 19).

In the *New Testament,* we can clearly discern the fulfillment of all these glorious prophecies in the person of *Jesus Christ,* the Messiah of Israel and the Light of the World. For example, Zechariah, the father of John the Baptist, recognizes that his son is destined to be "a prophet of the Most High" who will "go on before the Lord to prepare the way for him" who will be "the rising sun . . . come to us from heaven to shine on those living in darkness and in the shadow of death . . ." (Lk 1:76-79, NIV). And the aged Simeon acclaims the Child Jesus at his Presentation in the Temple as "a light for revelation to the Gentiles and for glory to your people Israel" (Lk 2:32, NIV). Later on, as a kind of central point between Jesus' baptism by John and his resurrection from the dead, Jesus is transfigured before his favored three Apostles, "his face . . . as dazzling as the sun, his clothes as radiant as light" (Mt 17:2; Mk 9:3; Lk 9:29).

But it is in *John's writings* that we find the greatest emphasis on light. In his Gospel, Jesus is identified and identifies himself as the "Light of the World" (Jn 1:4-5, 9; 3:19-21; 8:12; 9:5; 12:35, 46). Also in his Gospel, and in his First Letter as well, John refers to the followers of Jesus as "children of the light" (Jn 3:21; 8:12; 11:9; 12:35-36, 46), and children of God, for "God is Light" (1 Jn 1:5-7; 2:8-11). Finally, in his Book of Revelation, the Church (especially the seven churches of the Roman Province of Asia) is represented by the seven golden lampstands, in the midst of which is the risen Christ: "The hair of his head was as white as snow-white wool and his eyes blazed like fire. . . . His feet gleamed like polished brass . . . and his face shone like the sun at its brightest'' (Rv 1:12-16). And in the Book's triumphant final chapters, the Church is described as the fulfillment of the Isaian prophecies about the New Jerusalem, she and her members shining with and illuminated by the glory of God and the Risen Lamb (Rv 21:10-11, 23; 22:5). All of which brings us back to the challenging words of Jesus in his Sermon on the Mount, "You are the light of the world!'' (Mt 5:14). Why did Jesus use that expression? And why is it so full of meaning then and now?

In the ancient world, light (like salt) was precious indeed. Today, the wonders of electricity enable us to turn night into day, but in the time of Jesus (as still today in some parts of the world), life and work came to a standstill when darkness fell. *Olive oil lamps* were adequate for finding one's way around a room, but for little more. Hence, Jesus' repeated remarks about walking and working by daylight (Jn 8:12; 9:4; 11:9-10; 12:35-36). The first conclusion, then, from Jesus' statement in Matthew must be (as with the one about salt) that his followers are *indispensable* to the life of the whole world.

Even more than with his use of the salt symbol, however, Jesus goes on to expand his reference to light, "Let your light shine before men, that they may see your good deeds and praise your Father in heaven'' (Mt 5:16, NIV). Our second conclusion, then, is that our *good deeds,* our very lives, are to reflect God's love and life in the world today. This is especially so, since light came to signify in the ancient world, as it still largely does today, all that is true and good and holy, while darkness stood for error and evil and sin. Hence, in addition to John and Matthew, the great witness Paul frequently uses the symbolism of light to exhort us to Christian living in our surroundings (Rm 13:12; 2 Cor 4:4, 6; 6:14; Ep 5:8-14; Col 1:12; 1 Th 5:5). But there is still more to the picture than we have seen so far.

When Jesus proclaims in John 8:12 and 9:5, "I am the Light of the World,'' what is he really saying? What is the light of our world? *The sun,* of course! It is true that Israel tended to think of light as being independent of the sun (Gn 1:3-5, 14-19; Ec 12:2), no doubt because there was light before sunrise and after sunset, but other indications are that they did understand and appreciate the sun's responsibility, not only for light, but also for warmth, growth, and healing on the earth (Dt 33:14, NIV; Jos 10:12-13; Jb 8:16; Ps 19:7; Jr 31:35; Ml 3:20 [4:2 in RSV, NEB, NIV]). And such was their admiration of the glorious sun that they used it as a symbol of their own heroes, notably Samson (from Hebrew *shemesh* meaning sun — Jg 13-16; cf. also Ps 19:5-6) and David (Ps 89:37), even of Yahweh himself (Ps 84:12). What an impact, then, must the words of Jesus have carried when he declared, "I am the Light of the World!" But how much greater should be their impact on us in the twentieth century, who have come to learn so much more about the sun, especially that, directly or indirectly, it is the source of all our light, our warmth, our energy, in a sense even our life!

How aptly, then, does Jesus proclaim (Jn 8:12) "I am the light of the world! No follower of mine shall ever walk in darkness; no, he shall have the light of life!" How appropriately has Jesus come to be called the "Sun of Justice," "Sun of Righteousness," and "Sun of Salvation" in the worship of the Church, his glorious resurrection in particular being compared to the rising of the sun! And how suitably has the Church, not knowing the exact date of Jesus' birth, chosen to celebrate it on *December 25th,* which was the Roman *"Birthday of the Sun"!*

But what about that correlative statement, "You are the light of the world" (Mt 5:14)? In what sense can we be the light of the world? Like the sun? Hardly, for we are not at all the source of benefits to the world that the sun is. No, our role is much more like that of *the moon,* reflecting the light and warmth and energy of the sun, that is, the truth and love and life of the Risen Christ. Yet that is not quite accurate either, for we can and must, by the grace of God, do more than reflect. We must radiate! We must let Christ shine from the inside out! Is this not what Paul appears to be saying in 2 Corinthians 4:6?

> For God, who said, "Let light shine out of darkness," has shone in our hearts, that we in turn might make known the glory of God shining on the face of Christ!

And is this not rendered possible precisely through the indwelling of the risen Christ, his living in us (Jn 14:23; 17:22-23, 26; Rv 3:20) and transforming us into himself? Paul (with an allusion, not only to the veil over Moses' face in Ex 34:29-35, but also perhaps to the Transfiguration and Resurrection of Jesus) seems to declare as much in 2 Corinthians 3:18,

> All of us, gazing on the Lord's glory with unveiled faces, are being transformed from glory to glory into his very image by the Lord who is the Spirit!

By reflecting and radiating Christ, then, we witness to the world today in whatever state of life we are called to live. Young men and women exhibiting high moral values in spite of peer pressures, husbands and wives loving and faithful to each other for life, fathers and mothers dedicated to Christian parenthood, priests and religious committed to their consecration, monks and nuns living their lives in silent contemplation — all these and many more are witnessing Christ to a world which has never been so much in need of their witness. Perhaps the following anonymous reflection entitled, *"What is a Witness?"*[8] will make a fitting summary and conclusion of witnessing by our lives,

> *A Witness is*:
>
> Someone who stands out
>   because he is not afraid to stand up,
> Someone who outreaches others
>   because he reaches out to others,
> Someone who lifts others up
>   because he bends down to their weakness,
> Someone whose heart has grown great
>   because he has learned to become small.
>
> *A witness is all this and more. He is*:
>
> Someone who walks across the wastelands
>   of human lives and uncovers hidden springs,

Someone who opens windows everywhere
　　to let the sunshine and springtime fragrance in;
And, passing through the doors of self-filled hearts,
　　lights and leaves behind an everlasting FLAME!
Ultimately, a witness is all of these things —
　　because he is simply not afraid to LOVE!

Earlier, we noted that witnessing can be done in three principal ways: by our lives, by our words, and by our deaths. As indicated at that time, we have concentrated primarily on the first form of witnessing, namely by our lives. And that is as it should be. But at this point we need to say at least a few words about the other two ways of witnessing.

As with his shining life, so with his *words* and especially with his *death,* Jesus himself is the perfect witness. What an incomparable balance of fearless courage in speaking out against abuses of the powerful (Mt 23), extraordinary compassion for the needs of the powerless (Mt 12:15-21), and limitless patience in suffering the consequences (Lk 23:32-46)! The more we allow him to continue his life and ministry in us, the more we too will be able to witness with the same kind of balance. But, as an aid thereto, let us listen for a moment to some of his principal sayings in this matter. For example, in the same twelfth chapter of Matthew cited above, Jesus presents us with these sobering thoughts about our words,

Out of the abundance of the heart the mouth speaks. The good man out of his good treasure brings forth good, and the evil man out of his evil treasure brings forth evil. I tell you, on the day of Judgment men will render account for every careless word they utter; for by your words you will be justified, and by your words you will be condemned (Mt 12:34-37, RSV).

Sobering thoughts, yes, but also comforting ones because, if Christ truly lives in our hearts, then we will not have to worry about our words. The same is true of two other sayings of Jesus, both from his missionary discourse in Matthew,

> You will be brought to trial before rulers and kings, to give witness before them and before the Gentiles on my account. When they hand you over, do not worry about what you will say or how you will say it. When the hour comes, you will be given what you are to say. You yourselves will not be the speakers; the Spirit of your Father will be speaking in you (Mt 10:18-20).

> No pupil outranks his teacher, no slave his master. The pupil should be glad to become like his teacher, the slave like his master. If they call the head of the house Beelzebul, how much more the members of his household! Do not let them intimidate you. . . . What I tell you in darkness, speak in the light. What you hear in private, proclaim from the housetops (Mt 10:24-27).

"All well and good," many will say, "but I am just an ordinary person, just a 'little person.' I am only a learner, not a teacher; a hearer, not a preacher; a parent, not a prophet. I cannot speak out in public. I cannot even write a letter to the newspapers or magazines or to my elected representatives. Whatever is said about witnessing by word is not for me!"

Not for me? How do I know? Let us look at some of the possibilities. Take *parenting,* for example. Is there any greater influence, for good or evil, in a person's life than that of his or her parents? The influence of their example, above all, but also that of their words or lack of them! Because of his failure to correct his sons, who were stealing from the sacrifices, *Heli the High Priest* brought on the defeat of his people, the destruction of his house, and the capture of the Ark of the Covenant (1 S 2-4)!

Or take the example of *Aquila and Priscilla,* obviously "only laypeople" in the Church at Ephesus, who did not hesitate to "teach" the great Christian preacher, *Apollos,* even though he was "an authority on Scripture, . . . instructed [but not completely] in the new way of the Lord, . . . a man full of spiritual fervor." Of course, they did so with Christian kindness and tact. "They took him home and explained to him God's new way in greater detail" (Ac 18:24-26).

The key to success in witnessing by word is indeed the use of *kindness and tact* (albeit with firmness as necessary) in teaching, preaching, parenting, conversation, letter-writing, or any other form of communication. We must remember that, in whatever we say and do, or fail to say and do, we are communicating, whether we realize it or not! For example, one of our most powerful means of communication, of radiating Christ to others (2 Cor 4:6), is that of a warm and genuine *smile*. And what a negative communication when we fail to smile! Is it not much like the failure of Moses and Aaron to reflect the compassion of Yahweh in Numbers 20:12?

Our principal problem in witnessing by word is usually timidity or false humility which tends to wait for someone else to say or do something. There is an *anonymous saying* that is appropriate here, "I wondered why somebody didn't do something, then I realized that I was somebody!"[9] And another *anonymous* saying,

> I am only one, but I am one.
> I can't do everything, but I can do something.
> What I can do, that I ought to do.
> And what I ought to do,
> By the grace of God, I will do![10]

And what if I fail to do it? What if I fail to speak when I can and should, fail to write when the opportunity cries out for it? Does not *St. James* declare, in his usual blunt fashion, "When a man knows the right thing to do and does not do it, he sins!" (Jm 4:17)? Yes, I believe it may well be true that, in communication as in everything else, we sin more often through *omission* than through *commission*. But we have our share of the latter sins as well, and here *St. James* is particularly vivid in his instruction,

> We all stumble in many ways. If anyone is never at fault in what he says, he is a perfect man, able to keep his whole body in

check. . . . The tongue is a small part of the body but it makes great boasts. Consider what a great forest is set on fire by a small spark. The tongue also is a fire, a world of evil among the parts of the body. It corrupts the whole person, sets the whole course of his life on fire, and is itself set on fire by hell. . . .

With the tongue we praise our Lord and Father, and with it we curse men who have been made in God's likeness. Out of the same mouth come praise and cursing. My brothers, this should not be. Can both fresh water and salt water flow from the same spring? My brothers, can a fig tree bear olives, or a grapevine bear figs? Neither can a salt spring produce fresh water (Jm 3:2, 5-6, 9-12, NIV).

Strong words these, maybe even exaggerated. But maybe not, when one considers for a moment the irremediable harm that can be wrought by careless or vicious words, whether spoken or written. How many reputations have been destroyed! How many marriages and friendships ruined! How many suicides caused! How many cruel wars fought! And this can happen even when what is said or written is true! The truth is not always charitable. Rather, charity sometimes requires that we keep the truth to ourselves.

We would do well to adopt the policy of the Saints, "If we cannot think of anything good to say about someone, let us say nothing!" Otherwise, we run the risk of flouting what is possibly Jesus' most categorical and threatening prohibition, one unfortunately that is sometimes overlooked or ignored by otherwise "good Christians,"

Do not judge, or you too will be judged. For in the same way you judge others, you will be judged, and with the measure you use, it will be measured to you (Mt 7:1-2, NIV).

Finally, we can and should be prepared to witness, if necessary, by our *death*. There was a time when this was taken for granted by most Christians. As a matter of fact, the very word "witness" in

Greek is *mártys,* from which derives the English word *martyr.* Obviously, then, the ultimate form of witness is that of the martyrs, who gave their very lives in witness to their faith. This was true of the innumerable martyrs during the ten Roman persecutions, from that of Nero in A.D. 64-65 through that of Diocletian, which ceased in A.D. 311 with the Edict of Toleration by Galerius. It has been true of the many martyrs in the history of the Church since then. And it is still true today of the uncounted, almost unnoticed, martyrs who have given their lives in this "enlightened" twentieth century.

Even conservative estimates place the total of "liquidations or exterminations" under *Nazism and Communism* at well over thirty million, to which we would have to add a significant number of deaths under various other dictatorships of the left or right around the globe. How many of these deaths qualify as martyrdoms strictly speaking (that is, the ultimate witness because of our faith), is known only to God. For us, the more important and useful consideration is the stark reminder that to be a Christian is to be a candidate for martyrdom. There is a graphic poster that drives this truth home. It shows a lion, reminiscent of the wild beasts in the Roman arena, with the caption, "Christianity didn't use to be a spectator sport. It still isn't!"[11]

All of this notwithstanding, I cannot help wondering how many of us would be willing today to lose our lives for our faith. *James Breig,* a popular commentator on the situation of the Church in the world today, states, "There is evidence that contemporary Catholics have little respect for martyrdom,"[12] and would use almost any means to avoid it. I do hope that the "evidence" is either invalid or inconclusive, but how can I not be concerned?

From my own experience under *Communism in China,* when every day could have been my last, I know how strong yet subtle the instinct of self-preservation can be. And I had years of spiritual preparation for just that kind of situation. What about the majority of Catholics, especially in these United States, who have grown up in a soft and affluent society, who have never really been tested, who cannot even envision finding themselves in danger of death for their faith and who, instead of years of spiritual preparation, have been literally bombarded by the media with an endless barrage of self-preservation, self-fulfillment, and anti-sacred attitudes?

"Subject us not to the trial but deliver us from the evil one," we pray in the Lord's Prayer according to the New American Bible translation of Matthew 6:13. But what if the time comes when we must profess our faith and die, or renounce it and live? What will be our response? Only time will tell, of course, but I am a firm believer in being aware of just such an eventuality in today's world and being prepared to witness to our faith in Christ or, better still, to our love of him. For martyrdom is a form of fidelity, and fidelity is the triumph of love. To the extent, then, that we really live in the love of Christ, will we also be ready to die for the love of Christ. In fact, we might well ask ourselves, "If I am not willing to die for Christ, am I truly living for him? If *survival* is my top priority, am I really a Christian, a follower of him who declared, 'Anyone who does not take up his cross and follow me cannot be my disciple' (Lk 14:27)?"

Ultimately, I am convinced, the death of martyrs is the sacrificial *death of Christ himself* all over again. It is he himself, living in them, who enables them to die for their faith. "We know that Christ, once raised from the dead, will never die again; death has no more power over him" (Rm 6:9), yet he continues to suffer and die mystically in and through his followers (Ac 9:5; 22:8; 26:14; Col 1:24).

This is exemplified dramatically in the touching and highly authentic *Acts of Martyrdom of Sts. Perpetua and Felicitas,* who were thrown to wild beasts at Carthage in 203 A.D. Felicitas, Perpetua's servant girl, was pregnant when she was arrested and thus had to deliver her baby in prison. During the delivery, she moaned and cried out with the pangs of childbirth. Taunted by her jailer that she would never be able to face the greater pain of wild beasts in the arena, she quickly replied, "Now I suffer what I suffer, but then Another shall be in me who will suffer for me, because I too am ready to suffer for Him."[13] Obviously, then, the more we live Christ and allow him to continue his life in us, the more we will be ready, when necessary, for the ultimate witness of shedding our blood for Christ. In this, we will be living out *Jesus' categorical imperative* which, especially in Mark's Gospel, clearly refers to martyrdom,

> If anyone would come after me, he must deny himself and take up his cross and follow me. For whoever wants to save his life will lose it, but whoever loses his life for me and for the gospel will save it. . . .
>
> If anyone is ashamed of me and my words in this adulterous and sinful generation, the Son of Man will be ashamed of him when he comes in his Father's glory with the holy angels (Mk 8:34-35, 38 NIV).

Later in this chapter, we will return to the same subject when we reflect on sharing by suffering and sacrifice. For the time being, let us conclude this section on witnessing with the following beautiful and appropriate prayer of Cardinal Newman, entitled *"Radiating Christ,"*[14]

> Dear Jesus,
>> help me to spread Your fragrance
>> everywhere I go.
> Flood my soul with Your spirit and life.
> Penetrate and possess my whole being so utterly
>> that all my life may only be
>> a radiance of Your own.
> Shine through me, and be so in me
>> that every soul I come in contact with
>> may feel Your presence in my soul.
> Let them look up and see no longer me —
>> but only Jesus!
>
> Stay with me,
>> and then I shall begin to shine as You shine,
>> so to shine as to be a light to others.
> The light, O Jesus, will be all from You,

> none of it will be mine; it will be You
> shining on others through me.

Let me thus praise You
>   in the way that You love best,
>   by shining on those around me.

Let me preach You without preaching,
>   not by words but by example,
>   by the catching force,
>   the sympathetic influence, of what I do;
>   the evident fullness of the love
>   that my heart bears to You.   Amen.

SERVING:

The second form of sharing is that of serving. So important is this form that, in the minds of most Christians today, sharing and serving are synonymous. To some extent they are, but even synonyms have their shades of meaning. As we have already observed, there are other kinds of sharing such as witnessing. To use two outstanding examples among the Saints, *Francis of Assisi* witnessed to the poverty of Christ by his life; *Vincent de Paul* served Christ in the person of the poor. Each filled a real need, especially according to his time. And, in our own day, *Mother Teresa of Calcutta* is providing us with a shining example of both witness and service.

As for the terms *service and ministry,* they too are roughly synonymous, but the former is more general and comprehensive while the latter carries religious, ecclesial, or political connotations. The distinction is important, so much so that I will reserve my treatment of religious and ecclesial ministry until later, when we reflect on the Church, the Sacraments, and our calling in life. Meanwhile, let us examine, at least briefly, the important concept of service, particularly as we find it in the Bible.

By far, the most common words for *service* and *servant* respectively in the Old Testament are the Hebrew terms *'abad* and *'ebed.*

Their root meaning is clearly one of work or labor, whether it be that of a slave, a hired servant, or a devoted servant of God. By contrast, the Greek New Testament typically employs different words to express distinct ideas: *douleía and doûlos* for slavery and slave, *diakonía and diákonos* for hired service and servant (originally with the connotation of waiting on table). When used religiously, as they so often are in the New Testament, *douleía* normally refers to the service of God, *diakonía* to the service of fellow humans, in or outside the Church. In addition, but less commonly, the word *paîs* (boy or girl) can mean either slave or servant, while the words *latreía* and *leitourgía* (the source of our English word *liturgy*) normally signify religious service or *worship* of some kind.

A complete examination of the biblical references to service and servant would take us too far afield, but it can be very instructive to single out certain outstanding uses of the terms and the ideas involved as we see them in the Old and New Testaments. In the *Old Testament*, there are many beautiful uses of the expression *"servant"* (Hebrew *'ebed*, Greek *doûlos*), particularly as describing a person's proper attitude toward God. For example, in 1 Samuel 3:9-10, the boy *Samuel* is instructed by Heli to respond to Yahweh's call in those unforgettable words, "Speak, Lord, for your servant is listening!" Or note the touching attitude in Psalm 116:16, "O Lord, I am your servant; I am your servant, the son of your handmaid . . ." and Psalm 123:2,

> Behold, as the eyes of servants
> are on the hands of their masters . . .,
> So are our eyes on the Lord, our God,
> till he have pity on us.

But by far the most enigmatic and, at the same time, the most impressive use of the term "servant" in the Old Testament is undoubtedly that contained in the famous *"Songs of the Servant"* (Hebrew *'ebed*, Greek *paîs* or *doûlos* — Is 42:1-9; 49:1-7; 50:4-11; 52:13-53:12). These haunting songs have raised questions for centuries, as we see in Acts 8:32-34, where the Ethiopian eunuch, reading Isaiah 53:7-8, queries Philip the Deacon, "Tell me, please, who is the prophet talking about, himself or someone else?" Nor is this surprising, for they seem to fit their context, yet contrast with it; and the "servant," who seems at times to be identified with Israel (or even Cyrus the Persian!), nevertheless also is clearly sent as a guide to Israel and even a light to the Gentiles, ultimately suffering a humiliating death in vicarious atonement for the sins of others.

Enigmatic, haunting, even confusing as these songs are in their Old Testament context, they become surprisingly clear and clairvoyant in the revealing light of the life, death, and resurrection of *Jesus Christ*, detailed so simply and graphically in the Gospels. From the Old Testament (and from Jewish intertestamental literature), the Jews of Jesus' time inherited three highly diverse portraits of the Messiah which they were evidently quite unable to reconcile: the *Son of David* ([and Son of God?] 2 S 7; Is 9:5-6; 11:1-10; Mi 5:1-4; Zc 9:9-10 [and Ps 2?]), the *Suffering Servant of Yahweh* (Is 53 [and Ps 22?]), and the triumphant, heavenly *Son of Man* (Dn 7, especially verses 13-14). It remained for Jesus of Nazareth to reconcile them completely, not only in his mind and in his words, but also in his very life, death, and resurrection.

Of these three portraits, however, the ones which Jesus obviously preferred were those of *the Servant* (especially the Suffering Servant) *and the Son of Man* — not so much as a triumphant, heavenly being, but rather as identified with our weak human nature. Thus, he was especially fond of uniting these two portraits in single statements of profound meaning, not only regarding his own chosen role but also regarding the attitude which he expected and continues to expect of us who claim to be his followers. This is unquestionably true in the case of that landmark declaration of his (Mk 10:45 and Mt-Lk parallels), "The Son of Man has not come to be served but to serve (Greek *diakonéo*, from *diákonos*) — to give his life in ransom for the many." And, even more fully, it is true of his *three predictions* of his forthcoming suffering, death, and resurrection (Mk 8:31-33; 9:30-32; 10:32-34 and Mt-Lk parallels).

Nor is this all, for even when Jesus does not combine the two portraits, he still insists on his and our role of service (*diakonía*), as we see in this episode from the Last Supper (Lk 22:25-27),

> A dispute arose among them about who should be regarded as the greatest. He said: "Earthly kings lord it over their people. Those who exercise authority over them are called their benefactors. Yet it cannot be that way with you. Let the greatest among you be as the junior, the leader as the servant (*diákonos*). Who, in fact, is the greater — he who reclines at table or he who serves the meal? Yet I am in your midst as the one who serves you."

In fact, Jesus, in John's Last Supper account, evidently goes beyond the portrait in Luke, teaching that his Apostles and all of us his followers should be willing to serve, not only as waiters or hired servants (*diákonoi*), but even as foot-washers or slaves (*doûloi*) to one another,

> Do you understand what I just did for you? You address me as "Teacher" and "Lord," and fittingly enough, for that is what I am. But if I washed your feet — I who am Teacher and Lord — then you must wash each other's feet.

> What I just did was to give an example: as I have done, so you must do. I solemnly assure you, no slave (*doûlos*) is greater than his master; no messenger outranks the one who sent him (Jn 13:12-16).

What both portraits have in common, of course, is that quality which is basic to the biblical idea of service, namely *humility*. This is evident in *Mary's fiat* at the Annunciation, "I am the servant (*doúle*) of the Lord. Let it be done to me as you say" (Lk 1:38). It is evident also in her loving service toward her cousin Elizabeth (her immediate response to the news of her pregnancy) for in her canticle she exclaims, "He [Yahweh] has looked upon his servant (*doúle*) in her lowliness . . ." (Lk 1:48).

Even more instructive for us, this humility is the fundamental characteristic of Jesus' service throughout his entire life, as Paul reminds his readers (and us) in Philippians 2:3-8,

> Never act out of rivalry or conceit; rather, let all parties think humbly of others as superior to themselves, each of you looking to others' interests rather than to his own. Your attitude must be that of Christ:
>
> > Though he was in the form of God,
> >   he did not deem equality with God
> >   something to be grasped at.
> >
> > Rather, he *emptied* himself
> >   and took the form of a slave (*doûlos*)
> >   being born in the likeness of men.
> >
> > He was known to be of human estate,
> >   and it was thus that he *humbled* himself,
> >   obediently accepting even death,
> >   death on a cross!

It should be clear, then, that the very first and most basic quality of our service of God and others ought to be humility. Is this not what Jesus is inculcating in that lesson unique to Luke's Gospel?

> If one of you had a servant (*doûlos*) plowing or herding sheep and he came in from the fields, would you say to him, "Come and sit down at table"? Would you not rather say, "Prepare my supper. Put on your apron and wait on (*diakoneîn*) me while I eat and drink. You can eat and drink afterward"? Would you be grateful to the servant (*doûlos*) who was only carrying out his orders? It is quite the same with you who hear me. When you have done all you have been commanded to do, say "We are useless servants (*doûloi*). We have done no more than our duty" (Lk 17:7-10).

And does this not put into sharper relief the loving reward of our

"Master" to those who alertly await his "return from a wedding" (Lk 12:36)?

> Blessed are those servants (*doûloi*) whom the Master, on his return, will find watching. Amen I say to you that he will put on an apron, have them recline at table, and set about waiting (*diakoneîn*) on them! (Lk 12:37, WD)

As a footnote on humility, the first quality that must characterize our service of God and others, let me simply call attention to the extraordinary word for servant (*hyperétes*) with which Paul refers to himself and his fellow-missionaries in 1 Corinthians 4:1. To translate the Greek word literally, I would need an entire English sentence, for it denotes a galley slave rowing on the lowest bank of oars in a Roman trireme! How low can one get?

Ideally, in our service of Christ toward others and in others, there is absolutely no place for pride, vainglory, "eye service" (really "I service"), or desire for "self-fulfillment." I say "ideally" because, in reality, our innate self-centeredness has a way of infiltrating even our most altruistic deeds. For this reason, our service is a constant struggle, by God's grace, to be more and more emptied of self and filled with Christ, whose motives and deeds are always perfectly pure.

Ours should be the humble sentiment of John the Baptist, "He must increase, while I must decrease!" (Jn 3:30). And St. Paul's advice to Christian slaves in his day might well be applied to our Christian service in general,

> Do not render service for appearance only and to please men, but do God's will with your whole heart as slaves of Christ. Give your service willingly, doing it for the Lord rather than men (Ep 6:6-7).

Besides humility, the principal virtue that should characterize our service is, of course, that of *love*. After all, service is but the overflow of love. I do not think it would be twisting the thought of *St. Vincent de Paul,* the great Apostle of Love, to translate his beautiful statement about zeal[15] into one about service, "If love is a fire, service is its flame; if love is a sun, service is its ray." And indeed love is a fire which, unless it spreads outward to others, will soon consume itself and die. Love is a sun, enlightening, warming, energizing others, and if it should fail to emit its rays, to shine on others, then it becomes a burned out cinder in the sky or, worse still, a black hole, drawing everything inexorably into itself!

Yet "love is a many splendored thing" and, to be genuine, needs to evidence certain qualities, especially when it gives itself in service. As we have already seen, "to love is to give" (Ac 20:35; 2 Cor 9:7), and "to love deeply is to forgive completely" (Mt 18:21-35). Then, of course, Paul's lyrical description of *Christian agápe-love* (1 Cor 13:4-7) is particularly incisive when applied to service,

> Love is patient; love is kind. Love is not jealous, it does not put on airs, it is not snobbish. Love is never rude, it is not self-seeking, it is not prone to anger; neither does it brood over injuries.

> Love does not rejoice in what is wrong but rejoices with the truth. There is no limit to love's forbearance, to its trust, its hope, its power to endure.

But to St. Paul's unforgettable description of love in action, we should add another, one which is commonly overlooked, namely that of St. Peter (1 P 4:8-11),

> Let your love for one another be constant, for love covers a multitude of sins. Be mutually hospitable without complaining. As generous distributors of God's manifold grace, put your gifts at the service of one another, each in the measure he has received. The one who speaks is to deliver God's message. The one who serves is to do it with the strength provided by God. Thus, in all of you God is to be glorified through Jesus Christ; to him be glory and dominion throughout the ages.   Amen.

Both of these quotations call our attention to something which we need to consider at this time, the so-called *charismatic gifts*. Paul is extolling *agápe-love* as superior to all the charismatic gifts, while Peter is referring to these gifts as means of serving others. And we need to reflect on these gifts at this time precisely because they are "given for the common good" (1 Cor 12:7), to be used in "roles of service for the faithful to build up the body of Christ" (Ep 4:11).

God has bestowed on each of us certain gifts or talents, natural and supernatural, not for our own sakes but for those of others. Their generous and proper use, of course, will bring rewards for ourselves both in this life and the next, while their misuse or neglect will bring punishment, according to the clear lesson of Jesus' parable (Mt 25:14-30 and Lk 19:11-27). But it is also perfectly clear, especially in Paul's writings, that we must use these talents or gifts, not for our own self-glorification, not for our own self-fulfillment, not for our own spiritual perfection, but for the good of others. Unlike the "Seven Gifts of the Holy Spirit" (cf. Is 11:2) which are directly sanctifying, the charismatic gifts are *only indirectly sanctifying*; that is, they contribute to our sanctification only to the extent that we use them humbly and lovingly in the service of others.

Obviously, then, we need to discover our gifts, perfect them insofar as possible, value them according to their usefulness for others, and put them at the service of others inside and outside the Church. The teaching of the New Testament, it seems to me, is crystal clear in this regard. For example, Paul (1 Cor 12-14) deals with this very question of the "spiritual gifts" (1 Cor 12:1), evidently because they were becoming a source of pride, confusion, and division among his Corinthian converts. He may even have been thinking of them in his opening "Thanksgiving" (1 Cor 1:4-8) when, with a possible touch of *delicate irony,* he "thanks God" for richly endowing them "with every gift of speech and knowledge," the very roots of their divisions (1 Cor 1-4) and confusion (1 Cor 14).

Notice how masterfully Paul handles the situation. In 1 Corinthians 12, he lists the charismatic gifts, placing the less spectacular first and such gifts as prophecy (speaking in God's name) and the gift of tongues (ecstatic utterances) last. In 1 Corinthians 13, he insists on the superiority of *agápe-love* over all charismatic gifts. In 1 Corinthians 14, he treats the gift of tongues more as a problem than a great asset and lays down rules for the use of prophecy and especially tongues, so that all may be done "properly and in good order" (1 Cor 14:40). In Romans 12:3-8, Paul again warns against pride and disunity, then gives another list of the charismatic gifts, this time featuring prophecy, ministry, teaching, moral exhortation, and administration, and quite notably omitting the gift of tongues altogether. Finally Paul lists particularly those gifts which characterize the leadership of the Church: "apostles, prophets, evangelists, pastors, and teachers" (Ep 4:11), again totally omitting the gift of tongues. We have already seen St. Peter's reference to the gifts, where he emphasizes their loving use for others and mentions only speech and service. And finally in the longer ending of Mark, Jesus himself provides a "gift-list" of sorts, but obviously in a missionary context, and with a reference, not to ecstatic utterances, but to "new languages" (Mk 16:17).

Is all of this a rejection or denigration of charismatic gifts, especially the gift of tongues? Not at all! It is rather a plea to understand these gifts, which we all receive in varying amounts and degrees, and to use them as they are intended, namely for the loving service of others, rather than for our own private use or, worse still, for our own glorification. If the reader is interested in further exploration of the charismatic gifts, especially as they are mentioned in the Bible, I recommend the perusal of two of my articles in the *New Catholic Encyclopedia,* one on the *Charismatic Gifts* in general,[16] the other on the *Gift of Tongues.*[17]

Before concluding our treatment of the qualities and gifts which should characterize our service, let me call attention to three particular qualities or virtues which I have cherished ever since my days as a missionary in China. They are called *missionary virtues* in the *Maryknoll Spiritual Directory* compiled by *Bishop James E. Walsh,*[18] but I submit that they are extremely important in any and all kinds of loving service, as should be evident simply from a listing of them. The virtues, which can be easily remembered as "Triple A Virtues," are: *accessibility* or availability (being present, attentive, and willing to help), *adaptability* (being flexible, open-minded, and sensitive to the needs of others rather than our own), and *affability* (being open-hearted, cheerful, and able to laugh at ourselves). All three, I believe, are most important, but I have a special fondness for the third which, it seems to me, can go so far in making our service acceptable to those whom we are trying to help or, in the words of *St. Vincent,* to induce the poor to "forgive us"[19] for our charity to them in their need.

To these three virtues, *Bishop Walsh* wisely adds the virtue of *courage or fortitude,*[20] which is so important in confronting problems and persons in order to help those who are disadvantaged and oppressed. The Second Vatican Council, in its challenging *Constitution on the Church in the Modern World,*[21] wisely lists some of the principal causes of suffering in the world,

> The varieties of crime are numerous: all offenses against life itself, such as murder, genocide, abortion, euthanasia, and willful suicide; all violations of the integrity of the human person, such as mutilation, physical and mental torture, undue psychological pressures; all offenses against human dignity, such as subhuman living conditions, arbitrary imprisonment, deportation, slavery, prostitution, the selling of women and children, degrading working conditions where men are treated as mere tools for profit rather than free and responsible persons: all these and the like are criminal; they poison civilization; and they debase the perpetrators more than the victims, and militate against the honor of the Creator (n 27).

In a world beset with so many forms of injustice, it would be nothing short of sinful on our part to stand idly by and do nothing. To repeat the blunt words of James 4:17, "When a man knows the right thing to do and does not do it, he sins." However, the *virtue of prudence* and the *gift of counsel* require that we carefully study the situation, not as an excuse for inaction, but in order to be able to act responsibly and helpfully rather than "like a bull in a china shop!" In this, of course, we have the glowing example of Jesus and his Saints, e.g. St. Paul, who were able so admirably to combine courage with wisdom in the service of others.

For this delicate combination of virtues and gifts, we need special grace, and grace is normally gained through prayer. As an aid, then, in the fulfillment of our Christian love and service, I offer the following prayer, which is commonly known as the *"Christopher Prayer"*[22] after the marvelous movement for personal action in the world begun by the late *Father James Keller*, M.M.:

> Father, grant that I may be
>   a bearer of Christ Jesus, Your Son.
> Allow me to warm the often cold, impersonal
>   scene of modern life with Your burning love.
> Strengthen me, by Your Holy Spirit,
>   to carry out my mission of changing the world
>   or some definite part of it for the better.
> Despite my lamentable failures, bring home to me
>   that my advantages are Your blessings
>   to be shared with others.
> Make me more energetic in setting to rights
>   what I find wrong with the world
>   instead of complaining about it or myself.
> Nourish in me a practical desire
>   to build up rather than tear down
>   to reconcile more than polarize
>   to go out on a limb rather than crave security.
> Never let me forget that it is far better
>   to light one candle than to curse the darkness.
> And to join my light, one day, with Yours.   Amen.

SUFFERING AND SACRIFICE:

The third and final form of sharing for our reflection in this chapter is that of suffering and sacrifice. I prefer to use the two terms in conjunction with each other in order to make clear: (1) that suffering as such is spiritually neither good nor bad, but *indifferent,* for it is only *how* we accept suffering that can give it a vital value; and (2) that by sacrifice I do not mean a ritual or form of worship such as the temple sacrifices of the Old Testament and the Christian Eucharist, nor an act of self-denial (important as that is), but the *sanctifying of suffering* by a proper attitude of acceptance. In other words, I am using the term sacrifice according to its Latin etymology, in which it means quite literally "to *make sacred, to consecrate."*

In order to address ourselves to this question of suffering and sacrifice, I think it best if we stand back a moment and look at the *general attitude* toward suffering that is prevalent today. Because of our basic instinct of self-preservation, the comparatively soft and comfortable life we enjoy in our consumer society, and the seductive Siren's call of media commercials to avoid pain and discomfort at all costs in favor of pleasure and convenience, we tend to grow up with a distinct horror of suffering in all its forms: physical, emotional, mental, and spiritual. We seem to be far more afraid of pain than we are of sin!

But to compound the problem, the average Christian receives precious *little guidance* in the matter and, when it does come, it is quite likely to be *misguidance.* From many a pulpit and religious television program these days, the strange doctrine is being blared forth that our loving God does not want us to suffer in any way. If illness or injury or anything else occurs to cause or even threaten pain, then we should pray with all our might for a miracle of help and healing. If the miracle does not happen and we must undergo the suffering, that is a sure sign that we do not possess and pray with enough faith. What a travesty of Christianity! What an example of something I call "Cry-baby Christianity" and "Self-pity Spirituality"!

Please do not misunderstand my meaning. I am not advocating some kind of Christian masochism or a "martyr complex," still less am I proposing a modern form of Stoicism. No, I am simply calling attention to what is so very clear in the Word of God, that suffering is not the unmitigated evil we seem to consider it today, and that with the proper attitude it can and should become a *key means* of our own sanctification and of the service of others. Let us therefore look at the evidence of the Bible.

In the early history of the Israelites, basically up to the time of the Babylonian Captivity in the sixth century B.C., the so-called *Deuteronomic theology* of rewards and punishments prevailed. According to this teaching, if peoples as a whole or individual persons were faithful to God, then they could expect wonderful rewards of health, prosperity, and posterity in this life; if not, they would be punished in this life in many ways and go to an early grave without offspring. This kind of thinking seems to have resulted from two factors: (1) Israel was called as a people rather than as individuals; and (2) early Israel was given no clear revelation about any kind of afterlife, possibly because of the overemphasis on the afterlife and its gods in Egypt, from which Yahweh's People had been delivered. Their simplistic, even childish, attitude, therefore, was quite understandable and, indeed, forgivable. But one would hardly expect to find that same kind of simplistic and childish attitude among Christians today!

Even the Jews of the *Old Testament,* in the course of time, began to develop a far more mature theology of suffering. In the "questioning books" of *Job* and *Ecclesiastes or Qoheleth,* the traditional Deuteronomic theology is shown to be untrue in actual fact. In the *Prophets* generally, suffering is predicted as a punishment for covenant infidelity, yes, but also as a means of purification and future fidelity. In *Isaiah 53,* the supreme suffering of the Servant of Yahweh is clearly seen as expiatory and redemptive of the sins of others. And in Daniel (12:1-3), 2 Maccabees (6:12-7:41; 12:38-46), and Wisdom (2:1-3:12), there seems to be rather clear teaching about an *afterlife* where things are set right after the injustices of this life.

It is in the *New Testament,* however, that the full Theology of Suffering unfolds. For not only are resurrection and an eternal afterlife clearly taught, indeed almost taken for granted, but the unique *example and instruction of Jesus* about his own redemptive death (e.g. Lk 24:26; Mk 8:31 and parallels), and the necessity of his disciples to follow him even to the cross (e.g. Mk 8:34-38 and parallels) provide us with such a clear attitude about suffering that any contrary one would appear to be unthinkable. Like Paul, especially after his unsuccessful "philosophical" address at Athens (Ac 17), we should be determined to "speak of nothing but Jesus Christ and him crucified!" (1 Cor 2:2).

As children of the resurrection (Lk 20:36), we can and should be filled with joy, but a *spiritual joy* that also embraces the crucifixion which, after all, constitutes the condition of the resurrection for Jesus and for us. As a help in this regard, I would like to share with the reader a haunting poem by Elizabeth Cheney, entitled *There is a Man on the Cross,*[23] which was a great favorite of the late beloved Bishop Fulton Sheen,

> Whenever there is silence around me
> By day or by night —
> I am startled by a cry.
> It came down from the cross —
> The first time I heard it.
> I went out and searched —
> And found a man in the throes of crucifixion,
> And I said, "I will take you down,"
> And I tried to take the nails out of his feet.
> But he said, "Let them be
> For I cannot be taken down
> Until every man, every woman, and every child
> Come together to take me down."
> And I said, "But I cannot hear you cry.
> What can I do?"
> And he said, "Go about the world —
> Tell everyone that you meet —
> There is a man on the cross!"

We have already seen, earlier in this chapter, that to be a Christian means to be a candidate for *martyrdom*. That is certainly the unchanging teaching of Jesus to each of his followers, who must "take up his cross and follow" him (Mk 8:34; Mt 10:38; 16:24; Lk 9:23; 14:27). Here I want to emphasize that this applies also to every kind of suffering that may come our way. It is significant that *Luke,* who is concerned about the day-to-day life of Christians, adds the word "each day" or "daily" to Jesus' injunction about carrying our cross after him (Lk 9:23; cf. also Mt 5:10-12).

It may well be that Luke's "daily" requirement reflects his long association with *Paul,* who views his sufferings in union with Christ as both sanctifying and rewarding. In the eighth chapter of Romans, which comprises the very heart of Paul's Spiritual Theology, he assures us,

> The Spirit himself gives witness with our spirit that we are children of God. But if we are children, we are heirs as well: heirs of God, heirs with Christ, if only we suffer with him so as to be glorified with him. I consider the suffering of the present to be as nothing compared with the glory to be revealed in us (Rm 8:16-18; cf. also Rm 8:35-39).

But even more importantly, Paul sees his sufferings as the very *sufferings of Christ himself* in and through him for the sake of others,

> Continually we carry about in our bodies the *dying of Jesus,* so that in our bodies the life of Jesus may also be revealed. . . . Death is at work in us, but life in you (2 Cor 4:10-12).

> I have been *crucified with Christ,* and the life I live now is not my own; Christ is living in me (Gal 2:19-20). May I never boast of anything but the cross of our Lord Jesus Christ! Through it the world has been crucified to me and I to the world (Gal 6:14). Henceforth, let no man trouble me, for I bear the brand marks (Greek, *stigmata*) of Jesus in my body (Gal 6:17).

> Even now I find my joy in the suffering I endure for you. In my

own flesh I fill up what is lacking in the *sufferings of Christ* for
the sake of his body, the Church (Col 1:24).

One basic fact that we must keep clearly in mind is that Jesus did
not save the world by his teaching, still less by his miracles. He saved
the world by his redemptive sufferings, death, and resurrection. And,
according to Paul's Theology of Suffering, I believe that Christ, now
risen and glorified, desires to continue the *ongoing redemption* of the
world *through us*. Not that his death and resurrection did not suffice
for the redemption of a thousand worlds, but that the world continues
to need overwhelming grace in order to accept the redemption of
Christ. And this is precisely why our own acceptance of suffering in
union with Christ, our own sacrifice (making sacred) of the pains and
inconveniences that beset us, can be redemptive for ourselves and
others, because thereby Christ continues to suffer in and through us.

What a tremendous difference this can make in our lives! Suffering, of course, is part of our human existence, and any dream that
some may have of a perfect technological future when all pain and
suffering will be only a memory is certainly an illusion. It is *how we
suffer*, or rather *why we suffer*, that can make all the difference in the
world. *Viktor Frankl* learned in a Nazi concentration camp the truth of
Nietzsche's profound statement that, "He who has a why to live, can
endure almost any how!"[24]

If we suffer with a *purpose*, suffer in union with Christ out of
love and service to others, then not only are others greatly benefited
but we find that the suffering itself is far easier to bear. As with any
heavy object, the farther we try to keep the cross away from us, the
harder it is to carry, but if we embrace it and hold it close, then it
becomes surprisingly light and easy to bear. "My yoke is easy and my
burden light!" (Mt 11:30).

To express it another way, if we surrender ourselves to Christ
and allow him to suffer in and through us, then it is he who bears the
cross in us and, with Paul, we can exclaim, "Even now I find my joy
in the suffering I endure for you!" (Col 1:24). Perhaps this is most

vividly expressed in the following reflection which, to my knowledge, is anonymous,

FOOTPRINTS

One night a man had a dream. He dreamed he was walking along the beach with the Lord. Across the sky flashed scenes from his life. For each scene he noticed two sets of footprints in the sand, one belonging to him, the other to the Lord.

When the last scene of his life flashed before him, he looked back at the footprints in the sand. Then he noticed that many times along the path of his life there was only one set of footprints. He also noticed that it happened at the very lowest and saddest times in his life.

That really bothered him and he questioned the Lord about it. "Lord, you said that once I decided to follow You, You'd walk with me all the way. But I have noticed that during the most troublesome times in my life there is only one set of footprints. I don't understand why in times when I needed You most You would leave me."

The Lord replied, "My precious, precious child! I love you and would never leave you. During your times of trial and suffering, when you see only one set of footprints, it was then that I carried you!"[25]

SUMMARY AND CONCLUSION:

In this chapter we have reflected on the Outer Dimensions of our Spiritual Life, our wonderful challenge as Christians to share with others the love, the grace, the talents, and especially the life of the Risen Christ Himself in us, that our loving Father has so generously bestowed on us. We have seen that our sharing can take three principal forms, those of witnessing, serving and suffering. And even our witnessing can be accomplished by our life, our words, or possibly our death.

There is much food for meditation and contemplation here, but perhaps a final reflection by *Cardinal Newman,* at once inspired and inspiring, encouraging and consoling, may best serve as a capsule summary and conclusion,

REFLECTION 26

God has created me to do Him
    some definite service;
He has committed some work to me
    which He has not committed to another.

I have my mission . . .
    I am a link in a chain,
    a bond of connection between persons.

He has not created me for naught.

I shall be an angel of peace,
    a preacher of truth in my own place
    while not intending it —
    if I do but keep His commandments.

Therefore I will trust Him.

Whatever, wherever I am,
    I can never be thrown away.

If I am in sickness,
    my sickness may serve Him.

If I am in perplexity,
    my perplexity may serve Him.

If I am in sorrow,
    my sorrow may serve Him.

He does nothing in vain.

He knows what He is about.

RECOMMENDED READING LIST

1. Horbury, W. and McNeil, ed. *Suffering and Martyrdom in the New Testament,* Cambridge, England: Cambridge University Press, 1981.
2. Kelsey, Morton T. *Caring: How Can We Love One Another?* New York: Paulist Press, 1981.
3. Morris, Leon. *Testaments of Love: A Study of Love in the Bible,* Grand Rapids, MI: Wm. B. Eerdmans Publishing Co., 1981.
4. Nouwen, Henry. *The Living Reminder: Service and Prayer in Memory of Jesus Christ,* New York: Seabury Press, 1977.
5. Trites, A.A. *The New Testament Concept of Witness,* Cambridge, England: Cambridge University Press, 1977.

QUESTIONS FOR REFLECTION AND DISCUSSION

1. If we are striving to live a deeply Spiritual Life, how do we resolve the tension between the two commandments of love?
2. What does witnessing mean, and what are some of the general or special ways in which we can witness for Christ before others?
3. If called upon to witness for Christ with our lives, would we willingly do so or would we deny or compromise our faith?
4. If we are followers of Christ, who came "not to be served but to serve," what gifts do we have and use for serving others?
5. What is our attitude toward suffering and sacrifice in our own lives, and does it reflect the attitude of Christ?

SECTION THREE:
THE MEANS OF THE SPIRITUAL LIFE

CHAPTER TEN

SPECIAL MEANS OF THE RELATIONSHIP, PART I:
Encountering Christ in the Church and Her Liturgy

Years ago, I read an anonymous aphorism that has stuck in my mind ever since, "The trouble with life is that it's half over before we realize that it's a *do-it-yourself* proposition." How very true! And yet, if we stop to analyze that saying, we find that it is only half true. Life is, indeed, a do-it-yourself proposition in the sense that no one else can live it for us, but at the same time life, especially the Spiritual Life, is certainly not a do-it-yourself proposition for, of and by ourselves, we "can do nothing" (Jn 15:5). We need God's help at every turn, in every circumstance of our life. And if this is true of our natural life, how much more of our Spiritual Life. It takes supernatural means to accomplish supernatural ends. There is no such thing as a "self-made person" in the Spiritual Life!

We have already considered some of the principal means of living and growing in the Spiritual Life, such as self-discipline in Chapter Six and prayer in Chapter Eight. These are means that are common to any and all who are attempting to practice a Spiritual Life, whether they be Catholic, Protestant, Jewish, Moslem, Hindu, Buddhist, or whatever. So universal are they that I have chosen to treat them under the headings of qualities and dimensions of the Spiritual Life.

In these final chapters, however, we need to consider some of the *special means* which our loving God has provided for those of us who are trying to live the Spiritual Life as Christians, and especially as Catholic Christians. These means are primarily the Church and the Sacraments: the former as the general, the latter as the particular, means of our salvation, transformation, and sanctification.

Symbolic of the close, mutual relationship between the Church and the Sacraments in our Spiritual Life is one of the sacred sites in Galilee traditionally associated with the life of Jesus Christ. On the western shore of the Sea of Galilee, just south of the Mount of the Beatitudes, lies a small plain called *Et-Tabgha* containing two churches which have both been recently restored: that of the Multiplication of the Loaves and Fishes (Jn 6:1-15 and parallels) and that of the Primacy of Peter (Jn 21:9-19). What is particularly interesting about this site is that the name, *Et-Tabgha*, happens to be an Arabic corruption of a Greek word, *Heptápēgon (Chōrión)*, which literally means "(Place of) Seven Springs."[1] At one and the same time, we are reminded of the *Church*, founded by Christ on the rock of Peter (Mt 16:13-19; Jn 21:15-19) and the *Seven Sacraments* of the Church whereby, as through seven springs or streams, the risen Christ continues to impart to us the Life of the Spirit (Jn 7:37-39), with particular emphasis on those greatest of Sacraments, Baptism and the Holy Eucharist (Jn 6 and Jn 21:9-14).

If all of this seems too imaginative, too symbolic, too mystical, for a twentieth century Western reader, my reply is that without imagination, symbolism, and even mysticism, we will never begin to appreciate the New Testament, especially the writings of *St. John,* rich as they are in ecclesial and sacramental imagery. Multiple allusions and mystical symbols are so characteristic of Eastern mentality in general and of Johannine contemplation in particular that, if we are really looking for the meaning intended by the human authors of the Bible (which is the literal sense of Scripture), then we must be open, not only to their often matter-of-fact simplicity, but also to their frequent flights of creative imagination. Like *Harvey Cox,* we must be willing to leave the "Secular City"[2] for the "Feast of Fools"![3] And with *Zorba the Greek,* we need "a touch of madness"; for, unless we "cut the string," we'll "never really live!"[4]

In what follows on the Church and Sacraments, I will obviously have to limit my observations severely, confining myself largely to reflections stemming from my biblical studies and personal prayer. But this is as it should be. The wealth of considerations inherent in these subjects as well as the abundance of literature already available on them render extensive treatment on my part both impossible and unnecessary. That having been said, let us now address ourselves to these fascinating subjects of the Church and the Sacraments, which are so important and helpful as means in our Spiritual Life.

THE CHURCH:

One of the most dramatic moments in the life of Jesus occurred in the area of *Caesarea Philippi,* now called *Banyas,* an Arabic corruption of the Greek word *Paneas,* after *Pan,* the whimsical god associated with groves and streams. The present name fits admirably because, whatever may have been the magnificence of the city of Caesarea Philippi in the first century A.D., nothing remains today except groves and streams.

Jesus had taken his Apostles away from Jewish territory into the pagan district of *Tyre and Sidon* and then into the Greek area known as the *Decapolis* or Ten Cities (Mk 7:24-8:9 and parallels). The Gospels have very little to say about this mysterious excursion, but it seems quite possible, if not probable, that Jesus was using this opportunity to prepare his immediate followers to carry on after him. In other words, he was conducting a kind of peripatetic seminary, of which the climax would be a brief "final examination" at Caesarea Philippi, comprising two questions, "Who do people say that I am?" (Mk 8:27) and "Who do you say that I am?" (Mk 8:29).

After varied responses to the first question, *Peter* answers the second question correctly for all the Apostles, as we see in the Synoptic Gospels: "You are the Messiah" (Mk 8:29), "The Messiah of God'' (Lk 9:20), "You are the Messiah, the Son of the living God!'' (Mt 16:16). And, in John's equivalent at Capernaum, Peter again answers for all, "Lord, to whom shall we go? You have the words of eternal life. We believe and know that you are the Holy One of God!'' (Jn 6:68-69, NIV).

In Matthew's ecclesial Gospel, Jesus' response to Peter's profession of faith is his promise of the *primacy* in his Church,

> Blessed are you, Simon son of Jonah, for this was not revealed to you by man, but by my Father in heaven. And I tell you that you are Peter (rock), and on this rock I will build my church, and the gates of Hades will not overcome it. I will give you the keys of the kingdom of heaven; whatever you bind on earth will be bound in heaven, and whatever you loose on earth will be loosed in heaven (Mt 16:17-19, NIV).

It is not my purpose here to defend the Petrine and papal claims to the primacy in the Church. The context, the wording (clear in Greek and translations, but even more decisive in the *Aramaic* spoken by Jesus),[5] and subsequent confirmations in the New Testament and Church History[6] make such a defense unnecessary. Instead, I would like to concentrate on the *Church* itself, of which the mention above is the very first in the Gospels. By Church, I mean the *Christian* Church and especially, as a Catholic writing primarily for Catholics, the *Roman Catholic* Church.

The questions that Jesus asks of his Apostles about himself at Caesarea Philippi he continues to ask in each age about the Church or, to be more exact, about himself living in the Church, "Who do people say that I am?'' and "Who do you say that I am?''. And, just as at Caesarea Philippi, the answers to the first question vary greatly, depending largely on peoples' background and point of view.

To some, who are poorly educated and thoroughly indoctrinated, she is seen (through a wholesale misreading of the Book of Revelation)[7] as the beast, the dragon, the great harlot of the Apocalypse. To others, educated according to secular humanism, she is regarded as an irrelevant anachronism and a dying institution. But, on the other hand, there are a great number of others who admire, even envy, the tremendous longevity, prestige, and influence enjoyed by the Church, including the papacy, through the centuries. Noteworthy among these was the great English Protestant historian, *Lord Macaulay,* who penned the following eloquent tribute in 1840:

> There is not, and there never was on this earth, a work of human policy so well deserving of examination as the *Roman Catholic Church*. The history of that Church joins together the two great ages of human civilization. No other institution is left standing which carries the mind back to the times when the smoke of sacrifice rose from the Pantheon, and when camelopards and tigers bounded in the Flavian amphitheatre.
>
> The proudest royal houses are but of yesterday, when compared with the line of the *Supreme Pontiffs*. That line we trace back in an unbroken series, from the pope who crowned Napoleon in the nineteenth century to the pope who crowned Pepin in the eighth; and far beyond the time of Pepin the august dynasty extends, till it is lost in the twilight of fable. The republic of Venice came next in antiquity. But the republic of Venice is gone, and the papacy remains. The Papacy remains, not in decay, not a mere antique, but full of life and youthful vigour.
>
> The *Catholic Church* is still sending forth to the farthest ends of the world missionaries as zealous as those who landed in Kent with Augustin, and still confronting hostile kings with the same spirit with which she confronted Attila. The number of her children is greater than in any former age. Her acquisitions in the New World have more than compensated for what she has lost in the Old. Her spiritual ascendency extends over the vast countries which lie between the plains of the Missouri and Cape Horn, countries which, a century hence, may not improbably contain a population as large as that which now inhabits Europe. Nor do we see any sign which indicates that the term of her *long*

dominion is approaching. She saw the commencement of all the governments and of all the ecclesiastical establishments that now exist in the world; and we feel no assurance that she is not destined to see the end of them all. She was great and respected before the Saxon had set foot in Britain, before the Frank had passed the Rhine, when Grecian eloquence still flourished in Antioch, when idols were still worshipped in the temple of Mecca. And she may still exist in *undiminished vigour* when some traveller from New Zealand shall, in the midst of a vast solitude, take his stand on a broken arch of London Bridge to sketch the ruins of St. Paul's.[8] (italics added)

Helpful as is the answer to Jesus' first question applied to the Church, "Who do people say that I am?" our greater concern is with the answer to the second, "Who do *you* say that I am?". In other words, what is the image of the Church among her own members? And, for our special purposes, what is her image among those members who are seriously striving to live a deeply Spiritual Life? With this as with the first question, we hear a *variety of answers* rather than the one answer supplied by Peter. But perhaps the answers can at least be grouped into two principal types which we can label *Vatican I* and *Vatican II* images of the Church. This is admittedly a simplistic division which fails to note the many possible variations according to individuals, yet for our purposes it can serve to highlight some important general attitudes for our consideration and self-examination.

Having grown up as a *Vatican I Catholic* (I was forty years old and fifteen years a priest before Vatican II began), I can clearly remember our image of the Church during that period. To us the Church was, above all, a visible, perfect, supernatural society, "the pillar and bulwark of truth" (1 Tm 3:15), infallibly guided by the pope, and triumphantly exhibiting the four essential marks of oneness, holiness, catholicity, and apostolicity, which to us meant unchangeability. We felt proud, secure, even complacent in our Church

Did he meet T. DEC ? — CHINA

membership. All our emphasis was on the Church's *divine* origin, nature, and protection; little or none on her human membership, leadership, and nature. Consequently, anything that suggested imperfection or scandal was quickly "swept under the rug" of our idealism.

Thanks be to God, even *before Vatican II*, my image of the Church had already begun to change, principally from my China experience (1948-1951) which taught me *ecumenism,* and from my biblical studies, reflection, and teaching (1952-1960) which provided a more accurate and complete *profile of the Church* according to the Word of God. In fact, to me the whole secret of Vatican II was that, for the first time in centuries, everything was based on *Scripture.*[9] I use the word "secret" designedly because unfortunately the biblical basis of the Council has remained undiscovered even by many priests and unexplained to many of the laity, with the result that they continue to cling to their Vatican I image of the Church as if it were her official and traditional, her true and complete portrait. How sad! What is really needed today, particularly in regard to the Church, is *memory* of the past, yes, but also *understanding* of the present, and *vision* of the future. And nothing can supply this better than a grasp of *Salvation History* as it unfolds in Sacred Scripture and Church History.

The *biblical portrait* of the Church, which is so beautifully reflected in the *Constitution on the Church*[10] of Vatican II, shows her first of all in relation to God's Chosen People, *Israel.* Having given us a human nature that is naturally social and communal (Gn 1-2), it is not surprising that God has always called persons into relationship with himself, not as isolated individuals but as heads or members of a *community* of people. So it was with Abram (Gn 12:1-3), Isaac (Gn 25:23), and Jacob (Gn 35:9-12). So it was also, of course, with Moses and the Israelites (Ex 3, etc.).

Now, just as Israel was called out of Egypt (Ho 11:1) to be covenanted with and consecrated to God at Mt. Sinai as his Chosen People (Ex 19:3-6), his Congregation or Assembly (Hebrew *qahal,* Greek *ekklēsia* from *ek+kaleō*=to call out), so the Church has been *called* out of all the nations of the earth (Mt 28:19) to be *covenanted* with and *consecrated* through Christ with God the Father as his Chosen People (1 P 2:9-10), his Congregation or Assembly (Greek *ekklēsía*, Latin *ecclesia*, Italian *chiesa*, French *église*, Spanish *iglesia*, English *ecclesial*, etc).

The continuity between Israel and the Church may not seem as crucial to us in our twentieth century Western civilization as it was to first century Jewish Christians, but deeper reflection on this continuity reveals *important corollaries* which can help us achieve a clearer image of the Church in our own time:

(1) It places the Church in the mainstream of Salvation History, which *Luke* appears to see in three phases, namely those of Israel (the Old Testament), Jesus Christ (Luke's Gospel), and the Church (Luke's Acts of the Apostles).[11]

(2) It puts the emphasis where it belongs, namely on the Church as the People of God (*laòs toû theoû*, whence the word *laity*) rather than as a hierarchical institution.

(3) It reminds us that, *however stable* the Church may be, as a city which like Jerusalem stands firm forever (Ps 48; Mt 16:18; 28:20) and a building "built on the foundation of the apostles and prophets, with Christ Jesus Himself as the chief cornerstone" (Ep 2:20, NIV), as the "temple of God" (1 Cor 3:16-17; Ep 2:21-22), and "the pillar and bulwark of truth" (1 Tm 3:15), nevertheless, like the assembly (*qahal, ekklēsía*) of Israel in the desert (Ex, Nb), she is always on the move, always a *"Pilgrim Church"* (Lk 9:51-19:27; Ac 1:8; 1 Cor 10:1-13; Heb 3:7-4:11; 1 P 2:11), not so much a castle as a campaign, not so much a walled city as a wagon train![12]

(4) It instructs us that, as with Israel so with the Church, there is a divinely established and protected *leadership* (Ex 3:10; 4:14-16; 28:1; Nb 12, 16; Mt 16:13-19; 18:15-18; Lk 22:31-32; Jn 21:15-17; Ac 5:4, etc.), but it is to be the gentle and caring leadership of a *shepherd* (Ex 3:1; Nb 20:9-12; 1 S 16:11-13; 2 S 7:8; Ezk 34:23; Mt 18:10-14; Jn 10:11-18; 21:15-19; Ac 20:28; 1 P 5:1-4, etc.).

(5) It also instructs us that, just as God raised up two kinds of

leaders in Israel: *institutional,* such as priests and kings (Ex 28:1; 40:12-15; 2 S 7:11-16) and *inspirational,* such as "judges" and prophets (Jg, Is, Jr, etc.), and just as the latter were often more influential than the former, so also in the Church Jesus has raised up two kinds of leaders: institutional, such as Peter, the Apostles, and their successors as well as *episkopoi* (overseers, bishops), *presbyteroi* (elders, priests), and *diákonoi* (servants, deacons)—(e.g. in Mt 10:1-5 and parallels, 16:18-19; 18:18; 28:18-20; Ac 1-2; 6:1-6; 14:23; 20:17, 28; Ph 1:1; 1 Tm 3:1-12; Tt 1:5-9; 1 P 5:1-4); and inspirational, such as prophets, healers, etc. (1 Cor 12:1-11, 28-30; Rm 12:6-8; Ep 4:11-13; 1 P 4:10-11), and here again the latter can exercise greater influence than the former, as we see in the lives of outstanding inspirational leaders like St. Catherine of Siena, St. Teresa of Avila, St. Elizabeth Ann Seton, Frederick Ozanam, and Mother Teresa of Calcutta.

(6) It cautions us that both the leadership and the membership of the Church, as of Israel, are human and therefore, subject to very *human failures* and even scandals. This is patently evident in the history of Israel, where the human authors inspired by God draw a markedly candid picture of human failure and divine forgiveness, for example in the famous case of King David's adultery and murder (2 S 11-12). It is likewise evident in the early history of the Church, where once again the inspired human authors "tell it as it is," for example in the betrayal of Jesus by a trusted Apostle (Mt 26:14-16; Jn 13:18-30) and denial by his chosen Apostolic leader (Mk 14:66-72 and parallels). Why, then, should it surprise us to find, throughout all of Church History, clear evidence of human weakness, cowardice, sinfulness, and scandal? Did not Jesus himself clearly foretell this in his *Parable of the Wheat and the Weeds* (Mt 13:24-30) and in his *Ecclesial Discourse* (Mt 18:5-9)? Instead of "sweeping them under the rug," I now freely acknowledge them, adding that they constitute some of the strongest proofs of the Church's *divine origin and protection,* for with such human failures even at the highest levels of Church leadership, any purely human institution would long ago have gone out of existence!

(7) Finally, it humbles us to accept the fact that we have *no monopoly* on God's mercy and favor, any more than did the Chosen People of Israel. As Jesus himself pointed out to his fellow townspeople of *Nazareth,*

> There were many widows in Israel in the days of Elijah when the heavens remained closed for three and a half years and a great famine spread over the land. It was to none of these that Elijah was sent, but to a widow of Zarephath near Sidon. Recall, too, the many lepers in Israel in the time of Elisha the prophet; yet not one was cured except Naaman the Syrian (Lk 4:25-27).

And in the moral order, there is the magnificent parable of *Jonah,* apparently designed to remind the Jews after the Exile that God's mercy could extend even to the hated Assyrians who were regarded as the cruelest people of the ancient world. Wisely, then, does *St. Paul* quote Yahweh's statement to Moses, "I will show mercy to whomever I choose; I will have pity on whomever I wish" (Ex 33:19; Rm 9:15). And what about that clearly *ecumenical and interfaith declaration* of Jesus himself, which remained largely unnoticed for so many centuries of religious contentions, "Anyone who is not against us is with us" (Mk 9:40; Lk 9:50)?

Such are some of the principal lessons we can learn from the biblical portrait of the Church as the new Israel, and we have not even considered the many other rich images of the Church in the New Testament. But, before we go on to these, it will be helpful to dwell for a moment on *Church History,* which continues the story of the Acts of the Apostles in this final phase of Salvation History and clearly confirms the biblical portrait of the Church as divine and human, saintly and sinful.

Several years ago, when I was Rector of St. Mary's Seminary in Houston, Texas during the nine years immediately after Vatican II (and used to say facetiously, "Old Rectors never die; they just lose their faculties!"), I received the unusual request from parishioners of Holy Ghost Parish in Bellaire, a suburb of Houston, to present a *survey of Church History* in a single lecture. What? Almost two thousand years of history in one lecture of an hour or so? Impossible! Or so I thought at first. Then the Holy Spirit solved my problem with a flash of inspiration which made it not only possible but highly instructive.

It suddenly dawned on me that all of Church History can be divided into *periods* of some three or four hundred years each, every period beginning with *the letter "C"* as does the word *Church* and clearly exhibiting the divine and human, the ecstasies and agonies, so characteristic of the biblical portrait. Without going into the details in the interest of time and space, let me just indicate the periods, namely: the Cradle Church (1st to 4th century), the Constantinian Church (4th to 8th century), the Carolingian Church (8th to 12th century), the Crusading Church (12th to 16th century), the Catholic Reformation Church (16th to 20th century), and the Contemporary Church (20th century until?). These comprise six periods, but to round out the biblical perfect number of seven, we might also add the Coming Church.

In addition, it also struck me that the very *architecture* of the Church over the centuries tends to mirror her "Pilgrim's Progress" from a predominantly incarnational emphasis in the early centuries, featuring private homes, catacombs, and the highly proportionate Roman and Byzantine styles, through the increasingly transcendental Carolingian and Romanesque to the peak of the Gothic, then back down through the Renaissance, Mannerist, Baroque, and Neo-Classical to the current functional, incarnational, and liturgical emphasis in our contemporary ecclesial architecture.

We have now viewed the Church, at least briefly, in the light of Sacred Scripture and Church History. But the crucial question is, "How does the Church serve as a *powerful means* in our Spiritual Life?" For, like Israel of old (Ex 19:6), we are a "chosen race, a royal priesthood, a holy nation" (1 P 2:9), called to the pursuit of ever greater holiness (Lv 11:44-45; 19:2; 20:7, 26, etc.; Mt 5:48; 1 Th 4:3, etc.). How, then, does the Church help us to grow in holiness?

To this question a number of answers are possible. For instance, the example, encouragement, and support of our fellow *Church members,* especially in our parish community and in subcommunities such as prayer groups, discussion groups, base communities, etc., can and should contribute greatly to our Christian life. The same can be said of the example, instruction, and guidance available from dedicated *Church leaders* of various kinds: the pope, bishops, priests, deacons, religious, and lay ministers. Then, of course, there is the *wisdom of the centuries* which the Church has developed, preserved, and made available to us: the Sacred Scriptures, the writings of the Fathers, Doctors, and other scholars and, in a very special way, the lives and writings of the Saints. Finally, as we will see shortly in this chapter, the Church's *Liturgical and Sacramental System* enables us to grow in grace and holiness "from the cradle to the grave."

To me, however, the primary and central way in which the Church serves as a cardinal means of growth in our Spiritual Life is by enabling us through her to *encounter the Risen Christ* himself, to enter into union with him, to grow in him, to mature in him to "the measure of the age of the fullness of Christ" (Ep 4:13, WD), and to be totally transformed into him according to our destiny (Rm 8:29; 2 Cor 3:18). Or, to view it the other way around, the Church as our Spiritual Mother, in union with Mary the Mother of Jesus and through the dynamism of the Holy Spirit, enables the Risen Christ to be *incarnate anew,* to be "born again" in us (Jn 3:3, 7, NIV), and to grow with us "in wisdom, age, and grace before God and man" (Lk 2:52, WD). Borrowing the beautiful words of Paul, she can say to us with maternal tenderness, "My little children, with whom I am in labor again until Christ be formed in you" (Gal 4:19, WD).

How fitting, then, that at Vatican II the *role of Mary,* the Mother of Jesus and our Spiritual Mother, is described, not in a separate document, but in the *Constitution on the Church!*[13] For Mary is not only the Mother of the Church, as reflected in John 19:26-27, but the model and exemplar of the Church so completely that the one image is used interchangeably for both, as we see in Revelation 12,[14] introduced by the vision of the Ark of the Covenant (Rv 11:19), a Marian allusion in Luke's Visitation account (Lk 1:41-43; cf. 2 S 6:9-15).

To appreciate the essential union of the Risen Christ with the Church, whereby we are able to encounter him through her, we need only reflect briefly on some of the *other images* of the Church in the New Testament. For example, the designation of the Church as the (incipient) *Kingdom of God* — so common in the Synoptic Gospels, notably the Ecclesial Gospel of Matthew with its emphasis on Jesus as the Jewish Messiah or Christ (anointed king) establishing the Kingdom of Heaven — does not refer to the visible power and prestige of Christianity in the world (the third temptation in Mt 4:8-11) but rather to the *invisible reign and rule* of God, particularly in the person of the Risen Christ, within and among his followers. Hence the *Parable of the Leaven* (Mt 13:33 and parallels), and the famous *judgment scene* identifying Jesus and his "least brothers" (Mt 25:31-46). Hence also Jesus' flat declaration before Pontius Pilate, "My kingdom is not of this world!" (Jn 18:36, NIV).

Even more lucid in describing the union of Christ and the Church, and far more consonant with the tradition of the covenant union of Yahweh and Israel in Hosea, Isaiah, Jeremiah, Ezekiel, and the Song of Songs, is Paul's famous *marital analogy* in his Second Letter to the Corinthians (11:2) and especially in his Letter to the Ephesians, notably 5:25-27, RSV:

> Husbands, love your wives, as Christ loved the Church and gave himself up for her, that he might sanctify her, having cleansed her by the washing of water with the word, that he might present the Church to himself in splendor, without spot or wrinkle or any such thing, that she might be holy and without blemish.

Closely related to Paul's marital analogy, finally even identified with it, is his yet more famous analogy of the Church as the (mystical) *Body of Christ*. First stated in 1 Corinthians 12 as an antidote to disunity on the basis of charismatic gifts, it is repeated summarily and for the same purpose in Romans 12:3-8. Then, in the Captivity Letters

of Colossians and Ephesians, the additional note of Christ's headship
of the Body is added (e.g. in Col 1:18; 2:17-19; 3:15; Ep 1:10, 22-23;
3:6; 4:4, 15-16). But it is finally in *Ephesians 5:21-32*, partially
quoted above, that we see the full development of Paul's thought in
this matter, including the identity of the images of wife and body
stemming from the story of the formation of Eve and her union with
Adam in Genesis 2:18-25 (which should be read in full),

> Be subject to one another out of reverence for Christ. Wives, be
> subject to your husbands, as to the Lord. For the husband is the
> head of the wife as Christ is the head of the Church, his body,
> and is himself its Savior . . . (Ep 5:21-23, RSV).

> Even so husbands should love their wives as their own bodies.
> He who loves his wife loves himself. For no man ever hates his
> own flesh, but nourishes and cherishes it, as Christ does the
> Church, because we are members of his body. "For this reason
> a man shall leave his father and mother and be joined to his wife,
> and the two shall become one flesh." This mystery is a profound
> one, and I am saying that it refers to Christ and the Church . . .
> (Ep 5:28-32, RSV).

Paul's profound theology of the union of the risen Christ with his
Church was revealed to him directly by *Christ himself* in the famous
scene on the Damascus road which not only changed Paul's life
forever but also laid the foundation of his Christology and Ecclesiology: "Who are you, Lord?" . . . "I am Jesus, whom you are
persecuting!" (Ac 9:5; 22:8; 26:15). And so well did his friend and
disciple, *Luke the Physician,* learn that basic lesson from Paul that,
not content with recounting it three times in his Acts of the Apostles,
he also made it an underlying theme of the entire work, as seems
evident from the following indications:

(1) In the very opening sentence of Acts, which I have carefully translated from the Greek text, Luke clearly states,

The former work [the Gospel] I produced about all the things, O Theophilus, which Jesus began (*érxato*) to do and to teach until the day on which, having given orders through the Holy Spirit to the apostles whom he had chosen, he was taken up [to Heaven] . . . (Ac 1:1-2, WD).

To me, the unavoidable implication of Luke's thought-provoking declaration is that *Jesus Christ*, during his lifetime on earth before and after his resurrection, only *began* to do and teach those things which form the subject of the Gospel but *continues* to do and teach those things which form the subject of the Acts and indeed of the entire history of the Church, for he never ceases to do and teach through the Church itself.

(2)   There is a subtle but quite evident *parallel* between Luke's Gospel and his Acts of the Apostles, whereby what occurs in the life of *Jesus* in the former book is repeated in the life of the *Church*, or better still the life of Christ in the Church, in the latter work. And, while the Acts of the Apostles are primarily the Acts of *Peter and Paul* (with a running parallel also between them), these "Princes of the Apostles" clearly represent the Church. Therefore, the parallel mentioned above between the life of Jesus "in the flesh" and the life of Jesus in the Church is valid, as can be seen from the following *seven-point outline*:

(a) Prologue to Theophilus (Lk 1:1-4; Ac 1:1-3)
(b) Infancy Gospel of Jesus and the Church
     (Lk 1:5-2:52; Ac 1:4-26)
(c) Jesus and the Church anointed (baptized) by the Holy Spirit
     (Lk 3:1-4:13; Ac 2:1-13)
(d) Preaching and Miracles of Jesus and the Church
     (Lk 4:14-9:50; Ac 2:14-11:18)
(e) Great Journey of Jesus and the Church
     (Lk 9:51-19:27; Ac 11:19-21:14)

(f) Triumph in defeat of Jesus and the Church
     (Lk 19:28-24:51; Ac 21:15-28:28)
(g) Epilogue (Lk 24:52-53; Ac 28:30-31)

Finally, *St John*, the "Beloved Disciple," gives us some of our simplest yet most profound images of the union of Christ with his Church. Perhaps mainly reflecting *Psalm 80*, with its symbols of a flock and a vine in reference to Israel, John shows Jesus relating to his Church with the intimacy of *"the Good Shepherd"* to his flock (Jn 10:14-18, 25-30) and *"the True Vine"* to its branches (Jn 15:1-17), the latter image somewhat in parallel with the vision of Christ amid the *Lampstands* (Rv 1:12-20). And, as if this were not enough, John includes *Jesus' Prayer* at the Last Supper, with its tender references to his oneness with his Father and his followers, e.g.:

> I do not pray for them alone [the Apostles]. I pray also for those who will believe in me through their word, that all may be one as you, Father, are in me, and I in you; I pray that they may be in us, that the world may believe that you sent me.
>
> I have given them the glory you gave me that they may be one, as we are one — I living in them, you living in me — that their unity may be complete. So shall the world know that you sent me, and that you loved them as you loved me. . . .
>
> Just Father, the world has not known you, but I have known you; and these men have known that you sent me. To them I have revealed your name, and I will continue to reveal it so that your love for me may live in them, and I may live in them (Jn 17:20-23, 25-26).

As we reach the close of these reflections about the Church, I cannot help thinking that the reader may well be mystified by what may seem to him or her as *contradictions* in our treatment. For example, I have spoken of the humanness, even the sinfulness of the *Church*, and yet I have also quoted Paul in Ephesians 5:26-27 as using terms like "holy, glorious, immaculate, etc." of the Church. Here, the contradiction is only apparent, for Paul is referring to the Church as Christ has desired it to be, not necessarily as it actually is. A thornier problem may be that of emphasizing the union of *Christ* and the Church while, at the same time, recognizing the latter as prone to human weakness, sinfulness, and scandal. How is this possible? But is this any more difficult than the problem of reconciling Christ's living in us individually with our own propensity to human weakness and sin?

Is this not all part of his *indescribable love* of us, that love whereby he "emptied himself, taking the nature of a slave, becoming [one] in the likeness of men" (Ph 2:7, WD), that same love whereby, in Old Testament terms, "there was in him no stately bearing to make us look at him, nor appearance that would attract us to him" (Is 53:2)? Perhaps Paul expressed it best when he made the shocking statement in 2 Corinthians 5:21, "For our sakes God made him who did not know sin to be sin, so that in him we might become the very holiness of God!"

An old saying that "we like someone because, we love someone although"[15] may apply here. It is easy to like, even to glory in, the Church when we concentrate on all the wonderful and positive qualities she possesses. What is not so easy, what calls for real *agápe-love,* is to recognize and acknowledge her human shortcomings as well, but to love her nonetheless and to work courageously and patiently for her ongoing reform and renewal. *"Ecclesia semper reformanda est"* is still true today, "The Church is always in need of reform!"[16] We might well adopt toward the Church the humble but loyal attitude which *St. Vincent de Paul* inculcated in his followers toward their community, the Congregation of the Mission, namely that a good child loves his mother, however lacking in beauty she may be, simply because she is his mother.[17]

By way of *summary and conclusion* to this section, I hope the reader will bear with me if I repeat the final segment of my *"Creed of a Christian,"* which is especially appropriate here:

I believe in the Church, God's pilgrim People on earth,
So human yet divine, communal Body of the risen Christ,
Saved by Jesus' Blood, consecrated by His Covenant,
Guided by His Spirit and by chosen human leaders,
Serving all with truth and love, word and sacraments,
And leading us, through life and death and rising,
To our eternal home with God, our final End.   Amen.

THE CHURCH'S LITURGY:

In St. Paul's longest, most carefully written, and most theological letter, his great *Epistle to the Romans,* he first presents his doctrinal synthesis on justification and salvation in the first eight chapters and then, after three more doctrinal chapters on the mystery of the temporary rejection of the Jews and call of the Gentiles, he finally proceeds in Chapter Twelve to draw his moral and spiritual conclusions. His opening words of this important section, contained in Romans 12:1-2, are:

And now, my brothers, I beg you through the mercy of God to offer your bodies as a *living sacrifice* holy and acceptable to God, your *spiritual worship.* Do not conform yourselves to this age but be *transformed* by the renewal of your mind, so that you may judge what is God's will, what is good, pleasing and perfect.

Notice that the very first response Paul asks for, indeed begs for, from his readers is that they offer themselves as a *living and spiritual sacrifice in worship to God*; and the second is that, avoiding the false values of this world, they become *transformed, renewed,* and capable of recognizing (and doing) the will of God for them. In this brief introductory paragraph, Paul summarizes brilliantly the *twofold purpose* of the Church's Liturgy, namely her members' gift of themselves in the worship of God and their ongoing transformation, renewal, and growth in responsibility, the ability to respond generously to God's holy will.

The Greek word *leitourgía* has a fascinating etymology. Originally, it meant a public service which one rendered at his own initiative and expense. From this meaning, quite logically, it came to signify any public service, ministry, or worship, particularly one that was offered officially by an authorized priest or minister. As used by the Church, it comprises her entire life of official worship, prayer, and sacraments as well as sacramentals and blessings, calendar and whatever else pertains to the dual focus of the service of God and sanctification of her members.

To fully appreciate the Church's esteem for her Sacred Liturgy, I strongly recommend the careful and prayerful reading of the *Constitution on the Sacred Liturgy* from Vatican II, along with the various documents of implementation published therewith. For example, early in the document itself, the Church declares,

> It is the Liturgy through which, especially in the divine sacrifice of the Eucharist, "the work of our redemption is accomplished," and it is through the Liturgy, especially, that the faithful are enabled to express in their lives and manifest to others the mystery of Christ and the real nature of the true Church. . . .[18]

> From the Liturgy, therefore, and especially from the Eucharist, grace is poured forth upon us as from a fountain, and the sanctification of men in Christ and the glorification of God to which all other activities of the Church are directed, as toward their end, are achieved with maximum effectiveness.[19]

Between *Sacred Scripture and Sacred Liturgy*, there is a very special affinity, which is clearly delineated by the same *Constitution on the Liturgy*,

> Sacred Scripture is of the greatest importance in the celebration of the Liturgy. For it is from it that lessons are read and explained in the homily, and psalms are sung. It is from the Scriptures that the prayers, collects, and hymns draw their

inspiration and their force, and that actions and signs derive their meaning.

Hence in order to achieve the restoration, progress, and adaptation of the Sacred Liturgy it is essential to promote that sweet and *living love for Sacred Scripture* to which the venerable tradition of Eastern and Western rites gives testimony.[20]

As we might expect, the same conviction about the affinity of the Word of God and the Liturgy is echoed in the great *Constitution on Divine Revelation* from Vatican II,

> The Church has always venerated the divine Scriptures as she venerated the Body of the Lord, in so far as she never ceases, particularly in the Sacred Liturgy, to partake of the bread of life and to offer it to the faithful from the one table of the Word of God and the Body of Christ.[21]

The pure worship of God, the *"praise of his glory"* (Ep 1:6, 12, 14), offered at our *"own initiative and expense"* according to the etymology of the Greek word *leitourgia,* promotes not only the greater glory of God but also our own sanctification. But how can we achieve this pure worship of God? Certainly not by ourselves! No, Paul provides the answer in Romans 12:1-2 (already quoted) when, after he urges our "living sacrifice" and "spiritual worship," he then indicates the way in which we can accomplish it, "Do not conform yourselves to this age but be transformed by the renewal of your mind. . . ." The only way in which we can offer pure worship and service to God is through him who is "the way, and the truth, and the life" (Jn 14:6). We need to be so *transformed* into him, so *united* and *identified* with him, so *possessed* by him, that it is really he who lives and worships and serves through us.

And how is this transformation effected? One of the principal ways is through the *Sacraments,* which are primarily concerned with the second purpose of the Sacred Liturgy, our sanctification. According to an ancient saying of the Church, *"Sacramenta propter homines,"* that is, "The Sacraments are (instituted) for the sake of human beings."[22] In what follows, then, we will concentrate on these Sacraments, according to our constant purpose, *"To live the Word: Inspired and Incarnate."*

THE CHURCH'S SACRAMENTS:

About ten miles west of Athens on the road toward Corinth lies one of Greece's, and indeed the ancient world's, most famous religious sites, *Eleusis* (pronounced *Eléfsis* in modern Greek, possibly from *éleusis* meaning "coming" or "advent"), the center of the Eleusinian Mysteries.[23] Supposedly dating back to the Mycaenean epoch (12th century B.C.) or at least to the time of Homer (800 B.C.), but apparently popularized much later, in the 5th century and especially after 250 B.C., these and other Mysteries or Mystery Religions offered their devotees something which they could not find either in the public worship of the Olympian gods or in the study of the philosophers. That something was the hope that, through *personal initiation* into the "death and resurrection" of a god or goddess, they could be freed of their human weakness and guilt and achieve a happy *immortality.*

Unfortunately, the Mystery Religions were based entirely on *myth and legend,* usually with a strong element of the nature cycle, and with no historical foundation whatsoever. For example, the Eleusinian Mysteries stemmed from the legend of the abduction (through a cave at Eleusis) of *Kore or Persephone,* the daughter of *Demeter or Ceres,* the goddess of grain, by *Hades or Pluto,* the god of the underworld. Such was Demeter's fury over the loss of her daughter that she allowed no grain to grow, with the result that, through the intervention of Zeus, Kore was "resurrected" and returned to her but, since she had eaten seeds of a pomegranate in the nether world, she had to spend three months of each year there.

Quite probably, the religion began as an agricultural and fertility cult but, unlike some of the other Mystery rites which degenerated into drunken and sexual orgies, the Eleusinian Mysteries, like those of Orpheus as well as Isis, were refined over the centuries into a religion which, through initiation and other participatory rites, offered purity, perfection, and immortality.

Has all of this anything to do with Christian Sacraments? Yes and no! To begin with, our English word *sacrament* derives from the Latin *sacramentum*, which translates (among other things) the Greek term *mystérion* (mystery). In addition, it should be evident that our Christian Sacraments are designed to accomplish the very ends which the ancients hoped to achieve through the Mysteries: purity, perfection, and a happy afterlife. And, of course, they both involve certain *rites* in which individuals can personally participate, thus fulfilling a deep religious need of our human nature.

On the other hand, as I have already explained, the Mystery Religions were based entirely on myths or legends and often conjoined with the annual cycle of nature, while Christian Sacraments derive their efficacy from the *historical* life, death, and resurrection of *Jesus Christ*. Secondly, the word "mystery" is never used in the Bible in reference to rites but rather to secret or unfathomable *knowledge, revelation, or designs*, e.g. "the mystery of the reign of God" (Mk 4:11 and parallels), "the mystery of Christ" (Ep 3:4; Col 4:3). Even Paul, who undoubtedly was aware of Mystery Religions from his Greco-Roman environment and partial education at Tarsus in Southern Asia Minor (present-day Turkey), seems to have derived his use of the term "mystery" directly from his Jewish background and especially the *Old Testament*, where the "mysteries" or "secrets" of God, of wisdom, or of the heart are referred to (e.g. in Jb 11:6; 15:8; Ps 44:22; Dn 2:18-19, 22, 27-30, 47; 4:6; Amos 3:7) and where the Hebrew expression for "secret places" (*mistarim*) possesses a surprising resemblance to the Greek *mystéria* and the English *mysteries* (Pss 10:8-9; 17:12; 64:5; Jr 13:17; 23:24; 49:10; Lm 3:10; Hab 3:4).

What, then, is the principal connection, if any, between the Eleusinian and other Mysteries and the Christian Sacraments? To me,

Frederick C. Grant, in concluding the perceptive Introduction to his collection of documents on *Hellenistic Religions,* [24] sums it up admirably and, for our purposes, quite adequately,

> Little wonder that Judaism (in Philo, for example) found itself at home in such a world — or at least in part of it — and came to be looked upon as a highly philosophical religion; and that Christianity, a little later on, found a language at hand for the expression of its own highest concepts, and hearts ready for the proclamation of the Gospel.

> For increasingly throughout the later Hellenistic age (especially perhaps after 250 B.C. or thereabouts) and down through the Hellenistic-Roman age to the very end of paganism, there was a widespread, if more or less hidden, hunger for knowledge of the deity by a clear and incontestable *revelation;* a great desire for participation or *sharing in the divine life,* sacramentally or mystically; for *release from servitude* to the malevolent cosmic powers that hold mankind in leash; for *cleansing* from pollution and guilt, age-old and ingrained in human nature; and for the sure *guarantee* of a blessed future in the world to come or in some realm beyond this present evil one.

> The long process of Hellenizing the religions and cults of all mankind, with its consequent deepening and enrichment — and subjectivizing — of the religious life, viewed strictly historically, was in fact nothing less than what the Greek Fathers called it: *"the preparation for the Gospel."* To those who care deeply for both religion and philosophy, for the Jewish and for the Christian Church, and at the same time for the noblest elements in the ancient religions, this fact is one of perennial interest and inexhaustible meaning.

Many people today, who regard themselves as enlightened Christians therefore "free from religious superstition and magic," tend to look upon *Sacraments,* particularly the Seven Sacraments of the Roman Catholic Church, as inimical to that "authentic worship in

Spirit and truth'' which Jesus requires in John 4:23-24. Even some Catholic teachers and writers on spirituality seem to treat the Sacraments as if they exist primarily for the ''simple clergy, religious, and faithful'' and constitute, at best, traditional but comparatively unimportant appendages to their life of personal and communal prayer. Still others, who place a high premium on the ''social gospel,'' indicate by their neglect of the Sacraments in favor of the soup kitchen and the picket line, that these sacred rites hold little relevance for today's active Christians. Where do we stand? What is our own attitude about the Sacraments and their role in our Spiritual Life? Or, better still, what should it be, especially in the light of *Sacred Scripture* and, I might add, *Church History*?

At first glance, we might be inclined to dismiss the Sacraments as not at all prominent in the *New Testament*. For example, the word ''sacrament'' is never used there in its traditional meaning of ''an outward sign of inward grace.'' But further investigation reveals that two of the Sacraments, *Baptism* and the *Holy Eucharist,* are not only prominent; they are apparently *indispensable* if we accept Jesus' categorical statements in John 3:3-8 and 6:51-58. And still further investigation indicates that there is at least implicit and sometimes explicit New Testament evidence for all or most of the *other five* Sacraments.

But let us stop there for the time being, not only to avoid anticipating our examination of these Sacraments, but also and above all because this is not intended as a work of apologetics, let alone as a defense of the Seven Sacraments. Ironically, the most famous Defense of the Seven Sacraments was written by King *Henry VIII* of England[25] before he made his reputation for divorce and decapitation! No! What we really need, especially in our reflection on the Word of God, is not argument but discernment of the meaning and role in our Spiritual Life, first of the Sacraments in general, and then of each of the individual Sacraments.

Back in Chapter Two, we saw that our human nature, according to *biblical anthropology,* is one in three dimensions: flesh, person, and spirit. As spirit we are naturally oriented toward God. Our whole being hungers for relationship and even union with him. True, our dimension of flesh (as Paul explains in Gal 5:16-26 and Rm 8:1-17) is at odds with our natural aspirations of the spirit but cannot wholly extinguish them. "As the deer pants for streams of water, so my soul pants for you, O God!" (Ps 42:1, NIV).

Now, if we humans have a *natural hunger* for relationship and even union with God, then we also implicitly desire the *conditions* without which such a relationship and union will not occur. And what are these conditions? Frederick Grant has already enumerated some of the basic ones which appealed to the ancient world. Incorporating these and adding to them, I suggest that the following are *general conditions* which, consciously or unconsciously, our human nature instinctively recognizes and acknowledges:

(1) Some kind of *initiation* into personal relationship with God and with others who are also in relationship with him, both for this life and the next.

(2) Some possibility of ongoing self-giving and of *nourishment* of this relationship toward the goal of complete union with God.

(3) Some opportunity for *purification* and freedom from those manifestations of human weakness which present obstacles to growth toward complete union.

(4) Some special indication and assistance toward *maturity*, responsibility, and active implementation of this relationship, especially on behalf of others.

(5) Some ratification and consecration of the union of husband and wife in *love and life,* that it might help them, their children, and society in this relationship.

(6) Some provision for the commitment and consecration of certain ones to *special service* in the relationship with God and with others in that relationship.

(7) Finally, some additional help for those who have *advanced in years* or have been *struck by illness* or accident, that they may

be strengthened physically and/or spiritually and prepared for the life hereafter.

The reader will easily recognize that the seven conditions which I have just described are, as it were, made to order for fulfillment through the *Seven Sacraments* of Baptism, Eucharist, Reconciliation, Confirmation, Matrimony, Ordination, and Anointing of the Sick and Aged. But, before being accused of begging the question, let me point out that *Israel*, already from ancient times, had attempted to meet most of these conditions through her own "sacraments," for example the initiation rite of *circumcision*, established as a sign of God's covenant with Abraham and required of all his male descendants eight days after birth (Gn 17); the annual "sacrifice and sacrament" of the *Passover*, instituted at the time of the Exodus (Ex 12), and the annual Day of Atonement for sins, *Yom Kippur* (described in Lv 16), in addition to various other sacrifices and sin offerings detailed in Exodus, Leviticus, and Deuteronomy. Add to these the ceremonies of priestly *ordination* performed over Aaron and his sons (Ex 29 and Lv 8); the sacredness of *marriage* as an institution (Gn 2:18-25), as a covenant reflecting the Sinaitic Covenant in Hosea, Isaiah, Jeremiah, and Ezekiel, the spiritual interpretation of the Song of Songs, and the "marriage made in heaven" (Tb 7-8); the ceremony of *Bar Mitzvah* detailed in rabbinical literature and somewhat anticipated in Luke 2:41-52; and finally the instructions regarding *healing and purification* from illness, particularly leprosy (e.g. in Lv 13-14) — these and more make it evident that the Jewish people were, even more than people generally, "sacramentally" oriented throughout life.

It should come as no surprise, then, that *Christianity* (which clearly has its roots in Judaism) has been from its very inception a *sacramental religion*. In fact, even the most mystical of the Gospels, that of *John*, with its insistence on "worship in spirit and truth" (Jn 4:23-24), happens to be by far the most sacramental of all in its wealth of symbols and allusions.

First of all, John's Gospel contains only *seven prodigies* of Jesus, which are never called miracles but rather *signs*. And, while the use of the number seven is for Biblical rather than Sacramental reasons (since the Church apparently did not specify seven Sacraments until the Middle Ages),[26] the designation of "signs" clearly indicates John's symbolic preoccupation. Then, with regard to individual Sacraments, note the possible references to *Matrimony* and the *Eucharist* in John 2:1-11, the clear declaration on *Baptism* in 3:1-8 as well as the ongoing allusions to life-giving water in all of the first seven chapters, the strong *Eucharistic overtones* in chapter 6 (multiplication of food, walking on water, Eucharistic discourse), the solemn instructions on the *Holy Spirit* (and Confirmation?) in chapters 14-15, the possible implications of *Ordination* in 15:15-16 and 17:6-19, the symbolic intimation of the *Sacraments in general* and *Baptism and the Eucharist* in particular in the water and blood of 19:34 as well as the Paschal Lamb of 19:36, the unexpected but clear teaching on the *Forgiveness of Sins* (in the Sacrament of Penance or Reconciliation?) and perhaps *Ordination* in 20:21-23, and finally the *Eucharistic and Ordination* symbolism inherent in 21:1-19.

What, therefore, our human nature instinctively longs for, what some people of the ancient world sought in the Mystery Religions, what many of our Jewish brethren from time immemorial have found in their ceremonies or "sacraments," namely purification and perfection, transformation and "divinization," these have been available to all human beings for many centuries through the Christian Church (particularly the Roman Catholic Church) and her Sacraments. But, while there are obvious similarities among Greek Mysteries, Jewish "sacraments," and Christian Sacraments, there is one distinguishing note about Christian Sacraments which makes all the difference: the presence, power, and action of *Jesus Christ!*

From time immemorial, the Church has taught and we believe that the Christian Sacraments function *"ex opere operato"* (from the work worked).[27] What in the world does that mean? Do the Sacraments work like some kind of magic? Or are we dealing with some obscure and unnecessary Latin formula which has long been passé and has finally been shed at the time of Vatican II?

Not at all! What it means is simply this, that the Christian Sacraments are valid and fruitful provided that they be performed properly and with the right intention by qualified persons, independently of the worthiness or unworthiness of the minister. Why is this, and why is it important? Solely because *it is Christ himself who acts in the Sacraments,* and the efficacy of his action cannot be limited by the unworthiness of the one performing the Sacrament. In our reception of the Sacraments, we need not and do not depend on how good and holy the minister of the Sacraments may be (though this would be a plus in other ways) because we are in direct contact with Christ himself who acts through the Sacraments. And, of course, to benefit properly from the Sacraments, we ourselves, the recipients, need to be properly disposed. *St. Augustine* illustrates the principle of "ex opere operato" in his usual impelling fashion,

> Those who were baptized by John [the Baptist] were given baptism again. Now Jesus did not baptize Himself, but his disciples did, and Judas was still among them. How can it be that those who were baptized by John had to be baptized again, and not those baptized by Judas? Certainly . . . because those whom John baptized were baptized by John; those whom Judas baptized were baptized by Christ.[28]

Pope Pius XII, in one of his great encyclicals, *Mystici Corporis,* expresses the same thing even more succinctly, "It is He [Christ] who through the Church baptizes, teaches, governs, binds, absolves, offers, sacrifices."[29]

Earlier in this chapter, we contemplated the risen Christ continuing *"to do and to teach"* (Ac 1:1) in and through the Church. This he does in many ways, for example through the leadership of the Church which is especially entrusted with the responsibility of guiding and shepherding the flock (Jn 21:15-18; Ac 20:28; I P 5:1-4) and through the membership in their various roles of service to others (1 Cor 12:4-11; Ep 4:11-13; 1 P 4:10-11), including so-called "ordinary" roles such as parenting, witnessing, volunteer work, etc. But another and quite unique way in which the risen Christ continues to do and to teach in the Church is through the Sacraments. To appreciate this fact, it is helpful to *visualize Jesus* going about doing good during his earthly life and continuing to do the same sacramentally through the centuries, including our own time.

For example, did not Jesus go about forgiving sins (Mk 2:5 and parallels; Mt 9:13 and parallels; Lk 7:48; 15:1-32; Jn 8:11, etc.), and giving life, especially spiritual, supernatural life, called in Greek *zoé* (Jn 10:10), but also natural life (*psyché*) by restoring health (Mt 8:16-17, etc.)? Today, the risen Christ continues to forgive sins and give life through the Sacraments of *Baptism* (Ac 2:38-39; Rm 6:3-4; 1 P 1:1-5), *Reconciliation* (Mt 18:21-35; Jn 20:23; Jm 5:16) and *Anointing* of the Sick and Aged (Mk 6:13; 16:18; Jm 5:14-15), in which latter case he not infrequently restores physical health as well.

Did not Jesus, as the Good Shepherd, feed his hungry followers (Mk 8:1-9 and parallels) and, after his resurrection, first instruct the two disciples of Emmaus in the Scriptures and then reveal himself to them ''in the breaking of bread'' (Lk 24:13-35)? Today, the risen Christ continues to ''open the Scriptures for us'' (Lk 24:32, WD) and (wonder of wonders!) feed us with his own Body and Blood in the *Sacrament of the Holy Eucharist* (Jn 6:51-58; Ac 2:46; 20:7; 1 Cor 11:23-29).

Did not Jesus first promise and then confer the Holy Spirit on his followers (Jn 14-15; 20:22-23)? Thus, the risen Christ continues to pour out the Holy Spirit on us his followers all through our lives but, in a special way, in the Sacrament of *Confirmation* (Ac 2:1-12; 4:31; 8:14-17).

Did he not, in his lifetime, grace the wedding feast at Cana with his presence and his first miracle (Jn 2:1-11), uphold the sanctity of marriage against the dangers of divorce (Mt 5:31-32; 19:3-12 and parallels), and glory in the title of (spiritual) ''Bridegroom'' (Mt 9:14-15; 22:2-14; 25:1-13; Jn 3:29)? So, through the *Sacrament of Matrimony,* the risen Christ continues to uphold the sanctity and indissolubility of marriage (1 Cor 5:1-8; 7:1-11; 2 Cor 6:14-7:1; Ep 5:21-33).

And, finally, did Jesus not choose certain of his followers to fulfill a special leadership role in his Church (Mt 10:2-5 and parallels) and did he not in effect ordain them, among other things, for celebration of the Eucharist (Lk 22:19; 1 Cor 11:24-25; Jn 20:23)? Thus, to this day, the risen Christ continues to choose certain of his followers to fulfill special *leadership roles* as bishops, priests, and deacons in his Church (Ac 14:23; 20:17, 28; Ph 1:1; 1 Tm 3:1-10; Tt 1:5-9; 1 P 5:1-4).

But, granting that such a personal encounter with the risen Christ through the Sacraments could be most effective in terms of personal purification and transformation into "the image and likeness of God" (Gn 1:26-27) for which we were predestined and created (Rm 8:29; 2 Cor 3:18; Ep 4:24; Col 3:10), that "image and likeness" which is found in all its fullness only in Christ himself (Col 1:15-20; Heb 1:3), is it not naive to think that the risen Christ would actually use such *mundane things* as oil and water, bread and wine as means of his spiritual action in our lives? Naive? Yes, so it would seem except for one thing, that *"God is love"* and "God's love was revealed in our midst in this way: he sent his only Son to the world that we might have life through him!" (1 Jn 4:8-9).

Love does such things! Unlimited love does unbelievable things! After the incredible "leap of love" whereby Jesus Christ, "though he was by nature God . . . emptied himself, taking the nature of a slave, coming to be in the likeness of men" (Ph 2:6-7, WD), how can we possibly be surprised at any manner in which he chooses to come to us? When will we really begin to "believe in the love God has for us" (1 Jn 4:16)?

According to the late beloved *Fulton Sheen,* "Divinity is always where you least expect to find it!"[30] In the burning bush of Moses (Ex 3:2), with the gentle whispering sound of Elijah (1 K 19:12), among the sheep and sycamores of Amos (Am 7:14), in the manger of Jesus (Lk 2:7), on a cross of shame at Calvary (Mk 15:24)! And God has a way of choosing *unpredictable means* of helping us. Note, for example, his predilection for saving his Chosen People through the so-called *"weaker sex"* represented by Rahab the harlot (Jos 2), Debborah the prophetess (Jg 4:5), Judith the widow (Jdt 8:16), and Esther the timid queen (Est 2, 4 and 5). ''The weak things of the world has God chosen in order to shame the strong!'' (1 Cor 1:27). To which we might add God's use of water from the lowly Jordan River to cure Naaman, the Syrian general, of his leprosy (2 K 5:1-14), and Jesus' own use of such lowly means as spittle and mud in some of his cures (Mk 7:33; 8:23; Jn 9:6).

Part of our human problem, of course, is that we have grown up with such a *hard and fast distinction between material and spiritual things,* a distinction which has for so long been accepted and taken for granted from our Greco-Roman heritage. Because of this, it is naturally difficult for us to be open to the possibility of God's use of material things as symbols and even instruments in accomplishing spiritual effects. But this sharp distinction, as I have pointed out before, is not part of the Jewish and biblical heritage.

Recall, for example, that Paul's famous ''hostility between flesh and spirit'' (Gal 5:17 and Rm 8:5-9) is not a battle between our physical body and spiritual soul, as it has for so long been interpreted, but between our conflicting tendencies toward evil and good. Even from a scientific point of view, Teilhard de Chardin's pioneering theories, for example in his famous work, *The Phenomenon of Man,* [31] which are already implied in Romans 8:18-25, should help us understand how easy and even appropriate it is for God to use material things in order to spiritualize us, until that day when we and all creation will be completely spiritual.

The famous Protestant theologian, *Paul Tillich,* challenges all of us Christians along the same lines with these words,

> Let me ask you a question: are we still able to understand what a sacrament means? The more we are estranged from nature, the less we can answer affirmatively. That is why, in our time, the sacraments have lost so much of their significance for individuals and churches.
>
> For in the sacraments nature participates in the process of

salvation. Bread and wine, water and light, and all the great elements of nature become the bearers of spiritual meaning and saving power. Natural and spiritual powers are united — reunited — in the sacrament. The word appeals to our intellect and may move our will. The sacrament, if its meaning is alive, grasps our unconscious as well as our conscious being. It grasps the creative ground of our being. It is the symbol of nature and spirit, united in salvation.[32]

No wonder *George Maloney* describes the Sacraments as *"carriers of divine life!"*[33]

In a limited treatment of the Sacraments, such as I have perforce adopted in my comprehensive reflection on spirituality, there are obviously many facets of this intriguing subject which I must forego, but I urge the reader to pursue them further by referring to the list of recommended books at the end of this chapter. I have concentrated on what I believe to be the *essential feature of the Sacraments,* namely that they are acts of and encounters with the risen Christ himself. In doing so, I have tried to be faithful to the thrust of my entire work, *"To live the Word: Inspired and Incarnate."* However, some of the other dimensions that the reader is urged to explore are the following:

(1) The Sacraments not only as acts of and encounters with Christ but also as *celebrations* of what we are through Christ.

(2) The Sacraments in their *broader meaning* as including many things besides the official Seven Sacraments of the Church.

(3) The meaning and benefits of the kinds of grace received in the Sacraments, namely:

(a) *Uncreated grace* through the geater indwelling of God himself, especially in the person of Christ (Jn 14:23).

(b) *Sanctifying or habitual grace,* whereby as "sharers of the divine nature" (2 P 1:4), we grow in God's holiness.

(c) *Sacramental grace,* a "title" to all the help from God (actual grace) that we need to fulfill the responsibilities of individual Sacraments, e.g. Matrimony, Orders (1 Tm 4:14).

(4) The meaning of the permanent, even eternal, *"character or seal"* received with the three Sacraments of Baptism, Confirmation, and Holy Orders, so that these Sacraments cannot be repeated, primarily because they initiate us into three different degrees of the *eternal priesthood of Jesus Christ*[34] (Heb 4-8).

SUMMARY AND CONCLUSION:

By way of summary and conclusion, I propose to do something very unusual. Two of the most influential Catholic books on the Sacraments have been *Christ, the Sacrament of the Encounter with God* by the great Dutch theologian, *Edward Schillebeeckx, O.P.*,[35] and *Doors to the Sacred* by a rising American theologian, *Joseph Martos*.[36] I would like to make available to the reader some passages from the latter's sensitive appraisal of the former's landmark work which will serve to summarize and conclude our reflections in this chapter more effectively than any other way I can think of.

> Schillebeeckx suggests that the closest equivalent to what happens in a sacramental experience is an existential *encounter between persons*. When two people deeply encounter each other — in contrast to simply meeting each other — they discover something of the mystery that the other person is. Those who fall in love, for example, see beyond the physical appearance of the other person to a beauty and a value in that person that others cannot see. In the encounter of love they see the same *outward signs* that others see, but to them the words and gestures of the other person reveal a *depth of reality* that is ordinarily hidden from view.
>
> For Schillebeeckx the sacraments are outward signs that reveal a transcendent, divine reality. They open up, so to speak, the possibility of falling in love with God. Jesus himself when he lived in Palestine was that same kind of sacramental sign to many of those who knew him. . . . For them *Jesus was a*

sacrament through which they encountered the mystery of God. Even after he died Christ remained a sacrament to those who accepted his message and believed in him. . . .

In their turn the *community* of those whom Christ had called together were a *sacrament to others*. They preached his message and in their words God was present, touching people's hearts and transforming their lives. Through their actions Christ himself acted, healing the sick and bestowing his spirit. They were, as Christ had been, a sign of the mystery of God, and those who responded in faith to what they said and did encountered Christ as their Lord and acknowledged the gift, the grace, of God's redemptive power.

In time this Church came to see itself as making the divine mystery present in the world primarily in *seven ways,* corresponding to seven ways that Christ himself was a sacrament of God to others: in introducing others to new life, in sharing the power of his spirit with them, in healing their illness and forgiving their sinfulness, in ministering to their religious needs, in being faithful to his Father and his Church, ultimately in the action of sacrificing himself out of love.

The Church could have chosen other ways to collectively sacramentalize the redeeming presence and power of Christ — and indeed all Christians are called to be sacraments in the world — but as a matter of historical fact these seven were chosen as the ecclesial sacraments, the *official sacraments of the Church*. In these seven the Christian community recognized that the redemptive mystery of Christ was present, and that those who participated in these ritual actions could encounter the source of all salvation.

In this way Schillebeeckx traces the seven traditional *sacraments* to the *Church,* which is the sacrament of Christ, and to *Christ* himself, who is the sacrament of *God*. As official signs and acts of the Church they are also signs and acts of Christ.[37]

RECOMMENDED READING LIST

1. Bouyer, Louis. *The Church of God: Body of Christ and Temple of the Spirit,* Chicago: Franciscan Herald Press, 1982.
2. Irwin, Kevin W. *Liturgy, Prayer, and Spirituality,* New York: Paulist Press, 1984.
3. Martos, Joseph. *Doors to the Sacred: A Historical Introduction to Sacraments in the Catholic Church,* Garden City, NY: Doubleday & Company, 1982.
4. Stutfield, Hugh E. *Mysticism and Catholicism,* New York: Gordon Press, 1977.
5. Taylor, Michael, ed. *The Sacraments: Readings in Contemporary Sacramental Theology,* Staten Island, NY: Alba House, 1981.

QUESTIONS FOR REFLECTION AND DISCUSSION

1. What role does the Church fill in our Spiritual Life, personal as well as communal?
2. What is our attitude toward the Second Vatican Council and the current Church in the light of Scripture and Church History?
3. What is the meaning of Liturgy in itself, in the Church, and in our Spiritual Life?
4. What is the importance of Sacraments in our personal and communal Spiritual Life?
5. What is the meaning of the expression, ''ex opere operato,'' and what practical application does it have in our Spiritual Life?

CHAPTER ELEVEN

SPECIAL MEANS OF THE RELATIONSHIP, PART II:
Becoming Christ Through the Church's Sacraments

One of the characteristics of Catholicism that has been most affected by the changes since the Second Vatican Council is devotion to the *Saints*. The reason for this is not easy to discern. Perhaps it involves a variety of things: revision of the Liturgical Calendar with greater emphasis on seasonal and ferial Masses rather than those of the Saints, and the tendency of many priests to choose the former over the latter even when there is an option; liturgical change from subject sermons to biblical homilies, with corresponding reduction or even absence of references to the Saints; the shift from transcendent to incarnational religion, from promotion of fear to that of love toward God, accompanied by the lessening of a felt need for the intercession of Saints; greater concern about this life and this world, with diminished thought of heaven, the abode of the angels and the Saints. All of these and more may qualify as causes, but the result is the same: the Saints have almost become forgotten people, "non-persons," an "endangered species."

I, for one, am saddened by this widespread change. Whether or not it was inevitable, I fail to find it desirable. To me, it is one more instance of our penchant for going from one extreme to the other. As usual, we need a *middle way*. We need the Saints, not so much as helpers in our difficulties, but as heroes, models, and companions in our pilgrimage. We need, above all, the constant *example* of how the risen Christ can and does take possession of all kinds of persons in every kind of circumstance and succeed against all odds in *transforming* them into himself in the most interesting ways.[1] It is a never-ending revelation, the loss of which makes us the losers.

Like many other Catholics, I have had *my favorite Saints*. I still have. They include early Saints like tempestuous Peter and tireless Paul, courageous Stephen and contemplative John; second generation Saints such as gentle Clement of Rome and generous Ignatius of Antioch; later Saints and scholars like irascible Jerome and irresistible Augustine; medieval Saints such as lovable Bernard of Clairvaux, Francis of Assisi, and Catherine of Siena; post-medieval Saints like merry Thomas More and mystical Teresa of Avila, with those apostles of love Philip Neri, Francis de Sales, and Vincent de Paul; and modern Saints like the ascetic John Vianney and affable Don Bosco, the long-suffering Elizabeth Seton and self-effacing Catherine Laboure.

I also have my favorite saints who are *still uncanonized* at this writing, among them Cardinal Newman and Francis Thompson, Charles de Foucauld and Teilhard de Chardin, Padre Pio and Pope John XXIII, Sister Elizabeth of the Trinity and Mother Teresa of India. To these I would like to add *two Vincentian martyrs* in China in the past century, *Blessed Francis Regis Clet* and *Blessed John Gabriel Perboyre*. The former was an inspiration to the latter, who in turn has been a particular inspiration to me ever since I first heard the story of his life and martyrdom when I was twelve years old. One of the things that, along with *Pope Leo XIII* who beatified him, I find so attractive about Blessed John Gabriel is the extraordinary similarity between his martyrdom and that of Our Lord Jesus Christ himself.

Some *forty parallels* have been listed between the Passion account of Jesus and John Gabriel,[2] but time and space permit me to mention only a few. At thirty-eight years of age (quite possibly the real age of Jesus at his death and resurrection, according to reliable biblical studies),[3] and having labored in China under the most arduous conditions for approximately three years (corresponding to Jesus' public ministry), he was betrayed by a catechumen for thirty ounces of silver, dragged for an entire year from tribunal to tribunal for unbelievable interrogations and tortures, and finally died on a cross.

Here was a young man of whom it can truly be said that he was utterly *transformed into Christ*, freely allowing Jesus to continue his life, ministry, and martyrdom in and through him. How did this come about? What was his secret of sanctity? And was his such an exceptional case that the rest of us can hold no hope of following in his, and Jesus', footsteps? No, in reviewing his life and death, I have come to realize that basically the very *same means* which enabled him to be transformed into Christ are also available to me and indeed to most Christians, especially most Catholics.

And what are these means? *Prayer,* of course, and *self-denial,* but also the faithful and conscientious use of the *Sacraments of the Church.* If we add to these the regular reading of and reflection on the *Word of God,* which is now so much more available to us than it was to our martyr, should we not conclude that we have even more opportunities of transformation into Christ than he had, if only we grasp them?

We have already, of course, dwelt on Scripture reading, prayer, and purifying self-denial. We have also, in the previous chapter, considered the role of the Church and the Sacraments in general in our Spiritual Life, our predestined transformation into Christ (Rm 8:29). In this chapter, I propose to examine some of the individual Sacraments, particularly Baptism and the Holy Eucharist, under the following headings: *Initiation* (Baptism and Confirmation), *Healing* (Reconciliation and Holy Anointing), and *Union* (Holy Eucharist).

In our next and final chapter, when we consider our call to transformation according to our *vocation and state in life,* I will focus on the Sacraments of *Matrimony* and *Holy Orders,* with special segments also on Religious Consecration and Ministry based on *Vows,* as well as Lay Consecration and Ministry based on the Sacrament of *Confirmation.*

*SACRAMENTS OF INITIATION — BAPTISM
AND CONFIRMATION:*

In 1954, during my studies at the Pontifical Biblical Institute in Rome, I had the good fortune of making my first and most extensive tour of the lands of the Bible under the direction of *Father Robert North, S.J.,* our professor of Biblical Geography and Archaeology. Leaving Rome on June 20th, we first visited Egypt and the Sinai Peninsula then traveled by ship to Beirut and overland through Lebanon, Syria, Jordan, and Israel. Then, after our "Biblical Caravan" departed from Haifa for Rome on August 10th, I was privileged to stay on in Israel, make a twelve day *retreat at Nazareth,* and continue my biblical·journey with a fellow Vincentian, *Father John Murray, C.M.,* following the footsteps of *St. Paul* all around Cyprus, much of Turkey, and most of Greece, finally returning to Rome on October 4th.

That was truly the most unforgettable of the many journeys in my life. Today, thirty years later, I can still remember almost every detail as if it occurred yesterday. One of my most vivid memories is of our visit to *Jacob's Well* at ancient *Sichem,* near present day *Nablus* in central Israel. What stands out in my memory is the interesting coincidence between the cool, tasty water of the well, replete with memories of Jesus' discourse with the Samaritan woman in the fourth chapter of John's Gospel, and something very unusual which at that very time was hovering over neighboring *Mt. Garizim* — a cloud! The *very first cloud* we had seen since leaving Rome on June 20th. And here it was the middle of July! Not only no rain, but not even any clouds until now!

That is when the full force of Jesus' declaration to the Samaritan woman about *"living water"* (Jn 4:10) struck me like a bolt of lightning.

If you knew the gift of God and who it is that asks you for a drink, you would have asked him and he would have given you *living water* (Jn 4:10, NIV).

Everyone who drinks this water [from Jacob's Well] will be thirsty again, but whoever drinks the water I give him will *never thirst* (Jn 4:13-14,NIV).

Indeed, the water I give him will become in him a *spring of water* welling up to *eternal life!* (Jn 4:14, NIV).

Of course! "Living water" is rain or spring water; that is, water that flows and enables nature to come alive! This symbolizes the *new Life in the Spirit* which Jesus came to give, as we see in Jesus' later, and more public, utterance about water,

On the last and greatest day of the Feast [of Tabernacles], Jesus stood and said in a loud voice, "If a man is thirsty, let him come to me and drink. Whoever believes in me, as the Scripture has said, streams of living water will flow from within him."

By this he meant the Spirit, whom those who believed in him were later to receive. Up to that time the Spirit had not been given, since Jesus had not yet been glorified (Jn 7:37-39).

On the other hand, the water of *Jacob's Well,* like that of any well or cistern, was considered non-flowing, hence non-living water. In the same way as John shows Jesus, at the marriage feast of *Cana,* changing the non-living water of the six Jewish purification jars into the rich abundant wine of Messianic times (Jn 2:1-11; cf. Jr 31:12; Ho 14:8; Am 9:13-14), so here he has Jesus indicating the *replacement* of Jewish (and Samaritan) non-living water with his own living water of the Spirit.

An hour is coming, and is already here, when authentic worshippers will worship the Father in Spirit and truth. . . . God is Spirit, and those who worship him must worship in Spirit and truth (Jn 4:23-24).

From earliest times in the arid Middle East, water (especially the "living water" of rains and springs) has been a symbol of *life.* During the "early and late rains" (Dt 11:14), the land became alive; when the rains failed to materialize, the land became dry and dead (Dt 11:17). And water was especially dear to Israel as crucial in creation (Gn 1:2) and symbolic of that life lived in the favor of and in right relationship with God which later ages came to call (sanctifying) *grace* (Gn 2:10-14; Pss 42:2-3; 63:2-4; Ezk 47).

No wonder, then, that Jesus chooses water to symbolize Spiritual Life (*zoé*) and specifically *initiation* into that Life through the Sacrament of *Baptism,* "Amen, amen I say to you unless one (in Greek, *tis* meaning "anyone") is begotten of water and spirit, he cannot enter into the kingdom of God" (Jn 3:5, WD). No wonder that Paul speaks of initiation into the Christian life as a *"new creation"* (2 Cor 5:17; Gal 6:15) and the individual thus initiated into the new life as a *"new person"* (Ep 4:24; Col 3:10). Finally, no wonder that Paul, John, and Peter all refer to the life of the baptized as a *"new birth,* a birth from above" (Tt 3:4-7; Jn 3:3; 1 P 1:3-5). Moreover, John in his apocalyptic description of the *New Jerusalem,* borrows from Ezekiel 47 the impressive description of abundant, life-giving water flowing from the city (Rv 22:1-2).

This emphasis on the symbolism of "living water" also explains the preference in the early Church for "living or running water" in the Sacrament of Baptism according to the *Didache* or "Teaching of the Twelve Apostles"[4] dating from the second century,

> Baptize as follows: After first explaining all these points, baptize in the name of the Father and of the Son and of the Holy Spirit, in running water. But if you have no running water, baptize in other water; and if you cannot in cold, then in warm. But if you have neither, pour water on the head three times in the name of the Father and of the Son and of the Holy Spirit.

Life, therefore, seems to me (and others) to be the primary meaning intended, especially by John, Paul, and Peter, in the symbolic use of water in Baptism. But, of course, it is not the only meaning. Water has been used all through history for washing and *cleansing,* and use of the Greek verb *baptízo* and nouns *báptisma* or *baptismós* (all of which involve dipping, washing, immersing) would seem to favor this meaning. Hence the paramount importance attached by so many Christians to the other meaning of the baptismal water, namely to wash, cleanse, *purify from sin,* whether the reference is to "original" or personal sin.

However, as we have already seen in Chapter Five, *"Original Sin"* is not so much an historical sin which we have all somehow inherited from an historical first couple called Adam and Eve, as it is the sinfulness of the human race into which we are born or, to put it another way, the lack of sanctifying grace to which we are subject at our birth. It should be obvious, then, that even in the sense of cleansing from sin, the meaning of water as symbolizing life has a crucial place. Why? Because it is precisely by the *gift of the life of "sanctifying grace"* within us through Baptism that we are freed from the sinfulness of our human race. Nor does the word "baptize" necessarily weaken that conclusion, since it can as easily mean to *immerse in the new life of grace.* Does not Jesus himself speak of being immersed in his coming passion (Mk 10:38-39; Lk 12:50)? Hence *Jean Daniélou,* in his excellent work, *The Bible and the Liturgy,*[5] remarks,

> We generally interpret the rite of baptism by seeing in it a reference to water as cleansing and purifying. But this does not seem actually to be the most important meaning of the rite.

Some might assert that it is too difficult, in our area of the world, to put the emphasis on water as life-giving that the biblical people and writers found so easy. Perhaps that is so if ours happens to be one of the only areas of the world that is never afflicted by drought. But, even if that should indeed be the case, surely the *advances of science* in our time can provide us with ample appreciation of water as a perfect symbol of life.

Have not our explorations in space convinced us that our little *planet Earth,* beautiful as an agate when viewed from the moon, is the only body in our entire solar system that can support life because it alone possesses water? Do we not know also that some eighty percent of our planet is composed of water? For that matter, the same is true of *our own bodies,* with the result that it is far easier to die of thirst than of hunger. And are not biologists ecstatic over the amount of life in a single drop of water? No wonder scientists extol water as *"liquid life!"* [6]

It has been well noted that the choice which God sets before us is not so much one between good and evil, wisdom and folly, as it is between *life and death!* In Deuteronomy 30:19-20, Yahweh challenges his Chosen People, Israel, in these words:

> I call heaven and earth today to witness against you: I have set before you life and death, the blessing and the curse. Choose life, then, that you and your descendants may live, by loving the Lord, your God, heeding his voice, and holding fast to him. For that will mean life for you, a long life for you to live on the land which the Lord swore he would give to your fathers Abraham, Isaac, and Jacob.

Yes, Yahweh confronts Israel with a life and death choice, but the final sentence clearly indicates that, although the Greek word *zoé* is used in the Septuagint translation, the life referred to here is no more than the natural, physical life of the people of Israel. By contrast, when we get to the *New Testament* and, above all, the writings of John and Paul, it becomes unmistakably evident that the life in question is *supernatural, eternal, Spiritual Life* (e.g. Jn 11:25-26; 1 Jn 3:14; Rm 6:23; 11:15; Gal 6:8, etc.).

But what is this life that we are talking about? The life of grace? Yes. The Spiritual Life? Yes. The supernatural, eternal life of *zoé*? Yes, of course! Yet, however true all these answers are, they still do not give us the complete picture. For that, I believe, we must have recourse especially to the mystical thought and writing of *St. Paul.* To him, the real life that we receive and into which we enter through Baptism is nothing less than *the life of the Risen Christ* himself!

This may not seem so evident when we think of the *Trinitarian formula of Baptism* used in Matthew 28:19, in the Didache quoted above, and in Baptism throughout the ages, but most scholars readily agree that this was not the original formula. No, the earliest wording of the Sacrament of Baptism seems to have included only *the name of Jesus*. Thus, for example, Peter at the conclusion of his power-filled sermon on the Day of Pentecost, instructs the interested Jews with these words,

> You must reform and be baptized, each one of you, in the name of Jesus Christ, that your sins may be forgiven; then you will receive the gift of the Holy Spirit (Ac 2:38).

This is confirmed by the same usage in all the other places of the New Testament where the *formula of Baptism* seems to be indicated (Ac 8:16; 10:48; 19:5; Rm 6:3; 1 Cor 1:13, 15; 12:13; Gal 3:27). But there is still much more to the picture.

Unfortunately, our English translations do not reveal the rest of the picture to us, so we must have recourse to the Greek text. Now, of the New Testament references presented above, all but two use exactly the same preposition after the verb "baptize." The two exceptions are Acts 2:38 and 10:48. In the first instance, the preposition *epi* (usually "on, upon") is employed; in the second, the preposition *en* (normally "in, among, with"). In every other instance, even in the Trinitarian formula of Matthew 28:19, the chosen preposition is *eis,* whose basic and most common meaning is that of motion *"into."*

Prepositions are generally very small words and for that reason may not seem so important. In fact, it is not unusual to employ them rather loosely in our English language. But not so in Greek, even the *koine* or "common" international Greek in which the entire New Testament is written. Though there are scholars who disagree, to me the usage speaks for itself, particularly when we keep in mind that all but one of the references above are from *St. Paul* or his disciple, *St. Luke*. Remember that it was Jesus' simple yet profound words, "I am Jesus, whom you are persecuting!" (Ac 9:5, repeated in 22:8; 26:15) which not only converted Paul on the spot but also formed the cornerstone of his marvelous theology. To me, then, the inescapable conclusion is that, when Paul and his disciple Luke speak of "Baptism into Christ" or *"Baptism into the name of Christ,"* they mean exactly what they say: that the Sacrament of Baptism initiates us into *the very person of the Risen Christ!*

What a staggering thought! When we were baptized, whether as children or adults, we entered into *personal and lasting contact* with the self-same Jesus Christ who was born at Bethlehem, lived at Nazareth, traveled all over Palestine preaching, healing, and working miracles, died for our sins, rose from the dead, and is now in glory with the Father and the Holy Spirit as well as all the angels and saints. Mystery of mysteries, far surpassing even the wildest dreams and aspirations of the most devout initiates of the ancient Mystery religions! Yet it is true!

St. Paul, great mystic that he is, fleshes out his theology of our *Baptism into Christ* in Romans 6:3-4, 10-11,

> Are you not aware that we who were baptized into Christ Jesus were baptized into his death? Through baptism into his death we were buried with him, so that, just as Christ was raised from the dead by the glory of the Father, we too might live a new life. . . . His death was death to sin, once for all; his life is life for God. In the same way, you must consider yourselves dead to sin but alive for God in Christ Jesus.

To visualize fully what Paul is teaching here, we must remember that he has in mind *Baptism by immersion,* which was the most common form in the early Church and the most rich in symbolism, for descent into the water portrayed death and ascent from the water, life. That is why the Church today encourages the use of this form of Baptism as providing greater sign value. However, she leaves open the *option between immersion and infusion* or pouring, an option which (as we have seen) was practiced even in the early period of the Church's life, particularly because of the special symbolism of *"living or flowing water."*[7]

We have seen that Christian Baptism is a new birth, a new creation, and an initiation into the risen "body" or person of Christ. But is it not, first of all, an initiation and incorporation into the *communal "body" of Christ, the Church*? Yes, of course, the Sacrament of Baptism is the means whereby we (and, for that matter, *all validly baptized persons,* Ep 4:5) are initiated and incorporated into the Church. But "first of all"? That is another question, and one that is more serious than the well-known "chicken or egg" controversy. It makes a great deal of difference in our Spiritual Life whether our basic relationship is with the Risen Christ and therefore with the Church or with the Church and through the Church with Christ.

Perhaps the majority of Scripture scholars, theologians, and especially liturgists (in today's communal reaction against the individualism of yesterday) would maintain that, like the Israelites of the *Old Testament,* we Christians are called as a people, a living community, and therefore our prior relationship is with the Church, and it is only as members of the Church that we are in relationship with the risen Christ. But I, for one, respectfully disagree, and precisely for biblical reasons. Although there are many similarities, as I have already detailed in the previous chapter, between the two Israels, nevertheless there is one all important difference: *Jesus Christ!*

Christianity is not simply a movement or institution committed and consecrated to Jesus Christ as the Son of God, the Messiah of Israel, the Savior of the human race, and attempting to live as he taught us. *Christianity is Christ!* Through Baptism, we are united with the Risen Christ himself and, by that fact, we are also united with all others who are united with Christ. He is the hub, we the spokes; he is the vine, we the branches (Jn 15:1-8). Our personal and communal relationship with one another in the Church stems from and, I might add, is proportionate to our union with the risen Christ. However, this does not negate the fact that, for most of us, it is precisely *through the Church* that we have come to *know about* and to *know Christ*.

That Baptism is, first of all, initiation into the risen Christ is abundantly clear in the conversion experience, theology, and writing of *St. Paul,* who always speaks of Baptism into Christ rather than into the Church. Even when Paul focuses on *the Church* itself, he usually refers to it as *an extension* of Christ himself, *his "body"* (1 Cor 12; Rm 12; Col 1:18; Ep 1:22-23; 5:23, 29-30), *his "bride"* (2 Cor 11:2; Ep 5:22-33), *his "fullness"* (Ep 1:23); a *"living temple"* rising on the foundation of Christ (1 Cor 3:11, 16-17; Ep 2:20-22). Perhaps nowhere else does Paul make such a sharp distinction between the Old and New Testament situations, and so completely identify the Church with Christ as in Ephesians 2:11-18,

> You men of Gentile stock . . . , remember that, in former times, you had *no part in Christ and were excluded from the community of Israel.* You were strangers to the covenant and its promise; you were without hope and without God in the world.
>
> But now *in Christ Jesus* you who once were far off have been brought near through the blood of Christ. It is he who is our peace, and who made the two of us one by breaking down the barrier of hostility that kept us apart.
>
> *In his own flesh* he abolished the law with its commands and precepts, to create in himself one new man from us who had been two and to make peace, reconciling both of us to God *in one body* through his cross, which put that enmity to death.
>
> He came and "announced the good news of peace to you who were far off, and to those who were near"; through him we both have *access in one Spirit to the Father.*

Nor is the emphasis on our relationship with Christ as primary, and as the basis of our union with the Church, confined to the teaching of Paul. The Gospel according to *Matthew,* well named the "Ecclesial Gospel" because of its obvious emphasis on the Church, contains the same fruitful doctrine, if we but look for it, for example, in such passages as the following:

> You have heard that it was said. . . . But I say to you . . . (Mt 5:21-22, 27-28, 31-32, 33-34, 38-39, 43-44, RSV).

All things have been committed to me by my Father. No one knows the Son except the Father, and no one knows the Father except the Son and those to whom the Son chooses to reveal him. *Come to me,* all you who are weary and burdened, and I will give you rest. Take my yoke upon you, and learn from me . . . (Mt 11:27-29, NIV).

I asssure you, as often as you did it for one of my least brothers, *you did it for me.* . . . I assure you, as often as you neglected to do it to one of these least ones, *you neglected to do it to me* (Mt 25:40, 45).

St. Peter also, in his stirring First Epistle, generally regarded as a *baptismal homily or instruction,* couples his teachings on Baptism and on the Church with constant references to the *risen Christ,* as is evident especially in 1 P 1:1-9, 18-25; 2:1-10; 3:13-22; 4:12-16.

But it is *John* who, along with Paul, provides us with the most compelling evidence for the centrality of Christ in relation to the Church and everything else. So extensive is this evidence, in fact, that it runs like a golden thread all through the entire Johannine literature. In the interest of time and space, let me call attention to only two passages, as follows:

I am the true vine and my Father is the vinegrower . . . Live on in me, as I do in you. . . . I am the vine, you are the branches. *He who lives in me and I in him,* will produce abundantly, for apart from me you can do nothing . . . (Jn 15:1, 4-5).

I pray also for those who will believe in me through their word, that all may *be one as you, Father, are in me, and I in you;* I pray that they may be in us, that the world may believe that you sent me. I have given them the glory you gave me that they may be one, as we are one — *I living in them, you living in me* — that their unity may be complete. . . . To them I have revealed your name, and I will continue to reveal it so that your love for me may live in them, and *I may live in them* (Jn 17:20-23, 26).

In these two relatively brief passages, note how freely the wording moves back and forth between *our living in Christ and his living in us*. This is also thoroughly characteristic of Paul's thought and writing, but time does not permit us to pursue it further. Note, besides, that our *fruitfulness* in the first passage and our *unity* among ourselves in the second depend directly upon our personal and communal *union with Christ*.

The Sacrament of Baptism is extremely rich, both in the sign value of its *rites* and in the wealth of its *effects*. Before and after the central ceremony with water, the Church has placed *other symbols* to increase our understanding and appreciation, for example,

(1) Before the water, *optional anointing* with the Oil of Catechumens in imitation of ancient *athletes* who oiled their entire bodies for their contests, to symbolize the struggle between good and evil, grace and sin, within us (Rm 7:13-25).

(2) After the water, anointing with *Holy Chrism,* like *priests, kings,* and *prophets* of old, to symbolize our initiation into the eternal *Priesthood* of Jesus Christ (1 P 2:5, 9) and our *consecration* as living temples of the Holy Spirit (1 Cor 6:19), "living stones, built as an edifice of spirit, into a holy priesthood" (1 P 2:5).

(3) After the anointing with Chrism, the symbols of a *white garment* and a *burning candle*; the first, to remind us of the *purity and fidelity* which we are to carry through life (Rv 7:9), the second to remind us that we are called to be *"the light of the world"* (Mt 5:14-16).

But is not all this rich symbolism lost on us if we are baptized in *infancy*? Would it not be better to delay Baptism at least until we have reached the use of reason? In my answer to these questions, I trust the reader will not complain if again I resort to just summarizing certain important considerations:

(1) *Infant Baptism,* our initiation into the New Covenant, is perfectly in keeping with the Jewish covenant of *circumcision* on the eighth day after birth (Gn 17:12), as well as with the added notes of our being *children of God* (Jn 1:12-13; Gal 3:26; 4:1-7; Rm 8:14-17; Ep 1:5; 1 P 2:2; 1 Jn 3:1-3) and of *Jesus' special predilection for*

children (Mk 10:13-16; Mt 18:1-6; 19:13-15; Lk 18:15-17). After all, he himself came amongst us as a baby, so what could be more appropriate than his being "born again" in *our* infancy (Gal 4:19)?

(2)   Even though we may have been baptized as infants and therefore were not conscious at the time, the *effects* of Baptism, our Christian *privileges* and *responsibilities* still perdure. As brothers and sisters of Christ and adopted children of God, we should always be mindful of our royal roots. *"Noblesse oblige!"* St. Ignatius of Antioch has been quoted as exhorting us in these words, "Remember your dignity and you will not sin!"[8]

Moreover, Paul in particular, by using both the *indicative* and *imperative* moods in a given expression, challenges us to constantly become more and more what we have already been empowered to be.[9] For example, in Galatians 3:27, NIV, Paul declares, "All of you who were baptized into Christ *have been clothed* with Christ," a possible reference to the baptismal white garment or to the practice of wearing costumes and masks to portray characters in Greek theater. In Romans 13:14, NIV, he urges the Christians, *"Clothe yourselves* with the Lord Jesus Christ, and do not think about how to satisfy the desires of the sinful nature."

(3)   *The Sacrament of Confirmation,* which may at one time have been one with the Sacrament of Baptism (but may also have been separate as seems indicated in Acts 8:14-19), is now usually conferred several years after the reception of infant Baptism, for example in *late pre-teens* or *early teens.* This is a great help in *appreciating and accepting* the privileges and responsibilities acquired at Baptism and in successfully making the perilous journey to healthy *Christian adulthood* past the twin dangers, the Scylla and Charybdis, of self-indulgence and rejection of faith. At the same time, it initiates the recipient into a second degree of the *Eternal Priesthood* of Jesus Christ and empowers him or her to witness to Christ by a more mature life of *Christian example, service and sacrifice.*

This brief mention of Confirmation will have to suffice for now, but we shall return to this very special Sacrament when we reflect on *lay ministry* in the following chapter. Meanwhile, let us close our reflection on the Sacrament of Baptism with a brief beautiful quotation from the brilliant third century Christian writer, *Tertullian*,[10]

> Happy is our *sacrament of water,* in that by washing away the *sins* of our early blindness, we are set free and admitted into *eternal life* . . . . But we, little fishes, after the example of our *Ichthýs* [the Greek word for fish, the letters of which are also the initial letters of *Iesoûs Christòs theoû hyiòs sóter,* meaning "Jesus Christ, Son of God, Savior"], are born in water, nor have we safety in any other way than by permanently *abiding in water [the symbol of life]*.

SACRAMENTS OF HEALING — RECONCILIATION AND ANOINTING:

Shortly before I departed for China as a missionary in 1948, I heard or read this *true story* about a China missionary which, perhaps because of my heightened anticipation at the time, has always remained in my memory. It seems that an *outlying village* which contained no Christians had sent a message to this particular missionary, informing him that they were interested in learning something about Christianity and inviting him to come over and give them a talk. He gladly accepted the invitation but, being a prudent man, thought it best to check with one of his catechists whose wisdom he admired as to the best subject for his talk. What was his surprise when the catechist replied without hesitation that he ought to talk about *Confession.* "Confession! I want to convert these people, not drive them away!" But the catechist held his ground. "Father," he pointed out, "everybody needs to have his *sins forgiven.*" So, probably with fingers crossed, the missionary explained to the villagers the Catholic practice of confession and forgiveness of sins in the Sacrament of Penance (as it was then called) and, to his amazement, the entire village asked to become Catholic!

I have told this story here, not as an apologetic argument for the

Sacrament of Reconciliation, as we now usually call it, but to set the stage for some brief but crucial questions about this *"endangered Sacrament"* in the Church today. Why has there been such an obvious and apparently ever-increasing *decline* in the number of confessions since Vatican II? Are we Catholics sinning less than formerly? Or is it that we now realize we do not have to confess anything and everything? Are we merely stressing quality over quantity? Or using other means of forgiveness more, for example the penitential rite at the beginning of Mass? Perhaps all or most of these questions can be answered affirmatively, but I suspect there is far more to the situation.

As I wondered back in Chapter Five, have we simply lost our sense of sin? And if so, is it because we have lost our sense of God? Or is the problem that, even with a sense of God and of sin, we have been "weaned away by *pop psychology"* from such a "negative practice" as confessing our sins to another? Perhaps the replies to this second set of questions may bring us much closer to the truth but, whatever the answers, we do need to come to grips, personally and communally, with the thorny question of our whole attitude toward the *Sacrament of Reconciliation.* And I offer the following considerations as a help in doing so:

(1) The Spiritual Life is, at its heart, relationship with God, but that *relationship* cannot truly exist and grow if we ignore sin, which *sunders* (or at least strains) that relationship.

(2) If we are seriously pursuing a Spiritual Life, then we need a regular program of *purification,* so that the risen Christ may truly *take possession* of our whole being and *transform* us into himself. After all, we are *consecrated* persons!

(3) The special means which Christ, through his Church, offers us for that purification is primarily the Sacrament of Reconciliation, in which he desires to heal us as our *Savior,* our *Good Shepherd,* our *Divine Physician.*

(4) Besides the psychological and spiritual benefits of unburdening ourselves to someone else, experiencing forgiveness through sacramental *absolution,* and receiving practical *guidance,*

even besides the restoration or increase of *sanctifying grace* through our encounter with the healing Christ in confession and absolution, we also receive *sacramental grace* which enables us more quickly and completely to overcome our sins, including habitual sins.

(5) Under the guidance of the Holy Spirit, the Church has *revised the Rite of Penance* from a *formal juridical action,* with the penitent as self-accuser and the priest as judge, to an *informal interpersonal happening,* with the penitent desiring spiritual health, wholeness, and holiness from the priest who continues the ministry of Christ as Brother and Savior, Physician and Shepherd, Mediator and Reconciler.

Interestingly enough, while these five considerations may help in motivating more of us to take advantage of the Sacrament of Reconciliation on a regular basis, even to develop a healthy habit of confession, I cannot escape the thought that what may be the *single most effective remedy* for the current "back burner" attitude toward the Sacrament is a notable increase in the *qualifications and attitude* on the part of *the priest*. I suspect that, if more of us priests were completely qualified through *transformation* into Christ as well as thorough preparation in *counseling and guidance,* if more of us approached the hearing of confessions with *love* and *enthusiasm,* with the *humanity* of "wounded healers"[11] and the *patience* of ready listeners, striving to be true mediators and reconcilers between hurting Christians and the healing Christ, then we might begin to see a real *turnaround* in the use of the Sacrament of Reconciliation.

As a vivid illustration of Jesus' whole teaching about sin, repentance, and reconciliation, let us look for a moment at his touching *Parable of the Prodigal Son* (Lk 15:11-32), to which I promised in Chapter Five that I would return in this chapter. Notice, first of all, that this is the *third of three parables* in Luke 15, all of the *"lost and found"* theme: the Searching Shepherd and Lost Sheep, the Diligent Housewife and Lost Coin, and the Compassionate Father and Lost Son. The first two, as Jesus and Luke intended, appeal to men and women respectively. The third appeals to everyone, but especially parents and young people in their teens or just beyond.

The parable itself draws a perfect picture of four of the principal elements involved in the Sacrament of Reconciliation:

(1) *Sin* (Greek *hamartía*, "missing the mark, going astray") represented by the wayward action of the younger son in using the inheritance received from his generous father to *go astray*, to *estrange himself from his father, wasting* everything on his own pleasures.

(2) *Repentance* (Greek *metánoia*, "conversion, change of mind or attitude"), which occurs when the young man, looking honestly at his wretched situation, determines to swallow his pride and return to his father, humbly confessing his folly, seeking his forgiveness, and begging him to receive him back at least as a paid servant. This attitude of *humble sorrow for sin*, shown also in the familiar parable of the *publican* in contrast with the proud Pharisee (Lk 18:9-14), is at the heart of reconciliation.

(3) *Confession* (Greek *homología*, "saying the same thing; conceding, admitting the truth"), which the repentant young man proceeds to do in all humility and honesty, making no attempt to "beat around the bush" by excusing his conduct or cloaking it in euphemisms.

(4) *Reconciliation* (Greek *katallagé*, "changing, exchanging, e.g. coins, with another; restoring to favor"), accomplished primarily through the attitude and response of the *compassionate father* and celebrated with great *joy* by the entire household.

To fully appreciate the joy of reconciliation, it is helpful to think of it in very human terms, in the reconciliation, for example, of a *married couple* who have separated or even divorced, or of *parents with one or more of their children* who have run away from home because of real or imagined neglect and lack of communication; of *brothers and sisters* who have refused even to talk to one another for years; or of *friends* who have long been estranged over some silly peccadillo.

But there is still another part to the Parable of the Prodigal Son, one which can serve as a mirror in which we can take a good look at ourselves. While the festivities over the younger son's return are in progress, *the elder son* returns from the fields and, upon learning the reason for the celebration, becomes highly *indignant* and refuses even to enter the house. His father, full of loving concern, leaves the festivities to come outside and plead with his elder son.

Obviously, the son is totally deaf to his father's appeal. His heart is filled with *resentment,* which he has consciously or unconsciously been storing up since his younger brother's departure, and which now erupts in a torrent of *hurt feelings,*

> For years now I have *slaved* for you. I *never disobeyed* one of your orders, yet you never gave me so much as a kid goat to celebrate with my friends. Then, when this *son of yours* returns after having gone through your property with *loose women,* you kill the fatted calf for him! (Lk 15:29-30).

Now, deep down, do we not feel a sense of *solidarity* with the elder brother? After all, we might say, he does have a *legitimate complaint*! Here he has remained loyal to his father all this time, working hard on the farm and totally obedient to every one of his orders. Yet, in spite of all this, his father is celebrating over his wayward son rather than over him! But, if we look closer, we will see that this elder son is very much like *the Pharisee* in Luke 18:9-14 who proudly prays,

> I give you thanks, O God, that I am not like the rest of men — grasping, crooked, adulterous — or even like this tax collector. I fast twice a week. I pay tithes of all I possess!

Notice many of the same traits in the elder son as in the Pharisee: his *pride and self-righteousness* over his loyalty (evidently external like the Pharisee's), *his slavish and unloving obedience* to his father's orders (like the Pharisee's emphasis on law over love), his *presumption in judging and condemning* his brother (like the Pharisee's judgment and condemnation of the tax collector), and finally his utter *resentment* at his father's compassionate forgiveness of his brother (whom he refuses to forgive or even acknowledge as his brother, referring to him scornfully as "this son of yours").

All of these elements in the elder brother's behavior are pointed reminders to us of the *Pharisaic attitude* which we must avoid at all costs if we are to expect God's favor and forgiveness, an attitude of pride and self-righteousness, slavish and unloving obedience to law, judgment and condemnation of others, intolerant and unforgiving resentment. Remember that, according to the proper translation of the Greek, we ought to pray in the *Lord's Prayer,* "Forgive us our debts as we have *already forgiven* and *continue to forgive* (Greek *aphékamen,* in the perfect tense) our debtors!" To love deeply is to forgive completely!

When treating the Sacraments in general during the previous chapter, I believe that I gave sufficient indication of the *Scripture* references regarding the Sacrament of Reconciliation, especially the most familiar one of *John 20:23* on the very day of Christ's resurrection, when he breathed on his Apostles and said, "Receive the Holy Spirit. If you forgive men's sins, they are forgiven them; if you hold them bound, they are held bound." It is true that some today, even among Catholics, interpret this passage in reference to Baptism rather than Penance, but to me this is favored neither by the natural meaning of the words nor by the tradition of the Church. Jesus Christ, our loving Savior, who during his lifetime went about forgiving sins, and by his death and resurrection accomplished our *atonement* (in English, originally *at-one-ment*), continues his ministry of reconciliation down the centuries through the Church and her ministers, as we read in Paul's most self-revealing letter, Second Corinthians,

> If anyone is in Christ, he is a new creation. The old order has passed away; now all is new! All this has been done by God, who has *reconciled us* to himself through Christ and has given us the *ministry of reconciliation.*
>
> I mean that God, in Christ, was *reconciling the world* to himself, not counting men's transgressions against them, and that he has entrusted the *message of reconciliation to us.* This makes us ambassadors for Christ, God as it were appealing through us.

We implore you, in Christ's name: *be reconciled to God!* For our sakes God made him who did not know sin to be sin, so that in him we might become the very holiness of God (2 Cor 5:17-21).

Let us now turn, even more briefly, to the *Sacrament of Anointing of the Sick and Aged.* This we can do because much of what has already been said about Baptism, and particularly about Reconciliation, is applicable to this Sacrament as well. For example, all three can be called *Sacraments of healing.* Like Baptism, the Sacrament of the Sick involves anointing with oil; like Reconciliation, it is a special means for the forgiveness of sins committed after Baptism. But, unlike the other two Sacraments, it is intended specifically for the sick and the aged.

In this, it is especially easy and inspiring to recognize *Jesus Christ, the compassionate Physician,* who "cured all who were afflicted, thereby fulfilling what had been said through Isaiah the prophet: 'It was our infirmities he bore, our sufferings he endured' " (Mt 8:16-17), never ceasing through the Church and her ministers to visit, comfort, strengthen, and frequently heal those who are afflicted with illness or weakened by age.

Fortunately, unlike the Sacrament of Reconciliation, this rite of anointing, far from experiencing a decline, has enjoyed *greater appreciation and reception* than ever before, especially since it has been clearly separated from the onset of death and made available to all who are seriously ill or aged. If anything, there may be some failing on the side of *overuse* rather than neglect, since in practice many who are neither seriously ill nor getting along in years are anointed, particularly in communal anointing services, but I like to think that neither Christ himself nor the Church is inclined to turn anyone away from this consoling Sacrament.

The use of *olive oil* is especially fitting in the Sacrament of the Sick because, from time immemorial, it has been used as a soothing and curing agent. We see this clearly in the touching but challenging

Parable of the Good Samaritan, who approached the stricken man and "dressed his wounds, pouring in *oil and wine*" (Lk 10:34). Undoubtedly, the oil was for healing; the wine, for antiseptic purposes. Then in Mark 6:12-13, we see that the Apostles, in their missionary journey during Jesus' lifetime, "went off, preaching the need of repentance. They expelled many demons, *anointed the sick with oil,* and worked many cures."

And finally, we have that landmark text of *James 5:13-16* which we have already quoted in the previous chapter, but which certainly bears repeating here,

> If anyone among you is suffering hardship, he must pray. If a person is in good spirits, he should sing a hymn of praise. Is there anyone sick among you? He should ask for the *presbyters of the church.* They in turn are to *pray* over him, *anointing* him with oil in the Name [of the Lord].
>
> This prayer uttered in faith will reclaim the one who is ill, and the Lord will restore him to *health.* If he has committed any sins, *forgiveness* will be his. Hence, declare your sins to one another, and pray for one another, that you may find healing.

One of the noteworthy ideas in James' directives is the close connection between *the spiritual and the physical,* between forgiveness of sins and restoration of health. This, of course, is also quite characteristic of Jesus' cures, perhaps the most memorable example being that of the *paralytic* (Mk 2:1-12 and parallels). Not that illness is regarded as a punishment for sin, as Jesus clearly explains in John 9:1-3, but rather that the *Jewish anthropology,* which views each human being as existing in *three dimensions* (as distinguished from the Greek dichotomy of body and soul) practically demands an holistic approach to healing. It is, therefore, quite heartening to see this same approach becoming more and more common among physicians, psychologists, religious representatives, and people in general.

As with everything else, however, we humans tend to take a good thing and push it to *extremes.* I am referring to the growing preoccupation with healing in some religious, including Catholic circles. We all need spiritual or *inner healing,* especially of those anxieties, resentments, sometimes even hatreds, which eat away within us like a cancer, affecting us not only spiritually but emotionally and even physically. But we sometimes tend to get carried away and place such a premium on *physical health* that we make it the treasure where our heart is (Mt 6:21). It is almost as if we were back in pagan times when so many devotees flocked from all over the world to the shrines of *Asclepius* the Greek god of health (symbolized by a serpent, which still appears on the caduceus or medical insignia), whose greatest healing centers are still impressive at Epidaurus in Southern Greece and Pergamum in Western Turkey.

In this connection, I would like to call attention to what I have already written about suffering and sacrifice in Chapter Nine. As I suggest there, one of the great secrets of life is the realization that, while we must all expect to suffer in one way or another, we have the unique opportunity of offering our sufferings in union with those of Christ for the ongoing redemption of the world. Like St. Paul, we can "fill up what is lacking in the sufferings of Christ for the sake of his body, the church" (Col 1:24). This is a great *privilege*; in fact, a choice *vocation* which, unfortunately, even many who are striving to live a Spiritual Life do not fully understand. But those who do find that the same sufferings which once appeared unbearable can not only be borne; they can be borne with serenity and peace because they are no longer mere sufferings but *loving sacrifices,* as Paul intimates in Ephesians 5:1-2, NIV:

> Be imitators of God, therefore, as dearly loved children and live
> a life of love, just as Christ loved us and gave himself up for us as
> a fragrant offering and sacrifice to God.

THE SACRAMENT OF UNION — THE HOLY EUCHARIST:

We now come to the *pearl of the Sacraments,* the Blessed Sacrament of Love, the Holy Eucharist! To me, as to Catholics generally and many other Christians, this Sacrament is in a class by itself, for in it we not only encounter the risen Christ acting through visible signs, we possess him really and physically *present with us in his risen state* under the appearances of bread and wine. Even to those Christians who do not acknowledge the real presence of Christ in the Eucharist, this Sacrament remains nonetheless of unique importance for its powerful implications of *spiritual union* both with Christ and with fellow Christians.

In recent years, there seems to be a tendency among theologians and liturgists to downplay, or even ignore entirely, such questions as the *real presence* of Christ in the Eucharist and the *sacrificial character* of the Mass. True, in this age of ecumenism rather than apologetics and practical rather than speculative theology, we hardly need the extensive defenses and intricate distinctions that characterized an earlier time. Yet, on the other hand, it might be helpful if not downright necessary to look briefly at the biblical evidence for these "endangered subjects" regarding the Eucharist.

Christian belief about the real presence in and sacrificial nature of the Eucharist was certainly not born in a vacuum nor accepted without foundation. Some of the most *sacred Jewish celebrations,* such as the annual Feast of "the Passover Sacrifice" in private homes (Ex 12:21-27), the ratification of the Covenant at Sinai in Exodus 24:1-11 (observed annually on the Feast of Pentecost, Ac 2:1), and the daily sacrifices at the temple in Jerusalem (Lv 6, etc.), formed the providential Old Testament preparation for the institution and celebration of the Holy Eucharist, the *Passover Sacrificial Meal of the New Covenant.*

In the *New Testament,* the evidence for the Holy Eucharist as the Sacrifice and Sacrament of Christ's love and presence is both solid and convincing, from its *promise* by Jesus at the Capernaum synagogue (Jn 6:25-58, especially 51-58 — preceded by his multiplication of loaves and fishes and walking on water, evidences of his power over food and over his body, in Jn 6:1-24; Mk 6:32-52; 8:1-10; Mt 14:13-33; 15:32-39;Lk 9:10-17); to its *institution* (Mt 26:26-30 fol-

lowing Mk 14:22-26, and Lk 22:14-20 following 1 Cor 11:23-29); to
various indications of its *observance* in the life of the early Church
(e.g. in Ac 2:42, 46; 20:7, 11; 1 Cor 10:14-22; 11:17-22, 30-34), not
to mention such possible or even probable *allusions* to the Eucharist as
Jn 2:1-11; 19:34-36; 21:9-14 and Lk 24:13-35.

And, if I may add a page or two from *Church History* as well, it is
a significant fact that, while there were various doubts and denials in
the early centuries of the Church about the divinity of Jesus Christ, the
reality of his divine and human natures, and the three persons in the
Holy Trinity, it was not until the *ninth century* that the first Eucharistic
controversy arose between St. Paschasius and another monk named
Ratramnus, and not until the *eleventh century* that Berengar of Tours
actually denied the real presence of Christ in the Eucharist, finally
retracting his teaching not long before his death.[12] As it turned out,
the whole affair was a kind of *felix culpa* or "happy fault" because it
led to greater theological understanding of the Eucharist as well as to
the institution of the beautiful Feast of *Corpus Christi* or "Body of
Christ," for which St. Thomas Aquinas himself composed a magnificent Mass and set of hymns.

To summarize and complete this brief biblical and historical
survey, let me present the opening paragraph of Chapter Two, "The
Most Sacred Mystery of the Eucharist," from the first document to
issue from the Second Vatican Council, namely, the *Constitution on
the Sacred Liturgy*,[13]

> At the Last Supper, on the night he was betrayed, our Savior
> instituted the *eucharistic sacrifice* of his Body and Blood. This he
> did in order to perpetuate the *sacrifice of the Cross* throughout the
> ages until he should come again, and so to entrust to his beloved
> Spouse, the Church, a memorial of his death and resurrection: a
> *sacrament of love*, a *sign of unity*, a bond of *charity*, a *paschal
> banquet* in which Christ is consumed, the mind is filled with grace,
> and a pledge of future glory is given to us.

I have attempted to restrict the biblical and historical evidence for the Sacrament of the Eucharist to the minimum that I felt was indispensable. As for the *Theology of the Eucharist,* I propose to omit it altogether (referring the reader to works whose primary aim is theological), so that I may pass immediately to the double-barreled question which is much more relevant for my readers, "What is the *meaning* and the most effective *use* of the Holy Eucharist for our Spiritual Life?"

In replying to this question, I must continue to limit myself. There are many liturgical books and articles about the Eucharist as the primary public *worship* (in Greek, *leitourgía*) of the Church, as a *thanksgiving* (in Greek, *eucharistía*) for God's love in Creation and Salvation, as a *remembrance* (in Greek, *anámnēsis*) of the saving death and resurrection of his Son, Jesus Christ, and an anticipation of his glorious *return* (in Greek, *parousía*) in the eschatological Kingdom of God, and as a celebration of Christ's loving *presence* (also *parousía*) not only in *word and sacrament* but also within and among the *members and ministers* of God's People, especially when they are *gathered together* as a worshipping community (Mt 18:20).

What I want to focus on is the role of the Sacrifice and Sacrament of the Eucharist in our *personal living of the Word of God, both Inspired and Incarnate.* As I touched on previously, we have happily gone beyond an earlier *religious individualism* (whose whole concern was to "save my soul") and promoted a real sense of *community,* *"unity in diversity,"* which ought to characterize us as the People of God and Body of Christ. Unfortunately, we humans have an absolute genius for carrying a good thing to *extremes.* Thus, in our necessary emphasis on community, we sometimes tend to forget that every community is composed of persons, whom we cannot afford to *depersonalize,* even for the sake of the community. Have we unknowingly passed from individualism to communitarianism without promoting *a healthy personalism*? In all the hand-wringing about the problems of persuading people to form worshipping communities, are we overlooking their most basic need of personal union through Christ with God?

As we have already seen in discussing *Baptism,* we are first of all *initiated into the body or person of the Risen Christ* and by that fact we are also *initiated into his communal body,* which is the Church. Now, according to all liturgists, both *Confirmation and Eucharist* are, along with *Baptism, Sacraments of Initiation.* Baptism enables us to be Spiritually born into the risen Christ (and he into us), so that we live by his Life. In the Eucharist he feeds and nourishes that Spiritual Life in us with his own Body and Blood, transforming us more and more into himself. And with Confirmation, we can be strengthened in the Spirit so as to reach maturity in Christ and he in us.

The question is, then, *where and how* does the Holy Eucharist fit into this picture of our personal Spiritual Life? Just how, above all, does the Sacrifice and Sacrament of the Mass accomplish in us that *growth and transformation* to which we are predestined and called in our Spiritual Life of union with Christ? In brief, how does the Holy Eucharist help us *"to live the Word: Inspired and Incarnate"*? Let us, without further delay, explore the answer to that burning question.

The *first part* of the question admits of a fairly easy response. Not only the entire *Liturgy of the Word,* modeled after Jewish synagogue worship, but also the *complete Liturgy* of the Eucharist is permeated with references to *Sacred Scripture.* In fact, it is the Holy Eucharist which *re-presents* (makes present again) throughout the ages the great saving events of Jesus' life, death, and resurrection, anticipated in the Old Testament and detailed in the New, so that all of us can *participate* personally and communally *in our own time.* For this reason, Vatican II, in its *Constitution on the Sacred Liturgy,*[14] insists,

> *Sacred Scripture* is of the greatest importance in the celebration of the Liturgy. For it is from it that *lessons* are read and explained in the *homily,* and *psalms* are sung. It is from the Scriptures that the *prayers, collects, and hymns* draw their inspiration and their force, and that *actions and signs* derive their meaning.

Hence in order to achieve the restoration, progress, and adaptation of the Sacred Liturgy it is essential to promote that *sweet and living love for Sacred Scripture* to which the venerable tradition of Eastern and Western rites gives testimony.

And, in the *Constitution on Divine Revelation,*[15] the Council Fathers echo the same thought,

The Church has always venerated the *divine Scriptures* as she venerated the *Body of the Lord,* in so far as she never ceases, particularly in the Sacred Liturgy, to partake of the bread of life and to offer it to the faithful from *the one table* of the Word of God and the Body of Christ.

I trust that my readers will forgive me for repeating those two quotations, which I had already provided in the previous chapter. There, we were concerned with the relationship of Scripture and Liturgy in general; here, with that of Scripture and the Eucharist in particular.

Far more complex is the answer to the second part of our question, namely how does the Eucharist help in our personal *spiritual growth and transformation into Christ*? To arrive at it, we might have to do some *research and reflection.* But, while it can be helpful to understand the meaning of all the many details in the Eucharistic Liturgy, we must be careful not to "*miss the forest for the trees.*" For what it is worth and with apologies, if necessary, to my liturgist friends, I humbly offer the reader the following interpretation of the Eucharist which is the result, not so much of formal study, as of much prayer and reflection.

To me, the Mass is a *Sacred Drama,* as were many if not all of the great dramas of ancient Greece and certainly of medieval Europe. Just as a talented *playwright* might take a simple story and dramatize it to bring out all its latent power, or as an artistic *jeweler* might take a diamond and place it in an eye-catching setting in order to enhance its beauty, so the Church (or Christ in the Church) has taken the simple but powerful *institution account* of the Eucharist and placed it in a beautiful, *dramatic setting* to enable us all to appreciate the full extent of its dynamic splendor.

But the Mass is *not just play acting* (an actor is called in Greek *hypócritēs,* a "hypocrite"!); no, it is a *drama of real love and life,* filled with stimulating and transforming *action!* And in this action, this drama, we are all chosen to be *participants,* not just spectators. We all have a role to play, or rather to live, for by our *Baptism* we have all been *clothed* with Christ (Gal 3:27)! We are all *priests* (1 P 2:5, 9) as well as *victims* (Rm 12:1; Ep 5:2; Col 1:24). Let us listen again to the *Constitution on the Sacred Liturgy*[16] from Vatican II,

> The Church, therefore, earnestly desires that Christ's faithful, when present at this mystery of faith, should not be there as strangers or silent spectators. On the contrary, through a good understanding of the rites and prayers they should *take part* in the *sacred action,* conscious of what they are doing, with devotion and full collaboration.
>
> They should be instructed by God's word, and be nourished at the table of the Lord's Body. They should give thanks to God. Offering the immaculate victim, not only through the hands of the priest but also *together with him,* they should learn to *offer themselves.* Through Christ, the Mediator, they should be drawn day by day into ever more perfect *union with God and each other,* so that finally God may be all in all.

I hope I do not shock or scandalize the reader by referring to the Mass as a Sacred Drama. Actually, the heart of what I want to say does not really require use of this imagery, but I do feel that it is valid and helpful. Drama has been part of every culture in history, including the Judeo-Christian, as is evident from both the Old and New Testaments. The *Jewish Passover,* for example, was and is a dramatic celebration and re-presentation of Yahweh's deliverance of his Chosen People (Ex 12:21-27), so that the initial setting of the Eucharist was already dramatic.

In the New Testament, the *threefold temptations of Jesus* (Mt 4:1-11 and Lk 4:1-13) are, as I have already explained in Chapter Five, dramatic accounts of the fact that Jesus, as human, was certainly tempted. *Paul* refers to himself and his fellow preachers of the Gospel as "a *spectacle* (in Greek *théatron,* a theater or dramatic event) to the universe, to angels and men alike!" (1 Cor 4:9). And does not the *Apocalypse,* in presenting its "Theology of Church History," give every evidence of high drama, with its heavenly and earthly *stage settings*[17] and its highly *spectacular happenings*?

The Mass certainly contains all the *elements of theater*: dramatic *setting* and *action*; principal speaking and non-speaking *roles,* mostly in distinctive *clothing*; *music* and sometimes even *dancing, dialogue* throughout, with distinct *acts* and *scenes.* For example, the *two principal acts* are well-known as the Liturgy of the *Word* and the Liturgy of the *Eucharist.* What may not always be noticed is that each of those acts is divided into scenes.

The *first act* contains *two parallel scenes*: the opening one, in which *we begin* the drama, greet one another, and then address ourselves to God in penitence, praise, and petition; and the closing scene, in which *our God of love responds* to us in his own words from the Old and New Testaments, especially the Gospel, and in the words of the homilist. This is the first act of love and life, verbally exchanged between ourselves and God.

Thus far, we have had a dramatic exchange of love with God by means of the spoken and sung word, but the Beloved Disciple exhorts us in 1 John 3:18, "Dear children, let us not love with words or tongue but *with actions and in truth.*" So we move on to the *second act,* which is primarily action rather than word. But before we do, at least on Sunday, we have the interlude of the *Profession of Faith* and the *Prayers of Petition* which form a fitting transition between the first and second acts.

The *second act* comprises not two but *three scenes,* which are all important and well-known to us as the *Offertory* or Presentation of the Gifts, the *Consecration* or Eucharistic Prayer, and the *Communion* with Thanksgiving and Dismissal. *In the first scene,* after the collection and offertory procession (if they are held), the priest then proceeds to offer, in the name of all present and usually in dialogue with them, the bread and wine which will be consecrated in the Mass. But let us remember that we are not simply offering bread and wine; *we are offering ourselves — all we are,* all we *have,* all we *do,* all we *suffer* — represented and symbolized by the bread and wine. This is shown especially in two ways: the prayer immediately after the offering and the invitation to prayer after the priest washes his hands.

The prayer following the presentation of the gifts, while it has taken various forms in recent years, is still quite recognizable as a summary of the prayer of the *three young men* in the fiery furnace of Daniel 3:38-40. Being Jews, they were used to offering animal sacrifices at the hands of priests in the temple at Jerusalem. However, in their current situation they had none of these things, and so they *offered themselves,* as follows:

> We have in our day no prince, prophet, or leader, no holocaust, sacrifice, oblation, or incense, no place to offer first fruits, to find favor with you.
>
> But with contrite heart and humble spirit let us be received; as though it were holocausts of rams and bullocks, or thousands of fat lambs.
>
> So let our sacrifice be in your presence today as we follow you unreservedly; for those who trust in you cannot be put to shame.

The invitation to prayer is also illuminating, for it asks all present to pray that the common offering of priest and people may be acceptable to God. If the offering were merely of bread and wine, especially bread and wine which are about to become the Body and Blood of Christ, there would seem to be no need to pray for their acceptance, but if we are *offering ourselves,* then with a sense of our unworthiness and even sinfulness we certainly do need to be concerned about and pray for acceptance.

The second scene of the second act is that of the *Consecration,* whether that is understood as the *words of Jesus* recorded in the New Testament or as the *entire Eucharistic Prayer*. Our Catholic belief, based on Our Lord's own words, is that, in the Consecration, the bread and wine which we have offered become the *Body and Blood of Christ* or, to express it another way, become *the risen Christ sacramentally present*. Now, this is especially important for our Spiritual Life because, if the bread and wine which represent us become the risen Christ, does it not follow that we too are and should be *transformed into Christ*? Yes, through the miracle of the Eucharist, we are *sacramentally and mystically one with Christ* in his death and resurrection, for the glory of God, our own ongoing transformation and growth in holiness, and the continuing redemption of the world. And is this not vividly brought home to us if we make our own the words of consecration, "This is *my* body, this is *my* blood," uniting ourselves with Christ and with the priest as both *priest and victim*?

Finally, in our *third scene of the second act,* after the Great Amen, the Lord's Prayer, the Exchange of Peace, the Breaking of the Bread, and the other prayerful preparations, we are privileged to receive the *risen Christ in Holy Communion*. All through the centuries, such a *religious meal* has been regarded as uniting us in a special way with the god or the dead or anyone else in whose honor we eat and drink. That element is certainly present here, but with additional noteworthy considerations which make all the difference:

(1) We are not simply eating and drinking in honor of and in union with someone; we are sacramentally eating and drinking the very *Body and Blood of the risen Christ*; we are physically and spiritually receiving Christ himself in a way which he alone could make possible.

(2) As we know from nutritionists, *we are what we eat and drink*.[18] If that be true of natural foods, is it not true as well of the Spiritual Food and Drink of the Holy Eucharist? By receiving the risen Christ regularly in Communion, we can and should be more and more *transformed* into him. But also as with natural food, much will depend on our *general Spiritual health* as well as on our *Spiritual appetite*, our

hunger and thirst for Christ. If we are already filled with everything and everyone else, especially with ourselves, how can we really be hungry and thirsty for him?

(3) As Paul points out in 1 Corinthians 10:17, "Because the loaf of bread is one, *we, many though we are, are one body,* for we all partake of the one loaf." Yes, our whole participation in, and especially our reception of the Holy Eucharist, serve to unite us more and more, not only with the risen Christ, but also with his body the *Church* and with our *fellow members* of the Church. As a matter of fact, I like to think that we are justified in referring to one another as *"blood brothers and sisters"* insofar as we partake of the same Body and Blood. And the *Breaking of the Bread* before Communion can be a painful but salutary reminder of our brokenness within and among ourselves, and our desperate need for union with Christ, our "True Self," and with one another.

To bring our drama of the Eucharist to a conclusion, we have the Prayer of *Thanksgiving* (although the entire Mass, especially the Preface and Eucharistic Prayer, constitutes a magnificent Prayer of Thanksgiving), then a final *Greeting* and *Blessing,* followed by the *Dismissal* which is really more of a commission, a *Sacred Commission* such as the Prophets and Apostles received, to go forth from the church or chapel and live the Mass by allowing Christ in us to witness, serve, and suffer for the glory of our Father and the good of our neighbor.

Allow me to share a *final note* on the Mass, one taken from the story of *Heli's priest-sons* (1 S 2:12-17) who continually stole from the sacrifices offered by the people. The lesson for us is that, if we have truly offered ourselves in the Eucharist, then we too must be careful lest we become *"thieves of the holocaust"* and incur the same or a worse kind of punishment. After all, the sacrifice in which we are privileged to participate is infinitely greater than the animal sacrifices of Heli's time could ever be!

And before we leave the subject of the Holy Eucharist, let me underline once again (as I have earlier in this work) the precious opportunity that we have of *visiting Our Lord* in the Blessed Sacrament for shorter or longer periods as time permits. Not out of some kind of fear, as in the anonymous whimsical verse,

> Every time I pass a church,
> I always make a visit
> Lest, when at last they roll me in,
> The Lord won't say, "Who is it?"

Rather, out of love and *love's contentment in the presence* of the Beloved. Not that this is the primary purpose of the Eucharist, but can one think of a better *setting for prayer,* either *personal* or *liturgical,* for example in the *Liturgy of the Hours?*

SUMMARY:

In this chapter, we have concentrated on some of the *individual Sacraments,* especially Baptism and Holy Eucharist, with a fairly brief consideration also of the Sacraments of Confirmation, Reconciliation, and Anointing of the Sick. Our reflection has focused, above all, on the role of these Sacraments in bringing about our *union* with and *transformation* into Christ, so that he can be *incarnate anew in us* and thereby be able to continue his life of love, service, and suffering through us for the glory of God and the ongoing redemption of humankind. Thus we are enabled *"To live the Word: Inspired and Incarnate."*

There are, of course, *other matters* which we could include under the general heading of *Sacred Liturgy;* for example, the *Liturgical Year* and the *Liturgy of the Hours* (both of which are especially important in my own Spiritual Life) as well as the more misunderstood *Sacramentals* and *Indulgences.* Since, however, the scope of this book and the length of this chapter do not permit inclusion of these subjects, I can only refer the reader to other works, especially the *Constitution on the Sacred Liturgy* from the Second Vatican Council.

CONCLUSION:

In our conclusion, I would like to return for a moment to the *beginning* of this chapter. There, I reflected with regret on the drastic diminution of devotion to the Saints, and reminisced on the inspiration I had received over the years from one of my favorites, *Blessed John Gabriel Perboyre,* a beloved Vincentian missionary and martyr in China.

Now, I would like to conclude this important chapter with an *inspiring prayer* which Blessed John Gabriel wrote and which, for many years, has been a favorite of mine as well as of many Vincentians, Daughters of Charity, and others. The words and thoughts themselves clearly indicate how well this particular prayer focuses on the very *considerations* to which we have devoted this chapter, namely our initiation into the risen Christ through Baptism and Confirmation, our cleansing and healing from spiritual and possibly physical weakness through Reconciliation and Anointing, as well as our union with and transformation into Christ through the Holy Eucharist, the Sacrifice and Sacrament of Incarnate Love,

PRAYER OF BLESSED JOHN GABRIEL PERBOYRE [19]

O My Divine Savior,
Transform me into Yourself.

May my hands be the hands of Jesus.
May my tongue be the tongue of Jesus.
Grant that every faculty of my body
May serve only to glorify You.

Above all,
Transform my soul and all its powers
So that my memory, will and affections
May be the memory, will and affections
Of Jesus.

I pray you to destroy in me
All that is not of You.

Grant that I may live
But in You, by You and for You,
So that I may truly say,
With Saint Paul,

"I live — now not I —
But Christ lives in me!"

RECOMMENDED READING LIST

1. Barry, David. *Ministry of Reconciliation: Modern Lessons from Scripture and Sacrament*, Staten Island, NY: Alba House, 1975.
2. Empereur, James. *Prophetic Anointing: God's Call to the Sick, the Elderly, and the Dying*, Wilmington, DE: M. Glazier, 1982.
3. Lussier, Ernest. *Living the Eucharistic Mystery* and *Eucharist, The Bread of Life,* Staten Island, NY: Alba House, 1977, 1979.
4. Marsh, Thomas A. *Gift of Community: Baptism and Confirmation,* Wilmington, DE: Michael Glazier, Inc., 1984.
5. McGinley, Phyllis. *Saint Watching,* New York: Crossroad Books, 1982.

QUESTIONS FOR REFLECTION AND DISCUSSION

1. What is the connection, if any, between the Saints, the Sacraments, and our Spiritual Life?
2. What roles do the Sacraments of Baptism and Confirmation play in our personal and communal Spiritual Life?
3. Why and how does the Sacrament of the Holy Eucharist hold such a crucial place in our personal and communal Spiritual Life?
4. What are our thoughts and feelings about the drastic decrease in the use of the Sacrament of Reconciliation?
5. What is the place of physical and spiritual healing in our own Spiritual Life, and how does the Anointing of the Sick fit in?

CHAPTER TWELVE

SPECIAL MEANS OF THE RELATIONSHIP, PART III:
Living Christ in Our Vocation and Ministry

Years ago, I do not remember when or where, I read a fanciful anecdote, at once simple yet profound, which has somehow remained with me as part of my philosophy, or rather theology, of life. In thirteenth century France, a towering cathedral was under construction, one of those magnificent gothic testaments to a transcendent faith that continue to astonish us with the wonder of their structure while they remind us of our origin and our end, pointing their tapering fingers unwaveringly toward the heavens. Volunteer craftsmen and common laborers were carving, hauling, and fitting huge stones into their designated places. Among them was one aging worker who was obviously exhausting himself with the sheer physical strain of the work but who, nevertheless, showed no signs of wanting to cease, or even rest. A stranger who happened by could not help noticing his extraordinary efforts and felt obliged to challenge him, "Why do you insist on hauling those heavy stones at your age? Let the younger and stronger men do it." To his surprise, the old man immediately responded, "Sir, I thank you for your concern but, you see, I am not just hauling stones; *I am building a cathedral!*"

For me, the point of this anecdote is that, whatever we do, however small *our role in life* may seem, it is our own God-given role and it is important in the general scheme of things: important for the glory of God and the service of others, important for the ongoing hominization and Christification of the human race, important in the fulfillment of our destiny to union with and transformation into Jesus Christ. *Viktor Frankl,* the founder of Logotherapy, which is some-times called the third form of psychotherapy (beyond Freud and Jung), insists on this importance as central to our *"Search for Meaning,"*

> Everyone has his own specific vocation or mission in life; everyone must carry out a concrete assignment that demands fulfillment. Therein he cannot be replaced, nor can his life be repeated. Thus, everyone's task is as unique as his specific opportunity to implement it. [1]

Now, if this be true of everyone (and all that is written in the Scriptures, as I have tried to interpret and apply them, indicates that it is), then how much truer and more crucial for us Christians, who are personally and communally an "ekklesĭa," a People Called! Hence, in this our twelfth and final chapter, we will be concerned with the question of *our call or vocation,* not only in general but in particular, as *an essential means* in our Spiritual Life.

Until fairly recently, whenever the term *"vocation"* was em-ployed by Catholics, the reference was almost exclusively to the ministerial priesthood or to the religious life. It is still used in that manner, of course, but (thanks be to God!) it now carries a far wider connotation. *Each and every one* of us is called and therefore has a vocation: some to the priesthood and religious life, yes, but the vast majority to marriage and parenting, to some form of lay ministry in the Church and the world, or perhaps to the newly restored permanent diaconate. All of these will be considered in this chapter, though not in any order of primacy. To me, the centuries-old debate about which is the most perfect vocation is an exercise in futility because, for each of us individually, *the most perfect vocation* is the one to which God has called us and in which he desires to sanctify us.

The Bible, as we have already seen in Chapter Four, is filled with examples of God's call and commission to various persons, both men and women, whom he has chosen to fulfill some special role in Salvation History, usually one of liberation, consolidation, or reformation. Outstanding examples in the *Old Testament* are those of Abram, Jacob, and Joseph; Moses, Joshua, and the Judges or Liberators; Saul, David, and the Pre-Exilic Prophets; Ezra, Nehemiah, and the Post-Exilic Prophets; Judith, Esther, Daniel, and the Maccabees. In the *New Testament,* of course, the shining examples are those of Mary and Joseph, the Twelve Apostles and Seven Deacons, Matthias and Barnabas, Paul and Luke.

You and I can hardly presume or expect a call of such magnitude, but we can be certain of this: we are indeed called, and called to a life which will make a tremendous difference here and hereafter. Do we ever pause to realize the extent to which our lives can *affect the lives of others,* perhaps others whom we will never even meet? All we need do is recall how often and how deeply our own lives have been *touched by others,* usually without their knowledge.

In my own case, two persons in particular come to mind immediately in this regard. One was a little old lady living in a tiny hut at the back of a neighbor's yard in Uptown New Orleans. Our mother, in her deep concern for others, used to send my younger sister and me over to the little hut with food for this solitary soul. The radiant smile, the warm feeling of love, the words of gratitude and blessing, the sense of dignity and holiness which we received from that little old lady were for us unforgettable rewards.

The other influence which comes immediately to mind is that of the priest and pastor with whom I had the privilege of living and working during my three missionary years in China, two of them spent under Communist oppression. His name was Father Leo Fox, C.M. Plain as an old shoe, with a simple, direct, and totally dedicated love for God and others, he was the ideal friend and companion, model and counselor during those trying times. Whatever happened or threatened to happen, he never ceased to be the "Rock of Gibraltar," always ready with a hearty laugh, especially at himself.

These are but two of the many *indelible influences* for good in my life, to which I could easily add many more, above all, my father and mother, brothers and sisters, relatives and friends, teachers and students, confreres and colleagues, as well as a vast number of consecrated and self-giving priests and deacons, religious and lay people, plus quite a few other Christians and Jews, and even some Muslims, Oriental religionists, and self-declared agnostics and atheists. The list is almost limitless! And no wonder, for just as a wave, great or small, moves noiselessly along until it breaks on some unseen and distant shore, so whatever we do, whatever we are, whatever we are called to be, has an effect far beyond our wildest imagining on an almost limitless number of people. God grant that our own wavelets may benefit others at least half as much as we have been blessed by them!

"All well and good," I seem to hear you say, "but how do I know what I am called to be and to do in my life?" A valid question to which, frankly, there is no easy answer. This can often require a lengthy period of *prayerful discernment,* both alone and with a competent spiritual director. On the other hand, the answer may come in a sudden flash of light, as happened in Paul's case. The important consideration for us is to be attentive and ready to follow Jesus in whatever direction he calls us. And we will be far more attentive and ready the more we respond to our *general vocation,* as Christians, to surrender ourselves to his love, to be transformed into him, and to permit him to continue his life of love and service through us.

Are we not, by our very *Baptism,* incorporated into the risen Christ (Rm 6:1-11) and into his communal body, the Church (Rm 12:4-5)? Are we not members of "a chosen race, a royal priesthood, a holy nation, a people he claims for his own to proclaim the glorious works" (Ex 19:6) of the One who has called us "from darkness into his marvelous light" (1 P 2:9)? Are we not "consecrated in Christ Jesus" and "called (to be) saints" (1 Cor 1:2, WD)? And are we not called and even commanded to "be compassionate" and "perfect" like our Heavenly Father (Lk 6:36; Mt 5:48) and not only to love our God and neighbor with our whole being (Mk 12:29-31 and parallels) but even to love one another as Christ himself has loved us (Jn 13:34; 15:12)? Can we ask for any higher or more responsible vocation than this? Let us listen to Paul extol this, our incomparable general vocation,

> We know that God makes all things work together for the good of those who have been called according to his decree. Those whom he foreknew he predestined to share the image of his Son, so that the Son might be the first-born of many brothers. Those he predestined he likewise called; those he called he also justified. What shall we say after that? (Rm 8:28-31)

To which he seems to answer, after many labors and letters,

> Praised be the God and Father of our Lord Jesus Christ, who has bestowed on us in Christ every spiritual blessing in the heavens! God chose us in him before the world began, to be holy and blameless in his sight, to be full of love; he likewise predestined us through Christ Jesus to be his adopted sons — such was his will and pleasure — that all might praise the glorious favor he has bestowed on us in his beloved (Ep 1:3-6).

I have deliberately emphasized our general vocation before reflecting on possible individual vocations in life because I am utterly convinced that, of the two, it is far more important. Yes, we each have our own calling in life, but if we expended as much time, energy, and even prayer on growth and perfection in our general Christian vocation as we do in trying to discern our individual vocation, I am convinced that we would not only be better Christians but would also find it easier to recognize and embrace our personal God-given calling.

This has very *practical application* to the whole question of vocation. Before we can embrace any of the individual vocations, we must already have passed several years, usually at least twenty, in living and growing to *maturity* as human beings and Christians. To become mature human persons during that formative period of our lives, we need to develop from the *dependence* of childhood, through the struggles for *independence* of adolescence, and finally to the *interdependence* of responsible, loving adults. If, at the same time, we truly devote ourselves to spiritual growth and maturity (using all the means at our disposal, especially prayer and the Sacraments, notably Baptism and Confirmation, Reconciliation and the Eucharist), then we will be both open to and prepared for whatever life-calling God in his loving Providence has chosen for us.

Is this entirely too idealistic and unrealistic? Is it asking something of our *young people* which is humanly impossible to fulfill, given the flighty and morally polluted atmosphere in which they have to grow up? Many would say so without hesitation or qualification. Perhaps I am the eternal optimist, but I simply do not believe in "selling short" either the grace of God or the goodwill of our young people. I have personally witnessed the moral miracles, despite seemingly impossible odds, that the winning combination of grace and goodwill can achieve. Besides, if swimming, gymnastic, and tennis prodigies in their early teens can bedazzle the world with their stellar performances, which require almost superhuman dedication and discipline, how can it be too much to challenge young people generally, with or without physical talent, to accomplish things with God's superhuman grace which are far more important and lasting both for time and for eternity? Recall Paul's timeless remarks about physical and spiritual training in 1 Corinthians 9:24-27 and 1 Timothy 4:7-8.

Finally, there is the added consideration that, to achieve the level of *personal and spiritual maturity* needed to begin our life-vocation, we are not limited to our first twenty years, more or less, but can take thirty or even forty, as more and more people seem to be doing now. An athlete at thirty is almost "over the hill," but with longer life-expectancy now and in the future, waiting until that approximate age before embarking on marriage or any other vocation in life is not at all unreasonable. After all, *Jesus* himself, perfect human that he was, did not begin his public ministry until he was "about thirty years of age" (Lk 3:23)! As a matter of fact, despite a much shorter life-expectancy in the world of his time, one was generally not even considered an adult and ready for any kind of public career until he was at least thirty years of age!

What I have just been saying pertains as much to the most common particular vocation, that of *marriage,* as it does to a priestly, diaconal, or religious calling. A small child, asked in catechism class to define adultery, thought a moment and then replied, "Adultery is a sin done by adults!" We can smile at the naivete of this answer, but there is a kernel of truth here, for adultery involves married people, who indeed ought to be adults. It is a safe conjecture that the vast majority of annulments sought and obtained since Vatican II have been based on the immaturity of one or both of the marriage partners, stemming either from their youthfulness or arrested development, and resulting in their inability to make and live a lifetime commitment to each other. We all deplore the current epidemic of annulments and divorces, and hope that stricter programs of immediate preparation for marriage will help to diminish their number, but what is needed above all is better *long-range preparation* for marriage (and indeed for life in any vocation) through effective personal and spiritual growth leading to human and Christian maturity. "Happiness in marriage is less the result of finding the right partner, important as that is, than of being the right person!"[2]

In this connection, I am reminded of an article that appeared during or right after Vatican II in one of the most popular national magazines of the time. The author, who had recently left the Catholic priesthood and gotten married, wrote glowingly about his new-found happiness and, among other things, declared that, for the first time in his life, he really felt like a *whole* person. A week or so later, I happened to notice a letter in the same magazine which addressed itself specifically to the issue of *wholeness.* In it the writer, a wife and mother, made the astute comment that, if the author of the article was not a whole person before leaving the priesthood to marry, then he should have been neither a priest nor a husband, for it takes a whole person to be successful in either of those sublime but difficult vocations.

That wise observation serves to underline quite forcefully what I have been pointing out about the importance of living and growing in our general vocation as Christians, called to "profess the truth in love and grow to the full maturity of Christ" (Ep 4:15). It will also double as a kind of introduction to the particular vocation of marriage which, since it is the one to which most people are called (dating back to Gn 1:28; 2:15-24), logically suggests itself as the first for our reflection. However, since there is so much to be considered in this chapter, it will be best (in the interest of space and order) if we divide our treatment into *two principal parts*: the first concerning the state of marriage or celibacy to which God has called us, and the second regarding the kind of ministry in the Church and world in which Christ desires to continue his life of love and service through us today.

MARRIAGE OR CELIBACY:

The subject of marriage always recalls to my mind the first wedding that I was asked to witness in *China*. It happened sometime between early November of 1948 and Lent of 1949; in other words, in the limbo-like interval between the return to the United States of the other young priests with whom I had arrived in September and the invasion of South China by the Communist "People's Liberation Army." Father Leo Fox, C.M., the Pastor of our mission parish, asked me one day if I would not mind witnessing a forthcoming wedding which, for private reasons, he would rather not handle personally. Since I trusted him implicitly, I of course agreed, asking only that he teach me the right questions to ask and answers to expect. This he gladly did, so that I felt rather confident despite my short acquaintance with the people and language of China.

The wedding day arrived, and I really enjoyed the beauty of the scene. Both bride and groom, as well as the entire wedding party, were dressed in flaming red silk, the Oriental color of joy based on the *yin-yang* (female-male) philosophy traditional in China.[3] All went well until I asked the bride if she would take the groom as her husband. To my surprise, she said nothing. I asked her again, and again she was silent. Then I inquired of the "maid of honor" if the bride had perhaps answered affirmatively but too low for me to hear. She assured me that such was not the case. Suddenly, the unnerving possibility occurred to me that this girl really did not want to marry this boy, even though (or perhaps because) everything had been arranged by their parents and the usual "marriage broker." No wonder Father Fox had excused himself from officiating at such a questionable "marriage"! Determined not to panic, however, I decided to turn toward the altar, pray for help, and then ask the bride one more time. If she still refused to respond, I would have no alternative but to cancel the wedding and send everyone home, regardless of the ensuing "loss of face" for all concerned. To my unbounded relief, she finally answered clearly and, thanks be to God, affirmatively. The rest of the ceremony continued without further incident.

Later that day, Father Fox inquired how the wedding had gone. "Fine," I said, "except for one thing," and I proceeded to recount what had happened and how close I had come to calling off the wedding. "Oh," he replied, "I *am* sorry! I guess I was so concerned about teaching you the right words that I forgot to tell you about Chinese marriage customs. It is considered immodest, especially among 'high-born Chinese,' for the bride to give her consent right away!" To which I could not help blurting out, "Now you tell me, after I died a thousand deaths out there!" But later we just had a good laugh about the whole matter.

I like to relate this true story as a typical example of the wide differences that exist among various cultures regarding *marital customs*. How true is the immortal observation by Rudyard Kipling that "East is East, and West is West, and never the twain shall meet!"[4] But, important as these differences are, and as essential as it is to adjust our thinking to them, nevertheless, they do not negate the *basic unity* of the institution of marriage, not only horizontally around the world today, but even vertically throughout the sweep of human history.

In Salvation History, as we see it in Scripture and Church history, marriage has had a *three-stage development*. The Yahwist author of Genesis 2:18-24 describes it as an *institution* established by God in which woman is pictured as formed from man so that she might be his companion and even be reunited with him as one flesh. In this way, humanity would "be fertile and multiply; fill the earth and subdue it" (Gn 1:28). Here, from the very beginning of Scripture, we see the two sacred ends of human marriage: love and life, companionship and creativity.

During the Patriarchal Period, in the absence of other directives, Abram and Jacob in particular generally follow the *customs of the Middle East,* reflected in such documents as the Hurrian Nuzi Tablets and the Old Babylonian Code of Hammurabi.[5] This explains why childless Sarai offers her handmaid, Hagar, to her husband Abram as a "surrogate mother" to bear children for them (Gn 16) and why both Rachel and Leah do the same for their husband Jacob (Gn 30:1-13). With the *Covenant of Sinai,* however, the descendants of Jacob or Israel are to be "a kingdom of priests, a holy nation" (Ex 19:6), "sacred" to Yahweh (Ex 22:30). As such, they are forbidden to "commit adultery" (Ex 20:14) or even to "covet" their "neighbor's wife" (Ex 20:17); they cannot seduce a virgin with impunity (Ex 22:15-16); and bestiality is punishable by death (Ex 22:18).

In the course of Jewish history, many *other laws* and penalties concerning sex and marriage are added, especially those contained in the prophetic Book of Deuteronomy (e.g. Dt 22:13-29; 24:1-5) and the priestly Book of Leviticus (e.g. Lv 18, 20), all based on the fact that, as Yahweh's beloved People (Dt 4:32-40; 8:1-5; 10:12-22), the Israelites are to love him with their whole being (Dt 6:4-9; 10:12-13; 11:1) and to "be holy" as he "is holy" (Lv 11:44-45; 19:2; 20:7, 26).

The second stage of Israel's understanding of marriage begins with the Prophet *Hosea,* who introduces the idea of the *covenant* into the marital relationship by describing the Sinaitic Covenant between Yahweh and Israel in terms of a marriage. In fact, through his own ill-fated marriage with a "harlot-wife," he himself experiences (really or parabolically?) the agonizing sense of rejection which Yahweh "feels" over his spouse Israel's infidelities, but is willing to forgive and forget if she repents and returns (Ho 1-3). This same analogy between human marriage and the Covenant relationship of Yahweh with Israel continues in the prophecies of Isaiah, Jeremiah, and Ezekiel (Is 49-66, passim; Jr 2-3, 30-31; Ezk 16, 23) as well as in the mysterious Song of Songs, at least in its spiritual interpretation.

In the *New Testament,* the marriage analogy perdures but is now applied to the union of Christ and his followers, either individually or communally (stated explicitly in Rm 7:4; 1 Cor 6:17; 2 Cor 11:2; Ep 5:22-23; Rv 19:5-9; 21:2-3, 9; 22:17 and at least implicitly in Mt 22:1-14; 25:1-13 and Jn 3:29). At the same time, in both the Old and the New Testaments, the *sacredness and sublimity of marriage* (and family life) are strongly upheld (Pss 45; 128; Pr 18:22; 19:14; 31:10-31; Si 26:1-4, 13-18; Tb 7-8, plus 1 Cor 5-7; 2 Cor 6:14-18; Ep 5:22-6:4; Col 3:18-21; 1 Th 4:3-8; 1 P 3:1-7; Jn 2:1-11). Its *stability* is defended in a number of powerful statements against *divorce and remarriage* (Ml 2:13-17; Mt. 5:31-32; 19:3-12; Mk 10:2-12; Lk 16:18; and 1 Cor 7:10-11).[6] To these latter declarations, the so-called permissive wording of Matthew 5:32, 19:9 (re: Dt 24:1-4), and 1 Corinthians 7:15, seen in their proper text and context, offer no real exemptions.[7]

Finally, in *Christian times,* marriage has come to be understood and appreciated, not only as institution and covenant, but also as *Sacrament,* as an outward sign of inward grace. This comprises the third and final stage of development, in preparation for the afterlife when "people will neither marry nor be given in marriage" (Mt 22:30; Mk 12:25; Lk 20:35). However, the traditional teaching that Matrimony (along with all the Sacraments) was instituted directly by the historical Jesus Christ is no longer widely held by Scripture scholars and Theologians.[8] Nor is this of paramount concern. What is important, as we have already seen when discussing the Church, is that the Risen Christ only "began to do and to teach until the day he was taken up" (Ac 1:1-2); he continues "to do and to teach" all through the centuries of Christian history, especially through the

Church which he authorized to "bind and loose" (Mt 16:19; 18:18), commissioned to "make disciples of all the nations" (Mt 28:19), and empowered with his Holy Spirit (Jn 14; Ac 2).

According to *Doors to the Sacred,* by Joseph Martos,

> Relatively early in the history of Christianity, marriage was regarded as a sacrament in the broad sense, but it was only in the twelfth century that it came to be regarded as a sacrament in the same sense as Baptism and the other official sacraments.[9]

The compelling consideration for us is that, thanks be to God, marriage is now and has been for a long time a Sacrament of Jesus Christ and of his Church. Significantly, *St. Ignatius of Antioch,* who first referred to the Christian Church as Catholic (that is, universal), also seems to have been the first after the New Testament authors to emphasize the sacredness of Christian marriage. Writing to St. Polycarp of Smyrna around the year 110 A.D., he proposes this directive,

> It is fitting that men and women who are going to marry should contract their union with the counsel of the bishops, so that their marriage will take place in accordance with the will of the Lord and not according to passion. Let everything be done for the honor of God.[10]

Nothing could be more fitting than that the union of husband and wife for the sacred ends of love and life should indeed be a Sacrament. And one can hardly think of a more crucial consideration in preparing for, preserving, and growing in holiness through Christian Marriage than this note of sacramentality.

Like the Sacrament of Orders, Matrimony is a *Social Sacrament,* for its effects spread far beyond the couple and family involved to the Church and Society as a whole. Unlike all the other Sacraments, Matrimony is *unique* in that the Sacrament is conferred, not by the officiating priest or deacon (who are only the Church's witnesses) but by the bride and groom themselves. In fact, not only at the time of the wedding, but all through their lives, they are called to be *"sacraments" to each other,* living channels of God's special grace enabling them to grow in love and life until death.

So rich is the theology of Christian marriage, especially as recently developed by married theologians, that I cannot expect to do it justice in my limited amount of space. Therefore, I must content myself with referring the reader to the book list at the end of the chapter and summarizing further consideration on this important subject in a brief special reflection, which I like to call my *"One-Two-Three" of Christian Marriage.*

(1) In the fundamental statement about marriage (made first in Gn 2:24, upheld by Jesus in Mk 10:7 as well as Mt 19:5-6, alluded to by Paul in 1 Cor 6:16, and directly quoted in Ep 5:31), it is emphasized that, "A man will leave his father and mother and be united to his wife, and they will become one flesh" (NIV). Therefore, from the time of their wedding and for the rest of their lives, the husband and wife are to be *Number One to each other* under God.

At first, that is normally rather easy, but after a few years it becomes increasingly difficult. For example, if the couple have *children,* it can become almost natural and accepted, especially for the wife and mother, to give them priority over her husband. After all, they are so helpless! And yet the well-being and happiness of both the couple and the children demand that the union of husband and wife be given top priority. It is through their physical union that God brings new human life into the world, and it is through their personal and spiritual union that he enables that human life to grow to responsible maturity. The anonymous aphorism that "The greatest favor a father can do his children is to love their mother" is only half the truth, for it is just as essential for the mother to love their father, and for both to grow in their love and union throughout their lives.

By the same token, the husband's *work and career* can easily usurp the first place in his life, at the expense of his wife and children. After all, should he not provide for them to the fullest extent possible? How often does it happen that "devoted" husbands manage to provide their wives and children with all kinds of material comforts but fail to give them what they most need: love and presence, attention and affection. And, of course, the difficulty can easily be doubled if the wife also has a job away from home, perhaps a profession, a career. Other things as well can, because of their overriding importance in the life of a husband and wife, succeed in straining and finally destroying their basic union, for example: undue attachment to their individual families, friends, and clubs; addiction to leisure activities such as television or reading, tennis or golf, hunting or fishing (not to mention alcohol or drugs); even excessive dedication to time-consuming volunteer work for the Church or for society. But true Christian lovers in marriage, well aware of these dangers, are able through their mutual devotion and thoughtful communication to change threatening quicksand into the solid concrete of enduring union.

(2)   In the same fundamental statement on marriage quoted above, it is clear that the husband and wife, although "in one flesh," are still *"two" distinct persons.* They can and should never lose their individual identity and merge into a *"tertium quid,"* a third entity of some kind. This being so, as essential as it is to live a common life of love and union, it is just as crucial for both partners to respect each other's unique individuality and to help each other reach the fullness of their potential as persons and Christians. This too is part of love, particularly the love of *friendship,* which is absolutely necessary in marriage. No matter that a husband and wife may be the greatest of lovers, if they are not also the best of friends, their marriage has little chance of success. Hence, part of the tragedy of *premarital sex,* so prevalent today, is that a boy and girl may learn something about making love but little or nothing about making a life together, something about sexual compatibility but little or nothing about personal compatibility. They come to know each other as sex-partners but seldom as persons and friends, or even as lovers in the full sense of the word.

The love of friendship carries the implication of *equality,* which is also of great importance in marriage. Of course, the partners are sexually different, not only in body but in mind and emotions as well, and this basic difference must be constantly adverted to in mutual understanding and love. As the French say, *"Vive la difference!"* Nevertheless, difference is not at all the same as inequality. And if *St. Paul* is invoked (especially in 1 Cor 11:2-16; 14:34-36; Ep 5:22-24; and 1 Tm 2:11-15) to argue for male superiority and female submission, we need to keep several points clearly in mind: (a) Paul was writing over nineteen centuries ago, in a very different social and cultural milieu, in which women enjoyed precious few rights, let alone equality; (b) Paul, like Jesus himself, recognized the futility of condemning accepted social institutions (e.g. slavery) and the necessity of first changing people (especially through liberation from sin) who would in time change unjust institutions. That this has taken so long is not the fault of Jesus or Paul but of us Christians who have leavened the world so slowly; (c) Paul (again like Jesus) did lay down the basic principle of cultural, social, and sexual equality in his landmark declaration of Galatians 3:28, "There does not exist among you Jew or Greek [i.e. Gentile], slave or freeman, male or female. All are one in Christ Jesus!" (d) Paul's statements, when read in their original Greek language and in their cultural and epistolary context, do not sound nearly so harsh as they otherwise might. For example, the key word in Ephesians 5:22-24 is *hypotásso,* used in the middle or reflexive voice *hypotássomai,* literally "I arrange myself under, I defer to" with the connotation of "for the sake of good order." In fact, Ephesians 5:22 is actually a continuation of 5:18-21, which Paul addresses to *all his readers,* regardless of their nationality, sex, or social condition, and in which he urges sobriety, joyfulness, thanksgiving, and humility, "deferring to one another in the fear of Christ" (Ep 5:21).

Finally, mutual respect and the love of friendship between married partners includes two other ideas which must always be kept in balance, namely *mutual honesty* and *personal privacy.* In John 15:15, Jesus assures his Apostles, "I call you friends, since I have made known to you all that I heard from my Father." This trusting self-revelation is one of the most beautiful characteristics of friendship and is especially appropriate in marriage. Each partner should be able to bare his or her soul to the other with complete assurance of understanding, loving support, honest opinion, and total confidentiality. On the other hand, each must recognize the other's right to personal privacy as a distinct human being and child of God. None of us can totally possess another human being, for that belongs to God alone, hence possessiveness (and the jealousy which it begets) must be carefully avoided. The same loving trust which encourages self-disclosure should also allow personal privacy. The sensitive Lebanese poet, Kahlil Gibran, in his best-known work, *The Prophet,* provides married couples with sage advice in this matter,

> You were born together, and together you will be forevermore.
> . . . But let there be spaces in your togetherness, and let the winds of the heavens dance between you.[11]

And, in the same spirit, the German poet *Rainer Maria Rilke* cautions,

> A good marriage is that in which each appoints the other guardian of his solitude, and shows him this confidence, the greatest in his power to bestow. But once the realization is accepted that even between the closest human beings infinite distances continue to exist, a wonderful living side by side can grow up, if they succeed in loving the distance between them.[12]

(3)   Husband and wife, as we have seen, are "one yet two" in the mystery of marriage, but there is still more to the mystery. For, in the Sacrament of Holy Matrimony, it takes *three to get married.* Jesus Christ is the third partner in a Christian marriage. When the bride and groom, with their exchange of wedding vows, consecrate themselves to each other in Christ for life, he himself is a party to this sacred covenant, with extremely important consequences.

First of all, the risen *Christ himself,* who acts in all the Sacraments and empowers them to achieve their special effects, personally approves and ratifies the lifelong covenant by which the bride and groom knowingly and freely commit themselves to each other in a valid sacramental marriage. And even if, at some future time, the human partners decide to rescind their covenant, Christ who is not "alternately 'yes' and 'no,' " (2 Cor 1:19) but "the same yesterday, today, and forever" (Heb 13:8) does not rescind his ratification. That is why, in the teaching of Jesus, of Paul, and of the Church, marriage is *indissoluble*. In both Mark 10:9 and Matthew 19:6, Jesus states categorically, "What therefore God has joined together, let not man put asunder" (RSV). And in 1 Corinthians 7:10-11, Paul adds,

> To those now married, however, I give this command (though it is not mine; it is the Lord's): a wife must not separate from her husband. If she does separate, she must remain single or become reconciled to him again. Similarly, a husband must not divorce his wife.

As with Jesus' declaration about the Eucharist, so also with his prohibition of divorce and remarriage, "many of his disciples" then and now quickly counter with, "This is a hard teaching. Who can accept it?" (Jn 6:60, NIV). And, of course, the result is the "marriage-go-round" so much in evidence today, and its natural spin-off of just "living together" without the benefits, commitment, and stability of marriage. But, instead of looking only at the difficulties involved in the indissolubility of marriage, we need to recognize its *advantages,* for example: (a) the motivation it provides for personal preparation, careful choice of a partner, ongoing growth in love, mutual acceptance and forgiveness, and ready willingness to work things out together rather than giving up; (b) the secure and favorable environment it establishes for the rearing of children, with advantages that last for generations to follow; (c) the shining witness it offers to a world which has largely rejected the treasure of marital happiness for the pleasure of sex for its own sake; and (d) the assurance it carries of all the divine helps needed for a stable, successful marriage bringing happiness and holiness for time and for eternity.

Of course, indissolubility of itself does not guarantee a happy marriage. It needs the essential ingredient of *love*. The nagging fear of so many husbands and wives is "to be trapped in a loveless marriage." And according to many, whether Christians or otherwise, if "love has gone out of the marriage," it is already dead and the decent thing to do is to bury it through divorce and seek a new and loving union. That sounds natural and logical, does it not? Yes it does, and I for one would not want to wish a "twilight marriage" on anyone, but it ignores a fundamental truth, namely that there is *more than one kind of love!*

As we have already seen when treating love in Chapter Seven, there is "erotic love" (from Greek *érōs*), which is romantic, sexual, and physical, the kind of love which in general coincides with our being "flesh," and which is most often identified with "married love." In the minds of so many today, when erotic love begins to subside in a marriage, as it normally does with the passage of time because of psycho-biological changes, the fear begins to arise that "love is going out of the marriage." And if love is totally equated with eroticism, that fear may be justified. But, again as I have already explained, in addition to erotic love, there are two other kinds of love that should characterize marriage, especially Christian marriage: the love of friendship (in Greek, *philía*) characteristic of our nature as "person," and spiritual love (in Greek, *agápē*) crowning our nature as "spirit." And these two other loves, far from diminishing with the passage of time, can and should continue to grow throughout life and even into eternity, for they do not depend like erotic love on the emotional and physical. With these three loves, which can and ought to be interwoven in a marriage like strands in an unbreakable cable, love need never "go out of a marriage."

Since Christ is the third partner in Christian Matrimony, he brings to the marriage his own indescribable gift of love. He himself provides all the love necessary to make marriage not only indissoluble but extremely happy. For *agápē-love* is not only his gift but a sharing in his very love. If his "new commandment" of *agápē-love* is intended for us all, is it not especially appropriate for those called to the married state? "Love one another as I have loved you!" (Jn 13:34-35; 15:12, 17). And if Paul's lyrical descriptions of this *agape-love* are full of meaning and challenge for us all, how much more so for husbands and wives,

> Love is patient; love is kind. Love is not jealous, it does not put on airs, it is not snobbish. Love is never rude, it is not self-seeking, it is not prone to anger; neither does it brood over injuries. Love does not rejoice in what is wrong but rejoices with the truth. There is no limit to love's forbearance, to its trust, its hope, its power to endure (1 Cor 13:4-7).

> Get rid of all bitterness, all passion and anger, harsh words, slander, and malice of every kind. In place of these, be kind to one another, compassionate, and mutually forgiving, just as God has forgiven you in Christ (Ep 4:31-32).

> Because you are God's chosen ones, holy and beloved, clothe yourselves with heartfelt mercy, with kindness, humility, meekness, and patience. Bear with one another; forgive whatever grievances you have against one another. Forgive as the Lord has forgiven you. Over all these virtues put on love, which binds the rest together and makes them perfect (Col 3:12-14).

Did you notice how prominent in all three of these Pauline quotations is the note of *forbearance and forgiveness?* The reason is simple and salutary. We are imperfect beings in an imperfect world. And, since it is a truism that "love is blind," married partners must expect to find imperfections in each other which they had never noticed before. What is essential here is, first of all, to temper idealistic expectations of marriage with a healthy realism and, secondly, to cherish married life, not as a perpetual honeymoon, but as a blessed time of mutual giving and forgiving, growing and forgoing together "to the full maturity of Christ the head" (Ep 4:15). If my little *"formula for real living"* is valid for everyone, it is especially appropriate for married partners, namely: "To live is to love, to love is to give, and to love deeply is to forgive completely!"

Jesus Christ, our divine bridegroom and king of all hearts, graced the marriage feast at *Cana* with his blessed presence and, by his very first miracle, changed ordinary water into choice wine. May he likewise grace those whom he has called to the married state with his abiding presence and gradually transform the water of their human love into the rich wine of his own unfailing divine love!

So far, we have been reflecting at some length on the vocation of marriage. But by design the title of this section is *"Marriage or Celibacy."* It is time, then, to dwell on the latter, though not at the same length for two principal reasons: (a) It is not as general a calling as that of marriage, and (b) what has already been said in Chapter Six about the virtue of purity is certainly applicable in our discussion of celibacy.

The word *celibacy*, from Latin *caelibatus,* denotes an unmarried or single state and, by connotation, a state of abstention from all sexual activity. The term is most often used in a religious sense, that is, of those who have consecrated their lives to God by religious *vows* (public or private, solemn or simple) or by *ordination* to the diaconate or priesthood. But, in reality, it has much broader application than that, for (whether or not it is formally accepted as one's state in life) it is expected and required of *all in the single state*: those not yet or never married (including homosexuals and lesbians) as well as those who have been widowed or divorced. The term is sometimes expanded to include married couples in the broad sense of conjugal chastity and occasional abstinence, but this is really an inexact usage which will not be part of our brief reflection.

Between *marriage and celibacy* there is a *close bond*. Not only do they represent the two general states of life to which God calls us, but also the vocation to celibacy cannot be fully appreciated except in comparison with marriage. Thus, in Matthew 19:3-12, it was only after *Jesus'* categorical prohibition of divorce and remarriage that ''his disciples said to him, 'If that is the case between man and wife, it is better not to marry,' '' thereby occasioning Jesus' clearest declaration about celibacy in the Gospels,

Not everyone can accept this teaching, but only those to whom it has been given. For some are eunuchs because they were born that way; others were made that way by men; and others have renounced marriage because of the kingdom of heaven. The one who can accept this should accept it (Mt 19:11-12, NIV).

In the same way, *St. Paul* treats the whole issue of marriage or celibacy as one question put to him by the Corinthian Church and answers accordingly,

It is good for a man not to marry. But since there is so much immorality, each man should have his own wife, and each woman her own husband. . . . I wish that all men were as I am. But each man has his own gift from God; one has this gift, another has that.

Now to the unmarried and the widows I say: It is good for them to stay unmarried, as I am. But if they cannot control themselves, they should marry, for it is better to marry than to burn with passion. . . .

Nevertheless, each one should retain the place in life that the Lord assigned to him and to which God has called him. This is the rule I lay down in all the churches. . . . Brothers, each man, as responsible to God, should remain in the situation God called him to (1 Cor 7:1-24, NIV).

In the *ancient world* generally, celibacy was not highly regarded. Even a shrewish wife like Socrates' Xanthippe was considered to be better than none at all! And this was true also in the thinking of God's Chosen People, the Israelites, as we see in the *Old Testament*. The Book of Proverbs, for example, has some rather "choice" things to say about adulterous wives (6:24-7:27), rebellious wives (11:22), nagging wives (19:13), quarrelsome wives (21:9, 19; 27:15), odious wives (30:23); and Ben Sira is even more brusque in his treatment of certain kinds of women and wives (25:12-25; 26:6-12); but nowhere do they ever suggest foregoing marriage altogether.

The only examples of celibacy in the Old Testament, so far as I can determine, contain their own built-in explanations. The virgin daughter of Jephthah the Judge or Liberator, facing death because of her father's rash vow, asks to be spared for two months so that she might go off into the mountains to mourn her virginity with her companions (Jg 11:37-40). Jeremiah the Prophet is forbidden by God to marry as a sign of the impending catastrophe that will engulf the Jewish People (Jr 16:1-4). And the Prophet Ezekiel is suddenly widowed but forbidden to mourn over his deceased wife, as a sign of the coming destruction of Jerusalem (Ezk 24:15-23).

Whether this negative attitude about celibacy persisted in Israel up to the time of Jesus is a moot point, for there is archaeological evidence that the Jewish Essenes of *Qumran* may have practiced celibacy,[13] and biblical indications that John the Baptist remained unmarried throughout his life (Lk 1:80). However, with the perfect example of *Jesus* himself and of his virgin mother *Mary* (Mt 1:18-25; Lk 1:34-35), the celibate state quickly became for many Christians a chosen way of life. How many of the Apostles were celibate, we have no way of knowing, for only Peter is mentioned as having a mother-in-law (Mk 1:29-31 and parallels), but *Paul* certainly was (1 Cor 7:7-8), and probably John (Rv 14:4-5).

In the history of the Church, celibacy became so identified with the pursuit and attainment of perfection that the vast *majority of Saints,* canonized either popularly or formally and proposed for our emulation, have been celibate. Hopefully, with the current theological appreciation of the sacredness and sublimity of marriage, this *historical imbalance* will be somewhat corrected. I would hope, however, that we do not manage as usual to go to the other extreme, with the result that marriage and family life become the ideal Christian state, and celibacy just an abnormal and embarrassing anachronism.

Even now, as is well known, there is a kind of crusade among some Catholic priests and lay people to abrogate the requirement of celibacy for the priesthood, advocating instead that it be left to the personal choice of the individual. *Priestly celibacy* is, after all, a matter of ecclesiastical, not divine, law and has been a requirement only since the fourth century, as we see from the Council of Elvira in Spain (300-360 A.D.) and the Instruction of Pope Siricius to Himerius of Tarragona in 385 A.D. [14] What the Church has bound, she can as easily loose (Mt 16:19; 18:18) and, given the shortage of priestly vocations today, perhaps she will be forced to do so. But wait! This is only one side of the picture. There is another side which certainly deserves our attention, namely the case for *consecrated celibacy* as a special means of sanctity for those called to the single state, a powerful witness to a sensuous world, and a most appropriate condition of priestly orders and ministry.

Not only among Christians but among many others, especially devotees of *Oriental religions,* celibacy has been prized from time immemorial as a most effective means of living a deeply spiritual life. Why? Because it involves detachment from the greatest natural pleasure known to human beings, that of sexual love, and the conquest of our two most basic instincts, self-preservation and preservation of humanity, through our sacrifice of human love, marriage, and a posterity to perpetuate our earthly existence. And the more we appreciate the nobility of marriage and family life, in terms of institution, covenant, and Sacrament, the greater the value of our celibate sacrifice.

But why make such a sacrifice? Various reasons are suggested in the Bible. As we have seen, Jeremiah and Ezekiel are required by God to embrace celibacy in different ways because of the coming destruction of Jerusalem (Jr 16:1-4; Ezk 24:15-23). In the New Testament, *Matthew's Jesus* mentions celibacy ''for the sake of the Kingdom'' (Mt 19:12), while *Paul* suggests two practical motives: (a) the shortness of time before the Second Coming (1 Cor 7:25-31), and (b) the freedom offered by celibacy to those who desire to devote themselves to the service of God,

I would like you to be free from concern. An unmarried man is concerned about the Lord's affairs — how he can please the

Lord. But a married man is concerned about the affairs of this world — how he can please his wife — and his interests are divided. An unmarried woman or virgin is concerned about the Lord's affairs: Her aim is to be devoted to the Lord in both body and spirit. But a married woman is concerned about the affairs of this world — how she can please her husband. I am saying this for your own good, not to restrict you, but that you may live in a right way in *undivided devotion* to the Lord (1 Cor 7:32-35, NIV).

It is this final motivation, in conjunction with Jesus' reference to celibacy "for the sake of the Kingdom of God" that the Church, and in particular the Second Vatican Council, employs as the basis for her requirement of celibacy as a condition for priestly ordination (and for the "transitional diaconate" leading to the priesthood). And who is to say that she does not have the right to insist on such a requirement? If *athletes* are required to make all kinds of sacrifices so that they can devote themselves completely and competently to the ephemeral goal of winning a championship (1 Cor 9:24-27), is it unreasonable that the Church, or rather Christ himself in the Church, would require a sacrifice like celibacy of those who are called to special leadership among his followers? Hence, in Luke's Gospel, Jesus first demands and later commends *total detachment,* even from one's wife, as the condition of discipleship and the basis of great rewards here and hereafter (Lk 14:25-27; 18:28-29).

But there is much more to celibacy than we have seen so far. Not only does it provide the *freedom* to devote ourselves more fully to the service of Christ, whether in the priesthood, religious life, or dedicated single life, but above all it allows us to center our entire *love and life* on him, growing ever more closely in loving union with him as our Divine Spouse, and becoming in time so possessed by him and transformed into him that he may be able to continue his celibate life and love today through us. What a vocation! What a powerful means of sanctification! Is this not at least implied in the following mystical expressions of St. Paul?

Do you not know that he who unites himself with a [temple] prostitute is one with her in body? For it is said, "The two will become one flesh." But he who unites himself with the Lord is one with him in spirit! (1 Cor 6:16-17, NIV).

A married woman is bound to her husband by law while he lives, but if he dies she is released from the law regarding husbands. ... In the same way, my brothers, you died to the law through the body of Christ, that you might belong to the Other who was raised from the dead, so that we might bear fruit for God (Rm 7:2, 4).

To these quotations, I have deliberately not added the well-known and very beautiful Pauline declaration in 2 Corinthians 11:2, which is obviously not addressed to individuals but to the whole Church at Corinth, nor the even better known and more lyrical Ephesians 5:22-33, which clearly refers to the entire Church in its union with Christ as the model for the union of husband and wife. This latter, however, does serve as a timely reminder to us that deep spiritual or *mystical union* with Christ is not the sole prerogative of celibates. As we have already seen earlier in this chapter, the loving consecrated union of *married Christians* can serve as a powerful means of mystical union with Christ. Hence, St. Paul warns those who are called to marriage,

Do not be yoked together with [married to] unbelievers... What harmony is there between Christ and Belial [Satan]? . . . What agreement is there between the temple of God and idols? For we are the temple of the living God! (2 Cor 6:14-16, NIV).

The key, for celibate as for married life, is love! We are made in the image and likeness of a God who is love itself! (Gn 1:26-27; 1 Jn 4:8; 5:1-6). We are born to love, for it is of our very nature! And, unless I am mistaken, we are *born to love a person!* It has been truly said that celibacy frees us from the love of a single human being so that we can love many human beings. To me, however, the deeper truth is that celibacy enables us to rise beyond the limited love of a single human being (wonderful as that is!) so that we can more easily enter into a loving union with the source of all love in the person of *Jesus Christ,* whose love impels us (2 Cor 5:14) to love all others as well.

If, however, we embrace celibacy for *selfish reasons* (e.g., to avoid the responsibilities of marriage and family life, or to have more time to pursue our own pleasures and ambitions), we certainly cannot expect to reap the benefits of truly *consecrated celibacy.* Or if we generously give up the joys of human love and marriage, but fail to embrace wholeheartedly the love of God and of others in God, then we may end by loving and pleasing only ourselves. Ours would perhaps be the unhappy state of the man described by Jesus in Luke 11:24-26,

> When an unclean spirit has gone out of a man, it wanders through arid wastes searching for a resting place; failing to find one, it says, "I will go back to where I came from." It then returns, to find the house swept and tidied. Next it goes out and returns with seven other spirits far worse than itself, who enter in and dwell there. The result is that the last stage of the man is worse than the first.

In contrast with this deplorable condition, which may well be called a kind of "diabolical possession" and "anticipation of hell" because of its absence and even rejection of real love, consecrated celibacy embraced out of love for God and others deserves the name of *"angelic"* for it is an anticipation of heaven itself, as Jesus intimates in his reply to the Sadducees regarding resurrection from the dead, "When people rise from the dead, they neither marry nor are given in marriage but live like angels in heaven" (Mt 22:30; Mk 12:25; Lk 20:34-36).

This is not to argue for celibacy instead of marriage, for (as I have already shown from the words of Jesus and Paul in Mt 19:12 and 1 Cor 7:7, 17, 20, 24 respectively) the most perfect state for each of us is that to which God has called us. But, if it is argued (as it sometimes is these days) that marriage is in itself more perfect than celibacy because it is a Sacrament, whereas celibacy is not, my reply is based on Jesus' declaration to the Sadducees above. Celibacy is an *anticipation of the resurrection* and heaven, where we will no longer need Sacraments because we will already possess those eternal realities for which the Sacraments are intended to prepare us.

And, finally, if it is alleged (as it often is today) that such an "angelic" state is not only impractical but impossible in our world, I need only call attention to two important facts: (1)   that the *world* in which Christianity was born was, if anything, even more decadent than our own; and   (2)   that God's powerful *grace* is quite capable of enabling us to live and grow in this "angelic" state, especially if we center our life on loving union with Christ and make full use of such means as prayer, the Sacraments, and spiritual direction. Even *"involuntary celibacy"* such as that of persons who desire marriage but cannot find a suitable partner, or who feel obliged to postpone marriage until it is too late in order to care for parents or younger brothers and sisters, or who feel no desire to marry because of their homosexual orientation, need not be the tragic source of sadness and self-pity that our society often pictures. Rather, by divine grace and human acceptance, it can become *voluntary (even consecrated) celibacy*, embraced as a "blessing in disguise" and a special opportunity for total commitment to Christ in love and service.

The same can be said of *widows*, who are clearly regarded with predilection in the Bible, (evidently because of their precarious financial and social condition, as reflected for example in Ex 22:21-23; Dt 24:17; Jb 29:13; Is 1:17; Ml 3:5; Lk 2:36-38; 7:11-15; Ac 6:1; 1 Cor 7:39-40; 1 Tm 5:3-16; Jm 1:27). By extension, we may include *widowers*, especially permanent deacons (who according to the Church's traditional discipline do not remarry after ordination, 1 Tm 3:12), as well as the *separated and divorced*. In all of these instances, the positive embracing of celibacy can, by the grace of God, transform tragedy into triumph, loneliness into solitude, self-pity into sanctity.

Before passing on to the second general section of this chapter, which will be concerned with ministry, let me add just a few words about the inspiring life of those who are not only celibate but consecrated to God by the *three vows* of poverty, chastity, and obedience. Among some people today, inside as well as outside the Church, there is a strong tendency to de-emphasize or even reject these vows and their corresponding evangelical counsels as impractical and irrelevant in our present complex society. This may partially explain the "great exodus" of so many religious from their state of life since Vatican II, the radical change in lifestyle of so many who remain, and the drastic diminution of religious vocations today. To treat this question in full would take us far beyond our scope, but some basic and very valid considerations, it seems to me, can and should be briefly suggested.

First of all, what are the *motives* for the practice of consecrated poverty, chastity, and obedience? The pursuit of personal holiness, of course, especially in a communal setting, by commitment to the three "virtues of letting go" (See Chapter Six). That is not all, however, for there is also the desire of witnessing and ministering to the Church and the world by a way of life which, at one and the same time, runs directly counter to "the [world's] carnal allurements, enticements for the eyes, and life of empty show" condemned by St. John (1 Jn 2:16) and provides an ideal setting for effective Christian ministry.

We could occupy the remainder of this chapter with quotations from the New Testament regarding the evangelical counsels that form the basis of the three vows, but I prefer to go right to the heart of the matter, which is the very *life of Jesus* himself as reflected in the Gospels and indeed the entire New Testament. Celibate, obedient, and poor, he is totally detached from things of this world and consecrated to loving union with his Father, out of which flows his complete dedication to witnessing and ministering to all in physical, personal, and spiritual need. And he lives this life in community with his chosen *Apostles,* of whom he demands the same absolute detachment and commitment,

If anyone comes to me without turning his back on his father and mother, his wife and his children, his brothers and sisters, indeed his very self, he cannot be my follower. Anyone who does not take up his cross and follow me cannot be my disciple. . . . In the same way, none of you can be my disciple if he does not renounce all his possessions (Lk 14:26-27, 33).

Thus, it can be argued back and forth about the advantages and disadvantages of a vowed life in today's world, but those who are called to this life instinctively desire to be free from all other attachments in order to belong only to Jesus Christ. "Love does such things!" And just as human love seeks total commitment to the beloved through marriage vows, so love of Jesus just as surely tends to desire total commitment to him through religious vows. Far from being irrelevant and passé, the three vows continue to be for many chosen ones, both men and women, a powerful means of union with and transformation into Christ in *"spiritual marriage."* "Whoever is joined to the Lord becomes one spirit with him!" (1 Cor 6:17). And out of this union flows a powerful witness to the world and compassionate ministry to the needy, as well as the joy of community living for those called to it. In the inspiring words of the *Apostolic Exhortation on the Renewal of Religious Life,*[15]

Dear sons and daughters, by a free response to the call of the Holy Spirit you have decided to follow Christ, consecrating yourselves totally to him. The evangelical counsels of chastity vowed to God, of poverty and of obedience have now become the law of your existence. . . .

The faithful of Christ can bind themselves to the three previously mentioned counsels either by vows, or by other sacred bonds which are like vows in their purpose. Through such a bond a person is totally dedicated to God by an act of supreme love. . . .

It is true that through baptism he (or she) has died to sin and has been consecrated to God. However, in order to derive more abundant fruit from his baptismal grace, he intends, by the profession of the evangelical counsels in the Church, to free himself from those obstacles which might draw him away from the fervor of charity and the perfection of divine worship.

Thus he is more intimately consecrated to divine service. This consecration will be the more perfect to the extent that, through more firm and stable bonds, the indissoluble union of Christ with his Spouse the Church is more perfectly represented.

MINISTRY AND PRIESTHOOD:

In the Ninth Chapter, we have already reflected on sharing God's love and gifts with others through service. Now, in this chapter, we will consider that service of others which we call *ministry* because it is fulfilled within the context of the Church. Before Vatican II, ministry in the Catholic Church referred almost exclusively to the episcopate and priesthood or, by extension, to the (transitional) diaconate and subdiaconate or, by greater extension, to the so-called minor orders and the religious life. *Vatican II,* however, experienced an extraordinary broadening of the idea of ministry to include, as a matter of course, *every member of the Church.* Providentially, at the very same time that this was happening in Rome, I was undergoing my own personal expansion of ideas in this regard at St. Mary's Seminary in Houston, Texas.

It all began with an invitation to participate in a panel discussion with a Greek Orthodox priest and an Anglican priest on the subject of *"Priesthood in the New Testament."* While doing my research for this discussion, I naturally checked my Greek New Testament for those passages that spoke of the priesthood. What was my shock and dismay when it dawned on me that, in the entire New Testament, there is not a single use of the normal Greek term for *priest,* namely *hiereús* (from which the word *hierarchy* is derived) in reference to the Apostles or any other group of Christians ordained to a ministerial priesthood. The term was used solely in reference to *Jesus Christ,* most notably in the Epistle to the Hebrews, and to *all Christians*, especially in 1 Peter 2:5, 9, with allusions to the Israelites in Exodus 19:6.

Talk about an identity crisis! Here I was, a Catholic priest ordained almost twenty years, a former China missionary, and now a so-called Scripture scholar, and suddenly I discovered that my ministerial priesthood was apparently without biblical foundation. What was I to do? What else but pursue my research further? There simply had to be some other explanation! Surely, almost two thousand years of Catholic priesthood had to be reflected in the New Testament, which the Church itself had written, disseminated, and preserved! So I delved more deeply into the whole question.

It quickly became clear that, while the technical Greek word for *priest (hiereús)* was indeed not used in the New Testament of a select priesthood within the Church, the *role and functions* were certainly in evidence. For example, when Jesus instituted the *Eucharist* at the Last Supper and added, "Do this in remembrance of me" (Lk 22:19; 1 Cor 11:24-25), did he not in effect ordain his Apostles to perform the Passover sacrifice of the New Covenant in his body and blood (Mt 26:17-19, 26-30; Mk 14:12-16, 22-26; Lk 22:7-20; 24:30-31, 35; Jn 6:51-58; 13:1; 18:28, 39; 19:14, 31-36; Ac 2:42, 46; 13:2; 20:7; 1 Cor 5:7; 10:14-22; 11:23-34)? And when, on the very day of his glorious resurrection, "he breathed on them and said, 'Receive the Holy Spirit. If you forgive anyone his sins, they are forgiven; if you do not forgive them, they are not forgiven,' " (Jn 20:21-23, NIV; cf. also Mt 18:18), did he not empower them to forgive sins in his name and by his Spirit?

Delving further, I was struck by the numerous indications of priestly ministry on the part of the *Apostles* and those whom they commissioned or ordained for special ministry. *Paul*, for example, speaks of "the grace given him" by God "to be a liturgical minister (*leitourgós*) of Christ Jesus to the Gentiles, mediating (*hierourgéo*, literally, doing a priestly work) the Gospel (*euangélion*, good news) of God, so that the sacrifice (*prosphorá*, sacrifice or offering) of the Gentiles may be acceptable (*euprósdektos*), consecrated (*hagiázo*, to make holy, sanctify, consecrate) in (or by) the Holy Spirit" (Rm 15:15-16, WD). And, as Alois Stoeger points out in his article on *Priest(hood)* in J.B. Bauer's *Encyclopedia of Biblical Theology* (The Complete Sacramentum Verbi), "their [i.e. the Apostles'] mission consists not merely in *preaching the word* but in *mediating salvation* as well," especially through Baptism (Mt 28:19), the Eucharist and Reconciliation (as already noted), Confirmation (Ac 8:15-18) and Ordination, namely of presbyters (Ac 14:23; 20:17; Tt 1:5, etc.) and deacons (Ac 6:1-6; Ph 1:1; 1 Tm 3:12-13).

These presbyters (*presbýteroi,* literally "elders," from which is derived the English word "priests"), whose title is at first interchangeable with that of bishops (*epískopoi,* literally "overseers," from which is derived the English word "bishops" as we see in Ac 20:17, 28), are ordained or commissioned "with prayer and fasting" (Ac 14:23) and the laying on of hands (1 Tm 4:14; 5:22; 2 Tm 1:6) to *"shepherd the church of God"* (Ac 20:28) in all the priestly ways just mentioned as well as in that of the Anointing of the Sick (Jm 5:13-16).

Yes, the role of the ordained, ministerial priesthood is certainly there in the New Testament, but why is the specific Greek word for priest (*hiereús*) not used in regard to the Christian priesthood? Perhaps for a variety of reasons, not the least of which is the desire to avoid confusion with the Jewish priesthood, still functioning at least until the destruction of the Jerusalem temple in 70 A.D. and still remembered a long time afterward. And no wonder! For the *Jewish priesthood* had become, by the time of Jesus, not only purely functional but often highly political.

Recall, in Jesus' moving *parable of the Good Samaritan* (Lk 10:25-37), that a Jewish priest and Levite were both traveling on the same Jerusalem-Jericho road (*Wadi Qelt*), saw the stricken man, and "passed by on the other side" (Lk 10:31-32). Why did they ignore the injured man? Because they thought he was dead and wanted to avoid ritual defilement (Lv 21:1-4; 22:4-7; Nb 5:2-3)? Possibly, but I think it is just as likely that, having worshipped at the temple in Jerusalem, they felt that they had already fulfilled their service to God and therefore that the plight of the man on the road was of no concern to them. What a difference from the mission of Jesus' Apostles and, by implication, their overseers and elders (*epískopoi* and *presbýteroi*, bishops and priests), whom he empowered "to overcome all demons and cure diseases," and whom he sent forth "to proclaim the reign of God and heal the afflicted" (Lk 9:1-2; cf. also Mk 6:7, 12-13; 16:17-18). Remember also that the *Sadducees,* the priestly party or sect among the Jews, were in effect their political leaders, and often very expedient as we see in the person of Caiaphas, the High Priest (Jn 11:49-50).

But was there possibly a *deeper and more positive reason* for the New Testament absence of the exact Greek term *hiereús* for Christian priests? I suggest that there was, and a very good one at that! The key lies in *Jesus' own manner* of speaking about himself, his mission, and his followers. Although he was and is certainly our great High Priest with a "priesthood which does not pass away" and "therefore he is always able to save those who approach God through him, since he forever lives to make intercession for them" (Heb 7:24-25), nevertheless, he referred to himself, not as a priest, but as a *servant* and a *victim.*

After his favorite title, *"Son of Man,"* whereby he identified himself with the whole human race (Ps 8:5), with the people of Israel (Dn 7:13), and even with the Messiah (Dn 7:13 and Jewish Apocalyptic Literature),[16] he preferred the title of *servant,* as he indicates in Mark 10:45 and Matthew 20:28, "The Son of Man has not come to be served but to serve — to give his life in ransom for the many." In Luke 22:27 and John 13:3-5 respectively, he appropriates and demonstrates the same role of servant. And, in his three predictions of his coming death and resurrection, there are certainly allusions to the famous *"Suffering Servant"* in Isaiah 52:13-53:12. But is not all of this no more than what Paul summarizes so lyrically in his famous *Hymn of Christ* (Ph 2:6-11)?

To be a follower of Jesus the servant means, of course, to become *servants ourselves,* a truth which Jesus has to teach over and over again to and through his ambitious Apostles,

You know how among the Gentiles those who seem to exercise authority lord it over them; their great ones make their importance felt. It cannot be like that with you. Anyone among you who aspires to greatness must serve the rest; whoever wants to rank first among you must serve the needs of all (Mk 10:42-44).

Do you understand what I just did for you? You address me as "Teacher" and "Lord," and fittingly enough, for that is what I am. But if I washed your feet — I who am Teacher and Lord — then you must wash each other's feet. What I just did was to give you an example: as I have done, so you must do. I solemnly assure you, no slave is greater than his master; no messenger outranks the one who sent him (Jn 13:12-16; see also Mt 18:21-35; 20:26; Lk 17:7-10; 22:24-27, etc.).

The decisive reason, then, why Jesus does not emphasize the role and title of priesthood in his own life and that of his followers is simply this: that priesthood in the New Testament is part of a larger and more basic whole, namely that of service or *ministry*. And to ignore the relationship between priesthood and ministry as a whole is to distort the meaning of both. Each needs the other and, through the other, reaches its perfection: ministry as ecclesial service, and priesthood as leadership in that service.

In no way does the image of the priesthood as only part of ministry detract from its *uniqueness and sublimity*. Without the priest, we would not have the Mass, or the Šacrament of Reconciliation, or the Sacrament of the Sick. And so closely is the priest *identified with Jesus Christ* the High Priest, that in the Mass he does not say, "This is the body, this is the blood, of Jesus Christ." No, he says, "This is *my* body, this is *my* blood"! Likewise, in the Sacrament of Reconciliation, he says "I absolve you"! What a unique, sublime privilege and responsibility! No wonder that centuries of tradition have agreed in calling priests *"Other Christs"*! Yet through it all a priest is only a servant and steward to the People of God, the Body of Christ, as Paul insists in 1 Corinthians 4:1-2,

Men should regard us as servants [*hyperétai,* galley slaves] of Christ and administrators [*oicónomoi*] of the mysteries [*mystéria,* including Sacraments?] of God. The first requirement of an administrator is that he prove trustworthy.

In fact, not only is the ordained priesthood only part of ministry; it is also only *part of priesthood* in the Church. As we have already seen when reflecting on the Sacraments of Baptism and Confirmation, these two along with Ordination cannot be repeated because they are all initiations, in three different but related degrees, into the eternal priesthood of Jesus Christ.

The Sacrament of *Baptism* initiates us into the general priesthood of all the faithful (1 P 2:5, 9), that first degree of the priesthood of Jesus Christ (Heb 4:14-8:6) whereby we are one with him and with all others who are baptized into him; we are able (under the proper conditions) to participate in the entire life of the Church including the other Sacraments, especially the Eucharist (Ac 2:41-47); we are called and privileged to "worship in spirit and in truth" (Jn 4:23), offering ourselves "as a living sacrifice holy and acceptable to God, our spiritual worship" (Rm 12:1).

The Sacrament of *Confirmation* initiates us into a second and higher, a more mature and active degree of the priesthood of Jesus Christ whereby, under the abiding and guiding, nurturing and transforming action of the Holy Spirit (Mk 1:10-12; Jn 14:16-26; Ac 2:1-12; 8:17; Rm 8:9-27; Gal 4:3-7), we are able to ratify in our hearts and lives the promises, privileges, and responsibilities of our Baptism, growing to a certain maturity and adulthood in Christ (Ep 4:15), becoming more and more united with and transformed into him (Jn 15:1-17; Rm 8:29; 12:2; 1 Cor 6:17; 2 Cor 3:18; Gal 2:19-20, etc.), and allowing him to continue his life and ministry in us according to his holy will and spiritual gifts, as reflected in 1 Corinthians 12:4-7,

There are different gifts but the same Spirit; there are different ministries but the same Lord; there are different works but the same God who accomplishes all of them in everyone. To each person the manifestation of the Spirit is given for the common good.

One of the great needs of the Church today, with its long overdue emphasis on lay ministry and the priesthood of the faithful, is a new and greater appreciation of the Sacrament of Confirmation as the *consecration of the laity,*[17] the *sacrament of lay ministry and witness.*[18] And with this new appreciation may come a realization of the importance of thorough preparation and of conferral of the Sacrament at the ideal time for each individual according to his or her readiness and desire.

The Sacrament of *Holy Orders* initiates the recipient into a third and final degree of participation in the eternal priesthood of Jesus Christ, with certain far-reaching consequences for him as well as for the Church and Society. Hence, like Matrimony, it is a *social sacrament.* The consequences I refer to have been largely misunderstood and denigrated in our times, hence the necessity of arriving at a clear appreciation of their meaning. For example, Holy Orders introduces one into the *clerical state,* and clericalism has taken on a definitely pejorative connotation. But the root of the word is the Greek noun *kléros* meaning a lot or share and the reference is to the Old Testament tradition that the *Tribe of Levi,* from which Yahweh chose the hereditary priesthood of Aaron (Ex 4:14-16; 28:1-30:38; Lv 8-10, 21-22) and the auxiliary order of the Levites (Nb 1:47-54; 3:5-4:49; 8:5-26; 35:1-8), received no section of the Promised Land as their territory like the other tribes because *Yahweh himself* was their lot or share (Dt 18:1-8; Jos 21; Ps 16:5-6). What an inspiring thought and challenge for clerics today!

Likewise, Holy Orders inserts the recipient into the sacred *hierarchy* of the Church, another concept which is not especially popular in certain circles. What does it mean? Priestly rule. However, in the light of the foregoing reflection on the priesthood as a leadership of service, the word *hierarchy* ought to evoke the image of *shepherding concern* reflected in Ps 23; Is 40:11; Ezk 34:11-16, 23-24; Jn

10:14-18, 27-30; Ac 20:28; and especially St. Peter's exhortation in 1
P 5:1-4,

> To the elders (*presbyters*) among you I, a fellow elder, a witness
> of Christ's sufferings and sharer in the glory that is to be
> revealed, make this appeal.

> God's flock is in your midst; give it a *shepherd's care*. Watch
> over it willingly as God would have you do, not under con-
> straint; and not for shameful profit either, but generously.

> Be *examples* to the flock, not lording it over those assigned to
> you, so that when the chief Shepherd appears you will win for
> yourselves the unfading crown of glory.

Of course, the most important consequence of Holy Orders is the
authorization and empowerment to minister to the faithful in the three
general areas of the *Word,* the *Liturgy,* and *Service,* but each order
(diaconate, priesthood, and episcopate) in its own way. For these
three orders (partially indicated in Ph 1:1, more fully in 1 Tm 3:8-13;
5:17-22; 3:1-7, and still more so in the famous Letters of *St. Ignatius
of Antioch,* [19] who was martyred about 110 A.D.) are *three levels of
participation* in the third degree of the priesthood of Jesus Christ.

Deacons, whether transitional (i.e., preparing to pass on to the
priesthood) or permanent[20] (i.e., remaining deacons for life, usually
married men with families who retain regular jobs but are prepared
and ordained for official part-time service in the Church) are authorized by their order and office to read the Gospel and preach (as
well as teach, instruct, and counsel); to assist the priest at Mass,
conduct services of Holy Communion and Benediction of the Blessed
Sacrament, and be an official minister of Baptism, Matrimony, and
Christian funerals; and to be the presence of Christ and the Church to
the sick and imprisoned, the abandoned and needy. In addition to
these ministries of the Word, the Liturgy, and Service, permanent
deacons fulfill a providential role as a bridge between clergy and laity,
being ordained clergy whose lives are for the most part identified with
those of the laity.

As we have already seen earlier in this chapter, *priests*[21] are required to be celibate and are ordained to devote their lives entirely to the ministry of the *Word* in preaching, teaching, and counseling; the ministry of the *Liturgy* in dispensing the Sacraments, especially those reserved only to priests, namely the Holy Eucharist, Reconciliation, and the Anointing of the Sick; and the ministry of *Service* by being, so far as possible, "eyes to the blind," "feet to the lame," and "father to the needy" (Jb 29:15-16). *Bishops,* possessing the fullness of the priesthood of Jesus Christ, not only fulfill, through themselves or through others, the threefold ministry mentioned under deacons and priests but are also the ordinary ministers of Confirmation (Ac 8:14-17) and Holy Orders (Ac 14:23) and, in addition, bear a twofold responsibility: as overseers (*episkopoi*), the leadership, education and care of all the faithful of their individual dioceses (Ac 20:28); and as successors of the Apostles, the leadership, education and care (together with their fellow bishops and under the direction of the Pope) of all the members of the Church as a whole (Mt 18:18; 2 Cor 11:28).

As I have mentioned earlier in this section, before Vatican II, ministry in the Church was widely regarded as identified with Holy Orders and perhaps religious vows. The role of the laity was to "pray, pay, and obey!" But, as I came to learn personally through my study of priesthood in the New Testament and as the Council itself came to teach, particularly in its *Decree on the Apostolate of Lay People* and its *Pastoral Constitution on the Church in the Modern World,* ministry is the privilege and the responsibility of the entire Church.[22]

Ours is the ministering Church founded by Jesus Christ, and therefore *every member, every leader* of the Church is called to ministry according to his or her vocation in life, spiritual gifts, and ministerial opportunities. No one can beg off on the score of being too young or too old, too busy or too ill, belonging to the wrong parish or diocese, the wrong nationality or race, the wrong social class or sex. Ministry of some kind, formal or informal, institutional or inspirational, highly trained or untrained, is for everyone in the Church. It rests with each of us, through prayer, reflection, and consultation, to discover the particular ministry to which God is calling us.

What a *blessed time* in the history of the Church is unfolding all around us! What an exciting time in which to live and to be a member of the Church! True, many are wringing their hands over the decrease of vocations to the priesthood and the religious life, and in a sense it is indeed to be deplored, but might it possibly be a *blessing in disguise*? Would so many bishops, priests, and lay people have been so open to the permanent diaconate and lay ministry without that decrease? Who knows but that, when the restored diaconate and lay ministry are well established, not only in the United States but throughout the Church generally, priestly and religious vocations will again increase, perhaps as part of the generous blossoming of ministry as a whole?

I am fully aware that my optimism is not shared by all. In fact, some especially among my fellow-priests, aware of my eager promotion of the permanent diaconate and lay ministry, have expressed deep concern about the future. "Should we not have a *moratorium,*" they suggest, "on the training of lay deacons (sic!) and lay ministers? One of these days, they may outnumber us priests!" My first reaction, perhaps prompted by a little devil, is to dismiss their anxiety as mere "ground-keeping," that is, the fear of losing any of their priestly "territory." But quickly putting that reaction aside, I answer that, as a matter of fact, I sincerely hope the day will come when permanent deacons and lay ministers will far outnumber us priests. After all, look at the Church as a whole. Is it not, and should it not be, a great series of *concentric circles*? We have one Pope, the symbol and center of Church unity, almost twenty-five hundred bishops governing the Church with the Pope, and over four hundred thousand priests assisting the bishops in serving the faithful. Should there not be even more permanent deacons assisting the priests and many, many more lay ministers and religious assisting the clergy in building up and perfecting the life of the Church? Frankly, I cannot help seeing in Church ministry today an intriguing parallel to the "problem" with which St. Paul wrestles in *Romans 9-11,* namely the disappointing numbers of Jewish Christians and by contrast the booming influx of Gentile converts. And, like St. Paul, I believe that ours should be an attitude of faith and trust, accepting and admiring the providential wisdom of God,

> How deep are the riches and the wisdom and the knowledge of God! How inscrutable his judgments, how unsearchable his ways! For "who has known the mind of the Lord? Or who has been his counselor?" . . . For from him and through him and for him all things are. To him be glory forever. Amen (Rm 11:33-36; cf. Is 40:13; Ws 9:13).

However, to fully appreciate Christian ministry in all its forms, whether clerical or lay, we need to reflect for a moment on what it is essentially, so that we can fulfill it as perfectly as possible according to our Father's will. For example, *whom are we called to serve?* Obviously, *God himself.* But he does not need our service, in terms of practical help, does he? So, instead, he insists that we love and serve him in the persons of our fellow *human beings,* who do need our ministry. And, as we saw back in Chapter Two, human beings are *three-dimensional*: flesh, person, and spirit. It follows, then, that they have human needs in all three of these dimensions.

As *flesh,* human beings have the most basic needs of food and drink, clothing and housing, growth and healing, not to mention life itself and an environment suitable for living. As *person,* they need education and training, support and encouragement, as well as human dignity and personal freedom. As *spirit,* they are naturally oriented toward God, but need direction and assistance in finding him and living in relationship with him. All these needs we are to fulfill in our ministry to God in others (Is 58:6-11) or, more specifically, through our service of Christ in others. "I was hungry and you gave me food, etc." (Mt 25:35-40). And even greater than physical hunger or other bodily needs is that sense of abandonment and spiritual starvation from which so many suffer in today's world, as *Mother Teresa of India* so touchingly reminds us,

The biggest disease today is not leprosy or tuberculosis, but rather the feeling of being unwanted, uncared for and deserted by everybody. The greatest evil is the lack of love and charity, the terrible indifference towards one's neighbor who lives at the roadside assaulted by exploitation, corruption, poverty and disease.[23]

But how can we effectively "help carry one another's burdens" (Gal 6:2) and "do good to all men — but especially those of the household of the faith" (Gal 6:10)? How else but by "the *love (agápe) of Christ*" which "impels us" (2 Cor 5:14) "to present ourselves as ministers of God, acting with patient endurance amid trials, difficulties, distresses, . . . conducting ourselves with innocence, knowledge, and patience in the Holy Spirit, in sincere love, . . . with the message of truth and the power of God" (2 Cor 6:4-7)?

Yes, ours is a ministry to our fellow human beings, but it is not so much our ministry as it is *Christ's ministry* in and through us. Jesus Christ, our "Good Samaritan" (Lk 10:30-37) came among us as he did precisely to minister to the needs of our three-dimensional human nature. As our "Good Shepherd" (Jn 10:14) and "Divine Physician" (Mt 8:16-17; 9:2, etc.), he came to fulfill our pastoral needs as flesh. As preacher, teacher, and prophet (Mt 4:17, 23; 5-7; 13; 16:14 and parallels), he responded to our needs as person. And as our great and eternal High Priest (Heb 4:14-10:39), offering himself in sacrifice and mediating our salvation, he reconciled us with his Father (2 Cor 5:18), thus answering our greatest need as spirit.

The nature of our call to ministry, then, should be evident. Jesus Christ, who came among us to fulfill the basic needs of our three-dimensional human nature, continues to do so, but now through us. What a *sublime vocation,* and it belongs to each of us if we accept it! As we reflected in Chapter Three, Jesus Christ, in a kind of *new Incarnation* (a true "reincarnation"), desires to take possession of our human nature, unique in each of us like every leaf on the tree or every snowflake on the ground, so that through us he may continue to love and serve the needs of all.

Through us, he can be present and visible and touchable. Through our eyes, he can see the needs of all; through our ears, listen to their pleas for help. With our mind and our heart, he can pour out his understanding and his love. Through our tongue, he can speak words of consolation and peace; through our hands, he can work and lift up and heal. With our feet, he can hurry wherever there is need; yes, and with our whole body, he can suffer for the needs of all. As Paul asks, "Who is equal to such a calling?" (2 Cor 2:16, NEB). Of ourselves, none of us! But by the grace of God, especially the *"uncreated grace"* of Christ living and loving in us, every one of us regardless of our background or state in life!

SUMMARY AND CONCLUSION:

In *summary,* we have examined in this chapter our destiny to continue the life of the risen Christ through our *vocation* to marriage and family life through the Sacrament of Matrimony, or to celibacy in the single life, in Holy Orders, or in religious life through the vows and evangelical counsels. Whatever state in life God has called us to is, for each of us, the most perfect life that we can embrace. And whatever state in life he has called us to, each of us has the privilege and responsibility to continue the *ministry* of Jesus Christ in the Church and world of today as lay people, religious, or clerics in the diaconate, priesthood, or episcopacy. To this end, the Sacraments of Confirmation and Holy Orders provide us with the authorization and grace we need for effective ministry.

By way of *conclusion,* I would like, first of all, to refer those called to *lay ministry* (or ministry in the *religious life*) to the inspiring reflections and prayers, mostly from the saintly Cardinal Newman, already included in *Chapter Nine* on sharing through witnessing, service, and suffering. For those called to the *ordained priesthood,* I ask your indulgence and patience until the *General Summary and Conclusion* following this Chapter, when I will share with you my personal Prayer of a Priest. For those called to the *permanent diaco-*

nate, I would like to offer now in your name the following prayer, which I wrote in the early 1970's at the request of the permanent deacon ordinands of the Diocese of Galveston-Houston and which has been reprinted many times since then.

PRAYER OF A PERMANENT DEACON

Servant of Yahweh, though Master Divine!
Jesus, my Lord, bless this service of mine!

Make me a herald of your holy word,
Preaching and teaching your truth without fail,
Letting it first in my own soul prevail,
Conscious of bearing your trust, gentle Lord!

Make me a leader in your liturgy,
Off'ring my own life that others may live,
Sharing with others the life which you give,
Awed to be chosen for your ministry!

Make me a shepherd with your tender care,
Leading and feeding those lost or in need,
Finding new ways to turn love into deed,
Destined to keep only love which I share!

Let me but true to your service remain,
Helped by my family through failure and pain,
You my reward whom to serve is to reign!

Let me but hear when I come to my end:

Well done, faithful servant!
Welcome, faithful friend!

RECOMMENDED READING LIST

1. Mitchell, Nathan. *Mission and Ministry: History and Theology in the Sacrament of Orders,* Wilmington, DE: Michael Glazier, 1982.
2. Moloney, Francis. *Disciples and Prophets: A Biblical Model for the Religious Life,* New York: Crossroad Books, 1981.
3. O'Meara, Thomas. *Theology of Ministry,* New York: Paulist Press, 1983.
4. Thomas, David. *Christian Marriage: A Journey Together,* Wilmington, DE: Michael Glazier, 1983.
5. Von Speyr, Adrienne. *They Followed His Call: Vocation & Asceticism,* tr. Erasmo Leiva, Staten Island, NY: Alba House, 1979.

QUESTIONS FOR REFLECTION AND DISCUSSION

1. What, if any, is the relationship between our state of life or vocation and our Spiritual Life?
2. Depending on God's call, how can we develop a deeply Spiritual Life in either the married or celibate state?
3. What is the place of ministry in our Spiritual Life, and what connection does it have with the Sacrament of Confirmation?
4. Is the life of religious (or lay people) consecrated by vows a thing of the past in the Church and, if not, why not?
5. In the light of expanding lay ministry in the Church, what are the respective roles of permanent deacons and priests today?

GENERAL SUMMARY AND CONCLUSION

In the interest of time and space, I have no intention of composing such a detailed summary and conclusion that this will constitute another chapter. The book is certainly long enough as it is, and I do not want to try my readers' patience any more than necessary. Besides, who wants a Chapter Thirteen anyway? On the other hand, we have considered so many matters that a brief summary would seem to be helpful, if not absolutely necessary, for the sake of clarity and integration. The difficulty lies with that term "brief," but at least I can make a valiant effort.

SUMMARY:

After an *Introduction* which described the "Why, What, and How" of our endeavor, we divided our reflections into *three Sections*, uneven in number of chapters but remarkably even in length, comprising the *Nature*, the *Features*, and the *Means* of the Spiritual Life according to Sacred Scripture. Throughout the work, our *focus* has been twofold, *Biblical* and *Christological*, our emphasis dynamic and practical, as indicated by the title, *To Live the Word: Inspired and Incarnate*.

In *Section One*, on the *Nature of the Spiritual Life*, we learned from the entire Bible that the essence of Spirituality, like that of Religion itself, lies in *relationship*: our relationship with God and with others because of God. We then proceeded to "search the Scriptures" (Jn 5:39) for their graphic portraits of the *partners* of this relationship, our three-dimensional selves and our triune God, with special emphasis on our destiny to be the *"image and likeness of God"* (Gn 1:26-27) by allowing the *risen Christ,* the perfect "image of the invisible God" (Col 1:15; Heb 1:3; Ws 7:26) to be *incarnate anew in us,* so that through us he might continue his life and love and service in the world today (Jn 14:23; Ac 1:1; Rm 8:29; 2 Cor 3:18; Col 1:27, etc.). To complete our reflection on the Nature of the Spiritual Life, we traced in both the Old and New Testaments the *sevenfold Process* of divine initiative and human response in our relationship with God as well as the *principal obstacles* of that relationship, above all the sundering and estranging obstacle of sin.

In the *Second Section,* our study of the *Features* of the Spiritual Life comprised two chapters on the *Qualities* that should characterize our Relationship with God and others, primarily the *Virtues of Letting Go* (humility, purity, and poverty) and the *Virtues of Holding On* (faith, hope, and love). Then, we devoted two chapters to the *Inner and Outer Dimensions* of the Relationship, namely the *Prayerful Life of the Spirit* and the *Challenging Life of Sharing* through witness, service, and suffering. Our *final Section,* on the *Special Means* of the Spiritual Life, concentrated on the role of the *Church,* the *Liturgy,* the *Sacraments,* our Particular *Vocation* in Life, and our Ecclesial *Ministry* in accomplishing our birth, growth, and maturity in our Relationship with God and others, and especially in our continuation of the Life and Ministry of Jesus.

Finally, the *three Appendices* which follow this Summary and Conclusion will hopefully serve to clarify some of the more intricate matters which we touched on in our reflection but were unable to develop at length in the main body of the work. If the reader has not already taken the opportunity to peruse them, and does not care to penetrate such matters more deeply than we already have in their proper chapters, that is a decision I must respect. I simply wanted to provide the occasion for still more elucidation that the material seemed to warrant. In some instances, however, I did not want to multiply Appendices, and therefore I simply included brief remarks in the *end-notes,* which I recommend for the reader's consideration.

Invariably, there will be those who are disappointed that I did not treat at all, or at least did not treat sufficiently, certain *topics* which are making *headlines* today, for example: war and peace, conventional and nuclear disarmament, capitalism and communism, free enterprise and welfarism, birth control and abortion, racist and sexist attitudes, women in the Church and in ministry, and possibly many more. In response, I can only request *consideration of the following points*: (1) that this is not a work on moral theology or Church law, still less on social, economic, or political theory, but on spirituality, and *biblical spirituality* at that; (2) that an integrated, comprehensive examination of even the bare essentials of biblical spirituality has obviously required a rather *lengthy work* as it is; and (3) that, like Jesus and Paul, who did not engage themselves in burning issues of their day such as political, social, and economic freedom, I have been more concerned with our being changed inwardly, with our being *transformed into Christ,* confident that if enough of us become identified with him and guided by his Spirit, then whatever changes are needed in the Church and society will gradually but inevitably take place.

CONCLUSION:

To me a General Conclusion is something like a personal *farewell*. The reader and I have traveled a long and somewhat difficult road or way (Lk 9:51-19:27; 24:13-35; Ac 9:2; 16:17; 18:25-26, etc.), a *Way of Life and Love* lighted for us by the inspired Word of God (Ps 119:105) and led for us by the incarnate Word of God (Jn 14:6). Like *fellow wayfarers* everywhere, we have come to know and, I hope, to understand and respect, trust and love each other. True, I cannot know you as well as you may know me through my somewhat "autobiographical" work on Biblical spirituality, but if you have read this far, then I recognize you as one *who already knows and loves* our Blessed Lord Jesus, a seeker who "hungers and thirsts" (Mt 5:6) for closer union with our *divine Bridegroom,* and I love you for it. Like John the Baptist, it is my joy to be, in a way, "the groom's best man" (Jn 3:29) in furthering that sublime union.

Now that our sacred journey, our blessed pilgrimage, is coming to an end, it is time for us to say goodbye in the original meaning of "God be with you," or in the beautiful Spanish expression, *Vaya con Dios*, "Go with God!" Yes, I have tried to accompany you this far, and I shall continue to accompany you in my thoughts and prayers, that you may indeed go on your way with God! But, at least so far as this particular book is concerned, it is indeed time for us to say farewell.

Interestingly enough, and instructively for us, the great *farewell discourses* that immediately come to my mind from *Sacred Scripture* all seem to contain something about the *Word of God*. For example, in *Deuteronomy*, which purports to be *Moses' farewell* discourse(s) to the Israelites before his death on Mt. Nebo and their entry into the Promised Land, he reminds them that "not by bread alone does man live, but by every word that comes forth from the mouth of the Lord" (Dt 8:3; Mt 4:4; Lk 4:4) and that God's word "is not too mysterious and remote" but "something very near to you, already in your mouths and in your hearts" (Dt 30:11, 14; Rm 10:8).

Our beloved Lord *Jesus*, in his touching *farewell discourse* at the Last Supper according to *John*, continues the revealing references to the Word of God,

> Anyone who loves me will be true to my word, and my Father will love him; we will come to him and make our dwelling place with him. . . . Yet the word you hear is not mine; it comes from the Father who sent me (Jn 14:23-24).

And, in his tender "High Priestly" prayer to his Father, he mentions first of all his beloved Apostles, "These men you gave me were yours; they have kept your word . . . . I entrusted to them the message (*rhémata*, literally "words") you entrusted to me" (Jn 17:6, 8), and then all "those who will believe in me through your word, that all may be one as you, Father, are in me and I in you . . ." (Jn 17:20-21).

Finally, *St. Paul*, who has followed the risen Christ so faithfully ever since their encounter on the Damascus Road, continues to follow him in his emphasis on the Word of God in both his *verbal and written farewells*. The former, his unforgettable address to the Church leaders of the Roman province of Asia gathered at *Miletus,* contains this seldom noted but exquisite expression, "I commend you now to the Lord, and to that gracious word of his which can enlarge you, and give you a share among all who are consecrated to him" (Ac 20:32). The latter, his final letter to his cherished protege, *St. Timothy,* provides us with one of our most invaluable teachings about the importance and nature of the Word of God,

> You, for your part, must remain faithful to what you have learned and believed, because you know who your teachers were. Likewise, from your infancy you have known the Sacred Scriptures, the source of the wisdom which through faith in Jesus Christ leads to salvation.
>
> All Scripture is inspired of God and is useful for teaching — for reproof, correction, and training in holiness so that the man of God may be fully competent and equipped for every good work (2 Tm 3:14-17).

To these farewell expressions about the Word of God, which form a kind of *last will and testament* from Moses, Jesus, and St. Paul, I can only add God's brief but profound exhortation in Isaiah 55:3, *"Listen, that you may have life!"* But, as a personal memento of our adventuresome journey together, I would like to share with you, my dear reader, the following *Prayer of a Priest,* which I wrote for my Silver Jubilee as a priest in 1970, with the addition of these remarks: (1) I little dreamed at the time just how I would be permitted to share the *suffering* of Christ; (2) I am still so very far from becoming what I pray for in that prayer, that I must beg your *kindness* in remembering me if and when you use it; and (3) While it was initially and still is the personal prayer of an ordained priest shared with my fellow priests and seminarians, I have come to realize how well suited it is to the general priesthood and ministry of all the faithful. With *agápe-love,* I offer it to all my fellow Catholics and Christians.

PRAYER OF A PRIEST

Jesus, Shepherd of my soul,
Live in the soul of your shepherd:

In the depth of your humility,
In the breadth of your charity,
In the strength of your courage.

Reign in me whom you have called,
Choose for me what you have chosen:

The last and the least,
The lowest and the poorest,
The worst and the hardest,
The crib and the cross.

Give me this day my daily bread,
The grace to do my Father's Will:

With pure intention,
With full attention,
To each duty of love,
At each moment of service.

Grant that my only business in life
May be my Father's business till death,
My only eulogy:

"He was another Christ."   Amen.

SPECIAL APPENDICES

APPENDIX A

RESURRECTION AND THE LAST THINGS

In his thoughtful article on *Resurrection of the Dead* in the New Catholic Encyclopedia, *Hugh M. McElwain* wisely remarks,

> Christianity professes faith in the resurrection of the body, of the man, the enfleshed spirit, and this can come only from God's revealed Word and man's immersion into Christ's own death-resurrection. Once this is clear, then it is valid and, within limits, useful and necessary to *inquire into the manner of this resurrection and related problems.*[1]

And again,

> Even though the tenet of the creed, "I believe in the resurrection of the dead," has been an integral element in the Christian faith from the very beginning, yet a more ready response from Christians for many centuries to the question of man's fate after death has been, "I believe in the *immortality of the soul.*"[2]

Yes, influenced both by the Greek body-soul emphasis on immortality of the soul after death, and by the biblical references to "resurrection on the last day" (Jn 6:39-40, 44, 54; 11:24; see also 1 Cor 15:51-52; Ph 3:20-21; 1 Th 4:15-17), it has been traditional for Christians, especially Catholics, to think of the resurrection of the body as occurring only at the end of time, the departed soul meanwhile continuing a separate existence as an immortal being. But, as I mentioned before in noting the limitations of the Greek body-soul anthropology, a separated soul is not a person, and resurrection of our billions of bodies (many, if not most of them, totally disintegrated or transmuted) at the end of time involves an incredible number of miracles. Even in philosophical theology, there is a long-standing axiom, "God does not multiply miracles"!

Is there, then, another possibility? I suggest that there is, namely that *our resurrection takes place at the time of our death*! In other words, when we die, this body of ours is laid to rest, cremated, donated to science, or otherwise respectfully disposed of, and we do not have to worry about it anymore. God gives us *a new body just like our own, but with all the properties of spirit*: glorious, spiritual, incorruptible, immortal! (1 Cor 15:42-50, 53). In this we differ from Jesus Christ, who rose with his self-same body, and (in Catholic and Orthodox belief) from Mary who was assumed into Heaven with her self-same body. Thus, with our new, spiritual, and immortal body we continue to live as *persons* rather than as separated souls for an eternity of rewards or punishments according to our life here on earth (2 Cor 5:10). At this point, I would like to quote at length from *Ladislaus Boros, S.J.* in his book, *Living in Hope*:[3]

> Man will rise from the dead. What is a risen human being? We will preface this question with another preliminary one which may appear merely incidental but which will bring us close to the essential definition of man's resurrection. *When* does the resurrection from the dead take place? The ideas we are about to outline may perhaps appear hazardous, but we should like to put them forward as a basis for reflection.
>
> On the one hand we usually think of the death of a human being as the separation of soul and body. In view of our previous considerations, however, is such a separation possible at all? We have noted that the soul by its very essence stands in relationship to matter. The soul cannot exist without the body.

Man is one entity. It would be incongruous to say there was a soul without a body. Consequently the resurrection must take place straightaway at the moment of death. There is no soul separated from the body, there is only the one single human being. This is the first point which must be taken into account.

On the other hand, revelation repeatedly emphasizes that man's resurrection from the dead is an eschatological event. It coincides with Christ's second coming at the *Last Day*. Consequently man's resurrection can only be conceived as taking place at the end of time. We are clearly faced by an *aporia*, a blind-alley of thought.

Karl Rahner has suggested the following solution. In death the human soul does not become "noncorporeal" but enters into a pancosmic relationship, and is present everywhere in the universe. He takes the view that at the moment of leaving the body, the human soul enters into a new relation to matter and becomes omnipresent in the material reality of the universe. I appreciate Karl Rahner's profound insight here and accept it, but I wonder why we need stop at this half-way solution. Why should the resurrection not take place at the same time as death? The more radical solution would be to say that the resurrection takes place *immediately at death*, but that it is an *eschatological event* nevertheless. This is only an apparent contradiction. The risen human being needs the transformed and transfigured universe as his dwelling place. The transformation at the end of time would therefore involve the final completion of the resurrection that had already occurred at death. Consequently it would be meaningful to say both that the resurrection takes place immediately at death and that the resurrection is an eschatological event at the end of time. This would mean that the human soul is never without a body; immortality and resurrection are in fact one and the same.

But how does this square with *Scripture*? Quite well, it seems, particularly if we keep in mind two important facts: (1) that there has been very little clear and detailed revelation about the afterlife, and (2) that the whole Greek idea of separation and immortality of the soul was largely foreign to the Jewish and early Christian thinking. Actually, there are very few explicit references to "resurrection on the last day" and these can be explained as being fulfilled in a final great triumph of Christ and the Church in a transformed universe at the end of time, when all will have risen from the dead, though not necessarily at the same time.

Other mentions of resurrection fit quite well, perhaps even better, with resurrection immediately after death, e.g., Jesus' argument with the Sadducees (Mt 22:23-33 and parallels), perhaps the strange resurrection of many from the dead at the time of the crucifixion (Mt 27:51-53), and several references in *Luke,* especially the parable of the rich man and Lazarus (Lk 16:19-31), the promise to the good thief (Lk 23:43), and Jesus' own appearance (24:39), about all of which *Eduard Schweizer* in Kittel's monumental *Theological Dictionary of the New Testament* comments, "Luke seems to be interested in a bodily resurrection immediately after death and he thus avoids expressions which might suggest the mere survival of the soul."[4] Then, too, we have that mysterious statement in the Apocalypse of St. John about the "first resurrection" (Rv 20:4-6).

But to me it is *Paul* who provides the most cogent biblical foundation for "immediate resurrection," in his analogy of the seed and the plant, the natural and the spiritual body (1 Cor 15:35-44 and 51). After all, seeds do not wait for centuries to germinate and become plants! But Paul is particularly convincing when, perhaps in allusion to a similar expression in Hezekiah's prayer (Is 38:12), he refers to our earthly and heavenly tent or dwelling in 2 Corinthians 5:1-5:

Indeed, we know that when the *earthly tent* in which we dwell is destroyed we have *a dwelling provided for us by God,* a dwelling in the heavens, not made by hands but to last forever. We groan while we are here even as we yearn to have our heavenly habitation envelop us. This it will, provided we are found clothed and not naked. While we live in our present tent we groan; we are weighed down because we do not wish to be stripped naked but rather to have the heavenly dwelling envelop us, so that what is mortal may be absorbed by life. God has fashioned us for this very thing and has given us the Spirit as a pledge of it.

All well and good, my Catholic readers may be thinking, but how can this be reconciled with *Church tradition and teaching* down through the centuries? A relevant question, to which there is a very interesting answer.

Of the various kinds of documents that mention the matter, dating from the first (?) to the sixteenth century, the vast majority simply refer to the resurrection of the dead. Of the rest, only two add the words "on the last day," and neither statement is from a general council. Several add the idea, "with the same body which we have in this life," but on close examination they turn out to be the teaching of provincial councils or individual Popes in non-solemn declarations, or variant wordings of general councils, leaving just one document, the clear but not very formal declaration of the Fourth Lateran Council[5] in the thirteenth century, at the height of Scholasticism based on Greek philosophy. Is this enough to constitute the constant tradition and official teaching of the Church for all time? But even if we must believe that, somehow, our new body is numerically the same as the one we have in our earthly life, can we not understand this according to Paul's analogy of the seed and the plant (1 Cor 15:35-49), updated by our knowledge of cells? For biochemists tell us that each one of the hundred trillion cells in our body carries the entire DNA, the complete "instruction book" of a hundred thousand genes, from which the entire body can be reproduced.[6] Cannot God do this, along with spiritualization and glorification, far more easily at death than centuries later?

On the other hand, I submit that the possibility of resurrection immediately after death is remarkably consonant with the *present funeral liturgy* of the Church, which totally emphasizes resurrection (not death, nor burial, nor immortality of the soul), by lighting the paschal candle, wearing white vestments, and referring over and over again to the resurrection of Christ and of the dead.[7] An ancient tradition in the Church says that the prayer-life of the Church reflects her beliefs, "Lex orandi, lex credendi," meaning "The law of praying (is) the law of believing."[8]

As with the so-called "doctrine" of the limbo of unbaptized infants, which has now largely been discarded or at least recognized for what it is, namely theological speculation, so also with this question of resurrection: the time may have arrived when we Catholics need to revise our thinking in the light of *biblical rather than philosophical anthropology* and arrive at conclusions which are so much more consoling to the faithful generally and, above all, for the grieving family and friends of those who are deceased.

But what does this approach do to the Catholic doctrines of Purgatory, Heaven, and Hell? Nothing at all, except to make them more real and personal, since we are now talking about persons rather than separated souls. However, a few words about these *"Last Things"* are clearly in order.

PURGATORY:

First, let us remember that the word *Purgatory,* etymologically and theologically, refers to purification and expiation, especially after death. Is there any biblical evidence for such a concept? Yes, as a matter of fact, there is. In the *Old Testament,* there are many references to expiation for sin, even when the sin is already forgiven, e.g. God's prohibition of Moses and Aaron entering the Promised Land (Nb 20:12) and his punishment of David for his sins of adultery, murder, and pride (2 S 11-12 ff. and 2 S 24). Even more clearly, the *Second Book of Maccabees,* accepted by Catholics as inspired and by Jews and Protestants as holy and reflective of Jewish history, thought, and customs (e.g. the Feast of Hanukkah), contains a beautiful story in which some Jews who had died in battle were found to be wearing pagan amulets; whereupon Judas Maccabaeus, the Jewish general, took up a collection so that sacrifices might be offered at the temple in Jerusalem for the expiation of this sin. By way of commentary, the author adds,

> In doing this he acted in a very excellent and noble way, inasmuch as he had the resurrection of the dead in view; for if he were not expecting the fallen to rise again, it would have been useless and foolish to pray for them in death. But if he did this with a view to the splendid reward that awaits those who had gone to rest in godliness, it was a holy and pious thought. Thus he made atonement for the dead that they might be freed from their sin (2 M 12:38-46).

In the *New Testament*, we read that, in the *"Heavenly Jerusalem,"* there can be "nothing profane" or "deserving a curse" and "no one who is a liar" or "has done a detestable act" (Rv 21:27; 22:3). If this be so, and it would have to be because we are talking about the all-holy presence and vision of God (Rv 4-5 ff.), then the idea of a Purgatory makes a lot of sense. In *Isaiah 6*, the symbolic presence of Yahweh causes the Seraphim to sing out, "Holy, holy, holy is the Lord of hosts!" (Is 6:3) and moves the prophet Isaiah to bemoan his uncleanness, "Woe is me, I am doomed! For I am a man of unclean lips, living among a people of unclean lips; yet my eyes have seen the King, the Lord of hosts!" (Is 6:5). Whereupon, Isaiah undergoes his own "Purgatory" by means of a burning ember touched to his mouth by one of the Seraphim (Is 6:7). How much holier and utterly overwhelming must be the actual presence and vision of the almighty, all-holy God who dwarfs the universe, and of the Lamb triumphant! We certainly need to be purified before we are ready to encounter the very holiness of God. As John expresses it, "If we say, 'We are free of the guilt of sin,' we deceive ourselves" (1 Jn 1:8). We still need to be freed of all sin and guilt and debt in order to see God "face to face." And that purification and expiation is what we call Purgatory.

All right, we do need purification before entering the "Heavenly Jerusalem," but how does this happen? Ideally, in this life, where the "sufferings of the present" are "nothing compared with the glory to be revealed in us" (Rm 8:18) and where "the present burden of our trial is light enough and earns for us an eternal weight of glory beyond all comparison" (2 Cor 4:17). This is the "Purgatory" of the Saints. "Everyone who has this hope . . . keeps himself pure, as he is pure" (1 Jn 3:3).

But what if we are not saints? What if we have not been sufficiently purified in this life? Ah! Then there is Purgatory in the next life, which is not so much a condition of punishment as an opportunity for purification and expiation leading to a glorious eternity of bliss. The great *Dante Alighieri* assures us, "If you really want God's way with you, you will get it in Heaven, and the pains of Purgatory will not deter you, they will be welcomed as means to an end."[9]

What, then, is Purgatory? A place? A state? A length of time? We really do not know, do we? Maybe it is none of these, but rather a *process* of purification and expiation which God can accomplish *"in an instant, in the twinkling of an eye"* (1 Cor 15:52), the intensity of the process varying according to our individual need of purification and expiation. Would this not accord well with the funeral liturgy, which rejoices in the hope that the deceased are already with God forever? But what about prayers and sacrifices for the *"Poor Souls in Purgatory"*? Well, I said that God could accomplish the process of purification in an instant, but we do not know that he does, do we? Therefore, in our love for our dear departed ones, it is most appropriate that we continue to pray and make sacrifices for them.

HEAVEN AND HELL:

If Purgatory is a process, then what about Heaven and Hell? Are they places, states, or processes? And, if they are places, where are they? Again, we do not really know, do we? It is very interesting that, in both Testaments (especially the Old Testament), God has chosen to satisfy so little of our insatiable curiosity about the afterlife. But there are some possibilities which are worth considering:

(1) *Heaven* is where we will "behold the face of God" (Mt 18:10; 22:30 and parallels), where "we shall be like him, for we shall see him as he is" (1 Jn 3:2). But God is everywhere! So Heaven would seem to be *everywhere*. In our space age, we no longer think of Heaven as "up there" and Hell as "down there." Heaven is all *around us*, but we cannot see it or behold God with his saints and angels because we are still in a time of faith and hope, not of vision. We are like the audience in a theater where the entire cast may be on stage, but we cannot see them because the curtain has not yet been raised. In fact, we can even say that Heaven is *within us* because, as *Blessed Elizabeth of the Trinity* expresses it, "Heaven is God and God is in my soul!"[10] No wonder *St. Catherine of Siena* could say in all truth, "All the way to Heaven is Heaven!"[11]

(2) But if Heaven is everywhere, then where is *Hell*? And how can there be a Hell at all; that is, a place or state of estrangement and separation from God, if God is everywhere (Ps 139:7-8)? A very good question! To me, it is a matter not of location but of *relation*. One can be a stranger even in one's own home! And so Hell, like Heaven, is not a place, nor a process like Purgatory, but *a state*: the state of the damned (or rather *self-condemned*) in Hell contrasted with the state of the blessed in Heaven (Mt 25:31-46; also Mt 5:29-30; 18:8-9; Mk 9:43-48, etc.). The difference lies in the persons themselves. Perhaps an analogy will help. If we are healthy, if our eyes are clear and our skin youthful, if we are not at all allergic to sunlight, then we can literally bathe in the sunshine which fills us with joy. But if, on the other hand, we are ill and diseased, if our eyes are weak and our skin hypersensitive to sunlight, then the very same sun which gives such radiant joy to the healthy provides nothing but torture and suffering (like the "Hell" fire of radiation!) to the unhealthy. May this not be true of Heaven and Hell? The difference may well be, not one of place or divine attitude, but simply one of *spiritual health or sickness*, goodness or evil in ourselves.[12] And, of course, both states last

forever because we have chosen our state, we have opted to be with God or against him, to enjoy his presence or not — and the time for repentance has passed.

(3) Let us return for a moment to the question of *Purgatory* as a process.[13] Might it not be true that the *very presence of God himself,* which gives such joy to the blessed and pain to the damned, cleanses and purifies the person in Purgatory (the process of purification), rendering him or her fit and ready for the full exposure to the blazing sunshine of the Beatific Vision? "Our God is a consuming fire!" (Dt 4:24; Heb 12:29).

(4) Also, returning for a moment to the question of *Heaven,* we have grown up regarding the state of the blessed as one of "eternal rest," and rightly so in regard to the struggles of this life. As we read in the great Epistle to the Hebrews, "A sabbath rest still remains for the people of God. And he who enters into God's rest, rests from his own work as God did from his" (Heb 4:9-10). Hence our prayer, "May they rest in peace." However, I suspect that Heaven is not at all a state of restful inactivity, but a state and process of *restful activity.* In the divine presence and Beatific Vision, we are called to spend an eternity getting to know God better and better, thereby loving him more and more, and never reaching the end (certainly never becoming bored!) because we can never fully comprehend God and, above all, we can never actually become God in the total sense! What a Heaven of pure happiness! *B.F. Westcott*[14] comments thus:

> We make a great mistake if we connect with our conception of Heaven the thought of rest from work. Rest from toil, from weariness, from exhaustion — yes; rest from work, from productiveness, from service — no. That abundant and increasing vitality of spirit and of body which is poured into the saints from the glorified Christ, that life from the very source of life, is not to be spent in idle harping upon harps of gold, reclining on clouds, or wandering aimlessly through the paradise of God, clad in white robes and with crowned heads. These apocalyptic pictures

are symbols of a bliss that passes words; but there is another side to the picture, which is too often forgotten in our anticipations of the life to come. "They rest not day and night"; "they serve God day and night"; "his servants shall do him service."

(5) But *what about others*, especially those near and dear to us in this life? Will we be able to recognize them, to know them, to share our joy (or misery) with them in the afterlife? I do believe that we will, and I might add that this is far more likely if we continue our existence, not as separated souls, but as human persons with human, risen, immortal bodies. Then, both our joy and our misery, depending on our chosen state, will be shared and multiplied by the recognition of those whom we have known and loved in our earthly life. The great difference is again largely within ourselves, for in Heaven the presence of our loved ones will increase our love and happiness, whereas part at least of the suffering in Hell is, as Dostoevsky points out in *The Brothers Karamazov*, "the suffering of not being able to love."[15]

(6) When all is said and done, whatever Heaven and Hell and Purgatory may be like, we need to keep in mind that the *free choice* is up to us. *William Law* explains, "Men are not in Hell because God is angry with them; they are in wrath and darkness because they have done to the light which infinitely flows forth from God as the man does to the light of the sun who puts out his own eyes!"[16] *Jean Paul Sartre* used to insist that "Hell is others!"[17] but the truth of the matter is that both Heaven and Hell are ourselves, in the sense that we freely make our own Heaven and Hell both in this life and in the next. This is unforgettably expressed in the *Rubaiyat of Omar Khayyam*,

> I sent my Soul through the Invisible,
> Some letter of that After-life to spell;
> And by and by my Soul returned to me,
> And answered "I Myself am Heaven and Hell!"[18]

(7) "I myself am Heaven!" Little did Omar Khayyam realize the deeper truth that he was voicing! For, "if we have died with

Christ," (Rm 6:8) and can say with St. Paul, "It is no longer I who live, but Christ lives in me," (Gal 2:20), then Heaven is, in a very real sense, already ours! Christ is our life, and death our gain (Ph 1:21)! Since "Christ" our "hope of glory" (Col 1:27) is already with us and in us, then "when Christ our life appears," we "shall appear with him in glory" (Col 3:4). "Thanks be to God who has given us the victory through our Lord Jesus Christ!" (1 Cor 15:57).

*If Christ is infallable he is also
impeccable?
His infallibility comes from his divinity
not from his humanity.
Got him*

APPENDIX   B

HOW HUMAN WAS JESUS CHRIST?

p. 457

For most of the history of the Church, it seems that the major emphasis regarding Jesus Christ was concerned with believing, defending, and worshipping his divinity. Reflections on his humanity tended to stress its extraordinary *privileges* because of its hypostatic union with his divine person and nature. Thus, it was commonly held by many theologians that Jesus, in his human nature, must have enjoyed the Beatific Vision of God throughout his life, that he had all infused knowledge, and that he was not only sinless but absolutely incapable of sinning.[1] This approach, of course, contributed greatly to adoration and even awe, but it did have its *shortcomings,* for example: (1) It tended to portray Jesus as "larger than life" and more or less "play acting" the role of an ordinary human, particularly during his so-called hidden life at Nazareth; (2) It left us little possibility of truly imitating him in his human life because of the great disparity between his human nature and our own; and (3) It did not seem to square very easily with some of the indications in the New Testament, especially the Gospel of Mark, about the limitations of his humanity. For these reasons in particular, many if not most Scripture scholars and theologians in more recent years have taken a different tack, looking at the possible limitations to which the Son of God may have subjected himself out of love for us.

Before we proceed further, however, it is essential that we be absolutely clear about what we are not and what we actually are talking about. *Our question under discussion is not* whether Jesus Christ was *truly divine and truly human,* for that is a dogma or doctrine of the faith, as defined particularly at the Council of Chalcedon in 451 A.D.[2] Nor is there any question that Jesus, *as divine,* as the Son of God, possessed *all knowledge* from all eternity and was absolutely *incapable of sin* or even of genuine temptation. Finally, ours is not the question of whether Jesus, *as human, could* have possessed the Beatific Vision, all infused knowledge, and immunity from the possibility of sinning or, even without the Beatific Vision and all infused knowledge, *could* have been conscious of being the Messiah and unique Son of God, and could have been incapable of sinning.

What we are reflecting on is whether Jesus Christ, *as human,* could have been without the Beatific Vision and all infused knowledge, hence capable of ignorance, or at least nescience, that is, *lack of knowledge* about persons, places, or things that he did not need to know in order to fulfill his mission. Further, we need to ask whether, acccording to the evidence of the *New Testament,* particularly the Gospel of *Mark,* Jesus was, as human, actually without the Beatific Vision and all infused knowledge during his earthly life and therefore limited in knowledge and ignorant or nescient about certain persons, places, and things of the past, present, and future. Above all, we are asking whether Jesus Christ was *aware or conscious* during his earthly life of being the Son of God and the Messiah and, if so, was this awareness or consciousness throughout his life or only after a certain point of his life and, further, was it based on certain intellectual knowledge or on faith. Finally, we are concerned with the possibility and actuality of whether Jesus Christ, *as human,* could have been and was sinless, not because of incapability of sin or even true temptation, but rather because, though subject to temptations of all kinds and actually *capable of sinning* because of his free human will, he nevertheless rejected all temptations and remained totally sinless throughout his entire life.

In summary, then, our question is twofold:

(1) Whether Jesus Christ, in his *human intelligence,* was limited in knowledge, subject to ignorance or at least nescience, and, even if aware of his Messiahship and unique Divine Sonship, had to live by faith just as we do.

(2) Whether Jesus Christ, in his *human will,* was limited in power, subject to temptations of all kinds, and even capable of sinning, but through his free will strengthened by faith, love, and grace remained absolutely sinless his entire life.

Having examined the nature of the question under discussion, we next need to ask, "Why even bring up such a question? What is the point? What is its *importance?*" Certainly, it does not consist in the fact that most modern authors on the New Testament or on Christology (e.g. Raymond Brown, Bruce Vawter, Karl Rahner, Edward Schillebeeckx, etc.) have felt it necessary to discuss the matter, for our purpose is not primarily intellectual but spiritual. Rather, I perceive two basic and very valid reasons for this examination, reasons which are absolutely in accord with our principal purposes and emphasis in this work, namely: (1) to arrive (especially through Scripture) at a *true knowledge and appreciation of Jesus Christ,* the Word made Flesh, who is the primary subject and object (or, better still, partner) of our relationship, and whose risen life in us is a principal focus of this work, and (2) to develop our own confidence in, commitment to, and identification with Jesus Christ, whose life of humility and love can become much more realistically the proper object of our own love, gratitude, and imitation.

Specifically, as the result of our reflection, we Christians can far more truly and fully admire, love, and try with God's grace to imitate Jesus's self-emptying *humility* (Ph 2:7) in becoming as completely human as he possibly could, even though he was in person and nature divine (a mystery of hypostatic union); his matchless *love* for his Father and for us in identifying himself as closely as possible with our lowly and sinful human nature, even dying for us as a crucified criminal (2 Cor 5:21); and his incomparable *faith, trust, and holiness* in remaining totally faithful to his Father's will (Heb 4:15) in spite of lifelong temptations, opposition from others, and seeming abandonment by his Father (Mk 15:34).

Now that we have seen the nature and importance of this difficult but fruitful question, let us turn to the New Testament, especially the Gospel of Mark, and see what the *biblical evidence* indicates one way or the other. Why the Gospel of Mark? Because, as we have already mentioned in Chapter Three, *Mark's Gospel* is evidently the earliest and most authentic, the least refined and most candid portrait of the (divine and) human Jesus as he was and as he appeared to others, notably his Apostles, during his earthly life and ministry. What, then, is the evidence? Here, there is something of a *division* among Scripture scholars and, above all, theologians, stemming possibly from an ambiguity in Mark itself. Some maintain that, according to the indications in Mark's Gospel, Jesus knew quite clearly that he was the *Messiah* (Mk 1:1; 8:29-30; 14:61-62), the *Son of Man* reminiscent of Daniel 7:13-14 and of Apocalyptic literature (Mk 2:10, 28; 8:31, 38; 9:9, 31; 10:33, 45; 13:26; 14:21, 41, 62), and even the *unique Son of God* (1:1, 11; 3:11; 9:7; 12:6; 13:32; 14:36, 61-62). And, of course, the other Gospels, particularly that of *John*, are used for confirmation.

According to others, the evidence from the New Testament, especially the Gospel of Mark, seems to indicate that Jesus Christ was clearly *limited in knowledge*, e.g. about who touched him (Mk 5:30), about the proper identification of the high priest who helped David when he was fleeing from Saul (1 S 21:2, 9; 22:9, 11, 14, 16, 20-21; Mk 2:26), about his own divinity (Mk 10:18), and about the time of the eschaton or last day (Mk 13:32); that he was also limited in power, e.g. in his inability to work many miracles in Nazareth (Mk 6:5) and his utter devastation before and at his death by crucifixion (Mk 14:34-36; 15:34); and, finally, that he was truly subject to temptation (and therefore capable of yielding to temptation and sinning) apparently without any limitation (Mk 1:12-13). With regard to the last-named indication, proponents also invoke *Hebrews 4:15,*

He was not subject to temptation but was the object of temptation.

Before abraham was, I am

For we do not have a high priest who is unable to sympathize with our weakness, but one who was tempted in every way that we are, yet never sinned. So let us confidently approach the throne of grace to receive mercy and favor and to find help in time of need.

And, of course, they dismiss the use of *John's Gospel* as confirmation of the opposite position on the grounds that, in its "realized eschatology,"[3] it portrays Jesus exalted and triumphant throughout his earthly life, as if his resurrection has already occurred and therefore as if he already possesses the Beatific Vision and all knowledge, power, and freedom from any possibility of temptation and sin.

Such is, in brief, the biblical evidence, but what about *Tradition*? What does the Church say, especially in the form of defined doctrine? Here, of course, the principal Conciliar statements would be those of the Council of *Nicaea* (325 A.D.) on the divinity of Jesus Christ; the Council of *Ephesus* (431 A.D.) on the one person in two natures and on Mary who, as mother of that person according to his human nature, deserves to be called Mother of God; but above all the Council of *Chalcedon* (451 A.D.) on the distinction and uniqueness of the two natures in Christ. To grasp something of what the *Council of Chalcedon*[4] is saying, it will be helpful to quote its definition in full:

Therefore, following the holy fathers, we all teach that with one accord we confess one and the same Son, our Lord Jesus Christ, the same perfect in human nature, truly God and the same with a rational soul and a body truly man, *consubstantial with the Father according to divinity, and consubstantial with us according to human nature, like unto us in all things except sin (cf. Heb 4:15)*; indeed born of the Father before the ages according to divine nature, but in the last days the same born of the Virgin Mary, Mother of God according to human nature; for us and for our deliverance, one and the same Christ only begotten Son, our Lord, acknowledged in *two natures, without mingling, without change, indivisibly, undividedly, the distinction of the natures nowhere removed on account of the union but rather the peculiarity of each nature being kept,* and uniting in one person and substance, not divided or separated into two persons, but one and the same Son only begotten God's word, Lord Jesus Christ, just as from the beginning the prophets taught about Him and the Lord Jesus Himself taught us, and the creed of our fathers has handed down to us.

I do not pretend to be a Conciliar theologian but, without going into the meaning then and now of substance, person, and nature, it seems clear to me that the Council of Chalcedon, in declaring the two natures in the one Person of Jesus Christ, clearly insisted that there was *no mixture or fusion* between them, hence union with the divine did not necessarily result (as much of traditional theology later maintained) in total knowledge and impeccability in the human nature of Jesus Christ. Neither subsequent Councils, nor Popes (except possibly Gregory I, the Great) nor Church Fathers (except possibly Augustine) have taught otherwise. Hence, the attribution to the human nature of Jesus of all that was not metaphysically impossible (particularly the Beatific Vision and all infused knowledge) is simply theological speculation. My confrere, Bruce Vawter, C.M., puts it concisely as usual in his excellent work, *This Man Jesus,* "To say that Jesus in his earthly life knew and judged himself to be God's natural Son and very God is to assert the unprovable and, from the perspective of the New Testament, the improbable."[5]

Now that we have seen the evidence, can we draw any conclusions or must we simply bow down in adoration before the ineffable mystery of the Incarnation, without any particular helps for our knowledge and imitation, our union and identification, with the human Jesus? For myself, and with every desire to be in agreement with true Christian and Catholic doctrine as we see it in Scripture and Tradition, the following conclusions are not only well-founded but very revealing, inspiring, and livable.

(1) The apparent ambiguity, primarily in the Gospel of Mark,

between Jesus' consciousness of his Messiahship and Divinity on the one hand, and limitations to his knowledge on the other, is due, not so much to an ambiguity in Mark's account (as some declare), but to a failure to ask the *right question*. To my way of thinking, the proper question, in view of the evidence, is not whether Jesus, in his human consciousness, was aware of being the Messiah and Son of God (there are just too *many indications that he was aware,* at least from the time of his baptism by John the Baptist), but rather *how was he aware*? Did he know by certain knowledge, such as from the Beatific Vision or infused knowledge? Did he know by some kind of intuition, which is still a form of knowledge? Or did he believe by faith? The evidence seems to me to point strongly to the last-named possibility. And this is lucidly confirmed by James P. Mackey in *Jesus, the Man and the Myth,* [6]

> If one had a smattering of Greek, one would quickly realize that in many places where the New Testament talks in English about having faith in Jesus, the original Greek could just as easily, and even more literally, be read as recommending the faith *of* Jesus. . . . The New Testament gives more warrant than we have yet seen for speaking of the historical Jesus as himself a *man of faith.* . . . Such, then, is the life of Jesus, the only life of Jesus of any interest to the world. Such is the historical Jesus, who can be discovered at the end of any quest, old or new. A man of faith, a life of faith . . . , inspiring to similar faith those with whom he came into contact, so that they in turn could inspire others. That was his life. That was the faith for which he lived and died.

Reading the Gospel of Mark with this *possibility in mind, that Jesus realized his Messiahship and Divine Sonship, but only by faith,* not only brings the Gospel even more to life, but also invites us (along with the original readers, probably the Roman Christians persecuted by Nero after the Great Fire at Rome, 64-65 A.D.), to follow our Brother and Savior in faith, trust, and selfless love despite all difficulties, even to the Cross and Resurrection.

(2) As with his knowledge, so also with his power and sinlessness, we need to ask the *right question*: not so much what extraordinary privileges should be accorded Jesus' human nature because of the hypostatic union, but how far could he and did he go in his *"self-emptying"* (Greek *kénōsis*, Ph 2:7) out of love for us? How much greater humility, love, and obedience to his Father did the Son of God show if, in fact, he so emptied himself that, as human, he had to live by sheer faith, trust, and abandonment to his Father's Will (Mk 14:36), if his human power was not absolute but at times limited (as was his physical power in the crib!), and if he (mystery of mysteries!) could be tempted in every way as we are, could sin as we can, but unlike us never sinned in the slightest way throughout his entire life! To my knowledge, the New Testament never says that Jesus *could* not sin; rather that he *did* not sin (Mt 4:1-11; Lk 4:1-13; Jn 8:46; 14:30; Rm 5:19; 2 Cor 5:21; Heb 4:15; 7:26; 1 P 2:22). Let us listen to Piet Schoonenberg, S.J. in his very relevant work, *The Christ*,[7]

> An incapacity for sin would always have been determined before Jesus' human insertion of will; with such a course of affairs, however, his human will is not redemptive and our human will not redeemed. Jesus would then . . . stand outside history. In particular, we should then be doing wrong to what the New Testament tells us about his temptations.

And, more recently, Dermot A. Lane, building on Schoonenberg's work in his own *The Reality of Jesus*,[8] has this to say,

> The sinlessness of Jesus should not be conceived of in terms of an a priori projection of impeccability in a way that would destroy the reality of his humanity. The New Testament never says that Jesus could not sin; it states rather that Jesus in fact did not sin. The sinlessness of Jesus, therefore, should be understood as the achievement of a rich response by the man Jesus to the gift of God's grace throughout his life.

> By maintaining an unbroken bond of hypostatic union with God,

Jesus realized the graced capacity of his humanity for communion with God. In doing so, he revealed the image and likeness of
God within the heart of man. It is in this sense that we can say
that the perfection of his humanity through communion with
God mediates divinity and so suggest that Jesus is known to
reflect the image of God by being true man and that therefore his
divinity is disclosed through the fullness of his humanity. This
does not mean that the sinlessness of Jesus is his divinity. Rather
the sinlessness of Jesus is an expression, a negative one at that,
of his communion with God which is the basis of his humanity
revealing his divinity.

What love! What astonishing fidelity! What an example to imitate!
Or, better still, what a life to live as we allow him to continue to live
his life of humility, purity, and poverty, of faith, trust, and love in and
through us!

By way of *general conclusion,* then, it seems to me that it is
possible, permissible, and extremely salutary for us (especially in
reading the Gospel of Mark) to recognize, appreciate, and identify
with the complete humanness of Jesus Christ, who identified with us
in all our human limitations. And, while Jesus' humanness united
with his divinity is indeed a mystery beyond our comprehension,
perhaps we can appreciate it to some extent by recalling that, through
him, we too are *children of God* (not by nature but by the grace of
adoption, Rm 8:15-17; Gal 4:4-7), we too are temples of the Holy
Spirit (1 Cor 6:19), we have *Christ living his life in us* (Jn 14:23; Col
1:27), truths of which we are conscious only by faith, not by
knowledge or vision. Therefore, after his example, we too are challenged to live by sheer faith, trust, and love; to grow in this life in spite
of (or because of) the many obstacles which come our way, and to
persevere in this life even to crucifixion and resurrection.

I like the conclusion of Raymond Brown in his thoughtful study,
Jesus God and Man,[9]

If Jesus is not "true God of true God," then we do not know God in human terms. . . . Only if Jesus is God do we know that God's love was so real that He gave Himself for us. Only if Jesus is of God do we know that it is of His nature to redeem the creation that He brought into being. Only if Jesus is of God do we know what God is like, for in Jesus we see God translated into terms that we can understand. . . .

Unless we understand that Jesus was truly human, we cannot comprehend the depth of God's love. And if theologians should ultimately come to accept the limitations of Jesus' knowledge that we have seen reflected prima facie in the biblical evidence, then how much the more shall we understand that God so loved us that He subjected Himself to our most agonizing infirmities.

In the fourth and fifth centuries the question of Jesus as God and man was not an abstract question debated in the scholars' chambers; it was a question of what God and Christianity were all about. I submit that, if we take the trouble to understand, it remains all of that even in the twentieth century.

APPENDIX   C

JUSTIFICATION AND SALVATION

The thorny question of justification and salvation is far too complex to include under the treatment of Faith in Chapter VII, but it is certainly *important* enough to deserve an appendix of its own. Historically and ecumenically, it is important because it constituted the crux of difference and debate between *Martin Luther* and the Protestant Reformers on the one hand and the Roman Catholic Church on the other. Biblically, theologically, and spiritually, it is important for us today because it is concerned with the most crucial consideration of religion, Christianity, and the Spiritual Life, namely: "How do we enter into and continue in a *right relationship* with God?" But, because of the very complexity of the question, it will be necessary to view it, first in its general context, and then in the key text employed by St. Paul in Galatians and Romans, whose interpretation by Martin Luther and his early followers contributed so greatly (though not exclusively) to the division of Christianity in the Western World.

THE GENERAL CONTEXT:

It is essential to keep in mind that St. Paul, in his letters to the Galatians and Romans, is grappling with the *fundamental "bone of contention"* between Judaism and Christianity. The controversy first surfaced, of course, during the life and ministry of *Jesus* himself, particularly in regard to the Sabbath regulations (e.g. Mk 2:23-3:6), but also concerning such things as the laws of cleanliness (Mk 7:1-23). Then, after the death, resurrection, and ascension of Jesus, the dispute erupted again over the preaching of *St. Stephen*, the first Christian martyr, who was accused of "speaking blasphemies against Moses and God" (Ac 6:11) or, more specifically, of "making statements against the holy place and the law" (Ac 6:13). These skirmishes were between Jesus and Christians on the one hand, and Jews on the other. Soon, however, the conflict would occur among Christians themselves. This happened when *St. Peter* received the first Gentiles into the Church in the person of the Roman Centurion Cornelius, with his entire household, at Caesarea by the Sea (Ac 10). Immediately upon his return to Jerusalem, he was challenged by some of the *Jewish Christians*, even for having entered the house of Gentiles and eaten with them (Ac 11:2-3). Peter was able to convince them that he had acted as he did on the initiative of God himself, who had instructed Cornelius to send messengers to him, had provided Peter with the threefold vision of the clean and unclean animals on the rooftop of the house of Simon the Tanner at Joppa, and finally had poured out the (charismatic) gifts of the Holy Spirit on Cornelius and his household even before their sacramental Baptism. Peter's concluding question was unanswerable, "If God was giving them the same gift he gave us when we first believed in the Lord Jesus Christ, who was I to interfere with him?" (Ac 11:17). "When they heard this they stopped objecting, and instead began to glorify God in these words: 'If this be so, then God has granted life-giving repentance even to the Gentiles!' " (Ac 11:18).

Now, *dedicated Jews* of the first century A.D. were heirs to thirteen centuries of conviction that they were God's uniquely Chosen People and proud possessors of the "adoption, the glory, the covenants, the lawgiving, the worship, . . . the promises, . . . the patriarchs, and . . . the Messiah" (Rm 9:4-5) as well as the Sacred Scriptures (the Old Testament), which had spoken over and over again about Israel's being a sign and instrument whereby the Gentiles would some day come to the worship of Yahweh. They might indeed, by the grace of God, come to accept Jesus as their long-promised Messiah, and even rejoice at the entry of Gentiles into the "New Israel," the Church, but (apart from this "exceptional" case of the "religious and God-fearing" Cornelius and his household in Ac 10:1), they would find it extremely difficult to reconcile themselves to the conversion of the Gentiles except through the *medium of Judaism.* Thus, when *Paul and Barnabas* returned to Antioch after their first and highly successful mission, during which many Gentiles had embraced the Christian faith, "some men came down to Antioch from Judea and began to teach the brothers, 'Unless you are circumcised according to Mosaic practice, you cannot be saved' " (Ac 15:1).

To appreciate what Paul and Barnabas were up against, a brief explanation about the *Jewish* and, in some cases, *Jewish-Christian theology of justification and salvation* may be helpful. As we discussed earlier in Chapters One and Four, Yahweh had called the Israelites (later called Jews, after the tribe of Judah and the land of Judea) out of Egypt and entered into a special *relationship* with them by means of the Mosaic Covenant at Mt. Sinai, the conditions of which were the Ten Commandments, to which were added then and especially later many other precepts of law to ensure the keeping of the Commandments and therefore the Covenant. Unfortunately, due to the characteristics of human nature, *the Law* itself had, in the course of time, taken precedence over the Covenant, so much so that, according to Rabbinical writings, it was held that *even Abraham,* who lived some four hundred years before the Sinai event, was justified only by his fidelity to the Mosaic Law, which was revealed to him in advance![1] In keeping with this overemphasis on the works of the Law, it is interesting to compare *two vineyard parables*: one, a rabbinical parable in which, among all the workers of the world, Israel alone deserves a salary because she alone has really worked;[2] the other, the parable of Jesus (Mt 20:1-6), in which the Gentiles, called at the eleventh hour (late afternoon), receive the same salary as the Jews, called much earlier, because of the merciful, gratuitous goodness of the Master of the Vineyard.

Even when, at the so-called *"Council of Jerusalem"* under the leadership of St. Peter, the head of the Church at large, and St. James, the head of the Mother-Church at Jerusalem and of the Jewish Christians generally, the decision went unanimously in favor of Paul and Barnabas, some of the Jewish Christians, mostly former Pharisees, absolutely refused to accept it and, for the remainder of Paul's life, continued to "hound" his footsteps, trying to win his Gentile converts over to the practice of the Mosaic Law. These *"Judaizers,"* as they came to be called, simply could not lay aside their former attachment to the Mosaic Law as *the* means of justification and salvation. *Paul* himself had been a Pharisee and, if anything, even more attached to the Law than they, but his personal encounter with the risen Christ en route to Damascus (Ac 9; Gal 1) had changed all that and, during his initial desert experience in Arabia (Gal 1:17) and his subsequent extended wait at his home in Tarsus (Ac 9:30; 11:25-26), he had taken the opportunity to completely rethink the entire Old Testament in the light of Christ and had come to realize that, throughout Salvation History, justification (and salvation) came, not through the works of the Law, but through faith in God and his Messiah, Jesus. Sooner or later, Paul would have to deal with the Judaizers, not so much in direct argumentation with them (which was largely fruitless, and which they tended to avoid anyway), but with those of his converts whom the Judaizers were attempting to win over to the Mosaic Law.

This is exactly what happened in the case of a people known as the *Galatians*. These were a pagan people, related to the Gauls but living in that area of Asia Minor which is now centered around the modern Turkish capitol of Ankara. According to Luke's account in Acts, Paul seems to have evangelized them on his second missionary journey (Ac 16:6) before heading West to Troas and the principal cities of Greece (Ac 16:7-18:22).[3] Later, after again visiting the Galatians on the third missionary journey (Ac 18:23), Paul and his companions spent quite some time in Ephesus and its surroundings, one of the four great centers of the ancient world. During this period,

Paul was preoccupied, not only with the evangelization of Ephesus, but also with the deteriorating conditions of the Church in Corinth, so much so that he wrote no fewer than four letters, probably three from Ephesus and the fourth from Philippi. (Of these, we may have only the second and fourth, our 1 and 2 Corinthians, though it is quite possible that all the parts of the other two letters are contained in 2 Corinthians.) Either while in Ephesus or Philippi, or possibly even Corinth,[4] Paul seems to have learned of the *inroads of the Judaizers* among his Galatian converts. He was so upset and even angry that he quickly fired off a letter to the Church of Galatia. And what a letter! If the final chapters of 2 Corinthians (2 Cor 10-13, possibly the letter written "in great sorrow and anguish, with copious tears," 2 Cor 2:4) are deeply revealing and moving, what can we say about Galatians?

In this *hard-hitting polemic,* Paul "lays down a verbal barrage" which must have scorched the eyes and ears of his readers and listeners. So upset is he with his wayward Galatians that, instead of the thanksgiving, which he (after the manner of contemporary letter-writing) rarely omits, Paul immediately vents his emotions,

> I am *amazed* that you are so soon deserting him [God] who called you in accord with his gracious design in Christ, and are going over to another *"gospel."* But there is no other! . . . For even if we, or an angel from heaven, should preach to you a gospel not in accord with the one we delivered to you, let a *curse* be upon him! (Gal 1:6-8).

Then, after recounting his conversion and apostolic call by Christ himself and his prior scrape with the Judaizers at Antioch, when he even had to confront Peter, the head of the Church, for failing to live up to his own convictions by practicing "de facto segregation" against the Gentile converts in order to placate the Jewish Christians, Paul then proceeds to lay out, as calmly as he can under the circumstances, his theology of *justification by faith* in Christ rather than by the works of the Law,

We are *Jews* by birth, . . . Nevertheless, knowing that a man is not justified by legal observance but by *faith in Jesus Christ,* we too have believed in him in order to be justified by faith in Christ, not by observance of the law; for by works of the law no one will be justified. . . . It was through the law that I died to the law, to live for God. I have been crucified with Christ, and the life I live now is not my own; Christ is living in me. I still live my human life, but it is a *life of faith* in the Son of God, who loved me and gave himself for me. I will not treat God's gracious gift as pointless. If justice is available through the law, then Christ died to no purpose! (Gal 2:15-16, 19-21).

Then Paul lays down his "biblical barrage," featuring the example of *Abraham* himself, the father of the Jewish faith,

Consider the case of Abraham: he *"believed* God, and it was *credited* to him as *justice"* [Gn 15:6]. This means that those who believe are sons of Abraham. Because Scripture saw in advance that God's way of justifying the Gentiles would be through faith, it foretold this good news to Abraham: "All nations shall be blessed in you" [Gn 12:3]. Thus it is that all who believe are blessed along with Abraham, the man of faith (Gal 3:6-9).

The Letter to the Galatians contains much more, of course, but this is a good place to leave it for the time being. After sending this powerful letter, either from Philippi or Corinth, Paul apparently takes some more time to think his whole theology through, particularly with a view to sharing it with others in an organized fashion. This he does, when he takes the opportunity of a possible visit to *Rome,* to introduce himself to them by sharing his "Theology of Justification and Salvation." Writing almost certainly from Corinth, he draws up his doctrine and his argumentation in an exquisitely organized structure, which it would take us beyond our scope to explain. Gone is the Galatian polemic! In its stead is the careful development and expression of a truly great theologian. Nevertheless, Paul does use some of the same ideas and arguments with which he has bombarded the Galatians, and foremost of these, perhaps, is the biblical example of Abraham,

> What, then, shall we say of Abraham? Certainly if Abraham was justified by his deeds he has grounds for boasting, but not in God's view; for what does Scripture say? "Abraham *believed* God, and it was *credited* to him as *justice*" [Gn 15:6]. Now, when a man works, his wages are not regarded as a favor but as his due. But when a man does nothing, yet believes in him who justifies the sinful, his faith is credited as justice (Rm 4:1-5).

Over fourteen centuries later, it was this very text from Genesis 15:6 about Abraham's justification through faith that struck an Augustinian monk named *Martin Luther* as his spiritual lifesaver. Without going deeply into the psychological and spiritual state of Luther's soul, suffice it to say that, by his own declaration, he was tormented with scrupulous fears of God, whom he envisioned (possibly by transference from his own father) as an exacting and disapproving taskmaster.[5] How could he ever please and satisfy this all-holy, all-demanding God? How could he ever be in a right and peaceful relationship with him? Ah! Here was the solution! If, like Abraham, he simply believed, then he would be *regarded* by God as just and righteous and holy, even if he was not! His faith would be "credited to him as justice." Thus did Martin Luther find his "freedom," and, through a combination of many factors: moral, religious, ecclesial, social, economic, and political, Luther's "discovery" led eventually to the fragmentation of Western Christendom. This is, admittedly, an oversimplification in the interest of time and space, but it will have to suffice for our purposes.

THE KEY TEXT:

Before examining the meaning of the key text in Galatians and Romans which, as we have seen, is crucial both to Paul's argumentation against the Judaizers and to Luther's theology of justification and salvation, a few preliminary *clarifications* will be helpful:

(1) There is a *distinction between justification and salvation.* Strictly speaking, justification refers to entrance into a right relationship with God, what we Catholics would call entry into the state of sanctifying grace. Salvation refers to perseverance in that state of grace, that right relationship with God, even to death. Thus, Paul says in Romans 5:1-2, 9-10,

> Now that we have been *justified by faith,* we are at peace with God through our Lord Jesus Christ. Through him we have gained access by faith to the grace in which we now stand, and we boast of our hope for the glory of God. . . . Now that we have been justified by his blood, it is all the more certain that *we shall be saved* by him from [God's] wrath. For if, when we were God's enemies, we were reconciled to him by the death of his Son, it is all the more certain that we who have been reconciled will be saved by his life.

This is a crucial distinction for, while Paul rightly insists on the uselessness of our merely human works for achieving the state of grace or justification (that is, God's gratuitous sharing of his own life with us, 2 P 1:4), he also insists just as much on the necessity and merit of *'graced works'* for salvation. This is clear even in Galatians and Romans, e.g. Galatians 5:6, 21 and Romans 2:5-11, not to mention Matthew 25, James 2:26, and many other places. A careful reading of the Scriptures, both Old and New Testaments, will confirm this, despite the fact that, on occasion, both Paul and James do seem to use the terms *justification* and *salvation* synonymously, e.g. Ephesians 2:5 and James 2:24.

(2) Note also that, while Paul is more immediately talking about the works of the Mosaic Law as being useless for justification, what he has to say is actually *applicable to all law,* for the simple reason that law is an external directive which can in no way change a person but only point out his obligations. Only grace, accepted through faith,

can change a person inwardly and, for that matter, enable him to truly observe the law, whatever that may be. This, of course, does not constitute a condemnation of law as such, for law is unfortunately necessary. If we were all perfect, we would need no law, for we would do the right thing of ourselves; but we are not perfect and therefore, not only do we need the directives and restrictions of law for right conduct and good order but, above all, we need laws for the protection of the innocent.

(3) Finally, it is rather basic to Paul's argument that Abraham's faith and justification are recounted in the *15th chapter of Genesis,* before any covenant (Ch 17) and before his selfless act of fidelity and obedience in offering to sacrifice Isaac, his "son of the promise" (Ch 22).

Now, let us carefully examine the meaning of our text, "Abraham *believed* God and it was *credited* to him as *justice*" (Gn 15:6). And, since Paul was quoting from the Septuagint (Greek) translation of the original Hebrew, we shall have to see what the italicized words signify in those two languages.

Believed (Hebrew *he'emin,* Greek *episteusen*): Traditional Judaism translates the Hebrew word as "was faithful" and indeed that is the meaning of the basic verb *aman,* but here we have the Hiphil or Causative form *he'emin,* which almost invariably means *believed,* as does the Greek translation *episteusen,* with the added connotation of trust and hope. Interestingly, however, the Greek has Abram (sic) *believe God,* while the Hebrew has him *believe in God* (literally *in Yahweh*). To my mind, the distinction mirrors the intellectual tendency of the Greeks and the holistic tendency of the Jews. At any rate, both the immediate and remote contexts clearly indicate that what is meant here is neither fidelity as such nor a purely intellectual belief. The full, rich meaning of the expression is clearly indicated in the following quotations from Kittel's prestigious *Theological Dictionary of the New Testament*:

The *"Hiphil"* finds an analogous use as an expression for man's relation to God. . . . The *mutual relation between God and man* is of the very essence of faith. . . . It can come to embrace the total relation between God and man. . . . It denotes a relation to God which embraces the whole person in the totality of his external conduct and inner life. . . . (Theodore Weiser).[6]

In the *New Testament*, faith is the act in virtue of which a person, responding to God's eschatological deed in Christ, comes out of the world and makes a *radical reorientation to God*. It is the act in which the new eschatological existence of Christians is established, the attitude which is proper to this existence. As this attitude which constitutes existence, *pistis* governs the whole of life . . . *pistis* is man's *absolute committal to God*. . . . It is the radical decision of the will in which man delivers himself up . . . a surrender of one's own power, of the righteousness achieved in one's own strength. (Rudolph Bultmann)[7]

With this assessment of the meaning of faith in Genesis 15:6 (and usually elsewhere), Catholic Scripture scholars are in general agreement with their Protestant colleagues, in distinction from the so-called "traditional" Catholic understanding of faith as the acceptance of a certain body of truths. *Juan Alfaro, O.S.B.,* writing on the *Motive of Faith* in Karl Rahner's *Encyclopedia of Theology*, attests to this,

In the act of faith man enters into a *personal relationship* with the God who speaks to him. This is the kernel of faith, which is therefore essentially religious. When submitting to the divine word and confiding himself to it, *man gives himself to God*, who communicates himself to him and reveals himself and draws him to himself by an inward illumination.[8]

Credited (Hebrew *yah'she'beah*, Greek *elogisthe*): Here the Hebrew and Greek carry roughly the same meaning, which is that of a juridical or *forensic declaration* which, however, presupposes an *internal reality* and not just a legal attribution in Luther's sense. In other words, God credits justice or righteousness to a person because he has rendered that person just or righteous. And this is clearly confirmed by *F.W. Beare,* writing on *Romans* in the *Interpreter's Dictionary of the Bible,*

> The usual sense of the verb in Greek is to "declare righteous" or "pronounce *not guilty*" — the verdict of the judge, the antithesis of "find guilty," or "condemn." This is the *"forensic" interpretation* of the word, which has been all but unanimously upheld by Protestant theologians from Luther down. Despite this weight of authority, this interpretation is far from satisfactory here. It leaves us with the *monstrous notion,* which is not adequately defended by resort to the magic word "paradox," that "God pronounces men righteous" who are in fact guilty of sinning against him! It would be easier to defend the rendering "make righteous" (Goodspeed), which has at least the sanction of practically all pre-Reformation interpreters; indeed, if God's word does not go forth void, his pronouncement itself makes a man righteous; he speaks, and it is done. *Justification is not to be regarded as a legal fiction.* But in this context, the meaning of "justified" is substantially *"forgiven,"* with the addition of the positive factor that man is brought into a *right relationship with God.*[9]

To such a clear statement, let me only add that, not only is this "crediting of justice" not a legal fiction; it is also *not a legal action,* in the sense of rewarding someone for his work, because faith is certainly not considered as a work itself. It is rather the denial of any prior work or merit on the part of the one who believes.

Justice (Hebrew *se'daqah,* Greek *dikaiosúnē*): The Hebrew term signifies moral rectitude or, more precisely, *innocence,* especially the holiness and goodness of God which is imparted to and reflected in humans. Isaiah, for example, was the prophet of God's *se'daqah* and demanded Israel's *se'daqah* in response to him. Generally, in the Old Testament, this justice or innocence was attested to by a *moral or legal judgment* (Hebrew *mishpat*), but *never in a fictitious sense.* The Greek term, based on the noun *dike* (judgment) contains the Hebrew idea of justice or innocence attested to by moral or legal judgment, but as used by *Paul* (and as the word was used generally), it was not a legal fiction. Rather, in Paul, it is the very justice or *holiness of the Risen Christ* which is imparted to us through faith and Baptism, with the result that we are able to do the works of God, the works of Christ, who works in and through us. Hence, our works, done in a state of justice or righteousness, are meritorious of Eternal Life, not because they are our works but because they are *Christ's works in us*. Being the God-Man, his works are per se deserving of reward (*misthós*).

CONCLUSION:

From the foregoing, it should be evident that neither the Jewish idea of justification through works (especially the works of the Mosaic Law) nor the so-called classical Protestant idea of justice or righteousness legally or fictitiously attributed to sinful humans (who remain in their sins) is to be found in this famous text, which is at the heart of Paul's idea of justification by faith. By the same token, as we have seen abundantly, the "traditional" Catholic idea of faith as an intellectual assent to a body of truths, also falls short of the true meaning.

In addition, Martin Luther's term *"extrinsic justification"* in his *Lectures on Romans*[10] can and should be understood, not as justice fictitiously attributed to us, but as justice which we can in no way develop within ourselves and from ourselves but only from God. In this sense, his "extrinsic justification" is perfectly orthodox, signifying our justice from God, while his *"intrinsic justification"* refers (in his thinking) to the self-glorification whereby a person may think that he can be justified and holy by himself instead of from God. If Catholics and Protestants alike would come to grips with the semantics involved in this thorny question, it would be immediately evident, I do believe, that this "sword of division" has in fact already been sheathed.

Finally, the lesson in all this for our Spiritual Life should be clear, for it is a lesson of our nothingness of ourselves and God's everlasting goodness to us. In no way can we of ourselves merit his grace, his holiness; but he confers it on us freely and lovingly if only we commit ourselves to him by the gift and surrender of ourselves through faith in his Son, our Lord Jesus Christ. Then, the virtues of Christ become our virtues, his works become our works, his holiness becomes our holiness, for he is "our wisdom, our justice, our sanctification, and our redemption!" (1 Cor 1:30). "To him be glory for ever and ever! Amen" (Gal 1:5, WD).

FOOTNOTES

Introduction

1. Austin Flannery, ed., *Vatican Council II: The Conciliar and Post Conciliar Documents* (Collegeville, MN: Liturgical Press, 1975), pp. 1-37.
2. Ibid., pp. 283-292.
3. Ibid., pp. 903-1001.
4. Walter Abbott, ed., *The Documents of Vatican II* (New York: America Press, 1966), Appendix: Convocation Address, p. 709.
5. St. Augustine, *The Confessions of St. Augustine*, trans. F.J. Sheed (New York: Sheed and Ward, 1943), bk. 1, ch. 1, p. 3.
6. Austin Flannery, ed., *Vatican Council II*, pp. 750-765.
7. Ibid., p. 764.
8. Ibid., p. 762.
9. Ibid., p. 762.
10. Ibid., p. 765.
11. Warren Dicharry, *Greek Without Grief: An Outline Guide to New Testament Greek,* 4th rev. ed. (New Orleans, LA: Vincentian Evangelization, 1984).
12. John Milton, *The Complete Poems and Major Prose,* ed. Merritt Hughes (New York: Odyssey Press, 1957), Sonnet 19, p. 168.
13. Adolphe Tanquerey, *The Spiritual Life: A Treatise on Ascetical and Mystical Theology,* tr. Herman Braderis, 2nd. ed rev. (Tournai, Belgium: Desclee Company, 1952).
14. St. Ephrem, *Commentary on the Diatessaron,* tr. Armenian into Latin by Louis Leloir (Louvain, Belgium: Corp. Script. Christ. Orient., 1964), ch 1, par. 18, p. 9.; English translation in *Liturgy of the Hours* (New York: Catholic Book Publishing Co., 1975), vol. 3, p. 119.
15. St. Augustine, *The City of God,* tr. Marcus Dodds, int. Thomas Merton (New York: Modern Library, 1950), bk. 13, ch. 20, p. 431.
16. St. Jerome, "Homily on Ps. 1" in *The Homilies of St. Jerome,* tr. Sr. Marie Liguori Ewald, in The Fathers of the Church series, ed. R.J. Deferrari (Washington, DC: Catholic University Press, 1964), vol. 48, p. 9.
17. Walter Wink, *Transforming Bible Study: A Leader's Guide* (Nashville, TN: Abingdon Press, 1983); idem, *The Bible in Human Transformation: Toward a New Paradigm for Biblical Study* (Philadelphia, PA: Fortress Press, 1980).

Chapter One

1. John Godfrey Saxe, "The Blind Men and the Elephant," quoted in *Masterpieces of Religious Verse,* ed. J.D. Morrison (Grand Rapids, MI: Baker Book House, 1977), n. 1412, pp. 428-429.
2. Helen Keller, *The Story of My Life* (Garden City, NY: Doubleday and Co., 1954), part 3, suppl., p. 229.

3. Idem, in John Vitale, "Beauty is Everywhere," quoted in *Take Off Your Shoes*, ed. Mark Link (Niles, IL: Argus Communications, 1972), p. 100.

4. *Webster's Ninth New Collegiate Dictionary* (Springfield, MA: Merriam-Webster, Inc., 1984), p. 995.

5. John B. Noss, *Man's Religions* (New York: Macmillan Company, 1974), p. 2.

6. Richard McBrien, *Catholicism* (Minneapolis, MN: Winston Press, 1980), vol. 2, p. 1058.

7. Geo. E. Mendenhall, "Covenant" in *The Interpreter's Dictionary of the Bible*, ed. Geo. A. Buttrick (Nashville, TN: Abingdon Press, 1962), pp. 714-720.

8. Walter Abbott, ed. *The Documents of Vatican II*, Appendix: Convocation Address, p. 709.

9. Norbert Schiffers, "Religion" in *Encyclopedia of Theology*, ed. Karl Rahner (New York: Seabury Press, 1975), p. 1357.

10. Pierre Teilhard de Chardin, *The Future of Man* (New York: Harper & Row, 1964), pp. 276-280; idem, *Science and Christ* (New York: Harper & Row, 1968), pp. 215-219; idem, *Activation of Energy* (New York: Harcourt Brace Jovanovich, 1971), pp. 213-381, passim.

11. Francis Thompson, "The Hound of Heaven" in *Collected Works of Francis Thompson*, ed. Wilfred Meynell (Westminster, MD: Newman Press, 1949), vol. 1, pp. 107-113.

12. Louis Bouyer, *Introduction to Spirituality*, tr. Mary P. Ryan (New York: Desclee Company, 1961), pp. 8-9.

13. F.X. Durrwell, *In the Redeeming Christ: Toward a Theology of Spirituality*, tr. Rosemary Sheed (New York: Sheed and Ward, 1963), ch. 3, p. 41.

14. Austin Flannery, ed., *Vatican Council II*, p. 764.

15. St. Ambrose, "Duties of the Clergy" in *Some of the Principal Works of St. Ambrose*, tr. H. De Romestin, in The Nicene and Post-Nicene Fathers, (2nd Series), ed. Schaff and Wace (Grand Rapids, MI: Wm. B. Eerdmans Publishing Co., 1969), bk. 1, ch. 20, par. 88, p. 16.

16. Zeno of Citium, quoted in Diogenes Laertius, *Lives of Eminent Philosophers*, tr. R.D. Hicks, in the Loeb Classical Library series (Cambridge, MA: Harvard Univ. Press, 1950), vol. 2, p. 135.

17. William Shakespeare, "Hamlet, Prince of Denmark" in *The Complete Works of William Shakespeare* (New York: Avenel Books, 1975), act 1, scene 3, p. 1076.

18. Idem, "King Henry IV, Second Part," act 1, scene 2, p. 459.

19. *The Liturgy of the Hours*, tr. The International Commission on English in the Liturgy (New York: Catholic Book Publishing Co., 1975), vol. 1, p. 648 and parallels.

20. *The Sacramentary*, tr. The International Commission on English in the Liturgy (New York: Catholic Bk. Publishing Co., 1974), Mass for December 30, p. 52.

21. Thomas Merton, *Opening the Bible* (Collegeville, MN: Liturgical Press, 1970), pp. 8-9.

22. St. Jerome, "Commentaries on Isaiah" in *The Works of St. Jerome, Priest* in *Corpus Christianorum* (Turnhout, Belgium: Brepols, 1963), vol. 73, Prologue, par. 1, p. 1. (English translation in Flannery, ed., *Vatican Council II*, p. 764.)

23. Idem, "Commentary on Ecclesiastes" in *Works of St. Jerome*, in *Corp. Christ.*, vol. 72, On Eccles. 3:12-14, p. 278. (English translation in Durrwell, *In the Redeeming Christ*, p. 45.)

24. Flannery, ed. *Vatican Council II*, p. 762.

25. Ibid., p. 762.

Chapter Two

1. Plato, *The Dialogues of Plato*, tr. B. Jowett (New York: Random House, 1937), vol. 1, pp. 14-15.

2. Francis Quarles, "Hieroglyphics of the Life of Man," quoted in *The Home Book of Quotations*, ed. Burton Stevenson, 10th ed. (New York: Dodd, Mead, and Co., 1967), p. 1251.

3. Alexander Pope, "An Essay on Man" in *The Poems of Alexander Pope*, ed. John Butt (New Haven, CT: Yale Univ. Press, 1963), epistle 2, p. 516.

4. Hugh Wilgus Ramsaur, "Epitaph Found Somewhere in Space," cited in Morrison, ed., *Religious Verse*, no. 985, p. 311.

5. Blaise Pascal, *Pensées de Pascal: Sur la Vérité de la Religion Chrétienne*, ed. Jacques Chevalier, 2nd ed. rev. (Paris: Boivin et Cie., 1948), p. 278.

6. Plato, *The Dialogues of Plato*, vol. 1, pp. 15, 112, 235; vol. 2, pp. 383, 661, 757, 764, 768.

7. Jonathan Miller, *The Body in Question* (New York: Random House, 1978).

8. Gordon Rattray Taylor, *The Natural History of the Mind* (New York: E.P. Dutton, 1979).

9. Charles Panati, *Breakthroughs: Astonishing Advances in Your Lifetime in Medicine, Science, and Technology* (Boston, MA: Houghton Mifflin Co., 1980).

10. Paul Brand and Philip Yancey, *Fearfully and Wonderfully Made: A Surgeon Looks at the Human and Spiritual Body* (Grand Rapids, MI: Zondervan Publishing House, 1982).

11. Richard McBrien, *Catholicism*, vol. 2, 1091.

12. Jeremias Drexel, *The Heliotropium: Conformity of the Human Will to the Divine*, tr. and ed. Ferdinand Bogner (New York: Devin-Adair Co., 1912), passim.

13. William Shakespeare, "The Life and Death of King Richard the Third" in *The Complete Works of William Shakespeare*, act 1, scene 1, p. 627.

14. Ladislaus Boros, *Pain and Providence*, tr. Edward Quinn (Baltimore, MD: Helicon Press, 1966), pp. 45-47; idem, *Living in Hope: Future Perspectives in Christian Thought*, tr. W. O'Hara (New York: Herder & Herder, 1970), pp. 38-39; idem, *Christian Prayer*, tr. David Smith (New York: Seabury Press, 1976), pp. 53-54.

15. Pope Benedict XV, "The Encyclical Letter Spiritus Paraclitus: On the Fifteenth Centenary of the Death of St. Jerome" in *Rome and the Study of Scripture*, 7th ed. rev. & enlarged (St. Meinrad, IN: Grail Publications, 1962), pp. 43-79.

16. Pope Pius XII, "Encyclical Letter Divino Afflante Spiritu: On the Most Opportune Way to Promote Biblical Studies" in *Rome and the Study of Scripture*, pp. 80-107.

17. Austin Flannery, ed., *Vatican Council II*, "Dogmatic Constitution on Divine Revelation," pp. 750-765.

18. Daniel Day Williams, *The Spirit and the Forms of Love* (New York: Harper & Row, 1968), p. 135. Also found as "God and Man" in *Process Theology*, ed. Ewert H. Cousins (New York: Newman/Paulist Press, 1971), pp. 173-187.

19. Ibid., p. 138. (Cf. Cousins, ed. *Process Theology*, p. 183.)

20. Mark Link, ed., *Take Off Your Shoes*, p. 101.

21. St. Irenaeus, "Against Heresies" in *Patrologiae Cursus Completus*, ed. J.-P. Migne (Paris: Migne, 1857), vol. 7, part 1, bk. 4, ch. 20, par. 7, p. 1037. (English translation in the *Liturgy of the Hours*, vol. 3, p. 1499.)

22. William De Witt Hyde, "Creation's Lord, We Give Thee Thanks," quoted in Morrison, ed., *Religious Verse*, no. 966, p. 306.

Chapter Three

1. Thomas a Kempis, *Of the Imitation of Christ*, tr. Abbot Justin McCann (Westminster, MD: Newman Press, 1955), bk. 1, ch. 1, par. 3. (Note that, because of the variety of translations of this spiritual classic, I will refer to it as above, rather than by page number.)

2. Pope Leo XIII, "Encyclical Letter Providentissimus Deus: On the Study of Holy Scripture" in *Rome and the Study of Scripture*, par. 114, p. 17; Ibid., Pope Benedict XV, "Encyclical Letter Spiritus Paraclitus: On the Fifteenth Centenary of the Death of St. Jerome," par. 483, p. 66; "Dogmatic Constitution on Divine Revelation" in Flannery, ed., *Vatican Council II*, p. 764.

3. Phillis Trible, "God, Nature of, in the Old Testament," in *The Interpreter's Dictionary of the Bible*, Suppl., ed. Keith Crim (Nashville, TN: Abingdon Press, 1976), p. 368.

4. St. John Chrysostom, "Homily on the Epistle to the Romans, No. 32" in *All the Extant Works of John Chrysostom*, ed. Bernard de Montfaucon, 2nd ed. rev. & enl. (Paris: Gaume Freres, 1837), vol. 9, part 2, pp. 836-837. English translation in The Nicene and Post-Nicene Fathers (First Series), ed. Philip Schaff (New York: The Christian Literature Co., 1889), vol. 11, p. 563.

5. Robert Jastrow, *God and the Astronomers* (New York: W.W. Norton and Co., 1978), passim.

6. Ibid., p. 114.

7. Ibid., p. 115.

8. John Man, ed., *The Encyclopedia of Space Travel and Astronomy* (London: Octopus Books, Ltd., 1979), passim.

9. Richard Crashaw, "Hymn of the Nativity" in *The Complete Poetry of Richard Crashaw*, ed. George W. Williams (New York: New York University Press, 1972), p. 83.

10. Mark Link, "Love Does Such Things" in *He is the Still Point of the Turning World*, ed. Mark Link (Niles, IL: Argus Communications, 1971), p. 25.

11. Idem, "The Still Point" in Link, ed., *Still Point*, p. 9.

12. Raymond Brown, *Jesus God and Man: Modern Biblical Reflections* (New York: Macmillan Publishing Co., 1967), pp. 79-102; Jean Galot, *Who is Christ?: A Theology of the Incarnation* (Chicago: Franciscan Herald Press, 1981), part 5, pp. 319-404; Dermot Lane, *The Reality of Jesus: An Essay in Christology* (New York: Paulist Press, 1975), ch. 8, pp. 109-129; James Mackey, *Jesus the Man and the Myth: A Contemporary Christology* (New York: Paulist Press, 1979), pp. 159, 240-247; Karl Rahner, *Theological Investigations*, tr. K.-H. Kruger (New York: Seabury Press, 1966), vol. 5, pp. 193-215; Karl Rahner and Wilhelm Thuesing, *A New Christology* (New York: Seabury Press, 1980), pp. 143-159; Leopold Sabourin, *Christology: Basic Texts in Focus* (New York: Alba House, 1984), pp. 56, 59 and 101f; Edward Schillebeeckx, *Jesus: An Experiment in Christology* (New York: Seabury Press, 1979), pp. 652-669; Piet Schoonenberg, *The Christ: A Study of the God-Man Relationship in the Whole of Creation and in Jesus Christ* (New York: Herder and Herder, 1971), pp. 71-78, 127-135, 140-152; Bruce Vawter, *This Man Jesus: An Essay Toward a New Testament Christology* (Garden City, NY: Doubleday & Co. 1973), pp. 133-151.

13. Ernesto Cardenal, *The Gospel in Solentiname*, tr. Donald Walsh (Maryknoll, NY: Orbis Books, 1976), passim; Joseph Donders, *Jesus, the Way: Reflections on the Gospel of Luke* (Maryknoll, NY: Orbis Books, 1979), pp. 4-9, 55-59, etc.; John Linskens, *Christ, Liberator of the Poor: Secularity, Wealth, and Poverty in the Gospel of St. Luke* (San Antonio, TX: Mexican American Cultural Center, 1976); Juan Luis Segundo, *The Liberation of Theology* (Maryknoll, NY: Orbis Books, 1976), pp. 228-231.

14. Jn. Seldon Whale, cited in *A Treasury of Quotations on Christian Themes*, ed. Carroll E. Simcox (New York: Seabury Press, 1975), no. 1634, p. 136.

15. *The Sacramentary*, p. 459.

16. St. Thomas Aquinas, *Basic Writings of St. Thomas Aquinas*, ed. Anton C. Pegis (New York: Random House, 1945), vol. 1, q. 28-29, pp. 282-298.

17. Joachim Jeremias, *New Testament Theology* (New York: Charles Scribner's Sons, 1971), pp. 61-68.

Chapter Four

1. St. Thomas Aquinas, *Summa Theologica*, tr. English Dominicans (New York: Benziger Bros., 1947), vol. 1, part 1, quest. 6, ans. to obj. 1, p. 29.
2. Bernard E. Meland, *The Realities of Faith: The Revolution in Culture Forms* (New York: Oxford Univ. Press, 1962), p. 265.
3. W. Norman Pittenger, "Bernard E. Meland, Process Thought, and Significance of Christ" fr. *Religion in Life*, vol. 37 (1968), in Cousins, ed., *Process Theology*, pp. 205-206.
4. Jas. B. Pritchard, ed. *Ancient Near Eastern Texts Relating to the Old Testament* (Princeton, NJ: Princeton University Press, 1955), pp. 72-99.
5. Daniel Day Williams, *The Spirit and the Forms of Love* (New York: Harper & Row, 1968), t p. 136. (See "God and Man" in Cousins, ed., *Process Theology*, p. 180.)
6. Roland de Vaux, *Ancient Israel: Its Life and Institutions* (New York: McGraw-Hill Book Co., 1961), pp. 484-493.
7. Burton Bernstein, *Sinai: The Great and Terrible Wilderness* (New York: Viking Press, 1979), p. 153; J. Daumas, *La Péninsule du Sinái* (Cairo: Imprimerie Grunberg, 1951), p. 261.
8. Ibid., Bernstein, *Sinái*, p. 153; Daumas, *La Péninsule*, p. 77.
9. Geo. E. Mendenhall, "Covenant" in *The Interpreter's Dictionary of the Bible*, ed. Geo. A. Buttrick (Nashville, TN: Abingdon Press, 1962), pp. 714-720; Dennis J. McCarthy, *Old Testament Covenant: A Survey of Current Opinions* (Richmond, VA: John Knox Press, 1972), pp. 11-15.
10. Roland de Vaux, *Ancient Israel*, pp. 493-495.
11. Dietrich Bonhoeffer, *The Cost of Discipleship* (New York: The Macmillan Co., 1964), p. 53.
12. Gerard Manley Hopkins, "St. Thomae Aquinatis Rhythmus ad SS. Sacramentum" in *Poems of Gerard Manley Hopkins*, ed. Gardner & MacKenzie, 4th. ed. (London: Oxford Univ. Press 1967), p. 211.
13. Idem, "God's Grandeur" in Gardner & MacKenzie, ed., *Poems of Gerard Manley Hopkins*, p. 66.
14. Pierre Teilhard de Chardin, *Science and Christ*, pp. 168, 170. (Cf. Christopher Mooney, "Teilhard de Chardin and Christian Spirituality" in Cousins, ed. *Process Theology*, p. 316.)
15. Max Ehrman, *Desiderata: Found in Old St. Paul's Church, Baltimore;* Dated 1692 (Boston: Crescendo Publishing Co., 1954).
16. Pierre Teilhard de Chardin, *The Divine Milieu*, Torchback Edition, rev. (New York: Harper & Row, 1968), p. 66.
17. Elizabeth Barrett Browning, "Aurora Leigh" in *The Complete Poetical Works of Mrs. Browning* (Boston: Houghton Mifflin Co., 1900), bk. 7, 1. 821, p. 371.
18. Francis Thompson, "The Hound of Heaven" in Wilfrid Meynell, ed., *Collected Works of Francis Thompson*, vol. 1, p. 108.
19. St. Augustine, *The Confessions*, bk. 8, ch. 12, pp. 178-179.
20. Francis Thompson, *Saint Ignatius Loyola*, ed. John H. Pollen (Baltimore, MD: The Carroll Press, 1951), ch. 1, pp. 24-25.
21. St. Augustine, *The Confessions*, bk. 10, ch. 27, p. 236.

22. Joseph Mary Plunkett, "I See His Blood Upon the Rose," quoted in Morrison, ed., *Religious Verse*, no. 633, p. 201.

Chapter Five

1. St. Augustine, *The Confessions*, bk. 8, ch. 7, p. 170.
2. A.J. Langguth, "Jesus Christs," quoted in Link, *Still Point*, p. 50.
3. Richard S. Emrich, cited in *Living Quotations for Christians*, ed. Wirt and Beckstrom (New York: Harper & Row, 1974), no. 950, p. 72.
4. Joseph Cardinal Bernardin, quoted in Geo. W. Cornell, "Seldom Mentioned 'Sin' is Harsh Fact for Synod," *Associated Press* Article in *Rocky Mountain News*, Denver, CO., Saturday, Sept. 24, 1983.
5. Karl Menninger, *Whatever Became of Sin?* (New York: Hawthorn Books, 1973).
6. James P. Mackey, "New Thinking on Original Sin," Pierre Smulders, "Evolution and Original Sin," Piet Schoonenberg, "Original Sin and Man's Situation," Marcel Van Caster, "A Catechesis on Original Sin," all in *The Mystery of Sin and Forgiveness*, ed. Michael Taylor (Staten Island, NY: Alba House, 1971), part 3, pp. 215-277.
7. Jas. B. Pritchard, ed., *Ancient Near Eastern Texts*, p. 72-99.
8. W. Stewart McCullough, "Serpent" in Buttrick, ed., *The Interpreter's Dictionary of the Bible*, vol. 4, p. 290.
9. Gottfried Quell, *"hamartáno, hamártema, hamartía"* in *Theological Dictionary of the New Testament*, ed. Gerhard Kittel, tr. and ed. Geoffrey W. Bromiley (Grand Rapids, MI: William B. Eerdmans Publishing Co., 1964), vol. 1, pp. 267-268.
10. Ibid., pp. 270-271.
11. St. John Chrysostom, "Homily to the People of Antioch, No. 5" in de Montfaucon, ed., *Extant Works of St. John Chrysostom*, vol. 2, part 1, p. 71.
12. C.T. Onions, ed. *The Oxford Universal Dictionary on Historical Principles*, 3rd ed. rev. & enl. (Oxford: Clarendon Press, 1955), p. 117.
13. James F. Strange, "Crucifixion, Method of" in Crim, ed., *The Interpreter's Dictionary of the Bible, Suppl.*, pp. 199-200; J.B. Torrance, "Cross, Crucifixion" in *The Illustrated Bible Dictionary*, ed. J.D. Douglas (Wheaton IL: Tyndale House Publishers, 1980), vol. 1, pp. 342-344.
14. Pierre Barbet, *A Doctor at Calvary*, tr. The Earl of Wicklow (New York: P.J. Kenedy & Sons, 1953); John Walsh, *The Shroud* (New York: Macmillan Publishing Co., 1977); Ian Wilson, *The Shroud of Turin: The Burial Cloth of Jesus Christ?*, rev. ed. (Garden City, NY: Doubleday & Co., 1979); Kenneth Stevenson and Gary Habermas, *Verdict on the Shroud: Evidence for the Death and Resurrection of Jesus Christ* (Ann Arbor, MI: Servant Books, 1981).
15. Gerhard Kittel, "Die Religionsgeschichte und das Urchristentum" (1932), quoted in Walter Grundmann, "Sin in the N.T." in Kittel, ed., *Theo. Dictionary of the N.T.*, vol. 1, p. 316.
16. Leslie D. Weatherhead, *Psychology, Religion, and Healing*, revised edition (Nashville, TN: Abingdon Press, 1952), p. 19.
17. *The Sacramentary*, p. 184.
18. F.X. Durrwell, *The Resurrection: A Biblical Study*, tr. Rosemary Sheed (New York: Sheed and Ward, 1960), p. 35 ff.
19. Daniel Day Williams, "God and Man," from *The Spirit and the Forms of Love*, in Cousins, ed., *Process Theology*, p. 179.
20. Oscar Wilde, "The Picture of Dorian Gray" in *The Works of Oscar Wilde*, ed. John Gilbert (London: Spring Books, 1963), pp. 376-503.

21. Thomas a Kempis, *Of the Imitation of Christ*, bk. 1, ch. 24, par. 7.
22. St. Catherine of Siena, cited in Wirt and Beckstrom, *Living Quotations*, no. 1429, p. 105.
23. Georges Crespy, *From Science to Theology: An Essay on Teilhard de Chardin*, tr. George H. Shriver (Nashville, TN: Abingdon Press, 1968), p. 111.
24. Oscar Wilde, "The Picture of Dorian Gray" in Gilbert, ed., *The Works of Oscar Wilde*, ch. 2, p. 386.
25. Raymond E. Brown, *New Testament Essays* (Milwaukee, WI: Bruce Publishing Co., 1965), pp. 203-207.
26. Thomas a Kempis, *Of the Imitation of Christ*, bk. 1, ch. 13, par. 1.
27. Edwin Arlington Robinson, "Miniver Cheevy" in *Collected Poems of Edwin Arlington Robinson* (New York: The Macmillan Co., 1961), pp. 347-348.
28. Emmanuel Cardinal Suhard, *Priests Among Men* (Notre Dame, IN: Fides Publishers, 1960), p. 60. This ringing challenge, addressed here to priests, is certainly applicable to the whole body of Christians, especially Catholics.
29. Leon Bloy, *The Woman Who Was Poor: A Contemporary Novel of the French 'Eighties,'* tr. I.J. Collins (New York: Sheed and Ward, 1947), p. 356.
30. St. John of the Cross, *The Ascent of Mount Carmel*, tr. & ed. E. Allison Peers, 3rd ed. rev. (Garden City, NY: Doubleday & Co., 1958), bk. 1, ch. 11, pp. 145-146.
31. Stanislas Lyonnet, "Sin," tr. Robert C. O'Connor in *Dictionary of Biblical Theology*, ed. Xavier Leon-Dufour, 2nd ed. rev. & enl. (New York: Seabury Press, 1973), p. 550.

Chapter Six

1. Bergen Evans, ed., *Dictionary of Quotations* (New York: Avenel Books, 1978), no. 11, note, p. 727.
2. E.C. McKenzie, ed., *Mac's Giant Book of Quips and Quotes* (Grand Rapids, MI: Baker Book House, 1980), p. 534.
3. Alphonsus Rodriguez, *The Practice of Perfection and Christian Virtues*, tr. Jos. Rickaby (Chicago: Loyola U. Press, 1929).
4. William Wordsworth, "The Virgin" in *The Poems of Wm. Wordsworth*, ed. John Hayden (New Haven, CT: Yale U. Press, 1981), vol. 2, p. 474.
5. J.B. Boudignon, *St. Vincent de Paul: Model of Men of Action*, tr. P. Finney (St. Louis: Vincentian Press, 1925), p. 152.
6. Ibid., p. 155.
7. René Bazin, *Charles De Foucauld: Hermit and Explorer*, tr. P. Keelan (New York: Benziger Bros., 1923), p. 124.
8. St. Ignatius of Antioch, "To the Magnesians," in *The Apostolic Fathers*, ed. Ludwig Schopp, tr. Glimm, Marique, and Walsh (New York: Cima Publishing Co., 1947), par. 12, p. 100.
9. Richard Armstrong, ed., *Bits and Pieces: A Treasury of Christopher Quotes* (New York: The Christophers, no date), p. 13.
10. St. Thomas Aquinas, *Summa Theologica* (Cambridge, Eng.: Blackfriars, 1964), Pars I, Q. 1, Art. 8, ad 2, pp. 30-31.
11. Adrian van Kaam, *Personality Fulfillment in the Spiritual Life* (Wilkes-Barre, PA: Dimension Books, 1966), p. 17.
12. John Henry Cardinal Newman, "Development of Christian Doctrine," quoted in *Newman's Apologia: A Classic Reconsidered*, ed. Blehl and Connolly (New York: Harcourt, Brace, & World, 1964), p. 139.

13. Idem, *Apologia pro Vita Sua: History of my Religious Opinions* (New York: Longmans, Green, & Co., 1947), p. 5.
14. Richard Armstrong, ed. *Bits and Pieces*, p. 45.
15. Louis F. Hartman, "Sin in Paradise" in *The Catholic Biblical Quarterly* (Washington, DC: Catholic Biblical Ass'n.), vol. 20 (1958), pp. 26-40; John L. McKenzie, "The Fall" in *Dictionary of the Bible* (Milwaukee, WI: Bruce Publishing Co., 1965), pp. 270-271; Bruce Vawter, "Genesis" in *A New Catholic Commentary on Holy Scripture*, ed. Fuller, Johnston, and Kearns (London: Thomas Nelson & Sons, 1969), pp. 180-181.
16. William Wordsworth, "The Virgin" in Hayden, ed., *The Poems of William Wordsworth*, vol. 2, p. 474.
17. Richard Kugelman, "The First Letter to the Corinthians" in *The Jerome Biblical Commentary*, ed. Brown, Fitzmyer, and Murphy (Englewood Cliffs, NJ: Prentice-Hall, Inc., 1968), vol. 2 (New Testament), p. 254.
18. William Wordsworth, "The World is Too Much With Us" in Hayden, ed., *The Poems of Wm. Wordsworth*, vol. 1, p. 568.
19. Thomas a Kempis, *Of the Imitation of Christ*, bk. 1, ch. 1, par. 3.
20. Reinhold Niebuhr, quoted in Armstrong, ed., *Bits and Pieces*, p. 26.
21. Nathaniel Hawthorne, quoted in *Treasures of Inspiration*, ed. Mary Dawson Hughes (Kansas City, MO: Hallmark Cards, Inc. 1971), no page indication.

Chapter Seven

1. St. Ignatius of Antioch, "To the Ephesians" in Schopp, ed., *The Apostolic Fathers*, par. 14, p. 92.
2. St. Ambrose, "Enarratio in Ps. 40" in *Patrologiae Cursus Completus*, ed. J.-P. Migne (Paris: Vrayet de Surcy, 1845), vol. 14, par. 4, p. 1070.
3. Blaise Pascal, "The Memorial" in *The Essential Pascal*, tr. and ed. Robert E. Gleason (New York: New American Library, 1966), pp. 205-206.
4. I have been unable to verify this oft-quoted saying of Louis Pasteur, but two distinct and distinguished works certainly confirm the depth of the great scientist's humble faith, viz. Francis E. Benz, *Pasteur: Knight of the Laboratory* (New York: Dodd, Mead, & Co., 1938), p. 232; and Rene Dubos, *Louis Pasteur: Free Lance of Science* (Boston, MA: Little, Brown & Co., 1950), pp. 385-400.
5. Hugh of St. Victor, cited in Simcox, ed., *Treasury of Quotations*, no. 1068, p. 90.
6. *The Cloud of Unknowing*, tr. James Walsh (New York: Paulist Press, 1981).
7. Abbot John Chapman, "Spiritual Letters," cited in *The Book of Catholic Quotations*, ed. Jn. Chapin (New York: Farrar, Straus and Cudahy, 1956), p. 328.
8. St. Augustine, "Sermon No. 40," cited in Chapin, ed., *Catholic Quotations*, p. 328.
9. The First Vatican General Council, Third Session, "Dogmatic Constitution on the Catholic Faith" in *The Christian Faith*, ed. Neuner-Dupuis, rev. ed. (New York: Alba House, 1982), pp. 42-44.
10. Edward Carter, *Response in Christ: A Study of the Christian Life* (Dayton, OH: Pflaum Press, 1969), pp. 145-146.
11. St. Thomas Aquinas, "An Exposition of the Apostles' Creed" in *The Three Greatest Prayers*, tr. L. Shopcote (Westminster, MD: Newman Press, 1956), p. 39.
12. Kilian McDonnell, "Lutherans and Catholics on Justification" in *America Magazine* (New York: America Press), vol. 149, no. 18, Dec. 3, 1983, pp. 345-348, whose conclusion states:

Lutherans and Catholics in the dialogue have reached complete agreement on the principle behind justification (ultimate trust in God alone), a convergence on justification with the recognition that the remaining difficulties are not Church dividing. . .

13. John Henry Cardinal Newman, "The Pillar of Cloud" in *Newman: Prose and Poetry*, ed. Geoffrey Tillotson (Cambridge, MA: Harvard University Press, 1957), p. 807.

14. St. Cyril of Alexandria, "The Second Letter to Nestorius, Approved by the Council of Ephesus" in Neuner & Dupuis, ed. *The Christian Faith*, pp. 148, 201.

15. E.C. McKenzie, *Mac's Quips & Quotes*, p. 242.

16. Ibid., p. 242.

17. Emil Brunner, quoted in Wirt & Beckstrom, ed., *Living Quotations*, no. 1540, p. 114.

18. Viktor Frankl, *Man's Search for Meaning: An Introduction to Logotherapy*, tr. Ilse Lasch (New York: Washington Sq. Press, 1969), pp. 3-148.

19. Alexander Pope, "An Essay on Man" in Butt, ed., *The Poems of Alexander Pope*, ep. 1, p. 508.

20. Simone Weil, quoted in Simcox, ed., *A Treasury of Quotations*, no. 2143, p. 180.

21. Mitch Leigh and Joe Darion, "Man from La Mancha," quoted in *In the Stillness is the Dancing*, ed. Mark Link (Niles, IL: Argus Communications, 1972), p. 63.

22. Charles H. Spurgeon, cited in Wirt & Beckstrom, ed., *Living Quotations*, no. 3278, p. 246.

23. Frederick William Faber, *Spiritual Conferences* (Philadelphia, PA: The Peter Reilly Co., 1957), p. 241.

24. Alfred Wikenhauser, *Pauline Mysticism: Christ in the Mystical Theology of St. Paul*, tr. Joseph Cunningham (New York: Herder and Herder, 1960), pp. 71-72.

25. Simon & Garfunkel, "Bridge over Troubled Waters," in *Concert in Central Park* (New York: Record Plan Renote Truck, 1981).

26. Jean-Pierre de Caussade, *Abandonment to Divine Providence*, tr. John Beevers (Garden City, NY: Doubleday and Co., 1975), pp. 31, 81-82, 84-85.

27. Francis Thompson, "The Hound of Heaven" in Meynell, ed., *The Collected Works of Francis Thompson*, vol. 1, p. 107.

28. St. Teresa of Avila, "St. Teresa's Bookmark" in E. Allison Peers, *Mother of Carmel: A Portrait of St. Teresa of Jesus* (New York: Morehouse-Gorham Co., 1946), p. 196.

29. Gilbert Keith Chesterton, quoted in Link, ed., *Take Off Your Shoes*, p. 117.

30. Victor Hugo, quoted in Link, ed., *In the Stillness*, p. 64.

31. Francis Bourdillon, "Light and Love" quoted in Morrison, ed., *Religious Verse*, no. 1313, p. 403.

32. Harry S. Truman, "Season of Love," quoted in *The Treasure Chest*, ed. Charles L. Wallis (New York: Harper & Row, 1965), p. 169.

33. Barbara Jordan, quoted in Armstrong, ed., *Bits and Pieces*, p. 39.

34. Karl Menninger, cited in Wirt & Beckstrom, *Living Quotations*, no 1990, p. 148.

35. Ramon Lull, ibid., no. 1986, p. 148.

36. Ernesto Cardenal, *To Live is to Love: Meditations on Love and Spirituality*, tr. Kurt Reinhardt (Garden City, NY: Doubleday and Co., 1974), p. 40.

37. Thomas Merton, "Introduction" to Cardenal, ibid., p. 7.

38. Ibid., pp. 13-14.

39. Edward Carter, "Love is Forever" in *Everyday and Its Possibilities* (St. Meinrad, IN: Abbey Press, 1973), p. 1.

40. John Powell, *Unconditional Love* (Niles, IL: Argus Communications, 1978).

41. St. Bernard, *On the Love of God*, tr. Terence Connolly (Westminster, MD: Newman Press, 1951), p. 4.

42. J.B. Boudignon, *St. Vincent de Paul: Model of Men of Action*, pp. 332-365.

43. Lewis B. Smedes, *Love Within Limits: A Realist's View of lst Co. 13* (Grand Rapids, MI: Eerdmans Publishing Co., 1978).

44. Phyllis & David York and Ted Wachtel, *Tough Love: An Effective Program for Parents of Unruly Teenagers* (Garden City, NY: Doubleday, 1982).

45. Though I cannot identify this beautiful and practical saying, I can certainly recommend some sources of further reading and reflection on the important virtue of kindness, e.g.: Frederick William Faber, "Kindness" in *Spiritual Conferences*, I-IV, pp. 11-55; F.X. Lasance, *Kindness: The Bloom of Charity* (New York: Benziger Bros., 1938); Lawrence G. Lovasik, *Kindness* (New York: The Macmillan Co., 1963).

46. St. John of the Cross, "Sayings of Light and Love" in *The Collected Works of St. John of the Cross*, tr. Kavanaugh and Rodriguez (Wash., DC: ICS Publ., 1973), no. 57, p. 672.

47. Henri de Montherlant, cited in Simcox, ed., *Treasury of Quotations*, no 2300, p. 190.

48. Thomas a Kempis, *On the Imitation of Christ*, bk. 3, ch. 5, par. 3-4.

49. Teilhard de Chardin, cited in Link, ed., *Take Off Your Shoes*. p. 116.

50. Dom Bede Griffiths, "The Golden String," cited in Chapin, ed., *Catholic Quotations*, p.565.

51. Mitch Leigh and Joe Darion, "Man from La Mancha," quoted in Link, ed., *The Still Point*, p. 62.

52. Reinhold Niebuhr, cited in Link, ed., *Stillness*, p. 62.

Chapter Eight

1. *Webster's Ninth New Collegiate Dictionary*, p. 355.

2. St. Bernard of Clairvaux, *On the Love of God*, p. 4.

3. Thomas a Kempis, *Of the Imitation of Christ*, bk. 3, ch. 5, par. 4.

4. Idem, *Of the Imitation of Christ*, bk. 3, ch. 5, par. 5-6.

5. Mark Link, "Why Pray?" in Link, ed., *Still Point*, p. 68.

6. St. John of the Cross, "Sayings of Light and Love" in *The Collected Works of St. John of the Cross*, no. 57, p. 672.

7. St. Augustine, quoted in *Voice of the Saints*, ed. Francis W. Johnston (Springfield, IL: Templegate, 1965), p. 35.

8. Bl. Robert Southwell, "Ensamples of Our Saviour" in "Verses Prefixed to Short Rules of Good Life" in *The Book of Robert Southwell*, ed. C.M. Hood (Oxford: Blackwell, 1926), p. 157.

9. St. Vincent de Paul, cited in Abbe Maynard, *Virtues and Spiritual Doctrine of St. Vincent de Paul*, tr. and rev. Carlton Prindeville (St. Louis, MO: Vincentian Foreign Mission Press, 1961), p. 39.

10. St. John Eudes, quoted in Johnston, ed., *Voice of the Saints*, p. 35.

11. Peter Taylor Forsyth, cited in Simcox, ed., *Treasury of Quotations*, no. 256, p. 27.

12. Joachim Jeremias, *The Prayers of Jesus*, tr. various scholars (Naperville, IL: Alec R. Allenson, 1967), pp. 29-57; Idem, *New Testament Theology: The Proclamation of Jesus*, tr. John Bowden (New York: Charles Scribner's Sons, 1971), pp. 36-37.

13. Kahlil Gibran, "Jesus, the Son of God," quoted in Link, ed., *Still Point*, p. 25.

14. Robert Hugh Benson, "Bands of Love," quoted in Chapin, ed., *Catholic Quotations*, p. 720.

15. Clement of Alexandria, "Stromateis," cited in Chapin, ed., *Catholic Quotations*, no. 7, p. 715.

16. Sts. Gregory of Nyssa, Augustine, and Jerome, quoted in K.J. Healy, "The Theology of Prayer," in the *New Catholic Encyclopedia*, ed. The Catholic University of America (New York: McGraw-Hill Book Co., 1967), vol. 11, p. 671.

17. St. John Climacus, ibid. See the extensive material on prayer by this great Desert Father in St. John Climacus, "On Prayer" in *The Ladder of Divine Ascent* (New York: Paulist Press, 1982), pp. 274-281.

18. St. Teresa of Avila, *Autobiography*, tr. and ed. E. Allison Peers (Garden City, NY: Doubleday, 1960), ch. 8, p. 110.

19. St. Francis de Sales, "Treatise on the Love of God," quoted in Chapin, ed., *Catholic Quotations*, ch. 6, p. 719.

20. St. Vincent de Paul, cited in Maynard, *Virtues and Spiritual Doctrine*, p. 41.

21. St. Elizabeth Seton, quoted in Johnston, ed., *Voice of The Saints*, p. 37.

22. Alfred Lord Tennyson, "Idylls of the King: the Passing of Arthur" (Morte d'Arthur) in *The Poems and Plays of Alfred Lord Tennyson* (New York: Random House, 1938), p. 131.

23. Mohandas K. (Mahatma) Gandhi, cited in Simcox, ed., *Treasury of Quotations on Christian Themes*, no. 258, p. 27.

24. Wm. Culbertson, cited in Wirt & Beckstrom, ed., *Living Quotations*, no. 2422, p. 178.

25. Anonymous Prayer (found on a dead Confederate soldier?) cited in Simcox, ed., *Treasury of Quotes*, no. 261, pp. 27-28.

26. George Maloney, *The Breath of the Mystic* (Denville, NJ: Dimension Books, 1974), p. 49.

27. St. Ambrose, "De Officiis Ministrorum," cited in "The Constitution on Divine Revelation" in Flannery, ed. *Vatican Council II*, ch. 6, p. 764.

28. St. Jane Frances de Chantal, cited in Johnston, ed., *Voice of the Saints*, pp. 40-41.

29. St. Anthony of the Desert, cited in Chapin, ed., *Catholic Quotations*, p. 716.

30. Louis Bouyer, *Introduction to Spirituality*, tr. Mary Perkins Ryan (New York: Desclee Co., 1961), pp. 52-55.

31. Ibid., pp. 84-85.

32. Giacomo Cardinal Lercaro, *Methods of Mental Prayer*, tr. T.F. Lindsay (Westminster, MD: Newman Press, 1957).

33. George Maloney, *The Breath of the Mystic*, p. 38.

34. Louis Bouyer, *The Spirituality of the New Testament and the Fathers*, tr. Mary P. Ryan (New York: Seabury Press, 1963), pp. 380-384, 412-421.

35. St. John of the Cross, "The Dark Night, Book One: The Night of the Senses" in *The Collected Works*, ch. 10, p. 318.

36. W.F. Dicharry, "Charism in the Bible" in the *New Catholic Encyclopedia*, vol. 3, p. 460.

37. Mark Link, "With or Without Words" in Link, ed., *Still Point*, p. 71.

38. St. Teresa of Avila, *Autobiography*, ch. 22, pp. 208-219.

39. Louis Bouyer, *Introduction to Spirituality*, pp. 298-299.

40. Thomas Merton, "The Living Bread," cited in Chapin, ed., *Book of Catholic Quotations*, p. 629.

41. St. Irenaeus, quoted in Geo. Maloney, *The Breath of the Mystic*, p. 33.

42. Joseph Roux, *Meditations of a Parish Priest*, tr. I.F. Hapgood (New York: Thomas Y. Crowell & Co., 1886), p. 108.

43. Walter Savage Landor, "Imaginary Conversations: Lord Brooke and Sir Philip Sidney," cited in Stevenson, ed., *Home Book of Quotations*, p. 1871.

44. Eugene Ionesco, "Conversations," quoted in Link, ed., *In the Stillness*, p. 22.

45. This famous saying, generally attributed to St. Bernard, was certainly not original with him, for it was used by such ancients as Themistocles and Scipio Africanus, quoted in Burton Stevenson, ed., *Home Book of Quotations*, p. 1874.

46. Bl. Raymond of Capua, *The Life of Catherine of Siena*, tr. and ed. Conleth Kearns (Wilmington, DE: Michael Glazier, 1980), part 1, ch. 4, no. 49, pp. 46-47.

47. Thomas Merton, *New Seeds of Contemplation* (New York: New Directions Publishing Corp., 1972), pp. 52-53.

48. George Maloney, *The Breath of the Mystic*, p. 20.

49. Thomas a Kempis, *Of the Imitation of Christ*, bk. 1, ch. 20, par. 6.

50. St. John of the Cross, "Maxims and Counsels" in *The Collected Works*, no. 21, p. 675.

51. Menander, "Fragments," cited in Stevenson, ed., *Home Book of Quotations*, no. 818, p. 1822.

52. Wm. Penn, "Advice to His Children," cited in Stevenson, ed., *The Home Book of Quotations*, p. 1820.

53. Thomas Carlyle, *Sartor Resartus* (London: Macmillan & Company, Ltd., 1927), bk. 3, ch. 3, p. 186.

54. Alvin Toffler, *Future Shock* (New York: Random House, 1970), especially ch. 17, pp. 371-397.

55. Andrew Greeley, "The Critic," quoted in Link, ed., *Take Off Your Shoes*, p. 104.

56. Richard Card. Cushing, "Slow Me Down, Lord," quoted in Link, *In the Stillness*, p. 25.

57. Walt Whitman, "Song of Myself" in *Leaves of Grass*, ed. Bradley & Blodgett (New York: W.W. Norton, 1973), no. 48, p. 87.

58. Abraham Heschel, quoted in Link, ed., *Take Off Your Shoes*, p. 64.

59. Teilhard de Chardin, quoted in George Maloney, *The Breath of the Mystic*, p. 33.

60. Sr. Elizabeth of the Trinity, *Reminiscences*, tr. by a Benedictine of Stanbrook Abbey (Westminster, MD: Newman Press, 1952), Ch. 12, 109-118, Appendix I, pp. 210-211.

61. *The Sacramentary*, pp. 765-767.

62. St. Vincent de Paul, cited in Maynard, *Virtues and Spiritual Doctrine of St. Vincent de Paul*, p. 126. As always, St. Vincent was simply following the example of Jesus himself, when he immediately allowed his prayer to be interrupted in order to continue his ministry to others (Mk 1:35-39).

63. Thomas Merton, *New Seeds of Contemplation*, p. 216.

64. St. Vincent de Paul, quoted in *Thoughts from St. Vincent de Paul*, tr. & ed. Joseph Leonard (New York: Edw. O'Toole Co., 1935). The full statement is, "The practice of the presence of God is an excellent one, but I think that the practice of doing His holy Will in all things is even more so."

65. Robert Hugh Benson, *The Friendship of Christ* (London: Longmans, Green, and Co., 1914), pp. 55-56.

66. This wise saying, attributed to St. Bernard and other Saints, has more recently been adopted by some psychiatrists and psychologists in this form, "Whoever tries to be his own therapist has a fool for a therapist!"

67. Adrian van Kaam, *The Dynamics of Spiritual Self-Direction* (Denville, NJ: Dimension Books, 1976).

68. Robert Hugh Benson, *The Friendship of Christ*, pp. 40-41, etc.

69. Ira Progoff, *At a Journal Workshop: The Basic Text and Guide for Using the Intensive Journal* (New York: Dialogue House Library, 1975); idem, *The Practice of Process Meditation: The Intensive Journal Way to Spiritual Experience* (New York: Dialogue House Library, 1980).

70. Abram J. Ryan, "Song of the Mystic" in *Father Ryan's Poems* (New York: P.J. Kenedy & Sons, 1880), pp. 35-37.

Chapter Nine

1. Harry Emerson Fosdick, *The Meaning of Being a Christian* (New York: Association Press, 1964), n. 285, p. 314.
2. St. Francis of Assisi, "Prayer of Saint Francis," quoted in Armstrong, ed., *Bits & Pieces*, p. 58.
3. St. Augustine, "Epist. at Parthos" in *Patrologiae Cursus Completus*, ed. J.-P. Migne, vol. 35, p. 2055. English translation cited in Christopher Mooney, *Teilhard de Chardin and the Mystery of Christ* (Garden City: Doubleday & Co., 1968), page 233, "By loving, a man becomes a member; and by love, he fits into the structure of Christ's Body; and so there will be one Christ loving himself."
4. St. John of the Cross, "Sayings of Light and Love," in *The Collected Works*, p. 672.
5. Sir Roger L'Estrange, "Seneca's Morals II," cited in Evans, ed., *Dictionary of Quotations*, p. 547.
6. Plautus, "Pseudolus," act 1, sc. 1; John Milton, "Paradise Regained," bk. 3, 1. 9; both cited in Stevenson, ed., *The Home Book of Quotations*, p. 2227.
7. Emmanuel Cardinal Suhard, *Priests Among Men*, p. 60.
8. This *anonymous reflection* was given to me by a very dedicated Daughter of Charity of St. Vincent de Paul, who was herself a shining witness of Christ's love in a Dallas barrio.
9. Anonymous, quoted in Armstrong, ed., *Bits & Pieces*, p. 52.
10. Anonymous, ibid., p. 10.
11. Author and publisher *not indicated* on poster.
12. James Breig, "Martyrs: You-Bet-Your-Life Christians" in *U.S. Catholic Magazine* (Chicago, IL: Claretian Publications), vol. 47, no. 1 (Jan. 1982), p. 36.
13. "The Acts of Martyrdom of Sts. Perpetua and Felicitas," cited in Newman Eberhardt, *A Summary of Catholic History* (St. Louis, MO: B. Herder Book Co., 1962), vol. 1, p. 90.
14. John Henry Cardinal Newman, "Radiating Christ," quoted in *Cor Unum*, ed. Religious of the Sacred Heart (Sydney, Australia: Rose Bay Convent, 1962), pp. 164-165.
15. St. Vincent de Paul, quoted in Maynard, *Virtues and Spiritual Doctrine of Saint Vincent de Paul*, p. 62. St. Vincent's original statement, of course, is, "If love is a fire, zeal is its flame; if love is a sun, zeal is its ray." In practice, zeal and service are virtually interchangeable, but unfortunately the former has taken on pejorative overtones associated with words like zealot, fanatic, etc.
16. W.F. Dicharry, "Charism in the Bible" in *The New Catholic Encyclopedia*, vol. 3, p. 460.
17. Ibid., vol. 6, p. 473.
18. Bp. James E. Walsh, *Maryknoll Spiritual Directory* (New York: Field Afar Press, 1947), ch. 8, pp. 55-70.
19. St. Vincent de Paul, concluding words in the motion picture, "Monsieur Vincent" written by Jean Anouihl (1948), quoted in Philip Dion, *Monsieur Vincent: Questions and Answers* (Chicago, IL: St. Joseph Hospital, 1978), p. 18. The complete final sentence is, "It is only because of your love — and your love alone — that the poor will forgive you the bread you give them."
20. Bp. James E. Walsh, *Maryknoll Spiritual Directory*, pp. 79-81.
21. Austin Flannery, ed., *Vatican Council II*, "Pastoral Constitution on the Church in the Modern World," ch. 2, no. 27, p. 928.
22. Richard Armstrong, *Christopher Prayers for Today* (New York: Paulist Press, 1972), p. 14.
23. Elizabeth Cheney, "There is a Man on the Cross," quoted in Morrison, ed., *Religious Verse*, no. 626, p. 198.

452   TO LIVE THE WORD, INSPIRED AND INCARNATE

24. Friedrich Nietzsche, quoted in Viktor E. Frankl, *Man's Search for Meaning*, Preface, xiii.
25. Anonymous, *Footprints* (Allen, TX: Argus Communications, 1982).
26. John Henry Card. Newman, "Reflection," quoted in Armstrong, ed., *Bits & Pieces*, pp. 4-5.

Chapter Ten

 1. Jack Finegan, *The Archaeology of the New Testament* (Princeton, NJ: Princeton University Press, 1978), p. 48.
 2. Harvey Cox, *The Secular City: Secularization and Urbanization in Theological Perspective*, rev. (New York: Macmillan, 1966).
 3. Idem, *The Feast of Fools: A Theological Essay on Festivity and Fantasy* (Cambridge, MA: Harvard University Press, 1969).
 4. Nikos Kazantzakis, "Zorba the Greek," quoted in *Take Off Your Shoes*, p. 83. This is a rather free translation. The original reads more like this, "Boss, you've got everything — except one thing. You need a touch of madness; otherwise, you will never 'cut the rope' and be free!"
 5. The Aramaic word for rock is *kepha*, from which is derived the Greek transliteration, *Kephâs* (Cephas), the Semitic equivalent of the Greek word for rock, *pétra*, masculinized into the Greek name Pétros (Peter). The former seems to have been the earlier favorite, for example in Paul's Letters (1 Cor 1:12; 3:22; 9:5; 15:5; Gal 1:18; 2:9, 11, 14), but the latter prevailed in the Gospels, where Cephas appears only in John 1:42. Most scripture scholars, Protestant as well as Catholic, are in agreement that Cephas and Peter are interchangeable names with the same meaning, "rock," as emphasized in Matthew 16:18.
 6. I prefer not to delay on the primacy of Peter (and the Popes) but to leave this question to Catholic apologists and Christian ecumenists. However, for those who may wish to pursue it further, especially in a biblical and archaeological manner, I recommend the following: Raymond Brown, Karl Donfried, and John Reumann, ed. *Peter in the New Testament: A Collaborative Assessment by Protestant and Roman Catholic Scholars* (Minneapolis, MN: Augsburg Publishing House and New York: Paulist Press, 1973); Jocelyn Toynbee & John Ward Perkins, *The Shrine of St. Peter and the Vatican Excavations* (New York: Pantheon Books, 1957); John Evangelist Walsh, *The Bones of St. Peter: The First Full Account of the Search for the Apostle's Body* (Garden City, NY: Doubleday & Company, 1982).
 7. The secret of understanding the *Apocalypse* or Book of Revelation is to read it as it was written, namely as *apocalyptic literature*. This strange (to us) kind of writing is very different from prophetic literature (though it may contain some prophecy) and is best read as "underground or resistance literature," written to encourage those suffering persecution e.g. the Jews under *Antiochus Epiphanes* in the 2nd century B.C. (for whom the apocalyptic Book of Daniel was written) or the Christians under *Domitian* toward the end of the 1st century A.D. (for whom the apocalyptic Book of Revelation was intended). Thus understood, the mysterious language employed (most of it from various parts of the Old Testament) is seen as both helpful in boosting the spirits of the persecuted and necessary in avoiding detection by the persecutors. And when read with understanding, the Apocalypse is revealed as one of the richest books of the Bible, particularly in Christology, and one of the most encouraging in our "Age of Martyrs." For further reading and reflection, see Patrick J. Sena, C.PP.S., *The Apocalypse: Biblical Revelation Explained* (New York: Alba House, 1983).
 8. Thomas Babington Lord Macaulay, "Essay on Von Ranke's History of the Popes" in *The Work of Lord Macaulay*, ed. his sister, Lady Trevelyan (London: Longmans, Green, Co., 1900), vol. 6, pp.454-455.

9. My emphasis on Scripture, like that of Vatican II and of the contemporary Church generally, should not be misconstrued as a rejection of or even a deemphasis on *tradition*. For what is Scripture but written tradition? And what is tradition but an ongoing understanding, living, and development of what is explicitly or implicitly contained in the inspired Word of God? For confirmation, see Austin Flannery, ed., *Vatican Council II*, "Dogmatic Constitution on Divine Revelation," ch. 2, no. 9, p. 755.

10. Austin Flannery, ed., *Vatican Council II*, "Dogmatic Constitution on the Church," pp. 350-423.

11. Hans Conzelmann, *The Theology of St. Luke*, tr. Geoffrey Buswell (New York: Harper and Row, 1960), pp. 16-17.

12. A good description of "Pioneer vs. Settler Theology" is that of Wes Seeliger, quoted in Link, ed., *Still Point*, pp. 20-21.

13. Austin Flannery, ed., *Vatican Council II*, "Dogmatic Constitution on the Church," ch. 8, pp. 413-423.

14. Jean Cantinat, *Mary in the Bible*, tr. Paul Barrett (Westminster, MD: Newman Press, 1965), pp. 199-205; Raymond Brown, Karl Donfried, Joseph Fitzmyer, John Reumann, ed. *Mary in the New Testament: A Collaborative Assessment by Protestant and Roman Catholic Scholars* (Philadelphia, PA: Fortress Press and New York: Paulist Press, 1978), pp. 223-239.

15. Henri De Montherlant, cited in Simcox, ed., *Treasury of Quotations*, no. 2300, p. 190.

16. Austin Flannery, ed., *Vatican Council II*, "Decree on Ecumenism," ch. 2, no. 6, p. 459.

17. Charles Rice, ed., *Common Rules of the Congregation of the Mission* (Perryville, MO: The Miraculous Medal Ass'n., 1974), ch. 12, par. 10, p. 47.

18. Austin Flannery, ed., *Vatican Council II*, "The Constitution on the Sacred Liturgy," Introduction, no. 2, p. 1.

19. Ibid., ch. 1, sec. 1, no. 10, p. 6.

20. Ibid., ch. 1, sec. 3, no. 24, p. 10.

21. Ibid., "Dogmatic Constitution on Divine Revelation," ch. 6, no. 21, p. 762.

22. Ibid., "Constitution on The Sacred Liturgy," ch. 3, no. 59, p. 20.

23. Peter Levi, *Atlas of the Greek World* (New York: Facts on File, Inc., 1980), pp. 65, 69, 83, 113.

24. Frederick C. Grant, ed., *Hellenistic Religions: The Age of Syncretism* (New York: The Liberal Arts Press, 1953), Introduction, pp. xxxviii-xxxix.

25. Newman Eberhardt, *Catholic History*, vol. 2, p. 183.

26. Joseph Martos, *Doors to the Sacred: A Historical Introduction to Sacraments in the Catholic Church* (Garden City, NY: Doubleday & Company, 1982), pp. 65-69.

27. Ibid., pp. 57, 84, 88, etc.

28. St. Augustine, "Treatise on St. John's Gospel," quoted in Aime Georges Martimort, *The Signs of the New Covenant* (Collegeville, MN: The Liturgical Press, 1963), p. 38.

29. Pope Pius XII, "Encyclical Letter 'Mystici Corporis' on the Mystical Body of Christ" (1943), quoted in Aime Georges Martimort, *The Signs of the New Covenant*, p. 38.

30. Bishop Fulton J. Sheen, *Christmas Inspirations* (New York: Maco Publishing, Inc., 1966), p. 5.

31. Pierre Teilhard de Chardin, *The Phenomenon of Man* (New York: Harper & Row, Publishers, 1959).

32. Paul Tillich, cited in Simcox, ed., *A Treasury of Quotations*, no. 1781, p. 150.

33. George Maloney, *Breath of the Mystic*, p. 18.

34. Austin Flannery, ed. *Vatican Council II*, "Dogmatic Constitution on the Church," ch. 2, no. 10-11, pp. 360-362; also Aime Georges Martimort, *Signs of the New Covenant*, pp. 70-73.

35. Edward Schillebeeckx, *Christ the Sacrament of the Encounter with God* (New York: Sheed and Ward, 1963).
36. Joseph Martos, *Doors to the Sacred: A Historical Introduction to Sacraments in the Catholic Church* (Garden City, NY: Doubleday and Company, 1982).
37. Ibid., Joseph Martos, *Doors to the Sacred*, pp. 141-142.

Chapter Eleven

1. In this connection, St. Clement of Rome, the third successor of St. Peter as Bishop of Rome and Vicar of Christ, writes to the still troublesome Corinthians, "Cling to the saints, for they who cleave to them shall become saints!" ("The Letter of St. Clement of Rome to the Corinthians," tr. F.X. Glimm, in Schopp, ed., *The Apostolic Fathers*, ch. 46, p. 45).
2. Thomas Cawley, *Two Vincentian Martyrs in China: Blessed Francis Regis Clet, Blessed John Gabriel Perboyre* (Tainan, Taiwan, R.O.C.: Kao Ching Printing Co., 1979), pp. 52-56.
3. Geo. Ogg, "The Age of Jesus when He Taught" in *New Testament Studies*, ed. Matthew Black (Cambridge, England: Cambridge Univ. Press), vol. 5, (1958-1959), pp. 291-298.
4. "The Didache: Teaching of the Twelve Apostles" in Schopp, ed., *The Apostolic Fathers*, ch. 7, p. 177.
5. Jean Danielou, *The Bible and the Liturgy* (Notre Dame, IN: University of Notre Dame Press, 1966), pp. 6-7.
6. O.A. Battista, *God's World and You* (Milwaukee, WI: Bruce Publishing Company, 1957), p. 121.
7. "The Didache: Teaching of the Twelve Apostles" in Schopp, ed., *The Apostolic Fathers*, ch. 7, p. 177.
8. Unfortunately, I have not been able to find this quotation in the collection of St. Ignatius' famous Seven Letters, written on his way to martyrdom at Rome. (See "The Letters of St. Ignatius of Antioch" in Schopp, ed., *The Apostolic Fathers*, tr. Gerald G. Walsh, pp. 83-127.) Of course, the statement itself is intrinsically powerful and useful in our Spiritual Life.
9. George T. Montague, *Growth in Christ: A Study in Saint Paul's Theology of Progress* (Kirkwood, MO: Maryhurst Press, 1961), pp. 184-189.
10. Tertullian, "On Baptism," cited in Chapin, ed., *Catholic Quotations*, p. 49.
11. Henry J.M. Nouwen, *The Wounded Healer: Ministry in Contemporary Society* (Garden City, NY: Doubleday & Co., 1972).
12. Newman Eberhardt, *Catholic History*, vol. 1, pp. 609-610.
13. Austin Flannery, *Vatican Council II*, "The Constitution on the Sacred Liturgy," ch. 2, no. 47, p. 16.
14. Ibid., ch. 1, sec. 3, no. 24, p. 10.
15. Ibid., "Dogmatic Constitution on Divine Revelation," ch. 6, no. 21, p. 762.
16. Ibid., "Constitution on the Sacred Liturgy," ch. 2, no. 47-48, pp. 16-17.
17. John Wick Bowman, "Revelation, Book of" in Burkitt, ed., *The Interpreter's Dictionary of the Bible*, vol. 4, pp. 58-71.
18. Joseph L. Gardner, ed., *Eat Better, Live Better: A Common-sense Guide to Nutrition and Good Health* (Pleasantville, NY: The Reader's Digest Association, Inc., 1984).
19. Thomas Cawley, *Two Vincentian Martyrs in China*, p. 51.

Chapter Twelve

1. Viktor Frankl, cited in Armstrong, ed., *Bits & Pieces*, p. 56.
2. See similar thoughts by Wilbert Donald Gough, cited in Wirt & Beckstrom, ed., *Living Quotations*, no. 2023, p. 151; also Rabbi B.R. Brickner, cited in Simcox, ed., *A Treasury of Quotations*, no. 1139, p. 95.
3. Arnold Toynbee, ed. *Half the World: The History and Culture of China and Japan* (New York: Holt, Rinehart & Winston, 1973), pp. 118, 143; Bradley Smith & Wang-Go Weng, *China: A History in Art* (Garden City, NY: Doubleday & Co., no date), pp. 78-80.
4. Rudyard Kipling, "The Ballad of East and West" in *Kipling: A Selection of His Stories and Poems*, ed. John Beecraft (Garden City, NY: Doubleday and Company, 1956), pp. 425-427.
5. Jack Finegan, *Light from the Ancient Past: The Archaeological Background of the Hebrew-Christian Religion* (Princeton, NJ: Princeton University Press, 1956), pp. 58-67.
6. The texts of Jesus' words (*1 Cor 7:10-11*; *Mk 10:2-12*, and *Lk 16:18*) show quite clearly his categorical condemnation of divorce and remarriage. Other texts (namely 1 Cor 7:12-16 as well as Mt 5:31-32 and 19:3-9), are adduced as examples of a more lenient attitude on the part of Jesus and his early followers. Is this so? Closer examination of the text and context of *1 Corinthians 7:12-16* indicates an Apostolic decision allowing dissolution of a purely natural bond (between unbaptized persons) in favor of a (sacramental) Christian marriage, what we have traditionally called the Pauline Privilege.
7. The two texts in Matthew are more difficult. First, the context of the *lógion* (saying) in *Matthew 5:31-32* and the pronouncement story in *19:3-9* are clear evidence of Jesus' rejection of Jewish divorce practices — a rejection so surprising to his Apostles that they exclaim, "If this is the situation between a husband and wife, it is better not to marry!" (Mt 19:10, NIV). Why, then, the apparent exceptive clauses in 5:32 and 19:9? Two principal explanations have been given by Catholic scripture scholars: one, that the Greek word *porneía* (uncleanness), which emerges in various English translations as "unchastity" (RSV, NEB), "marital unfaithfulness" (NIV), "lewd conduct" (NAB), or "fornication" (JB), actually refers either to (incestuous) concubinage (as in 1 Cor 5:1) or perhaps to marriage within forbidden degrees of kinship, according to Jewish law, which may be the meaning of *porneía* in Acts 15:20 and 29; the other explanation, that the so-called exceptive clauses are actually rejection clauses which eliminate from consideration the whole rabbinical question of what constitutes an uncleanness (Hebrew, *ervath davar*; Greek Septuagint, *áschemon prágma*) for which Deuteronomy 24:1 (dating centuries after Moses) permitted divorce and remarriage.

    This last explanation is especially appropriate on account of the then current debate between the liberal Rabbi Hillel and the conservative Rabbi Shammai on the meaning of the Deuteronomic "uncleanness" justifying divorce, which seems to be the whole background of the pronouncement story in Matthew 19:3-9 and Mark 10:2-12. Jesus rejects both rabbinical positions and insists on the lifelong, monogamous marriage reflected in Genesis 2:24 and Malachi 2:14-16. For further reading, see R. De Vaux, *Ancient Israel: Its Life and Institutions* (London: Darton, Longman & Todd, 1962), pp. 34-36; Bruce Vawter, "The Divorce Clauses in Mt 5:32 and 19:9" in *The Catholic Biblical Quarterly*, vol. 16, (1954), pp. 155-167.
8. David M. Thomas, *Christian Marriage: A Journey Together* (Wilmington, DE: Michael Glazier, Inc., 1983), pp. 20, 85 ff.
9. Joseph Martos, *Doors to the Sacred*, p. 399.
10. St. Ignatius of Antioch, "To Polycarp" in Schopp, ed., *The Apostolic Fathers*, par. 5, p. 126; cited also in Aime Georges Martimort, *The Signs of the Covenant*, p. 292.

11. Kahlil Gibran, *The Prophet* (New York: Alfred A. Knopf, 1964), p. 15.

12. Rainer Maria Rilke, quoted in David R. Mace, "Marital Spirituality: A Personal Account" in *Marital Spirituality*, ed. David Thomas (St. Meinrad, IN: Abbey Press, 1978), p. 35.

13. Raymond Brown, "Qumran Dead Sea Scrolls" in *The Jerome Biblical Commentary*, vol. 2, art. 68, par. 95, p. 554.

14. Henry Denzinger, *The Sources of Catholic Dogma*, tr. Roy J. Deferrari (St. Louis, MO: B. Herder Book Co., 1955), pp. 25 and 38-39.

15. The Sacred Congregation for Religious and Secular Institutes, "Apostolic Exhortation on the Renewal of Religious Life," in Flannery, ed., *Vatican Council II*, Doc. 53, no. 7, p. 683.

16. William Barclay, *Jesus as They Saw Him: New Testament Interpretations of Jesus* (Grand Rapids, MI: Wm. B. Eerdmans Publishing Co., 1962), pp. 68-92; Oscar Cullmann, *The Christology of the New Testament*, tr. Shirley Guthrie & Charles Hall, rev. (Philadelphia, PA: Westminster Press, 1963), pp. 137-192; Sigmund Mowinckel, *He That Cometh: The Messiah Concept in the Old Testament and Later Judaism*, tr. G.W. Anderson (Nashville, TN., 1954), pp. 346-450.

17. Max Thurian, *Consecration of the Layman: New Approaches to the Sacrament of Confirmation*, tr. W.J. Kerrigan (Baltimore, MD: Helicon Press, 1963); Thomas A. Marsh, *Gift of Community: Baptism and Confirmation* (Wilmington, DE: M. Glazier, 1984).

18. Bp. Emile-Joseph De Smet, *The Priesthood of the Faithful*, tr. Jos. F.M. Marique (New York: Paulist Press, 1962); Edw. Schillebeeckx, *Ministry: Leadership in the Community of Jesus Christ* (New York: Crossroad Publ. Co., 1981); Thos. F. O'Meara, *Theology of Ministry* (New York: Paulist Press, 1983); Norman Pittenger, *The Ministry of All Christians: A Theology of Lay Ministry* (Wilton: CT: Morehouse-Barlow Company, 1983).

19. St. Ignatius of Antioch, "The Letters of St. Ignatius of Antioch" in Schopp, ed., *The Apostolic Fathers*, pp. 97, 100, 102, 113, 121.

20. Austin Flannery, ed. *Vatican Council II*, "Dogmatic Constitution on the Church," ch. 3, no. 29, p. 387, "Apostolic Letter Containing Norms for the Order of Diaconate," pp. 433-440.

21. Ibid., "Dogmatic Constitution on the Church," ch. 3, no. 28, pp. 384-387, "Decree on the Ministry and Life of Priests," pp. 863-902.

22. Ibid., "Dogmatic Constitution on the Church," chs. 4-5, nos.30-42, pp. 388-402, "Decree on the Apostolate of Lay People," pp. 766-798, "Pastoral Constitution on the Church in the Modern World," pp. 903-1014.

23. Mother Teresa of Calcutta, cited in Armstrong, ed., *Bits and Pieces*, p. 9; cf. Georges Gorree & Jean Barbier, *Love Without Boundaries: Mother Teresa of Calcutta*, tr. Paula Speakman (Huntington, IN: Our Sunday Visitor Press, 1979).

Appendices

APPENDIX A:

1. Hugh M. McElwain, "Resurrection of the Dead" in *The New Catholic Encyclopedia*, vol. 12, p. 427.

2. Ibid., p. 424.

3. Ladislaus Boros, *Living in Hope: Future Perspectives in Christian Thought*, tr. W.J. O'Hara (Garden City, NY: Doubleday and Co., 1973), pp. 37-39.

4. Eduard Schweizer, "Psyche" in Kittel, ed., *Theological Dictionary of the New Testament*, vol. 9, p. 656.

5. Henry Denzinger, *The Sources of Catholic Dogma*, par. 429, p. 169.
6. Dr. Paul Brand & Philip Yancey, *Fearfully and Wonderfully Made: A Surgeon Looks at the Human and Spiritual Body* (Grand Rapids, MI: Zondervan Publishing House, 1982), p. 45.
7. *The Roman Ritual: Rite of Funerals*, tr. Int'l. Comm. on English in the Liturgy (New York: Catholic Book Publishing Co., 1971); *The Sacramentary* (1974), pp. 527-537, 952-987; *The Lectionary*, tr. I.C.E.L. (New York: Catholic Book Publishing Co., 1974), pp. 965-988.
8. Henry Denzinger, *The Sources of Catholic Dogma*, par. 139, p. 56; par. 2200, p. 571.
9. Dante Alighieri, cited in Simcox, ed., *A Treasury of Quotations*, no. 2767, p. 229.
10. Sr. Elizabeth of the Trinity, *Reminiscences*, Appendix IV, p. 255. The complete quotation in well worth including,
    We carry our heaven about with us, since He who satisfies the glorified soul in the light of vision gives Himself to us in faith and mystery. It is the same thing. It seems to me that I have found my heaven on earth, since heaven is God and God is in my soul.
11. St. Catherine of Siena, cited in Simcox, *A Treasury of Quotations*, no. 2759, p. 228.
12. Cardinal Newman, it seems to me, expresses much the same idea in his Miscellanies, no. 309, quoted in Chapin, ed., *Catholic Quotations*, p. 425, "Heaven would be hell to an irreligious man!"
13. George A. Maloney, S.J., *Death, Where Is Your Sting?* (New York: Alba House, 1984), p. 35ff.
14. Brooks Foss Westcott, cited in Simcox, ed., *Treasury of Quotations*, no. 2774, pp. 229-230.
15. Fyodor Dostoevsky, "The Brothers Karamazov," cited in Simcox, ed., *Treasury of Quotations*, no. 2775, p. 230.
16. William Law, ibid., no. 2770, p. 229.
17. Jean Paul Sartre, *No Exit*, tr. S. Gilbert (New York: Alfred A. Knopf, Inc., 1948), p. 61.
18. Omar Khayyam, "Rubaiyat of Omar Khayyam," tr. Edw. Fitzgerald, cited in Evans, ed., *Dictionary of Quotations*, p. 310.

APPENDIX B:

1. Ludwig Ott, *Fundamentals of Catholic Dogma*, tr. P. Lynch, ed. J. Canon Bastible (St. Louis, MO: B. Herder Book Co., 1957), bk. 3, sec. 1, pp. 162-172.
2. Henry Denzinger, *The Sources of Catholic Dogma*, par. 148, pp. 60-61.
3. Raymond E. Brown, *The Gospel According to John* (Garden City, NY: Doubleday & Co., Inc., 1966), vol. 1, intro., p. cxvii.
4. Henry Denzinger, *The Sources of Catholic Dogma*, par. 148, pp. 60-61.
5. Bruce Vawter, *This Man Jesus: An Essay Toward a New Testament Christology* (Garden City, NY: Doubleday & Co., 1973), p. 134.
6. James P. Mackey, *Jesus, the Man and the Myth: A Contemporary Christology* (New York: Paulist Press, 1979), pp. 163, 165, 171.
7. Piet Schoonenberg, *The Christ: A Study of the God-Man Relationship in the Whole of Creation and in Jesus Christ* (New York: Herder and Herder, 1971), p. 142.
8. Dermot A. Lane, *The Reality of Jesus: An Essay in Christology* (New York: Paulist Press, 1975), pp. 123-124.

9. Raymond E. Brown, *Jesus God and Man: Modern Biblical Reflections* (New York: Macmillan Publishing Co., 1978), pp. 103-105.

APPENDIX C:

1. This "pious Jewish belief" (reflected in Si 44:19-23; 1 M 2:52; Ws 10:5), and especially in rabbinical writings, is abundantly confirmed in Strack-Billerbeck, *Kommentar zum Neuen Testament aus Talmud und Midrasch* (Munich: Oscar Beck, 1926), vol. 3, Der Brief an die Roemer, pp. 204-206, as well as in Stanislas Lyonnet, *Quaestiones in Epistulam ad Romanos, Prima Series,* ed. rev. & enl. (Rome: Pontificio Istituto Biblico, 1962), ch. 3, pp. 90-94.
2. This parable, from rabbinical literature, is also abundantly confirmed, not only in Lyonnet, *Quaestiones,* p. 94, but also in Joseph Bonsirven, *Palestinian Judaism in the Time of Jesus Christ,* tr. Wm. Wolf (New York: Holt, Rinehart, and Winston, 1964), ch. 3, p. 65. It reads as follows:

   'I will look with favor upon you' (Lv 26:9). Here is a parable. A king hired many laborers, and among them was one who had worked with him for a long time. The workers came to get their wages, and this man was with them. The king said to him: 'My son, I will look with favor upon you. The others have done little work with me and I will give them a small salary, but I shall pay you a large salary.' In like manner, Israel claims its reward before God, and the other nations claim their reward. And he says to the Israelites: 'My sons, I will look with favor upon you. These nations of the world have done little work with me and I will give them only a small salary, but I will give you a large salary.' That is why it is said: 'I will look with favor upon you, and I will make you fruitful and numerous, as I carry out my covenant with you.'
3. This is according to the so-called *"North Galatian Theory,"* which I personally favor as being more consonant with indications in Acts, e.g. Acts 16:6. See Dillon and Fitzmyer, "The Acts of the Apostles," in the *JBC,* vol. 2, p. 197.
4. To me, both the content and the tone of Galatians fits best between Second Corinthians, written at Philippi, and Romans, written at Corinth.
5. Carl S. Meyer, "Luther, Martin" in *The New International Dictionary of the Christian Church,* rev. ed. J.D. Douglas, (Grand Rapids, MI: Zondervan Publishing House, 1978), pp. 609-611; Bamber Gascoigne: *The Christians* (William Morrow & Company, 1977), pp. 158-159.
6. Theodore Weiser, *"Pistis,"* in Kittle, ed., *Theological Dictionary of the New Testament,* vol. 6, p. 187.
7. Rudolph Bultmann, *"Pistis,"* ibid., vol. 6, p. 216.
8. Juan Alfaro, "Motive of Faith" in Rahner, ed., *Encyclopedia of Theology,* p. 511.
9. Frank W. Beare, "Romans, Letter to the" in Buttrick, ed., *The Interpreter's Dictionary of the Bible,* vol. 4, pp. 116-117.
10. Martin Luther, *Lectures on Romans,* tr. and ed. Wilhelm Pauck (Philadelphia, PA: Westminster Press, 1961), p. 124.

TOPICAL INDEX

BIBLICAL SPIRITUALITY BOOKS from ALBA HOUSE

THE APOCALYPSE:
Biblical Revelation Explained
Patrick J. Sena, C.PP.S.

In a clear, concise fashion the author unfolds the significance and message of the book of Revelation. At one and the same time, the author refutes many of the fundamentalistic beliefs about the book and presents an intelligent, accurate interpretation that is in accord with the latest data of biblical scholarship.

It answers the basic questions, "How does one interpret the book of Revelation?", "Who is the beast?", "Is there such a thing as rapture?", "How do I know that this is a book of hope and not of woe?", "What are the meanings of the numbers in the book?". This work will no doubt become the standard introductory text for adults on this fascinating and important topic.
116 pages   **$6.95**

JOHN: THE DIFFERENT GOSPEL
A Reflective Commentary
Michael J. Taylor, S.J.

The reasons for John's unique relationship with Jesus are clearly explained and outlined in this exciting and original work which reflects the best and most current insights of contemporary biblical exegesis. A careful reading not only will increase your understanding of his Gospel but also your love for it. It is an outstanding text, sure to enlighten and move the reader. Anyone who has utilized any of Taylor's superb anthologies will be delighted to discover that this latest work measures up in every way to his own consistent and very high standards. Excellent for adult education, seminary courses and university classes.

"When the four gospels are compared, most readers readily recognize that John's book and his Jesus are 'different' in many ways from the others. Not all commentators, however, speak about the reasons for John's 'difference' as clearly and understandably as Fr. Taylor. The book should prove valuable to all students of John who seek a deeper understanding of Jesus as God's Word incarnate." *Pastoral Life*
269 pages   **$9.95**

A COMPANION TO JOHN:
Readings in Johannine Theology
(John's Gospel and Epistles)
Michael J. Taylor, S.J.

". . . a compilation of articles dealing with the Gospel of John produced by some of the best scholars in the world. It is ecumenical in outlook and includes studies by Americans as well as by Europeans." *Pastoral Life*
281 pages $6.95

A COMPANION TO PAUL:
Readings in Pauline Theology
Michael J. Taylor, S.J.

"Although one could spend a lifetime investigating the themes and theological concepts of Paul, Taylor has put together a one-volume anthology which does justice to all of Paul's writings. By carefully selecting a number of articles written by various scholars, he presents an excellent overview of the gospel of Paul for those who want or need an introduction to this thought." *Theological Studies*

"The college and seminary teacher will want to take note of this collection of articles by Michael J. Taylor. Nineteen articles on various facets of Pauline theology, mainly by Catholic scholars, are handily and economically presented here under one cover." *Donald Senior - The Bible Today*
251 pages $6.95

PAUL'S EARLY LETTERS:
From Hope Through Faith To Love
A Study Guide to I and II Thessalonians, Galatians and
I and II Corinthians
Paul Wrightman

This book is recommended for all those who want to grow in their understanding and appreciation of the Apostle Paul. Few parts of the Bible give us a more comprehensive picture of the biblical roots of our faith than do Paul's letters to the Thessalonians, Galatians and Corinthians. This book highlights the way in which these letters teach us about the Resurrection, the Second Coming, the connection between faith and works, the Eucharist and the nature of the Christian community.
148 pages $6.00

PAUL'S LATER LETTERS:
From Promise to Fulfillment
Paul Wrightman

Written in the closing decade of his life, Paul's letters to the Romans, Colossians, Ephesians and Philippians (as well as those to Philemon, Titus and Timothy) reflect the inspired insights of one who has "run the race and kept the faith." To embark on a study of these letters is to begin in a theological and spiritual adventure of major proportions for here we encounter Paul's full scale treatise on faith, his profound concept of marriage and his deep understanding of the nature of Christ, the Church and community. A follow-up to *Paul's Early Letters: From Hope Through Faith to Love* by the same author, this work retains the practical, easy-to-read approach that made the first book so popular in parish bible study groups everywhere. As in his earlier work, the author provides helpful suggestions on how to most effectively use the book for personal study or group discussion along with down-to-earth questions for reflection and application of the biblical text to everyday life.

238 pages   **$9.95**

WHO DO YOU SAY THAT I AM?
An Adult Inquiry Into the First Three Gospels
Rev. Edward J. Ciuba

". . . a work of sound biblical scholarship with an appealing, eminently readable style. The work is excellent. There is up to the minute presentation that is in line with the most recent hermeneutical attempts 'to get at the literal meaning' which the inspired gospel writers intended to convey . . . the result is splendid scholarship put to the service of most attractive—and most timely—exposition of the Synoptic Gospels and their contemporary relevance." *Pastoral Life*

155 pages   **$5.95**

Available at your local BOOK STORE or from:

> **Alba House Publications**
> **2187 Victory Blvd.**
> **Staten Island, N.Y. 10314-6603**